Mastering Cloud Security Posture Management (CSPM)

Secure multi-cloud infrastructure across AWS, Azure, and Google Cloud using proven techniques

Qamar Nomani

BIRMINGHAM—MUMBAI

Mastering Cloud Security Posture Management (CSPM)

Group Product Manager: Preet Ahuja

Publishing Product Manager: Prachi Sawant

Book Project Manager: Uma Devi

Senior Editor: Sayali Pingale

Technical Editor: Nithik Cheruvakodan

Copy Editor: Safis Editing

Proofreader: Safis Editing

Indexer: Rekha Nair

Production Designer: Shankar Kalbhor

Marketing Coordinator: Rohan Dobhal

First published: January 2024

Production reference: 1100124

Published by

Packt Publishing Ltd.

Grosvenor House

11 St Paul's Square

Birmingham

B3 1RB, UK

ISBN 978-1-83763-840-6

www.packtpub.com

To my wife, Lubna. Thank you for your patience, your kindness, and your friendship.
Most of all, for your unwavering support in the new country and throughout.
I couldn't have asked for more.
This book is dedicated to you with deepest gratitude and love.

Foreword

As a fellow cyber practitioner, friend, and former colleague, I am honored to introduce this pivotal book by Qamar Nomani, a remarkable cybersecurity architect and previously an integral part of the product security team I led at Sophos. Qamar's expertise was instrumental in securing the cloud infrastructure that supported our extensive cloud product portfolio, which safeguarded over 500,000 customers worldwide. When it comes to high-stake cloud environments, he knows what to do.

This book is a treasure trove of insights for cloud security professionals. It meticulously unpacks the complex landscape of **Cloud Security Posture Management** (**CSPM**), offering practical strategies, techniques, and best practices for securing multi-cloud infrastructures. Its comprehensive content spans from fundamental cloud security concepts to advanced topics such as CSPM tool selection and implementation, vulnerability and compliance management, and future trends in cloud security.

What sets this book apart is Qamar's hands-on experience and deep understanding of real-world challenges in cloud security. He skillfully bridges the gap between theoretical knowledge and practical application, making this book a must-read for cybersecurity managers, security leads, cloud security architects, and professionals at all levels. By incorporating vendor-neutral perspectives, Qamar ensures that the content is educational and highly applicable in diverse cloud environments.

Reading this book will empower you to improve your organization's security posture, ensure compliance, and stay abreast of the ever-evolving cloud security landscape. It is an essential guide for anyone committed to mastering cloud security and shaping the future of this critical domain.

Julie Davila

Technology and Cyber Security Practitioner

I have had the privilege of working with Qamar Nomani, an esteemed cybersecurity expert who draws from his extensive experience securing cloud environments to guide readers on an illuminating journey of CSPM.

As cloud computing has become ubiquitous, its convenience and flexibility have also introduced new vulnerabilities that many organizations are ill-equipped to address. With sensitive data and vital applications migrated to the cloud, a robust and proactive security strategy is essential to safeguard these critical assets.

This definitive guide equips cybersecurity managers, cloud architects, and DevOps engineers with the practical knowledge to comprehend the unique threats posed by the cloud landscape and implement robust CSPM tools and solutions to minimize risk exposure.

Methodically organized in four parts, this book establishes the CSPM fundamentals, evaluates leading products against pertinent criteria, supplies technical deployment blueprints tailored for organizations of varying sizes, and provides actionable direction on inventorying cloud assets, harnessing infrastructure-as-code, configuring policies-as-code, and integrating security across the development life cycle.

The chapters provide detailed CSPM product evaluation criteria, security capability features, and technical deployment designs that are appropriate for organizations of any size. They cover a practical framework for onboarding cloud accounts and containers, discovering cloud asset and inventory management, and infrastructure-as-code examples.

Most importantly, this book will be super helpful for cloud security administrators and security engineers in configuring security policies as code and enabling the CSPM configurations and deployment architecture. For DevOps and DevSecOps practitioners charged with enabling continuous compliance, this book covers policy as code automation blueprints and remediation workflows that accelerate integrating security across the development life cycle.

With insightful analysis of the evolving threat landscape and innovative approaches to cloud security controls, this definitive guide provides indispensable direction to advanced cloud security.

I'm confident this book will establish itself as vital reading for anyone serious about protecting critical assets residing in the cloud.

Rehman Khan

Security Architecture and Engineering Executive, CISSP, and CCSP

Contributors

About the author

Qamar Nomani is a cybersecurity expert and **Microsoft Certified Trainer** (MCT). He is currently working as a cloud security architect for one of the world's leading mobility companies from their Paris office. With over 10 years of experience as an IT professional in various domains, his expertise lies in security architecting and design for multi-cloud infrastructure. With his passion for solving complex problems, Qamar has worked for security product companies, financial institutions, and automotive companies with their security teams, helping to achieve top-notch industry-standard security practices for multi-cloud environments.

Along with his master's degree in computer applications from Jamia Millia Islamia, New Delhi, Qamar also holds several cloud security certifications. Being an avid learner and a passionate technology trainer, he has trained thousands of professionals across the globe on cloud security topics. Qamar is an active member of various cybersecurity communities and forums and often gets invited to universities and NGOs to speak about cybersecurity awareness and career guidance topics. In his free time, Qamar writes articles on Infortified (`https://infortified.com`), his personal tech blog, and a bi-weekly LinkedIn newsletter (`https://www.linkedin.com/newsletters/7050538814062108672/`)

Journey of writing a book has fulfilled a lifelong dream, and only through the immersive experience did I realize the depth and comprehensiveness of this endeavor. This book is a testament to the collaborative efforts and unwavering support of many individuals, each playing a vital role in bringing it to life. My heartfelt thanks go out to those who contributed to this project, and I express immense gratitude for their invaluable support.

My heartfelt appreciation to my family, with a special mention to my father and brother Neyaz Nomani. Their unwavering support for my education, even in the face of very limited resources, touches me deeply and means the world to me.

I express my heartfelt gratitude to all my teachers and professors, with a special acknowledgment to my high school gurus, Mr. Alam Sir and the late Mr. Khusru Alam Sir for being not only guiding lights but also being my godfathers, playing a pivotal role in supporting me during my transition from the village to the city for further studies.

Special thanks to friends, colleagues, managers, mentors, and dedicated cloud security professionals. Your groundbreaking research has paved the way for a deeper understanding of CSPM. This book stands on the shoulders of giants, and I'm grateful for the collective wisdom of the cybersecurity community.

I would also like to thank the team at Packt Publishing, whose commitment to excellence and passion for disseminating knowledge have made this project a reality. Their expertise and support have been indispensable in giving this book life.

Finally, heartfelt thanks to readers joining this educational journey. Your interest in cloud security fuels my commitment to contributing to the dynamic field of cybersecurity.

Thank you to everyone who has played a role, big or small, in making this book possible. Your contributions are deeply appreciated.

With gratitude and lots of love,

Qamar Nomani

About the reviewers

Rahul Gupta is a distinguished authority and expert in the field of cybersecurity. He brings a wealth of knowledge and experience to the world of cybersecurity, privacy, and compliance. With over 15 years at the forefront of protecting organizations from digital threats, Rahul has cemented his reputation as a trailblazer in the domain of InfoSec leaders. Throughout his career, Rahul has held pivotal roles in a diverse array of industries, ranging from Fortune 500 companies to cutting-edge start-ups. With a strong academic background and many industry certifications, including CISSP, Rahul has contributed extensively to the cybersecurity community and is very passionate about shaping the future of cybersecurity strategies and products.

Manas Mondal is a principal cloud architect with 29 years of experience, and specializes in app layouts, app migration, modernization of apps, ERP migration, and advanced analytics.

With substantial transformation experiences in both technology and business, Manas is a result-oriented, purpose-driven, problem-solving leadership personality. He has expertise in Software Engineering, Enterprise Architecture, Cloud Transformation, Application Disposition, CTO Strategy, ERP modernization, and Fast Data Engineering.

Table of Contents

Part 1: CSPM Fundamentals

1

2

Understanding CSPM and the Threat Landscape   37

3

CSPM Tools and Features   51

4

CSPM Tool Selection   71

Part 2: CSPM Deployment Aspects

5

Deploying the CSPM Tool   99

6

Onboarding Cloud Accounts   121

7

Onboarding Containers   137

8

Exploring Environment Settings   151

Part 3: Security Posture Enhancement

9

10

11

12

Investigating Threats with Query Explorers and KQL   235

13

Vulnerability and Patch Management   259

14

Compliance Management and Governance   281

15

Security Alerts and Monitoring   315

Part 4: Advanced Topics and Future Trends

16

Integrating CSPM with IaC   339

17

DevSecOps – Workflow Automation   359

Preface

Welcome to the world of *Mastering Cloud Security Posture Management*. In today's ever-changing tech world, where organizations heavily rely on cloud technologies, keeping digital assets safe is more important than ever. Think of this book as your friendly guide, helping you navigate through the complexities of **Cloud Security Posture Management (CSPM)** to strengthen how your organization stays secure across different cloud setups.

As we dive into the heart of things, know that this book is your companion in understanding the essentials. We start with the basics in *Chapter 1, Cloud Security Fundamentals,* laying the groundwork for what's to come. Each subsequent chapter peels back layers, revealing insights, strategies, and practices tailored for the multi-cloud landscape.

One thing that sets this book apart is its vendor-neutral stance. We're not pushing a particular tool. Instead, in *Chapter 3, CSPM Tools and Features,* we explore the broader world of tools, ensuring you have the freedom to choose what suits your needs. This journey is about your mastery, not brand loyalty.

In *Chapter 6, Onboarding Cloud Accounts,* we seamlessly transition into the practical side, making sure you're ready to safeguard your digital treasures. We demystify complex concepts, from *Exploring Environment Settings (Chapter 8)* to managing your digital assets in *Exploring Cloud Asset Inventory (Chapter 9)*.

The emphasis here is on your journey. No matter your background, from *Reviewing CSPM Dashboards (Chapter 10)* to mitigating *Major Configuration Risks (Chapter 11)*, we've got your back. Become a digital detective in *Investigating Threats with Query Explorer and KQL (Chapter 12)* and fortify your defenses with *Vulnerability and Patch Management (Chapter 13)*.

But this book isn't just about the present; it's about preparing for the future. Join us in exploring *Future Trends and Challenges (Chapter 19)* to stay ahead in the ever-evolving landscape.

So, why pick up this book? Because it's your gateway to mastering cloud security without bias, a journey into understanding, and a toolkit for securing your digital kingdom across multiple clouds. Get ready to embark on a captivating adventure!

Who this book is for

This book is crafted for a diverse audience seeking to improve their understanding of cloud security and navigate the intricate realm of CSPM. This book is aimed at the following people:

- **Cybersecurity champions**: Seasoned practitioners looking to deepen their expertise in cloud security, understand CSPM intricacies, and implement robust strategies across multi-cloud environments

- **IT and cloud trailblazers**: Technology specialists and cloud architects seeking practical insights to enhance the security posture of their organization's cloud infrastructure

- **Developers and DevOps engineers**: Professionals involved in the development and deployment processes, aiming to integrate security seamlessly into their workflows through the principles of DevSecOps

- **Students and aspiring cloud security enthusiasts**: Those embarking on their educational journey in cloud security, eager to grasp the fundamentals and best practices from a real-world perspective

- **Business leaders and decision-makers**: Executives and decision-makers aiming to grasp the essentials of CSPM to make informed choices regarding the security of their organization's cloud assets

Whether you are a seasoned professional, a technology enthusiast, or someone keen on securing digital assets in the cloud, this book is designed to be a comprehensive guide, offering practical strategies and proven techniques. Embrace this resource to elevate your knowledge, empower your practices, and safeguard your digital landscape in the era of multi-cloud technologies.

What this book covers

Chapter 1, Cloud Security Fundamentals, Let's start with the basics! This chapter lays the foundation, ensuring everyone is on the same page when it comes to keeping things safe and sound in the cloud.

Chapter 2, Understanding CSPM and the Threat Landscape. This chapter *decodes the language of CSPM* and explores the potential threats hiding in the digital shadows.

Chapter 3, CSPM Tools and Features, Meet your digital allies. This chapter helps you explore the tools and features integral to CSPM, arming you with the resources needed for a robust security strategy.

Chapter 4, CSPM Tool Selection, Choose wisely. This chapter guides you through the process of selecting the right CSPM tool for your organization's unique security needs.

Chapter 5, Deploying the CSPM Tool, Put theory into practice. This chapter covers the practical steps involved in deploying your chosen CSPM tool effectively across your cloud infrastructure.

Chapter 6, Onboarding Cloud Accounts. This chapter explains how you can unify your cloud accounts seamlessly with a CSPM tool. *Master the onboarding process* to ensure comprehensive protection across your digital landscape.

Chapter 7, Onboarding Containers, Safeguard your digital treasures. This chapter covers secure methods for onboarding and protecting valuable containers in your cloud environment.

Chapter 8, Exploring Environment Settings. This chapter empowers you to manage your cloud environment effectively.

Chapter 9, Exploring Cloud Asset Inventory, Know your assets inside out. This chapter dives into managing and tracking your cloud assets with precision and efficiency.

Chapter 10, Reviewing CSPM Dashboards, Command your security hub. This chapter explains how to navigate and interpret CSPM dashboards, providing valuable insights into your security status.

Chapter 11, Major Configuration Risks, Stay ahead of potential risks. This chapter covers identifying and mitigating major configuration risks, ensuring a secure and resilient cloud environment.

Chapter 12, Investigating Threats with Query Explorer and KQL, Become a digital detective. This chapter shows you how to uncover hidden risks and investigate their potential impact through advanced attack path analysis.

Chapter 13, Vulnerability and Patch Management, Protect your digital fortress. This chapter explores the vulnerabilities that emerge within cloud environments, emphasizing the dynamic nature of the cloud and how it necessitates a proactive approach to security. We will also explore the role of **Cyber Threat Intelligence** (**CTI**) in enhancing vulnerability management.

Chapter 14, Compliance Management and Governance. This chapter guides you through compliance management and governance for a secure cloud.

Chapter 15, Security Alerts and Monitoring, Be the guardian of your digital realm. This chapter covers the art of real-time alerts and proactive monitoring to stay one step ahead of potential security threats.

Chapter 16, Integrating CSPM with IaC, Merge security seamlessly with code. This chapter covers the integration process, aligning security practices with modern development workflows.

Chapter 17, DevSecOps – Workflow Automation, Join the revolution. This chapter explores how DevSecOps principles can be employed for seamless security integration in development workflows.

Chapter 18, CSPM-Related Technologies, Explore the tech landscape surrounding CSPM. This chapter provides insights into related technologies that complement and enhance cloud security posture management.

Chapter 19, Future Trends and Challenges, Peek into the future of cloud security. This chapter covers emerging trends and will help you to anticipate challenges, preparing yourself for the evolving digital landscape.

Your journey to mastery begins now!

Whether you're a seasoned professional or a newcomer to cloud security, *Mastering Cloud Security Posture Management* is your comprehensive guide. Elevate your knowledge, embrace practical strategies, and safeguard your digital realm across the exciting era of multi-cloud technologies. The journey begins now!

To get the most out of this book

Before you embark on this journey through *Mastering Cloud Security Posture Management*, let's ensure you're well prepared for the adventure ahead. This book assumes a foundational understanding of cloud concepts, basic cybersecurity principles, and a familiarity with cloud environments such as AWS, Azure, and Google Cloud. If you're new to these concepts, consider brushing up on these areas to maximize your comprehension. *Chapter 1* helps with revisiting those fundamental concepts.

To make the most of your learning experience, ensure that you have access to a cloud environment for hands-on exercises. Additionally, be ready to explore CSPM tools practically, so having a trial or demo environment for these tools will enhance your learning. Install any specified software or tools mentioned in the chapters to follow along seamlessly.

> **Note**
> *If you do not have access to any CSPM tool, the easiest way to explore CSPM tools is by setting up a free Microsoft Azure cloud environment and starting a free trial of Microsoft Defender for Cloud.*

This book is designed for active participation, so keep your curiosity alive, engage with the practical examples, and don't hesitate to experiment in your cloud environment. By embracing a hands-on approach, you'll gain a deeper understanding of the strategies, techniques, and best practices presented. Let's dive in and elevate your mastery of cloud security posture management!

Conventions used

There are a number of text conventions used throughout this book.

`Code in text`: Indicates code words in text, database table names, folder names, filenames, file extensions, pathnames, dummy URLs, user input, and Twitter handles. Here is an example: "You can find the latest CIS benchmarks for cloud providers such as Alibaba, AWS, and Azure, as well as various other technologies, at `https://www.cisecurity.org/cis-benchmarks`."

A block of code is set as follows:

```
resource "aws_instance" "web_server" {
  count = var.instance_count
  instance_type = "t2.micro"
  ami = "ami-xxxxxxxxxxxxxx"
}
variable "instance_count" {
  default = 3
}
```

Bold: Indicates a new term, an important word, or words that you see onscreen. For instance, words in menus or dialog boxes appear in **bold**. Here is an example: "More than 50% of organizations will have explicit strategies to adopt cloud-delivered **Secure Access Service Edge (SASE)**, up from less than 5% in 2020."

> **Tips or important notes**
> Appear like this.

Get in touch

Feedback from our readers is always welcome.

General feedback: If you have questions about any aspect of this book, email us at `customercare@packtpub.com` and mention the book title in the subject of your message.

Errata: Although we have taken every care to ensure the accuracy of our content, mistakes do happen. If you have found a mistake in this book, we would be grateful if you would report this to us. Please visit `www.packtpub.com/support/errata` and fill in the form.

Piracy: If you come across any illegal copies of our works in any form on the internet, we would be grateful if you would provide us with the location address or website name. Please contact us at `copyright@packt.com` with a link to the material.

If you are interested in becoming an author: If there is a topic that you have expertise in and you are interested in either writing or contributing to a book, please visit `authors.packtpub.com`.

Share Your Thoughts

Once you've read *Mastering Cloud Security Posture Management (CSPM)*, we'd love to hear your thoughts! Scan the QR code below to go straight to the Amazon review page for this book and share your feedback.

https://packt.link/r/1837638403

Your review is important to us and the tech community and will help us make sure we're delivering excellent quality content.

Download a free PDF copy of this book

Thanks for purchasing this book!

Do you like to read on the go but are unable to carry your print books everywhere?

Is your eBook purchase not compatible with the device of your choice?

Don't worry, now with every Packt book you get a DRM-free PDF version of that book at no cost.

Read anywhere, any place, on any device. Search, copy, and paste code from your favorite technical books directly into your application.

The perks don't stop there, you can get exclusive access to discounts, newsletters, and great free content in your inbox daily

Follow these simple steps to get the benefits:

1. Scan the QR code or visit the link below

https://packt.link/free-ebook/9781837638406

2. Submit your proof of purchase
3. That's it! We'll send your free PDF and other benefits to your email directly

Part 1: CSPM Fundamentals

In this part, you will discover the essentials of **Cloud Security Posture Management (CSPM)**. From cloud security fundamentals to navigating the threat landscape, we provide insights into potential challenges. You will explore CSPM tools and features, empowering organizations to enhance their cloud security. *Chapter 4* will take you through informed tool selection, laying a crucial foundation for readers new to cloud security or seeking a deeper understanding. These chapters set the stage for a confident and comprehensive exploration of CSPM.

This part contains the following chapters:

- *Chapter 1, Cloud Security Fundamentals*
- *Chapter 2, Understanding CSPM and the Threat Landscape*
- *Chapter 3, CSPM Tools and Features*
- *Chapter 4, CSPM Tool Selection*

1

Cloud Security Fundamentals

In the age of digital innovation, cloud computing has become the backbone of modern business operations. The convenience, scalability, and cost-efficiency of the cloud have revolutionized how we store, process, and share data. As we embrace the cloud's potential, we must also acknowledge the growing importance of cloud security. Protecting our digital assets from a range of threats is paramount in this interconnected world. Cloud security encompasses a wide range of concerns, including data protection, access control, compliance with regulatory requirements, and the overall integrity and confidentiality of information stored and processed in the cloud.

This chapter focuses on building baseline understanding of cloud security, which means understanding the key principles and strategies that underpin our ability to operate securely in the cloud. You will learn about some of the most important topics of cloud security, such as the shared responsibility model, defense in depth, the Zero Trust model, compliance concepts in the cloud, and the Cloud Adoption Framework.

The following main topics are covered in this chapter:

- What is cloud computing?
- Exploring cloud security
- The shared responsibility model
- Defense in depth
- The Zero Trust model
- Compliance concepts
- Cryptography and encryption in the cloud
- The Cloud Adoption Framework

Let us get started!

Technical requirements

To get the most out of this chapter, you are expected to have the following:

- A baseline understanding of cloud computing concepts.

- A general understanding or experience of working in an IT environment. To have a better understanding, you can use the sandbox environment of the organization's CSPM tool, if available.

What is cloud computing?

Cloud computing is a technology that allows organizations and individuals to access and use computing resources such as processing power, storage, and software over the internet without having to buy and maintain physical infrastructure. **Cloud service providers** (**CSPs**) such as **Amazon Web Services** (**AWS**), Microsoft Azure, **Google Cloud Platform** (**GCP**), and many other providers offer these services. Cloud offerings empower traditional IT offerings by adding many other services such as **artificial intelligence** (**AI**), **machine learning** (**ML**), **Internet of Things** (**IoT**), and security.

Cloud computing is a powerful technology for organizations of all sizes. Here are some of the key features of cloud computing:

- **Agility**: Cloud computing allows organizations to rapidly deploy and scale computing resources up or down as needed, which means they can be more agile and respond quickly to changing business requirements. With cloud computing, businesses can avoid the time and expense of building and managing their IT infrastructure, allowing them to focus on developing and delivering their products and services.

- **Productivity**: Cloud computing can improve productivity by providing access to computing resources and software from anywhere, on any device, and at any time. This flexibility allows employees to work remotely and collaborate more easily, which can lead to increased productivity and efficiency:

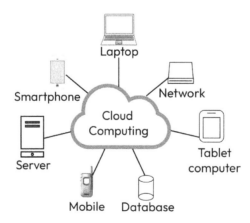

Figure 1.1 – Cloud computing

- **Resiliency**: Cloud computing can improve resiliency by providing redundancy and failover options, which means that if one computing resource fails, others can take over seamlessly. This reduces the risk of downtime and improves the availability and reliability of applications and services.

- **FinOps**: Cloud computing offers **Financial Operations (FinOps)** capabilities that allow organizations to manage and optimize their cloud spending. This includes tools for monitoring cloud usage, forecasting costs, and optimizing resource allocation to reduce costs and maximize value.

- **Pay-as-you-go model**: Cloud computing is often priced on a pay-as-you-go basis, which means that organizations only pay for the computing resources they use. This allows businesses to avoid the capital expense of buying and maintaining their IT infrastructure, and instead, pay for computing resources as an operational expense.

In summary, cloud computing provides organizations with agility, productivity, resiliency, FinOps, and a pay-as-you-go model, making it an attractive option for businesses looking to optimize their IT operations and focus on delivering value to their customers.

Gartner estimates the following by 2025 (`https://www.gartner.com/en/newsroom/press-releases/2021-11-10-gartner-says-cloud-will-be-the-centerpiece-of-new-digital-experiences`):

- More than 95% of new digital workloads will be deployed on cloud-native application platforms, up from 30% in 2021

- 70% of the new applications developed by companies will use low-code or no-code technologies

- More than 50% of organizations will have explicit strategies to adopt cloud-delivered **Secure Access Service Edge (SASE)**, up from less than 5% in 2020

- 85% of organizations will embrace cloud-first principles

While these fact-based estimations look very overwhelming, there is no doubt that the cloud provides extraordinary benefits to the data-driven business world.

Cloud computing service model

Cloud service models are different types of cloud computing services that are provided by CSPs to customers or users. There are three main types of cloud service models:

- **Infrastructure-as-a-Service (IaaS)**: In this service model, the CSP provides the infrastructure or computing resources such as servers, storage, and networking, which can be used by customers to build and manage their applications or services. The customer has control over the operating system, applications, and security, while the CSP is responsible for the underlying infrastructure.

- **Platform-as-a-Service (PaaS)**: In this service model, the CSP provides a platform for customers to develop, run, and manage their applications without the need to manage the underlying infrastructure. The customer can focus on building and deploying their applications while the CSP takes care of the infrastructure, operating system, and middleware.

- **Software-as-a-Service (SaaS)**: In this service model, the CSP provides a complete software application or service that can be accessed and used by customers over the internet. The customer does not need to install or manage the software as it is provided by the CSP as a service. Examples of SaaS include email, online storage, and **customer relationship management** (**CRM**) software.

In simple terms, cloud service models are different types of cloud computing services that are provided by CSPs to customers. These services can range from providing infrastructure resources to complete software applications, with varying degrees of control and management by the customer.

Next, let us talk about cloud security.

What is cloud security?

Cloud security refers to the set of practices, technologies, policies, and measures designed to safeguard data, applications, and infrastructure in cloud environments. Security in clouds is crucial because it addresses the unique security challenges and risks associated with cloud computing, which includes services such as IaaS, PaaS, and SaaS.

> **Important note**
>
> Gartner reports (`https://www.gartner.com/en/newsroom/press-releases/2021-11-10-gartner-says-cloud-will-be-the-centerpiece-of-new-digital-experiences`) that 99% of cloud breaches are traced back to preventable misconfigurations or mistakes by cloud customers.

It is evident that cloud computing services bring some overriding concerns too, and most of them can be prevented if they are configured correctly. This includes network and system misconfigurations, IAM misconfigurations, and accidental exposure of resources. We will read more about major configuration risks in *Chapter 11*, but some of them are explained in the following subsection.

Security concerns with the public cloud

There are several overriding concerns associated with cloud computing that organizations should be aware of:

- **Unauthorized access**: Public cloud services can be vulnerable to unauthorized access, which can lead to data breaches and the exposure of sensitive information.

- **Insider threats**: Cloud providers have access to users' data, which means that insider threats can pose a risk to security.

- **Data loss**: Public cloud services can suffer from data loss, which can occur due to hardware failures or other technical issues:

Figure 1.2 – Cloud security concerns

- **Compliance issues**: Public cloud services may not always meet regulatory and compliance requirements for data storage and security.

- **Multi-tenancy risks**: Public cloud services are often multi-tenant, which means that multiple users share the same physical infrastructure. This can increase the risk of data leakage or unauthorized access if they're not managed properly.

- **Vulnerabilities in third-party tools**: Public cloud services often rely on third-party tools and vendors, which can create vulnerabilities if these vendors are not properly vetted or have weak security measures in place.

- **Lack of control**: Public cloud services are managed by the cloud provider, which means that users have limited control over the security measures that are implemented.

- **DDoS attacks**: Public cloud services can be vulnerable to **distributed denial of service (DDoS)** attacks, which can disrupt service availability.

- **Data breaches through APIs**: Public cloud services often use APIs to enable integration with other systems, which can create vulnerabilities if these APIs are not secured properly.

- **Data exposure through misconfigured services**: Public cloud services can be vulnerable to data exposure if services are misconfigured, or access controls have not been set up properly.

It is important to understand these risks and take appropriate measures to mitigate them, such as implementing strong authentication and access controls, regularly monitoring and auditing activity, and using encryption to protect sensitive data. It is also important to work with reputable cloud providers who have a strong track record for security and compliance, be aware of the overriding concerns, and take steps to mitigate these risks through careful planning, risk assessment, and ongoing monitoring and management.

Now that you understand cloud computing and the security concerns around it, let us learn about the shared responsibility model.

The shared responsibility model

Cloud security is a tricky area. There are many myths about securing the cloud. Some think that once you have moved to the cloud, it is the cloud provider's responsibility to protect everything in the cloud, while others think that nothing is secure in the cloud and it is not safe to move to the cloud, especially when you are dealing with sensitive data. The fact is security and compliance in the cloud is a shared responsibility between cloud providers and cloud customers.

This brings a lot of questions to our minds. Who is responsible for what? How do you define the responsibility matrix between cloud providers and customers? Who defines those responsibilities and on what basis?

Let us understand this with a simple and fun analogy of a Pizza-as-a-Service model. The cloud's shared responsibility model can be explained using the analogy of ordering pizza in different ways: making it at home, ordering a Take and Bake pizza, ordering a pizza for delivery, or dining out at a restaurant:

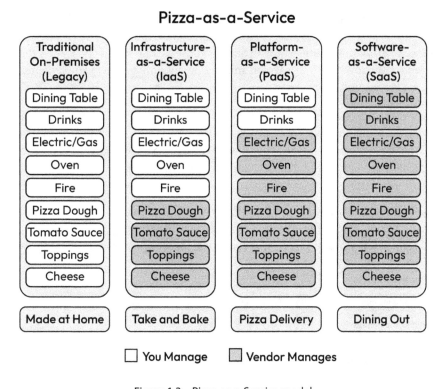

Figure 1.3 – Pizza-as-a-Service model

- **Making pizza** at home is like managing your IT infrastructure. You are responsible for everything, including buying the ingredients (hardware and software), preparing the dough and toppings (setting up the infrastructure and applications), cooking the pizza (maintaining the infrastructure), and cleaning up afterward (managing security, backups, and disaster recovery).

- **Ordering a Take and Bake pizza** is like using **IaaS**. You order the pizza with the toppings you want, but the pizza is not cooked yet. You must take it home and cook it yourself. Similarly, with IaaS, you are provided with a virtual infrastructure that you configure and manage yourself, including installing and configuring the operating system, middleware, and applications.

- **Ordering a pizza for delivery** is like using **PaaS**. You order the pizza with the toppings you want, and it is delivered to you fully cooked. You do not have to worry about the cooking process, but you still have control over the toppings. Similarly, with PaaS, you are provided with a platform for developing and deploying applications, and the CSP takes care of the underlying infrastructure.

- **Dining out at a restaurant** is like using **SaaS**. You order the pizza, and it is delivered to you fully cooked and ready to eat. You do not have to worry about cooking or toppings as the restaurant takes care of everything. Similarly, with SaaS, you use a cloud-based application that is fully managed by the cloud service provider, and you do not have to worry about the underlying infrastructure, security, or backups.

In all these scenarios, the shared responsibility model applies. You, as the customer, are responsible for selecting the pizza toppings you want, just as you are responsible for configuring and securing your data and applications in the cloud. The cloud service provider is responsible for providing a secure and reliable environment for your data and applications, just as the restaurant is responsible for providing a clean and safe dining experience.

Now that you have understood shared responsibility via an interesting analogy, let's understand the concept with the help of an actual responsibility model provided by every cloud provider for their customers. This responsibility is also known as security *of* the cloud versus security *in* the cloud:

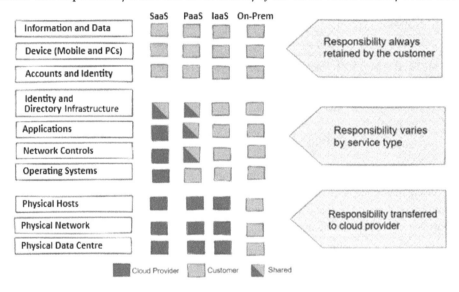

Figure 1.4 – Shared responsibility model

Let us quickly discuss what security of the cloud and security in the cloud mean:

- **Security of the cloud**: Security of the cloud means protecting the infrastructure that runs all the services offered by the cloud provider, which is composed of the hardware, software, networking, and facilities that public cloud services use. Cloud providers are responsible for the security *of* the cloud, which includes protecting the cloud environment against any security threats.

- **Security in the cloud**: This refers to the responsibility held by customers and is solely determined by the cloud services that customers choose for consumption and where those workloads are hosted, such as IaaS, PaaS, SaaS, **Database-as-a-Service (DBaaS)**, **Container-as-a-Service (CaaS)**, or even **Security-as-a-Service (SECaaS)**.

Customers must carefully consider the services they choose from different providers as their responsibilities vary depending on the services they use, the integration of those services into their IT environment, and applicable laws and regulations.

The responsibility model makes responsibility clear. When an organization does not have a cloud footprint, the organization is 100% responsible for the security and compliance of the infrastructure. When an organization moves to the cloud in a hybrid or cloud-native setup, the responsibility is shared between both parties.

Division of responsibility

Let us understand how the division of responsibilities varies from one service model to another:

- **On-premises data centers**: In an on-premises infrastructure (hardware and software), the customer is responsible for everything, from the physical security of data centers to the encryption of sensitive data.

- **IaaS**: Virtual machines as services, which are offered by cloud providers such as Azure VM, AWS EC2, and Google Compute Engine, can be taken as examples of IaaS. If a customer decides to use VMs in the cloud, the cloud provider is responsible for the security of the physical data center, physical network, and physical host where the VM is hosted. As per *Figure 1.4*, security to the operating system (vulnerabilities and patches), network controls, applications hosted in the VM, identity and directory infrastructure, devices through which VMs are accessed, and information and data in the VM are all the customer's responsibility.

- **PaaS**: A wide range of services is offered by cloud providers under the PaaS category. Azure Web App, Logic Apps, Azure Functions, Azure SQL, Azure Service Bus, AWS Lambda, AWS Elastic Beanstalk, and Google App Engine are a few services under the PaaS category. As the service name suggests, PaaS provides an environment for building, testing, and deploying software applications. The most useful benefit of PaaS for its customer is that it helps create an application quickly without the need to manage the underlying infrastructure, such as hardware and operating systems. This becomes easy for customers as they are only responsible for securing the application and data.

- **SaaS**: SaaS is a readymade, subscription-based application made available by cloud providers for its customers. Microsoft 365, Skype, Google Workspace, ERP, Amazon Chime, Amazon WorkDocs, and Dynamics CRM are some common examples of SaaS offerings. Out of all the service offerings, SaaS requires the least security responsibility from customers. The cloud provider is responsible for everything except data, identity access, accounts, and devices.

> **Important note**
>
> No matter which service is availed by the customer, the responsibility to protect accounts and identity, devices (mobile and PCs), and data is always retained by the customer.

The shared responsibility model is one of the most important topics to understand in the cloud security domain. Now that you understand it, let us understand another important topic – defense in depth.

Defense in depth

Defense in depth (**DiD**) is a cybersecurity strategy that uses a layered security approach to protect organizations' critical assets from cyber criminals by utilizing a series of security measures to slow the advance of an attack. This was originally inspired by the military strategy, where each layer provides protection so that if one layer is breached, a subsequent layer will prevent an attacker from getting unauthorized access to data.

Defense in depth guiding principle

The guiding principle of DiD is the idea that a single security product will not ensure the safety of critical data. Implementing multiple security controls at distinct levels reduces the chance of breaches caused by external or internal threats. The following diagram depicts the concept of the DiD layer. This approach is designed to provide a layered defense that can stop attackers at multiple points in the attack chain, rather than having to rely on a single point of failure:

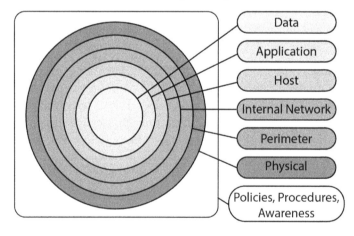

Figure 1.5 – Defense in depth (http://3.bp.blogspot.com/-YNJp1PXeV0o/
UjpD7j1-31I/AAAAAAAADJE/O_6COIge7CA/s1600/TechnetDinD.jpg)

The guiding principle of DiD is a strategy that is used to provide multiple layers of protection for a system or organization. Some important security practices that are used in DiD are as follows:

- **Least-privilege**: Least-privilege access is the practice of granting just enough access to the user so that they can perform their designated task in the organization and restrict their access to all other resources and systems. Limiting permissions on a user's identity helps minimize risk in case credentials are compromised and an unauthorized user attempts to access sensitive data.

- **Multi-factor authentication (MFA)**: This is a security mechanism that requires users to provide two or more factors of authentication to access a system or application. This approach adds an extra layer of security to the authentication process, making it more difficult for attackers to gain unauthorized access. They can use either software or hardware tokens to provide an additional layer of security beyond a user's password:

  - **Software tokens** are typically generated by a mobile app or software program. Once the user has entered their username and password, they are prompted to enter a one-time code generated by the app or software. This code is typically valid for only a short period and changes frequently, making it difficult for attackers to intercept and reuse.

  - **Hardware tokens**, on the other hand, are physical devices that generate one-time codes that the user must enter to complete the authentication process. These tokens may be in the form of key fobs, smart cards, or USB devices. The user inserts the hardware token into a device or presses a button to generate a code, which they then enter into the system or application being accessed.

  Both software and hardware tokens provide an additional layer of security by requiring something in addition to the user's password to gain access to a system or application. However, hardware tokens are generally considered more secure as they are not susceptible to attacks that can compromise software-based tokens, such as malware or phishing attacks. They also require physical possession of the token, making it more difficult for attackers to gain access, even if they have compromised the user's password.

- **Network segmentation**: This is the practice of dividing computer networks into smaller parts to limit the exposure of internal systems and data to vendors, contractors, and other outside or inside users. This also helps the security team protect sensitive data from insider threats, limit the spread of malware, and comply with data regulations.

- **Intrusion detection and prevention**: Intrusion detection and prevention systems can be used to detect and prevent attacks on a system or network. These systems can be configured to alert security personnel or take automated action when an attack is detected.

- **Security training**: Providing security awareness training to employees is an important security practice to ensure that they understand the importance of security and are aware of common threats and attack vectors.

These are just a few examples of the security practices that are part of DiD. Implementing these practices in a comprehensive and layered approach can help improve the overall security of an organization.

Security products and strategies at different layers

Let us take a closer look at what security products and strategies are appropriate and applied at different layers:

- **Physical security**: Physical security controls are an important part of DiD as they help protect an organization's physical assets, such as its buildings, servers, and other infrastructure. Here are some examples of physical security controls that are applied in the same way:

  - **Perimeter security**: Perimeter security controls are used to control access to the organization's property. Examples include fences, walls, gates, and barriers.

  - **Access control**: Access control measures are used to control who has access to the organization's physical assets. Examples include ID badges, security guards, and biometric authentication systems.

  - **Surveillance**: Surveillance measures are used to monitor the organization's physical assets for potential security threats. Examples include CCTV cameras, motion detectors, and security patrols.

  - **Environmental controls**: Environmental controls are used to protect the organization's physical assets from damage caused by environmental factors such as fire, water, and temperature. Examples include fire suppression systems, water leak detection systems, and temperature control systems.

  - **Redundancy**: Redundancy measures are used to ensure that the organization's physical assets remain operational even in the event of failure. Examples include backup generators, redundant HVAC systems, and redundant network connections.

- **Identity and access**: This implements security controls such as MFA, condition-based access, **attribute-based access control** (**ABAC**), and **role-based access control** (**RBAC**) to protect infrastructure and change control.

- **Perimeter**: A protection mechanism that is used across your corporate network to filter large-scale attacks such as DDoS so that the resources are not exhausted, causing a denial of service.

- **Network**: Security techniques such as network segmentation and network access control are used to segregate different resources together and to limit communication between resources to prevent lateral movement.

- **Compute**: This involves limiting access to VM from limited/whitelisted IPs only and also restricting certain ports and opening only the required ones.

- **Applications**: Four primary techniques can be used to secure applications, each with its strengths and weaknesses. Let us take a look:

  - **Runtime Application Self-Protection (RASP)**: RASP is an application security technology that is designed to detect and prevent attacks at runtime. RASP integrates with the application runtime environment and monitors the behavior of the application to identify potential threats. RASP can detect attacks such as SQL injection, **cross-site scripting** (**XSS**), and buffer overflow attacks, and can take action to block the attack or alert security personnel.

  - **Interactive Application Security Testing (IAST)**: IAST is an application security testing technique that combines aspects of both SAST and DAST. IAST is a real-time security testing technology that provides feedback on vulnerabilities during the testing process. IAST can detect vulnerabilities such as SQL injection and XSS attacks by monitoring the application during testing.

  - **Static Application Security Testing (SAST)**: SAST is an application security testing technique that analyzes the application's source code for security vulnerabilities. SAST can identify vulnerabilities such as buffer overflows, SQL injection, and XSS attacks. SAST is typically run during the development process and can help developers identify and fix vulnerabilities before the application is deployed.

  - **Dynamic Application Security Testing (DAST)**: DAST is an application security testing technique that analyzes the application while it is running. DAST can identify vulnerabilities such as SQL injection, XSS attacks, broken authentication, and session management. DAST is typically run after the application is deployed to identify vulnerabilities that may have been missed during the development process.

  Overall, these techniques can be used in combination to provide a comprehensive approach to securing applications. Each technique has its strengths and weaknesses, and the choice of which technique to use depends on the specific needs of the organization and the application being secured.

- **Data**: RBAC and ABAC are both access control models that are used to enforce data security:

  - In an RBAC model, access to resources is granted based on the user's role or job function within an organization. This means that users are assigned specific roles, and those roles are granted permission to access specific resources. For example, an administrator role might be granted full access to a system, while a regular user role might only be granted access to certain parts of the system.

  - In an ABAC model, access to resources is granted based on a combination of attributes, such as the user's job function, location, and time of day. This means that access control policies can be more flexible and granular than in an RBAC model. For example, a policy might be created to grant access to a resource only if the user is accessing it from a specific location and during specific hours.

Both RBAC and ABAC can be used to enforce data security by ensuring that only authorized users are granted access to sensitive data. Which model to use depends on the specific needs of the organization and the level of granularity and flexibility required for access control policies.

At this point, you should have a clear and baseline understanding of DiD. Now, let's try understanding a benchmark model in information security famously known as the **confidentiality, integrity, availability (CIA)** triad.

The CIA triad

Not to be confused with the central intelligence agency of the same acronym, **CIA** stands for **confidentiality, integrity, and availability**. It is a widely popular information security model that helps an organization protect its sensitive critical information and assets from unauthorized access:

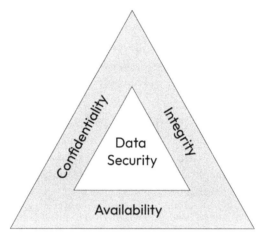

Figure 1.6 – The CIA triad (https://devopedia.org/images/article/178/8179.1558871715.png)

The preceding diagram depicts the CIA triad. Let's understand its attributes in detail.

Confidentiality

Confidentiality ensures that sensitive information is kept private and accessible only to authorized individuals. This attribute focuses on keeping sensitive information private and accessible only to authorized individuals or entities. It aims to prevent unauthorized disclosure of information, protecting it from being accessed or viewed by unauthorized users. Let's understand this by looking at an *example* of the payroll system of an organization. The confidentiality aspect of the payroll system ensures that employee salary information, tax details, and other sensitive financial data is kept private and accessible only to authorized personnel. Unauthorized access to such information can lead to privacy breaches, identity theft, or financial fraud.

Integrity

Integrity maintains the accuracy and trustworthiness of data by preventing unauthorized modifications. The integrity aspect ensures that information remains accurate, trustworthy, and unaltered. It safeguards against unauthorized modifications, deletions, or data tampering efforts, ensuring that the information's integrity is maintained throughout its life cycle. Let's understand integrity using the same example of the payroll system of an organization. The integrity aspect of the payroll system ensures that the data remains accurate and unchanged throughout its life cycle. Any unauthorized modifications to payroll data could lead to incorrect salary payments, tax discrepancies, or compliance issues.

Availability

Availability ensures that information and services are accessible and operational when needed without disruptions. This aspect emphasizes ensuring that information and systems are available and operational when needed. It focuses on preventing disruptions or denial of service, ensuring that authorized users can access the information and services they require without interruptions. Let's understand availability by using the same example of the payroll system of an organization. The availability aspect of the payroll system ensures that it is accessible and functional when needed. Payroll processing is critical for employee satisfaction and business operations, and any disruptions to the system could result in delayed payments or other financial issues.

Overall, the CIA triad provides a framework for organizations to develop effective cybersecurity strategies. By focusing on confidentiality, integrity, and availability, organizations can ensure that their systems and data are protected from a wide range of threats, including cyberattacks, data breaches, and other security incidents.

Why is it important to maintain confidentiality, integrity, and availability?

Cybersecurity professionals and cybercriminals work on the same strategy; the former works to develop the strategy to protect the confidentiality, integrity, and availability of a system, while the latter put all their effort to disrupt it. Maintaining the CIA triad is crucial because it serves as a comprehensive framework for addressing and balancing critical aspects of information security. Here is why it is essential to maintain the CIA triad:

- **Comprehensive security**: The CIA triad covers three fundamental dimensions of information security. By considering all three aspects, organizations can ensure a holistic approach to protecting their data and systems from a wide range of threats.

- **Risk management**: The triad helps organizations identify and prioritize potential risks. By understanding the vulnerabilities associated with confidentiality, integrity, and availability, they can implement appropriate security measures to mitigate these risks effectively.

- **Compliance and regulations**: Many laws and industry regulations mandate the protection of sensitive data and information. Adhering to the CIA triad assists organizations in complying with these legal requirements and demonstrating due diligence in safeguarding information.

- **Trust and reputation**: Maintaining the CIA triad instills confidence and trust among stakeholders, customers, and partners. Organizations that prioritize security and protect information gain a reputation for being reliable and trustworthy.

- **Business continuity**: Ensuring availability through the CIA triad helps organizations maintain operations even in the face of disruptions or attacks, thus safeguarding business continuity and reducing the impact of potential downtime.

- **Intellectual property protection**: The triad's integrity aspect is particularly vital for safeguarding intellectual property, trade secrets, and proprietary information. Maintaining data integrity prevents unauthorized changes or theft of valuable assets.

- **Incident response and recovery**: The CIA triad aids in developing effective incident response and recovery plans. Understanding how confidentiality, integrity, and availability may be compromised allows organizations to respond swiftly and appropriately to security incidents.

- **Defense against evolving threats**: As cybersecurity threats continue to evolve, the CIA triad remains a fundamental principle for guiding security strategies. By continually assessing and adapting security measures, organizations can stay ahead of emerging threats.

- **Competitive advantage**: Demonstrating a strong commitment to the CIA triad can become a competitive advantage. Organizations that effectively protect their data and systems may gain a competitive edge by inspiring trust and attracting security-conscious customers and partners.

- **Proactive security culture**: The CIA triad encourages organizations to cultivate a security-focused culture. By embedding security principles into their practices, employees become more aware of their role in protecting information and are better prepared to respond to security challenges.

In short, maintaining the CIA triad is vital for establishing a robust and resilient information security foundation. It helps organizations protect sensitive data, maintain business continuity, comply with regulations, and build trust among stakeholders, ultimately contributing to their overall success and longevity. Now, let us understand how organizations can maintain the CIA triad.

How do organizations ensure confidentiality, integrity, and availability?

Finding and maintaining the right balance of the CIA triad is challenging due to the diverse threat landscape, competing priorities, the complexity of IT systems, human factors, budget constraints, regulatory compliance, rapid technological advancements, and data sharing complexities. Organizations must proactively assess risks, prioritize assets, implement multi-layered (DiD) security strategies, and adapt to emerging threats. Collaboration among stakeholders is crucial for achieving a robust and effective security posture. It also requires a holistic approach to security and continual efforts to stay ahead of evolving security challenges. Organizations employ a combination of technical, administrative, and physical security measures to strike the right balance. Here are some common practices:

- **Confidentiality**:

  - **Access controls**: Implementing RBAC to ensure that only authorized individuals have access to sensitive data and information.

  - **Encryption**: Encrypting data during transmission (for example, using SSL/TLS for web traffic) and at rest (for example, encrypting data in databases or on storage devices) to protect against unauthorized access

  - **Secure Authentication**: Using strong authentication methods such as passwords, MFA, or biometrics to verify the identity of users.

- **Integrity**:

  - **Data validation**: Implementing validation checks to ensure that data is accurate, complete, and free from errors when it is entered into systems.

  - **Audit trails**: Creating logs and audit trails to track changes made to data and detect any unauthorized modifications.

  - **Version control**: Using version control mechanisms for critical documents to track changes and prevent unauthorized alterations.

- **Availability**:

  - **Redundancy**: Implementing redundant systems and infrastructure to ensure high availability and fault tolerance. This includes redundant servers, network links, and power sources.

  - **Load balancing**: Using load balancing techniques to distribute traffic across multiple servers, preventing overload and ensuring continuous service availability.

  - **Disaster recovery and business continuity planning**: Developing comprehensive plans and procedures to recover from system failures, natural disasters, or other emergencies, thus minimizing downtime and maintaining service availability.

Additionally, organizations can achieve the CIA triad through various administrative practices and security policies:

- **Security awareness training**: Conducting regular security awareness training for employees to educate them about security best practices, risks, and the importance of maintaining confidentiality, integrity, and availability

- **Risk assessment and management**: Identifying potential security risks and vulnerabilities through risk assessments and implementing measures to mitigate those risks effectively

- **Incident response**: Establishing incident response teams and procedures to quickly respond to and mitigate security incidents, ensuring the continuity of operations

- **Regular security audits**: Conducting periodic security audits and assessments to evaluate the effectiveness of existing security measures and identify areas for improvement

Achieving the CIA triad is an ongoing process that requires continuous monitoring, updates to security measures, and adaptations to address emerging threats. Organizations must strike a balance between security requirements and business needs and implement appropriate security controls to safeguard their information, systems, and operations effectively.

Now, let us understand another important topic of cybersecurity – the three pillars.

The three pillars of cybersecurity – people, process, and technology

People, process, and technology are the three most important pillars of cybersecurity that are essential for creating a comprehensive and effective cybersecurity strategy. If any of the people, process, or technology pillars are missing or inadequate in a cybersecurity strategy, it can significantly weaken the overall security posture of an organization and increase the risk of cyber threats. It will be as effective as a two-legged stool, unable to bear the full weight of an organization's security requirements. The following figure explains how each pillar is crucial for cybersecurity and, if missing, what impact it can bring to defect cybersecurity:

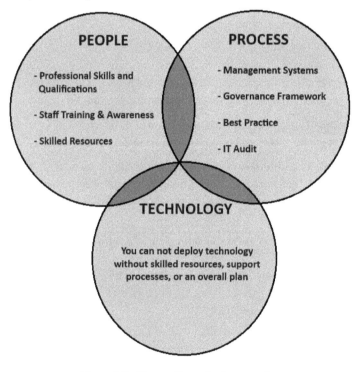

Figure 1.7 – Three pillars of cybersecurity

Let us look at these areas in detail:

- **People**: The people pillar refers to the human element of cybersecurity, including employees, contractors, and other stakeholders. People are an important part of any cybersecurity strategy because they can be both the weakest link and the strongest asset. Properly trained and aware employees can help prevent security breaches and quickly respond to incidents, while employees who lack awareness and training can inadvertently create security risks. To ensure the people pillar is strong, organizations should provide cybersecurity training to all employees, implement policies and procedures for cybersecurity best practices, and establish a culture of security awareness.

  If the people pillar is missing or inadequate, it can lead to security risks such as human error, insider threats, and social engineering attacks. Employees who lack cybersecurity awareness and training may inadvertently click on phishing emails or download malware, putting sensitive data at risk. Insider threats, where employees intentionally steal or leak data, can also be a significant risk if proper access controls and monitoring are not in place.

- **Process**: The process pillar refers to the policies, procedures, and standards that govern an organization's cybersecurity strategy. Effective processes are important for ensuring that security controls are consistently applied, security incidents are identified and responded to promptly, and risks are managed effectively. To ensure the process pillar is strong, organizations should implement a cybersecurity framework such as NIST or ISO, conduct regular risk assessments, establish incident response plans, and regularly review and update policies and procedures.

  If the process pillar is missing or inadequate, it can lead to inconsistent or ineffective security controls and responses to incidents. Without established policies and procedures, organizations may not know how to respond to security incidents, which could result in delays and increased damage. Risk assessments, vulnerability management, and incident response plans are all essential components of a strong process pillar.

- **Technology**: The technology pillar refers to the hardware, software, and other technological solutions that are used to protect an organization's systems and data. Technology is an important part of any cybersecurity strategy because it can help automate security controls and provide real-time threat intelligence. However, technology alone is not enough to ensure security. To ensure the technology pillar is strong, organizations should implement a layered DiD approach, including firewalls, intrusion detection and prevention systems, endpoint protection, encryption, and other security controls.

  If the technology pillar is missing or inadequate, it can leave systems and data vulnerable to a wide range of cyber threats. Without proper security controls, such as firewalls, intrusion detection systems, and encryption, cybercriminals may be able to breach systems and steal or damage sensitive data. Additionally, outdated software and systems can leave vulnerabilities open for exploitation.

Overall, by focusing on the three pillars of cybersecurity – people, process, and technology – organizations can create a comprehensive and effective cybersecurity strategy that is designed to protect against a wide range of cyber threats. Weakness in any of these pillars can have significant implications for an organization's cybersecurity. However, it is easier said than done when it comes to building a well-balanced program between these three pillars. Too often, organizations lack a solid foundation in all three pillars, which makes them vulnerable. In many cases, organizations look for **managed service providers** (**MSPs**) to get a more stable cybersecurity platform to protect their critical assets.

Now that you understand the three important pillars of cybersecurity, let us understand another important concept called the Zero Trust model.

The Zero Trust model

With exponential growth in cloud technology and the mobile workforce, the corporate network perimeter has been redefined. The traditional perimeter-based security approach is found to be ineffective as the resources are hosted in multi-cloud and hybrid scenarios. Today, organizations need a new security model that can provide secure access to their resources, irrespective of where they are accessed from and regardless of user or application environment. A Zero Trust security model helps in embracing the mobile workplace and helps in protecting identities, devices, apps, and data wherever they are located.

The Zero Trust model operates on the principle of *"trust no one, verify everything, every time."* This means that all users, devices, applications, and data that flow within an organization's network should be verified explicitly before being granted access to resources:

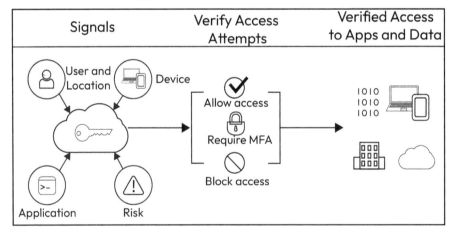

Figure 1.8 – The Zero Trust model (https://www.itgovernance.co.uk/blog/
wp-content/uploads/2015/07/PPT-Diagram-Blog.png)

Zero Trust guiding principles

The Zero Trust model has three principles based on NIST guidelines:

- **Verify explicitly**: The "verify explicitly" principle of Zero Trust means that access should be granted only after a user or device's identity and security posture have been verified and authenticated. This requires the use of strong authentication mechanisms, such as MFA, that require users to provide additional forms of authentication beyond just a password, such as a fingerprint scan, facial recognition, or a one-time code. In the case of devices, they must be assessed and verified before they are granted access to resources within an organization's network. This involves evaluating the device's security posture to ensure that it meets a minimum set of security standards, such as having the latest security patches, running up-to-date antivirus software, and having strong passwords or other authentication mechanisms in place. Devices that do not meet these security standards are either denied access or granted limited access until they can be remediated and brought up to the required security standards.

- **Least privilege access**: Least privilege access refers to **Just-in-Time** (**JIT**) access, which means elevating the permission as and when required to perform some tasks and then bringing back the default access with **Just Enough Administration** (**JEA**) to perform day-to-day tasks.

- **Minimize the blast radius**: This refers to the assume breach mindset, where you build your defense while keeping the worst-case scenario in mind so that even if some external or internal breach occurs, there is a minimum impact on the organization. Network segmentation, end-to-end encryption, advanced threat detection, and deeper analytics visibility are some practices to minimize the blast radius.

These guiding principles help us in understanding the baseline on which we define the conditions for the Zero Trust model. Now, let's understand which guidelines apply to which pillars.

The six foundational pillars

The following are the six pillars of the Zero Trust model. They work together to provide overall robust security for your infrastructure:

- **Identities**: Identities can refer to users, devices, or applications/services. It is important to verify and secure each identity with strong authentication across your entire digital estate. When an identity (user/device/service) attempts to access a resource, it must be verified with strong authentication and follow the least privilege principle.

- **Endpoints**: These are the carriers through which data flows on-premises and in the cloud; hence, they are the reason for creating large attack surfaces in many cases. It is important to have the visibility of devices accessing the network and notice their activities. A device's security posture and health, from a compliance perspective, is an important aspect of security.

- **Applications**: Discovering the shadow IT and in-app permissions is critical because applications are the way organizations' data is consumed. Not all applications' access management is managed centrally, so it is important to put a stringent process for access reviews and **privileged identity management (PIM)** in place.

- **Data**: Cloud computing services and offerings have completely changed the way data was managed traditionally, which resulted in perimeter-based whitelisting not being effective anymore in current hybrid/multi-cloud/SaaS-based systems. Many organizations do not have complete visibility of what kind of data they are dealing with, the most critical data, and where it resides in the organization. That is why it is important to discover, classify, label, and encrypt data intelligently based on its attributes. The whole effort is to protect the organization's critical data and ensure that data is safe from both internal and external threats. This is critical especially when data leaves devices, applications, infrastructure, and the network controlled by the organization.

- **Infrastructure**: Threats and attack vectors are very much a reality, whether they are on-premises or in the cloud. You can use intelligence-based telemetries such as JIT access, location, devices, and version to detect anomalies and attacks for ensuring security. This helps allow/block or automatically take action for any risky behavior almost at runtime, such as continuous failed login attempts.

- **Networks**: To make this pillar stronger, it is important to ensure that the devices are not trusted by default, even if they are in a trusted network. Implementing end-to-end encryption, reducing the attack surface by policy, network segmentation, in-network micro-segmentation, and real-time threat detection are some of the critical practices to keep in place.

Implementing all six pillars strongly is extremely hard to achieve. It becomes even more challenging when organizations have an enormously complex and hybrid infrastructure where they do not include security as a priority at an early stage. Now, let's understand the difference between security and compliance.

Compliance concepts

We are in the age of data analytics and data science, where data has become more precious than ever. Organizations, institutions, and businesses now rely on data to function on a day-to-day basis. It has become even more crucial to take extra care when dealing with data when organizations are moving their data to the cloud. To protect **personally identifiable information (PII)**, health-related data, and financial data, government agencies, regulatory authorities, and industry groups have issued regulations to help protect and govern the use of data.

Security and compliance are not the same concepts, even though they are very well interconnected and the line between them is blurred. **Security** refers to the set of policies, processes, and controls that a company implements to protect its assets, while **compliance** refers to the meeting that some regulatory body or third party has set as a best practice or legal requirement.

Some of the compliance concepts in cybersecurity include the following:

- **Regulatory compliance**: This refers to adherence to legal requirements, such as the **General Data Protection Regulation** (**GDPR**) and the **California Consumer Privacy Act** (**CCPA**). Regulatory compliance involves implementing security measures and protocols to protect sensitive data and ensure that organizations are following established legal requirements.

- **Industry-specific compliance**: This refers to adherence to specific security requirements established by particular industries, such as the **Payment Card Industry Data Security Standard** (**PCI DSS**) for organizations that handle credit card information. Industry-specific compliance involves implementing security measures and protocols that are specific to the requirements of a particular industry. Another significant example would be the **Health Insurance Portability and Accountability Act** (**HIPAA**) as it ensures the protection and confidentiality of individuals' sensitive health information, providing them with greater control over their medical data and promoting trust in the healthcare system. Its regulations establish standards for securely handling the protected health information of healthcare providers, insurers, and other entities in the United States.

- **Standards compliance**: This refers to adherence to established security standards, such as the ISO/IEC 27001 and the **National Institute of Standards and Technology** (**NIST**) standards for information security management systems. Standards compliance involves implementing security measures and protocols that meet or exceed established industry standards.

- **Best practices compliance**: This refers to adherence to established best practices for cybersecurity, such as the **Center for Internet Security** (**CIS**). Best practices compliance involves implementing security measures and protocols that are widely accepted as effective in the cybersecurity community. You can find the latest CIS benchmarks for cloud providers such as Alibaba, AWS, and Azure, as well as various other technologies, at `https://www.cisecurity.org/cis-benchmarks`.

Here are some important topics associated with data compliance:

- **Data residency**: This refers to the physical or geographical location of the data. It sounds normal in the case of on-premises but it's challenging to achieve when data is stored in the cloud. Some countries have regulations that their data must be stored on a server physically located within the country.

- **Data sovereignty**: This refers to the laws and governance structures that data is subject to, due to the geographical location of where it is processed.

- **Data privacy**: This refers to providing notice and being transparent about collecting, using, and sharing personal data. These are fundamental principles of laws and regulations.

Compliance in cybersecurity is important because it helps organizations establish a baseline of security measures and protocols that can protect sensitive data and ensure the security of computer systems and networks. Compliance can also be used to demonstrate to stakeholders that an organization is taking the necessary steps to protect data and mitigate cybersecurity risks.

Now, let's understand another interesting and important topic: cryptography.

Cryptography

In today's digital world, even with the utmost efforts to safeguard data, there remains a risk of losing control, especially when data is transmitted over the internet. To mitigate this risk, one effective method is encryption. By encrypting data, it becomes incomprehensible and unusable to unauthorized parties who lack the means to decrypt it.

> **Note**
> Cryptography is a comprehensive and well-covered subject in numerous cybersecurity books. To maintain a focus on the topics of cloud security, this book will only address its crucial and pertinent aspects in the context of cloud environments.

Cryptography is the science and practice of securing information by converting it into a secret code, making it unreadable and unusable to unauthorized parties. It plays a crucial role in ensuring data confidentiality, integrity, authentication, and non-repudiation, making it a fundamental tool for protecting sensitive information and communication in various digital systems, including computer networks, cloud computing, and online transactions.

Encryption

Encryption is a specific process within the field of cryptography. It is the technique of converting plaintext data into ciphertext using cryptographic algorithms and keys. The purpose of encryption is to protect data during transmission or storage by making it unreadable and unintelligible to unauthorized individuals or entities.

Encryption is pure mathematics. There is a defined complex method/formula to encrypt messages and decrypt those messages; you should have the same method *or* formula to decrypt them. Over time, encryption has achieved complexity due to attackers continuing to find ways to decrypt messages.

There are two different types of encryption: symmetric and asymmetric.

In symmetric encryption, the same secret key is used for both encrypting and decrypting data. This means that both the sender and the receiver need to possess the same secret key to securely communicate and exchange information:

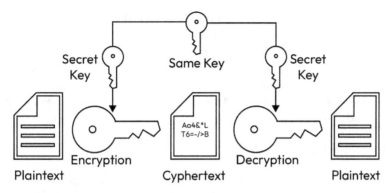

Figure 1.9 – Symmetric encryption (https://binarycoders.files.wordpress.
com/2020/07/01_symetric_encryption.png?w=1024)

Asymmetric encryption, also known as public-key encryption, is a cryptographic technique that uses a pair of keys (public key and private key) for secure communication and data exchange. The public key is used for encryption, while the private key is used for decryption:

Figure 1.10 – Asymmetric encryption (http://www.giuseppeurso.eu/wp-content/
uploads/2014/11/giuseppe-urso-asymmetric-key-encryption-in-java-03.png)

Let's look at how asymmetric encryption works:

- **Key generation**: A user generates a key pair consisting of a public key and a corresponding private key. The public key is made openly available, while the private key is kept secret.

- **Encryption**: If someone wants to send a confidential message to the key pair owner, they use the recipient's public key to encrypt the message.

- **Decryption**: Only the recipient who possesses the corresponding private key can decrypt the encrypted message that was sent to them using their public key.

The security of asymmetric encryption relies on the mathematical properties that make it computationally infeasible to derive the private key from the public key. As a result, the public key can be freely shared with others for encryption purposes, while the private key remains securely held by its owner for decryption. This makes asymmetric encryption a fundamental component of secure communication, digital signatures, and authentication in various applications, such as secure web browsing (HTTPS), email encryption, and digital certificates. Now that you understand the different types of encryption, let us understand another important concept: encrypting data in different stages.

Encrypting data in different stages

Data can be classified into different stages based on its level of activity or usage. The three main stages of data are data at rest, data in transit, and data in use. Encryption is a crucial technique that's used to protect data in these states:

- **Data at rest**: Data at rest refers to data that is stored on storage devices, such as hard drives, databases, or cloud servers, when it is not actively in use or being transmitted. Encryption at rest ensures that even if someone gains physical or unauthorized access to the storage medium, they won't be able to read or understand the data without the appropriate decryption key. For example, when you store sensitive files on your computer's hard drive, encrypting the files will protect them from unauthorized access if your device is lost or stolen.

- **Data in transit**: Data in transit refers to data that is being transmitted over networks between different devices or systems. Encryption in transit ensures that data is secured while it is moving from one location to another, preventing interception or eavesdropping by unauthorized parties. **Secure Sockets Layer** (**SSL**) or **Transport Layer Security** (**TLS**) protocols are commonly used for encrypting data during its transmission over the internet. For example, when you access a website using HTTPS, the data that's exchanged between your browser and the website's server is encrypted in transit.

- **Data in use**: Data in use refers to data that is actively being processed or accessed by an application or user. Encryption at this stage involves protecting the data while it is being used to prevent unauthorized access or disclosure. This can be achieved using techniques such as memory encryption or secure enclaves. For example, when you open a password-protected document, the data in the document is decrypted in memory for you to view and edit it. When you close the document or log out, the data is encrypted back in memory to protect it from potential unauthorized access.

Now that we have briefly covered encryption, let's understand the importance of encryption in the context of a cloud environment.

Importance of encryption for a multi-cloud hybrid environment

The importance of encryption in securing the cloud cannot be overstated. Encryption plays a vital role in ensuring the confidentiality, integrity, and privacy of sensitive data and communication within cloud environments. Here's why encryption is essential for cloud security:

- **Data confidentiality**: Encryption ensures that sensitive data stored in the cloud remains unreadable to unauthorized parties. Even if a security breach occurs, encrypted data appears as ciphertext, protecting it from exposure and misuse.

- **Secure communication**: When data is transmitted between cloud services and users, encryption guarantees secure communication. It prevents interception and eavesdropping, ensuring that sensitive information remains private during transit.

- **Data integrity**: Cryptographic techniques, such as digital signatures and hash functions, verify data integrity in the cloud. This prevents unauthorized modification or data tampering, maintaining its accuracy and reliability.

- **Access control**: Encryption enables robust access control in the cloud. By encrypting data and managing cryptographic keys effectively, cloud providers can enforce access restrictions, ensuring that data is accessible only to authorized personnel.

- **Regulatory compliance**: Many industries are subject to data protection regulations that require the use of strong cryptographic measures. By employing encryption, cloud providers can comply with these regulations and safeguard sensitive data.

- **User authentication**: Cryptographic mechanisms such as digital certificates and **public key infrastructure** (**PKI**) facilitate secure user authentication in the cloud. This ensures that users and services are legitimate and authorized to access cloud resources.

- **Key management**: Cloud environments involve managing a vast number of cryptographic keys for different purposes. Proper key management is essential for maintaining the security of encrypted data and protecting against unauthorized access.

- **Multi-tenancy security**: In a cloud environment, multiple users and organizations share the same infrastructure. Cryptography helps ensure that data from different tenants remains isolated and inaccessible to others, even if they share the same physical resources.

- **Data residency and sovereignty**: Encryption helps maintain data residency and sovereignty. Data can be encrypted in such a way that it remains unreadable to unauthorized entities, even if it's stored in different jurisdictions or countries.

- **Data sharing and collaboration**: With encryption, cloud users can securely share and collaborate on sensitive data with other authorized users or organizations without the risk of exposing the data to unauthorized parties.

Overall, encryption provides a critical layer of protection for cloud data and services.

Now, let's understand how encryption is achieved in cloud environments.

Encryption in cloud environments

In cloud environments, responsibility for encryption is typically shared between the cloud service provider and the customer. The cloud service provider is responsible for providing the underlying infrastructure and tools to enable encryption, while the customer is responsible for implementing encryption practices for their data and managing access to the encryption keys.

Encryption in a cloud environment can be achieved through a multi-step process that involves various responsibilities and tools. A cloud customer must understand these points. Let's break down the process:

1. **Data classification and encryption strategy**: The customer is responsible for classifying their data based on sensitivity and compliance requirements. They need to determine what data needs to be encrypted and what encryption algorithms to use. No specific tool is involved in this step. It's more of a policy and decision-making process.

2. **Data encryption**: The customer is responsible for encrypting their data before sending it to the cloud or storing it in the cloud service. Various encryption libraries and tools are available for data encryption, such as OpenSSL and HashiCorp Vault, as well as cloud provider-specific encryption via a **software development kit (SDK)**.

3. **Key generation and management**: The cloud service provider is responsible for providing a **Key Management Service (KMS)** that allows customers to create and manage encryption keys securely. Cloud service providers offer their own KMSs, including AWS KMS, Azure Key Vault, and Google Cloud KMS.

4. **Customer Master Key (CMK) creation and protection**: The customer is responsible for creating and managing their CMKs within the cloud provider's KMS. CMKs are used to protect and control access to data encryption keys. The KMS provided by the cloud service provider is used to create and manage CMKs.

5. **Data upload and storage**: The cloud service provider is responsible for securely receiving and storing encrypted data. No specific tool is involved here. The cloud provider's storage infrastructure handles the encrypted data.

6. **Data retrieval and decryption**: The customer is responsible for retrieving the encrypted data from the cloud and decrypting it using the appropriate **Data Encryption Key (DEK),** which is decrypted using the CMK. The decryption process is performed using encryption libraries or tools, along with the cloud provider's KMS to retrieve and use the necessary keys.

7. **Key rotation and life cycle management**: The customer is responsible for regularly rotating encryption keys and managing their life cycle to minimize the risk of unauthorized access. The cloud provider's KMS offers APIs and tools to facilitate key rotation and life cycle management.

8. **Monitoring and auditing**: Both the cloud service provider and the customer share the responsibility of monitoring and auditing encryption-related activities to detect and respond to security incidents or unauthorized access. **CSPM tools** provide the visibility of risk associated with keys.

In summary, encryption in the cloud involves collaboration between the cloud service provider and the customer. The customer is responsible for data classification, encryption, key management, and data decryption, while the cloud provider is responsible for providing a secure KMS and ensuring the secure storage and retrieval of encrypted data. Various encryption libraries, KMSs, and CSPM tools play crucial roles in achieving a robust encryption process in the cloud environment.

Now that you have a fundamental understanding of encryption and its relevance in cloud environments, let us understand another important topic: the **Cloud Adoption Framework (CAF)**. This is one of the most important topics for organizations planning to adopt the cloud for their infrastructure.

The Cloud Adoption Framework

CAF is a collection of guidelines, best practices, tools, and templates from all major public cloud providers to accelerate an organization's cloud adoption journey. Every organization has a diverse set of on-premises resources, critical data that they deal with, and regulatory compliance that they need to adhere to, and hence no one cloud adoption formula fits all. It is extremely important to have a strategy to adopt the cloud, and CAF helps business leaders and technology managers define the path of their adoption using CAF. All leading public cloud service providers have developed a version of CAF, which helps make the journey smoother for their potential customers moving into the cloud. It is a useful place to start your journey to understand your needs and do the initial assessment – that is, the *maturity assessment*. This maturity assessment helps you understand your existing infrastructure, processes, and readiness to adopt the cloud. It also helps the customer in choosing the right service model and IaaS, PaaS, and SaaS offerings.

Microsoft's CAF involves the following steps. You should also refer to the other cloud frameworks from AWS and GCP:

1. **Strategy**: This phase involves establishing the business case for cloud adoption and defining the organization's cloud strategy. It includes defining the organization's goals, identifying potential benefits and risks, and selecting the appropriate cloud service provider.

2. **Plan**: In this phase, the organization develops a detailed plan for migrating to the cloud. This includes identifying the workloads to be migrated, assessing their suitability for cloud deployment, and determining the appropriate migration strategy.

3. **Ready**: This phase involves preparing the organization's environment for cloud adoption. This includes establishing the necessary infrastructure, networking, and security requirements to ensure a smooth transition to the cloud. This also includes setting up the landing zone for the cloud infrastructure and defining the best practices to expand as the need arises.

4. **Adopt**: In this phase, the organization deploys its workloads to the cloud environment. This includes configuring and evaluating the cloud infrastructure and applications to ensure they are functioning as expected.

5. **Govern**: In this phase, the organization establishes governance policies and processes to manage its cloud-based solutions. This includes monitoring and managing cloud resources, ensuring compliance with regulatory requirements, and establishing security controls to protect against cyber threats.

6. **Manage**: This final phase involves ongoing management and optimization of the cloud environment. This includes monitoring performance, managing costs, and continually improving cloud-based solutions to meet the organization's evolving needs.

Overall, CAF provides organizations with a structured approach to adopting cloud computing technologies. By following the framework, organizations can better plan, implement, and manage their cloud-based solutions, enabling them to realize the full benefits of cloud computing while minimizing risks and costs. Now that you understand CAF, let us understand the last but very important topic of this chapter: landing zones.

Landing zone concepts

In the past, a common practice was to manage all cloud operations within a single cloud account, including various stages such as *development*, *testing*, *staging*, and *production*. This approach posed several challenges, particularly regarding security management. The absence of proper security measures raised concerns about the integrity of sensitive data and resources across different environments within the same account. Additionally, this setup hindered scalability, making it difficult to accommodate new teams and applications seamlessly. Moreover, the lack of centralized control and monitoring prevented efficient oversight of cloud resources.

To overcome these limitations and enhance the cloud adoption process, the concept of a "landing zone" emerged.

A **landing zone** refers to a well-architected, standardized, and secure foundation that organizations establish to facilitate the migration of workloads to the cloud or to enable the deployment of new workloads in the cloud. It serves as the starting point for cloud adoption and provides the necessary building blocks to ensure a smooth and controlled transition to the cloud. CAF and the landing zone are closely related and complement each other in the process of migrating to the cloud.

CAF versus the landing zone

CAF and the landing zone are interrelated components of a comprehensive cloud migration strategy. Here is how they relate to each other:

*   **Planning phase**: In the planning phase of CAF, organizations evaluate their current IT landscape, business goals, and technical requirements. As part of this planning, they also define the landing zone architecture that aligns with their cloud strategy. The landing zone becomes the technical foundation based on the strategic decisions made in CAF.

- **Design and architecture**: CAF addresses high-level architectural considerations, while the landing zone is more specific to the technical design and implementation. CAF sets the direction and objectives, and the landing zone translates those objectives into tangible technical solutions.

- **Governance and security**: Both CAF and the landing zone emphasize governance and security. CAF establishes the policies and controls that govern cloud adoption, while the landing zone enforces these policies at the technical level, ensuring consistent security measures, compliance, and best practices.

- **Execution and deployment:** Once CAF's planning phase is complete, the organization can use the defined landing zone architecture as the blueprint for implementing the initial cloud deployment. The landing zone serves as a ready-to-use template, accelerating the migration process while maintaining a standardized and secure environment.

The importance of a landing zone

Implementing a landing zone is a recommended approach when adopting the cloud and migrating workloads. Here are some of the advantages of implementing a landing zone:

- **Isolation and security**: With a landing zone, you can segregate different environments (development, test, staging, production, and so on) into separate accounts or sub-accounts. This isolation helps in containing any security breaches or issues, minimizing the impact on other environments.

- **Scalability and flexibility**: A landing zone architecture is designed to be scalable and flexible. It allows you to easily onboard new teams and applications, providing a consistent and well-defined environment for them to work in.

- **Centralized control and monitoring**: By using a landing zone, you can establish centralized governance and control over all cloud resources. This ensures that security policies, compliance requirements, and best practices are uniformly enforced across the organization.

- **Resource management**: A landing zone often includes resource templates, predefined policies, and automation scripts that simplify resource provisioning, management, and deployment. This streamlines the process of creating and managing cloud resources.

- **Cost management**: A well-designed landing zone can include cost management features, helping you track and optimize cloud spending across different accounts and environments.

- **Compliance and auditing**: By adopting a landing zone, you can better address compliance requirements and facilitate auditing processes since all resources are organized and managed while following a standardized approach.

- **Risk reduction**: Isolating environments and implementing security best practices in a landing zone helps reduce the risk of data breaches, unauthorized access, and other security-related issues.

Overall, a landing zone provides a solid foundation for an organization's cloud environment, enabling them to deploy workloads in a secure, efficient, and cost-effective manner while ensuring consistency and compliance with organizational policies and standards.

The core components of a landing zone

The primary goal of a landing zone is to ensure consistent deployment and governance across various environments, such as **production (Prod)**, **quality assurance (QA)**, **user acceptance testing (UAT)**, and **development (Dev)**. Let us understand the core concepts associated with landing zones:

- **Network segmentation**: Network segmentation is a critical aspect of a landing zone architecture, and it involves dividing the cloud environment into distinct network segments to ensure isolation and security between different environments and workloads. Each environment (Prod, QA, UAT, and Dev) has a dedicated network segment. These segments are logically separated to prevent unauthorized access between environments. Network segmentation ensures that activities in one environment do not impact others and that sensitive data is adequately protected.

- **Isolation of environments**: The network segments for each environment are isolated from each other to minimize the risk of data breaches or unauthorized access. This can be achieved through various means, such as **Virtual Private Clouds (VPCs)** in AWS, **Virtual Networks (VNets)** in Azure, or VPCs in GCP.

- **Connectivity between environments**: While isolation is crucial, there are specific scenarios where controlled connectivity is required between environments, such as data migration or application integration. This connectivity should be strictly controlled and monitored to avoid security risks.

- **Identity and access management (IAM)**: IAM policies and roles are implemented to regulate access to cloud resources within each environment. This ensures that only authorized users have access to specific resources based on their roles and responsibilities.

- **Security measures**: Each landing zone environment should have security measures, including firewall rules, security groups, **network access control lists (NACLs)**, and other security-related settings. This helps safeguard resources and data from potential threats.

- **Centralized governance**: A landing zone architecture also implements centralized governance and monitoring to maintain consistency, compliance, and visibility across all environments. This involves using a central management account or a shared services account for common services.

- **Resource isolation**: Within each environment, further resource isolation can be achieved by using resource groups (Azure), projects (GCP), or organizational units (AWS) to logically group resources and manage access control more effectively.

- **Monitoring and auditing**: To maintain the health and security of the landing zone, comprehensive monitoring and auditing practices should be implemented. This includes monitoring for suspicious activities, resource utilization, and compliance adherence.

Overall, a landing zone architecture provides a solid foundation for an organization's cloud deployment by enforcing security, governance, and network segmentation across different environments. This architecture is cloud provider-agnostic and can be adapted to various cloud platforms such as Azure, AWS, and GCP while following their respective best practices and services. To read more about it, you can search for Cloud Adoption Framework, followed by the cloud provider's name, via your favorite search engine – you will get plenty of resources.

Summary

Cloud security is an interesting topic and fun to learn. I hope you enjoyed it as much as I enjoyed writing some of these fundamental concepts. In this chapter, we introduced you to some important security and compliance concepts. This included shared responsibility in cloud security, encryption and its relevance in a cloud environment, compliance concepts, the Zero Trust model and its foundational pillars, and some of the most important topics related to cryptography. Finally, you were introduced to CAF and landing zones. All the terms and concepts discussed in this chapter will be referred to throughout this book. I encourage you to deep dive into these topics as much as you can.

In the next chapter, we will learn about **cloud security posture management** (CSPM) and the important concepts around it. Happy learning!

Further reading

To learn more about the topics that were covered in this chapter, look at the following resources:

- *Certificate of cloud security knowledge*: `https://cloudsecurityalliance.org/education/ccsk/`

- *CIS benchmarks list*: `https://www.cisecurity.org/cis-benchmarks`

- *Shared responsibility model*: `https://aws.amazon.com/compliance/shared-responsibility-model/`

2

Understanding CSPM and the Threat Landscape

Having a proper understanding of what **Cloud Security Posture Management (CSPM)** is and its importance in the cloud infrastructure is crucial to all stakeholders. A security leader or CISO's clear understanding of the role of CSPM in the cloud infrastructure is just as important as it is for security managers, architects, designers, and cloud security administrators or engineers. After setting the baseline understanding of cloud security in *Chapter 1*, this chapter focuses on building the concepts, and the importance and need of CSPM tools for multi-cloud infrastructure. This chapter also highlights Gartner's view on CSPM and key elements where Gartner emphasizes focusing more.

The following main topics are covered in this chapter:

- What is CSPM?
- Threat landscape and the importance of CSPM tools
- Key capabilities of CSPM and its working functions
- Common cloud misconfigurations and how they occur
- Best practices to safeguard from cloud misconfigurations
- Are CSPM tools enough to protect the cloud environment?
- Other cloud security technologies and tools

Let us get started and dive deep into the topics!

What is CSPM?

CSPM is a type of security tool or solution that helps organizations assess, monitor, and manage the security posture of their cloud environments. The term *CSPM* was coined by the Gartner research firm in its 2019 innovation paper (`https://www.gartner.com/reviews/market/cloud-security-posture-management-tools`) and is defined as follows:

> *"Cloud security posture management tools help in the identification and remediation of risks across cloud infrastructures, including Infrastructure as a Service (IaaS), Software as a Service (SaaS), and Platform as a Service (PaaS). These tools continuously assess the security posture across multi-cloud environments by maintaining a current inventory of the cloud assets for proactive analysis and risk assessment to detect any misconfigurations. Once these misconfigurations are identified, security controls are developed and implemented. CSPM solutions also integrate with DevOps tools, streamlining the incident response process and ensuring continuous compliance with regulatory requirements and security frameworks by providing visibility of the cloud environment's security posture."*

Gartner also notes that CSPM solutions can be integrated with a variety of other security tools and solutions, such as **Cloud Access Security Brokers** (**CASBs**), DevOps tools, **Security Information and Event Management** (**SIEM**), and **Data Loss Prevention** (**DLP**) to provide a comprehensive view of the security posture of cloud environments. Most CSPM tools come with inherent features of vulnerability management; however, they can also integrate with existing vulnerability management solutions to ensure that vulnerabilities are identified and addressed in the cloud environment. CSPM solutions can provide visibility into the cloud environment and identify vulnerabilities that could be exploited by attackers.

Gartner also highlights in that research paper that *"nearly all successful attacks on cloud services are the result of the customer side of misconfiguration, mismanagement, and mistakes."*

Gartner refers to CSPM as a new market sector for vendors. Here are some features that a CSPM should have as per Gartner's recommendations:

- **Asset discovery**: CSPM solutions should be able to identify all assets in the cloud environment, including virtual machines, containers, storage, and network resources. This helps organizations to ensure that their cloud environment is secure and compliant with relevant regulations and standards.

- **Configuration management**: CSPM solutions should be able to identify misconfigurations in the cloud environment and provide guidance on how to remediate them. This includes ensuring that cloud resources are configured in line with best practices for security and compliance.

- **Vulnerability management**: CSPM solutions should be able to detect vulnerabilities in the cloud environment and provide guidance on how to address them. This includes prioritizing vulnerabilities based on the severity of the risk they pose and providing recommendations for remediation.

- **Compliance monitoring**: CSPM solutions should be able to monitor compliance with relevant regulations and standards, including HIPAA, PCI DSS, and GDPR. This includes providing reports and alerts on compliance status and identifying areas where improvements can be made.

- **Threat detection and response**: CSPM solutions should be able to detect potential security incidents in the cloud environment and provide guidance on how to respond to them. This includes identifying **Indicators Of Compromise (IoCs)** and providing recommendations for incident response.

- **Cloud governance**: CSPM solutions should provide organizations with the ability to manage cloud governance policies and automate compliance workflows. This includes providing templates for cloud governance policies and automating compliance assessments and remediation.

- **Integration with other security solutions**: CSPM solutions should integrate with other security solutions, such as SIEM, DLP, and IAM solutions, to provide a comprehensive approach to cloud security. This includes sharing threat intelligence and security information across different security solutions to improve overall security posture.

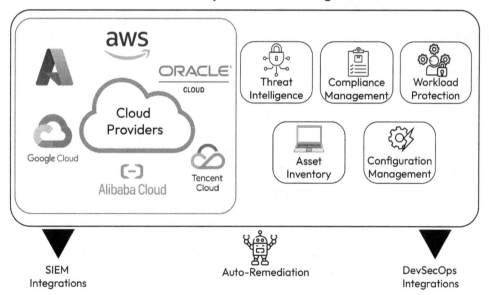

Figure 2.1 – Cloud Security Posture Management

CSPM tools empower organizations by identifying and remediating the risk through security assessments and automated compliance monitoring for **Infrastructure as a Service** (IaaS), **Platform as a Service** (PaaS), and **Software as a Service** (SaaS) across the Azure public cloud, AWS, Google Cloud, and hybrid clouds. CSPM tools are also growing over time in terms of their features and capabilities. Initially, CSPM tools helped in visualizing the IaaS and PaaS asset inventory; however, their most recent version is richer and more robust, with auto-remediation capabilities that reduce overhead.

In short, CSPM is a crucial tool for organizations that are leveraging cloud services, as it helps to ensure that their cloud environment is secure and compliant with industry standards and best practices. Now that you have an understanding of CSPM, let us understand the importance of CSPM tools.

Threat landscape and the importance of CSPM tools

Many organizations lack the visibility of their resources in the cloud, which can cause misconfigurations to go unnoticed for a longer period. This can make applications vulnerable. For example, organizations are unaware of how many cloud resources they are running and how they are all configured.

Gartner reports that by 2025 (`https://www.gartner.com/smarterwithgartner/is-the-cloud-secure`), the following will apply:

- 90% of organizations will inappropriately expose their sensitive data if they fail to control public cloud use

- 99% of cloud security failures will be the fault of cloud customers

Threat landscape refers to the evolving and dynamic state of security threats and vulnerabilities, including the types of threats, their sources, and the ways they can be carried out. The threat landscape changes frequently, and organizations need to continuously monitor and update their security measures to stay ahead of the latest threats.

In the cloud, the threat landscape includes a wide range of risks, such as unauthorized access to data, misconfigured cloud services, and compromised cloud accounts. CSPM helps organizations to stay on top of these threats by providing continuous visibility and control over their cloud security posture, allowing them to detect, respond to, and mitigate security risks in real time.

Security breaches are growing every year and regulatory compliance policies are becoming more stringent day by day. Thus, many security breaches carry huge monetary consequences, but more than that, they bring reputational damage as well.

Figure 2.2 is from Statista, and it describes the average cost of data breaches in the United States between 2006 and 2022. Let us take a close look:

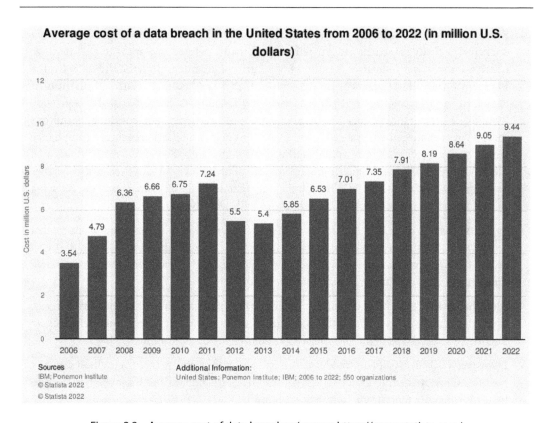

Figure 2.2 – Average cost of data breaches (source: https://www.statista.com/
statistics/273575/us-average-cost-incurred-by-a-data-breach/)

With these trends, predictions, and day-to-day headlines, it is evident that organizations need to be more attentive toward their security posture. This is where CSPM comes into the picture to bridge the gap. Let us explore some of the reasons CSPM is important:

- **Compliance benchmarks**: Compliance benchmarks are sets of guidelines or best practices that are designed to help organizations achieve a specific level of security. Compliance benchmarks are often created by organizations such as the **Center for Internet Security** (**CIS**) and are intended to help organizations meet specific compliance requirements or address specific security risks. CSPM solutions can help organizations achieve compliance with compliance benchmarks by providing visibility into their cloud environment and identifying security misconfigurations and vulnerabilities that could lead to compliance violations. CSPM solutions can also automate the assessment process, reducing the manual effort required to ensure compliance.

- **Security standards**: Compliance benchmarks and security standards are related but distinct concepts. Security standards are typically more broadly defined and apply to a wide range of organizations and industries. Examples of security standards include ISO/IEC 27001, the **Payment Card Industry Data Security Standard** (**PCI DSS**), and the **National Institute of Standards and Technology** (**NIST**) Cybersecurity Framework. Security standards provide a framework for organizations to establish, implement, maintain, and continually improve their security management systems. CSPM solutions help organizations achieve compliance with security standards by providing continuous visibility into their cloud environment and identifying security misconfigurations and vulnerabilities that could lead to security breaches or compliance violations. Most CSPM solutions also automate the assessment process, reducing the manual effort required to ensure compliance with security standards.

- **Protects sensitive data**: With the increasing use of cloud services, it is important to ensure that sensitive data is protected from cyber threats such as data breaches, hacking, and unauthorized access. CSPM helps organizations secure their data in the cloud by monitoring the environment for vulnerabilities and implementing security controls.

- **Identifies risks**: CSPM helps organizations identify potential risks in their cloud environment, such as misconfigured security settings, outdated software, and unpatched vulnerabilities, so that they can take steps to mitigate these risks before they become a threat.

- **Improves visibility**: CSPM provides organizations with visibility into their cloud security posture, allowing them to understand what resources are in place and what changes need to be made to ensure that the environment is secure.

- **Continuous monitoring**: CSPM continuously monitors the cloud environment, which enables organizations to detect and respond to security incidents in real time, reducing the risk of damage to the environment and the business.

Overall, CSPM is important because it helps organizations secure their cloud environment, maintain compliance with regulations, and protect sensitive data. By implementing a robust CSPM program, organizations can enhance their security posture, protect their critical assets, and reduce the risk of data breaches and other security incidents in the cloud. Let us take a look at the key capabilities and core components of CSPM tools.

Key capabilities and core components of CSPM

Cloud environments are becoming too large and complex for organizations, so it has become almost impossible to rely on manual processes. A robust CSPM tool is driven by automation. It automatically and continuously checks for misconfiguration and helps protect organizations from data breaches and leaks. Let us now look at some of the best features offered by CSPM in general, which are also depicted in *Figure 2.3*:

Figure 2.3 – CSPM features

Here are some of the core capabilities of a typical CSPM tool:

- **DevSecOps integration**: CSPM tools interact with existing DevOps tools sets along with SIEM and SOAR toolsets, allowing for quicker remediation and reaction inside the DevOps toolsets

- **Asset discovery and management**: CSPM tools allow organizations to discover and inventory their cloud assets, including compute resources, storage, databases, and networking components

- **Configuration management**: CSPM tools help organizations manage the configuration of their cloud assets, ensuring they comply with security best practices and company policies

- **Threat detection and response**: CSPM tools use machine learning, behavior analysis, and other advanced techniques to detect security threats in real time and provide automated remediation recommendations

- **Compliance management**: CSPM tools help organizations ensure their cloud infrastructure complies with industry regulations and standards such as PCI DSS, HIPAA, and SOC 2

- **Access control**: CSPM tools allow organizations to manage and control access to their cloud assets, including user authentication, authorization, and role-based access control

- **Activity monitoring**: CSPM tools provide visibility into user activity and resource usage, including API calls, network traffic, and resource utilization

- **Reporting and analytics**: CSPM tools generate reports and analytics that provide insights into the security posture of an organization's cloud infrastructure, including trends, anomalies, and areas of improvement

These are some of the key capabilities of CSPM tools, but the specific features and capabilities may vary depending on the tool. Now that you understand the core capabilities of CSPM tools, let us understand the workings of CSPM tools.

How do CSPM tools work?

CSPM tools work by continuously monitoring the security posture of an organization's cloud environment. They use various techniques such as vulnerability scanning, asset discovery, and configuration analysis to identify and assess the security risks in the cloud infrastructure. The tools analyze the cloud environment and identify potential security threats, misconfigurations, and vulnerabilities. They then provide actionable insights and recommendations to help organizations resolve security issues and improve their overall security posture. Additionally, the tools can also automate security remediation processes and provide real-time monitoring and reporting capabilities. By continuously monitoring and assessing the cloud environment, CSPM tools help organizations maintain a secure cloud infrastructure and meet security compliance requirements.

Now that you understand how CSPM tools work, let us now try to understand the common cloud misconfigurations and the reasons for their occurrence.

Common cloud misconfigurations and their causes

Several common cloud misconfigurations can lead to security and data privacy issues. Some of these are shown here:

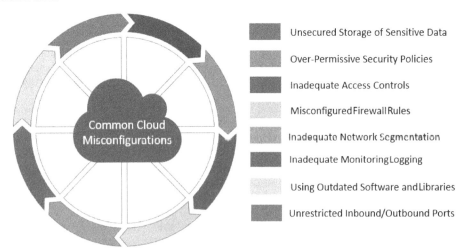

Figure 2.4 – Common cloud misconfigurations

Let's look at them in detail:

- **Unsecured storage of sensitive data**: This includes storing sensitive data such as credentials and confidential information in an unencrypted format, which can leave it vulnerable to theft.

- **Over-permissive security policies**: Allowing overly permissive security policies, such as granting full access to all users or resources, can increase the risk of data breaches and other security incidents.

- **Inadequate access controls**: Improperly configured access controls can allow unauthorized access to sensitive data and systems, potentially leading to data breaches and other security incidents.

- **Misconfigured firewall rules**: Misconfigured firewall rules can leave systems and networks exposed to threats, making it easier for attackers to gain access.

- **Inadequate network segmentation**: A lack of proper network segmentation can allow attackers to move laterally within a network and gain access to sensitive systems and data.

- **Inadequate monitoring and logging**: A lack of proper monitoring and logging can make it difficult to detect and respond to security incidents in a timely manner.

- **Using outdated software and libraries**: Using outdated software and libraries can leave systems and applications vulnerable to known security exploits and attacks.

- **Unrestricted inbound/outbound ports**: Having unrestricted inbound and outbound ports can pose a significant security risk for a network. It is essential to restrict inbound and outbound ports to minimize the risk of security incidents and maintain the integrity of a network. This can be done through proper firewall configuration and the implementation of security best practices:

  - **Inbound ports**: When inbound ports are unrestricted, it makes it easier for malicious actors to exploit vulnerabilities in network-connected devices, such as servers, laptops, and other internet-connected devices. This can lead to unauthorized access, data theft, and other security incidents.

  - **Outbound ports**: Unrestricted outbound ports allow malware to communicate with command-and-control servers or exfiltrate sensitive data. Malicious software can use these ports to transmit data and receive commands, making it more difficult for network administrators to detect and prevent security incidents.

It is important to take a proactive approach to cloud security and to regularly assess and update your configurations to avoid these and other common cloud misconfigurations. Now that you know the common misconfigurations in clouds, let us try to explore the reason behind these misconfigurations.

Why do misconfigurations occur?

Cloud misconfigurations occur when the settings, configurations, or deployment of cloud resources are not effectively managed or executed. Some common causes of cloud misconfigurations include the following:

- **Human error due to skill gap**: One of the most common causes of cloud misconfiguration is human error. This could be due to a lack of understanding of the cloud environment, incorrect manual settings, or typos in configuration files.

- **Insufficient access controls**: If the right access controls are not in place, unauthorized users may be able to access sensitive data or modify critical settings.

- **Automation issues**: Automated processes and scripts can sometimes cause unintended changes to the cloud environment. This can happen if the automation process is not thoroughly tested or if it is not set up to handle changes in the environment.

- **Lack of monitoring and maintenance**: Cloud resources that are not properly monitored and maintained can quickly become misconfigured. Regular checks and updates can help to prevent misconfigurations from happening.

- **Improper deployments**: Cloud resources that are not deployed properly can also lead to misconfigurations. This can be due to a lack of planning or understanding of the deployment process.

- **Legacy systems**: Legacy systems can sometimes cause issues when they are integrated into a cloud environment. This is because they may not be designed to work with cloud-based systems and may require manual configuration.

This can be solved through regular monitoring and maintenance, implementing proper access controls, and having a thorough understanding of the cloud environment. Now that you understand the misconfigurations and the reason behind their occurrence, let us now try to understand some of the best ways to safeguard from cloud misconfiguration.

Best practices to safeguard from misconfiguration

Cloud misconfiguration can result in serious security threats, data breaches, and financial losses. Here are some best practices to help you safeguard your cloud environment from misconfiguration:

- **Use access controls**: Implement strict access controls to limit who has access to your cloud resources. Use **role-based access control** (**RBAC**) to define the permissions and actions that different users and groups can perform within your cloud environment.

- **Encrypt sensitive data**: Encrypt all sensitive data, both at rest and in transit, to protect it from unauthorized access. You can use encryption tools provided by your cloud service provider, or you can implement encryption yourself.

- **Monitor and audit changes**: Regularly monitor and audit changes made to your cloud environment to detect misconfigurations and prevent them from being exploited. Use tools such as AWS CloudTrail, Azure Activity Logs, or Google Cloud Logging to track changes and detect misconfigurations.

- **Implement security policies**: Develop and implement security policies that define the standards and procedures for securing your cloud environment. This includes guidelines for password management, access control, and data protection.

- **Automate security scans**: Automate security scans to detect misconfigurations and vulnerabilities in your cloud environment. This can be done using security tools and services such as Amazon Inspector, Azure Security Center, or Google Cloud Security Scanner.

- **Use multi-factor authentication (MFA)**: This helps to reduce the risk of unauthorized access and helps prevent misconfigurations from being exploited.

- **Train employees**: Train employees on cloud security best practices, including how to identify and prevent misconfigurations. Make sure that employees are aware of the potential consequences of misconfigurations and the importance of following established security policies.

By following these best practices, you can help ensure the security and integrity of your cloud environment and prevent cloud misconfigurations from resulting in security threats and data breaches. The key question is, is it possible to implement all these best practices using CSPM tools? Or are CSPM tools enough for the overall security of the cloud environment? Let us understand now.

Are CSPM tools enough to protect the cloud environment?

The effectiveness of CSPM tools depends on the specific needs and requirements of your organization. While CSPM is an important tool for securing a cloud environment, it is not enough on its own to provide complete protection. CSPM is designed to help organizations identify and remediate security risks in their cloud environment, but it does not address all of the potential security threats that can arise in the cloud. This topic is comprehensively discussed in *Chapter 18, CSPM-Related Technologies*.

Here are some reasons why CSPM alone may not be enough to protect a cloud environment:

- **CSPM only focuses on the security posture of cloud resources**: CSPM tools are designed to scan cloud resources for misconfigurations, vulnerabilities, and other security issues. While this is an important part of cloud security, it does not address other types of security threats such as malware, phishing, or insider threats.

- **CSPM does not provide real-time protection**: CSPM tools are typically used to scan cloud resources periodically, often on a daily or weekly basis. This means that security issues may not be detected and remediated in real time, leaving the environment vulnerable to attacks.

- **CSPM does not address all cloud security concerns**: CSPM tools focus primarily on the security posture of cloud resources, but there are other security concerns that may need to be addressed in a cloud environment, such as network security, data protection, and user access management.

To address these concerns, organizations should consider using additional security tools alongside CSPM, such as the CASB for real-time monitoring and control of cloud traffic, cloud DLP for protecting sensitive data in the cloud, **Identity and Access Management** (**IAM**) for managing user access, and **Cloud Native Application Protection Platform** (**CNAPP**) for securing cloud-native applications.

Overall, CSPM is an important tool for securing a cloud environment, andit should be used in combination with other tools to provide comprehensive protection against a range of potential security threats.

What are other cloud security technologies and tools?

However, CSPM is just one part of a comprehensive cloud security strategy. There are several other tools that work together with CSPM to improve an organization's security posture in the cloud. Here are some examples:

- **CASB**: A CASB is a security tool that helps organizations enforce security policies across their cloud environment. It acts as a gatekeeper between the organization's on-premises infrastructure and its cloud environment, monitoring traffic and enforcing policies to ensure that data is protected. A CASB can work together with CSPM by providing additional visibility into cloud activity and enforcing policies to prevent security risks.

- **Cloud DLP**: Cloud DLP tools help organizations protect sensitive data in the cloud by identifying, monitoring, and preventing the unauthorized sharing or leakage of data. These tools can scan cloud storage, email, and other cloud-based applications to detect and prevent data breaches. By working together with CSPM, cloud DLP tools can provide additional protection against data breaches and unauthorized access to sensitive information.

- **CNAPP**: CNAPP is a security tool that provides protection for cloud-native applications. It is designed to address the unique security challenges that come with building and deploying applications in a cloud-native environment, including containerization and microservices architecture.

- **Cloud Infrastructure Entitlement Management** (**CIEM**): CIEM is a security tool that helps organizations manage user access to their cloud environment. It provides visibility into user permissions and access control policies and helps organizations enforce least privilege access to reduce the risk of data breaches and other security incidents.

- **Vulnerability management**: Vulnerability management tools help organizations identify and remediate security vulnerabilities in their cloud environment. These tools can scan cloud resources for vulnerabilities, prioritize vulnerabilities based on risk, and provide guidance on how to remediate them. By working together with CSPM, vulnerability management tools can provide additional visibility into security risks and help organizations prioritize and remediate vulnerabilities to improve their security posture.

- **Data Security Posture Management (DSPM) and SaaS Security Posture Management (SSPM):** DSPM and SSPM are two relatively newly introduced terminologies, and many vendors are now marketing their products as DSPM or SSPM or announcing the new features as DSPM and CSPM capabilities. Though we will discuss these terminologies in detail in later chapters, let's briefly cover both now:

  - The term *DSPM* is believed to have emerged in response to the increasing adoption of cloud computing and the need for organizations to manage their data security posture comprehensively and proactively across multiple environments, including on-premises and cloud-based systems. This involves identifying and mitigating security risks and vulnerabilities, monitoring for unauthorized access and data exfiltration, and ensuring compliance with relevant regulations and industry standards.

  - Similarly, the term *SSPM* is believed to have emerged in response to the growing use of SaaS applications and the need for organizations to manage their security posture concerning these applications, including managing access and permissions for users and monitoring for potential security threats. SSPM is focused on managing an organization's security posture in relation to SaaS applications. This includes identifying and monitoring SaaS applications in use, managing access and permissions for users, ensuring compliance with security policies and regulations, and monitoring for potential security threats.

Overall, these tools and technologies work together with CSPM to provide a more comprehensive approach to cloud security. By combining these tools with CSPM, organizations can improve their visibility into security risks, enforce security policies, and reduce the risk of data breaches and other security incidents.

Summary

CSPM, or Cloud Security Posture Management, is a process used to manage and monitor the security of cloud-based systems. This process involves the assessment of cloud security and the implementation of security measures to protect cloud-based systems from potential threats. This can include regular security audits, risk assessments, and the implementation of security protocols such as encryption and access controls. CSPM also involves the integration of DevSecOps for faster auto remedial deployment and with SIEM/SOAR tools for the management of security incidents, ensuring that they are handled quickly and effectively. The goal of CSPM is to ensure that cloud-based systems are protected from potential threats and remain secure, while also ensuring that the user experience is not impacted by security measures.

In this chapter, we discussed some of the most useful information about CSPM, such as what this tool is about, its importance and capabilities, common misconfigurations, and the reasons they occur. We also understood some of the best practices to protect cloud environments, and we learned about why CSPM alone cannot be enough to protect the cloud and what other tools work with CSPM for the overall security of an organization.

In the next chapter, we are going to learn about some of the most popular and leading CSPM tools available in the market. We will also explore their key features, some of the good features, and the not-so-good features as well.

Further reading

To learn more about the topics covered in this chapter, you can visit the following links:

- *How to Protect Your Clouds with CSPM, CWPP, CNAPP and CASB*: https://www.gartner.com/en/documents/4001348

- *Cloud Security Posture Management (CSPM)*: https://ermetic.com/solution/more-robust-cloud-security-posture-management-cspm/

3

CSPM Tools and Features

Cloud security posture management (**CSPM**) tools enable businesses to continuously monitor their cloud environments, identify security risks, comply with industry standards such as the **Center for Internet Security** (**CIS**), and take appropriate action to mitigate those risks. As growing numbers of organizations move their applications and data to the cloud, they face new and complex security challenges. CSPM tools can provide a centralized view of an organization's cloud infrastructure and resources, enabling security teams to quickly identify and address security issues before they become major threats. It becomes imperative to understand the specific need to choose the right tool as it comes with significant costs, especially the third-party ones.

This chapter highlights the importance of understanding the CSPM tools. It also compares and highlights the significance of cloud-native CSPM tools and cloud-agnostic CSPM tools. The previous chapter helped you identify your needs regarding CSPM and this chapter helps you map those needs with the right CSPM tool.

The following main topics are covered in this chapter:

- Cloud-native CSPM tools versus cloud-agnostic CSPM tools
- Agent-based versus agentless CSPM solutions
- Open source CSPM tools
- Understanding the Gartner Magic Quadrant

Let us get started with deep-diving into these topics!

Technical requirements

It is important to note that the specific technical requirements may vary depending on the CSPM tool you are using and the cloud platform you are working with. Therefore, it is recommended to review the documentation and training materials provided by the tool vendor to get a better understanding of the technical requirements.

Here are some things that it would be helpful to have:

- Familiarity with cloud computing platforms and services, such as **Amazon Web Services (AWS)**, Microsoft Azure, or **Google Cloud Platform (GCP)**

- Understanding of networking concepts, such as subnets, routing, and firewall rules

- Knowledge of cloud-native services and orchestration technologies

- Understanding of security best practices and threat modeling methodologies

Understanding CSPM tools

CSPM tools have specific requirements to effectively assess and enhance the security posture of cloud environments. As businesses increasingly adopt cloud services, the complexity of managing cloud security also rises, and thus organizations need CSPM tools to ensure the security and compliance of their cloud environments. In the previous chapter, we explored why CSPM can be a critical requirement. In this section, let us explore the available types of CSPM tools.

There are two main types of commercial CSPM tools: native CSPM tools provided by **cloud service providers (CSPs)** and third-party CSPM tools developed by independent vendors. There are some open source CSPM tools available, which are discussed as well.

Cloud provider native CSPM tool

A cloud provider's native CSPM tool is a security solution offered directly by the CSP, integrated into their cloud platform. These tools are designed to help users assess and enhance the security posture of their cloud resources within that specific provider's ecosystem. Some examples of cloud provider-native CSPM tools are **AWS Config**, **Microsoft Defender for Cloud**, **Google Cloud Security Command Center (SCC)**, and **Cloud Guard by Oracle Cloud**. We will discuss these tools in a later section of this chapter. Let us now try to understand some of the benefits of using CSPM tools offered by cloud providers.

Advantages and use cases of using a cloud provider's CSPM tool

A cloud provider's native CSPM tool can be a suitable option under specific circumstances. Here are some situations when it might be appropriate to opt for the native CSPM tool provided by your CSP:

- **Simplicity and ease of integration**: If your organization primarily uses a single cloud provider for most of its cloud services, the native CSPM tool can offer a straightforward and integrated solution. Since it is developed by the cloud provider, it seamlessly integrates with their services, reducing the complexity of setting up and managing security configurations.

- **Basic security needs**: If your cloud environment is relatively small or straightforward, and you require only basic security features, the native CSPM tool might be sufficient to meet your requirements. Cloud providers often offer essential security checks and best practice recommendations that can help you address common security issues.

- **Cost efficiency**: Some cloud providers include basic CSPM features as part of their service offerings without additional costs. If budget is a significant concern and the native CSPM tool provides the necessary security checks, it can be a cost-effective option. For example, Oracle Cloud has recently launched Cloud Guard as a free CSPM tool for their specific environments.

- **Vendor trust and support**: Native CSPM tools are developed and supported by the cloud provider itself. If your organization has a strong relationship with the cloud provider and trusts their security capabilities, using their native CSPM tool can provide a sense of confidence in the overall security of the cloud environment.

- **Leveraging cloud ecosystem features**: Native CSPM tools are designed to work seamlessly with other cloud-native services and features. If your organization intends to take advantage of specific cloud ecosystem features or services, the native CSPM tool might complement them more effectively.

- **Limited integration requirements**: If you don't have a complex security infrastructure and your organization doesn't require extensive integrations with other security tools or platforms, the native CSPM tool can be a straightforward choice.

Overall, it would be a wise decision to use a cloud-native CSPM tool when an organization primarily uses a single cloud provider, their cloud environment is simple, the cost is a significant factor, and the organization can work within the limitations of the cloud provider's native CSPM offering.

Concerns and disadvantages of using a cloud provider's CSPM tool

While cloud provider-native CSPM tools offer various security benefits, they may also come with certain concerns or disadvantages:

- **Limited cross-cloud support**: Cloud provider-native CSPM tools are primarily designed to work within their own cloud ecosystem. If your organization uses multiple cloud providers or operates in a multi-cloud environment, you may not get consistent security monitoring and management across all platforms.

- **Feature limitations**: Cloud provider CSPM tools might lack certain advanced security features or customization options that are available in third-party solutions. This can be a limitation for organizations with complex security requirements or specific compliance needs.

- **Integration challenges**: Integrating a cloud provider's native CSPM tool with existing security infrastructure or third-party security tools may not be as seamless as working with a single, unified third-party solution.

- **Delayed feature updates**: Cloud providers may not release updates or new features for their native CSPM tools as frequently as dedicated third-party security vendors. This could lead to delays in getting access to the latest security enhancements.

- **Vendor lock-in**: Relying solely on a cloud provider's CSPM tool might lead to vendor lock-in, making it challenging to switch to a different cloud provider or third-party solution if needed.

- **Security tool overload**: Cloud providers often offer a variety of security tools and services, and using multiple native tools for different aspects of security can become overwhelming and difficult to manage.

- **Potential bias:** There may be a perceived bias in security assessments provided by cloud providers, as their native CSPM tools might not be as critical of their own services as an independent third-party solution would be.

- **Compliance considerations**: For organizations with specific compliance requirements, the native CSPM tools might not cover all the necessary controls and regulations, necessitating additional security measures.

- **Lack of focus on multi-cloud**: Some cloud providers might prioritize features and updates for their primary cloud service, which could result in less focus on multi-cloud security concerns.

- **Data privacy concerns**: Organizations may be cautious about using a cloud provider's native CSPM tool if they have concerns about data privacy or the potential access cloud providers might have to security assessment data.

It's essential for organizations to carefully assess their security needs, consider the specific limitations of a cloud provider's native CSPM tool, and evaluate whether a third-party CSPM solution might offer more comprehensive and tailored security features to meet their requirements. In some cases, a combination of both native and third-party CSPM tools might be the optimal approach to achieve a robust and flexible cloud security posture.

Third-party CSPM tool

A third-party CSPM tool is developed and provided by independent security vendors, offering security management and monitoring across multiple cloud platforms and environments. These tools often provide more advanced and customizable security features compared to cloud provider-native solutions. Some popular third-party CSPM tools are discussed later in the chapter.

Advantages and use cases of using a third-party CSPM tool

Using a third-party CSPM tool can offer several advantages over relying solely on a cloud provider's native CSPM tool. Here are some of the key advantages:

- **Multi-cloud support**: Third-party CSPM tools typically support multiple cloud platforms, allowing organizations to manage security consistently across different cloud providers. This is especially beneficial for companies operating in multi-cloud or hybrid cloud environments.

- **Advanced security features**: Third-party CSPM tools often offer more advanced security capabilities, such as behavioral analysis, anomaly detection, and AI-driven threat detection. They may also provide customizable security policies to meet specific organizational needs and industry compliance standards.

- **Independent validation**: Third-party CSPM tools offer an additional layer of validation and verification of the cloud provider's security controls. As independent tools, they can provide unbiased assessments of security posture.

- **Customization and flexibility**: Third-party CSPM tools typically offer more flexibility in configuring and customizing security policies according to an organization's unique requirements. This level of customization may not be available in cloud provider-native tools.

- **Centralized visibility**: Third-party CSPM tools can provide a centralized view of security across all cloud environments, even if the organization uses multiple cloud providers. This unified view simplifies security monitoring and management.

- **Specialized expertise**: Third-party CSPM tool providers focus solely on cloud security and invest heavily in research and development. As a result, they may be at the forefront of security advancements, offering more up-to-date and comprehensive security solutions.

- **Data security posture management (DSPM)**: Some third-party CSPM tools include DSPM features that focus on protecting sensitive data within the cloud environment. This can be crucial for organizations that handle sensitive data and need advanced data protection measures.

- **Integration with existing security infrastructure**: Third-party CSPM tools can often integrate seamlessly with an organization's existing security infrastructure, including SIEM solutions and **Security Operations Centers (SOCs)**. This enables a more comprehensive security ecosystem.

- **Additional insights and recommendations**: Third-party CSPM tools may provide more detailed insights, recommendations, and actionable steps to remediate security issues effectively. They might offer a deeper level of analysis beyond what cloud provider-native tools provide.

- **Flexibility in licensing and pricing**: Some third-party CSPM tools offer flexible licensing models, allowing organizations to choose the features and scale that fit their needs and budget.

While cloud provider-native CSPM tools can be valuable in certain situations, third-party CSPM tools are often preferred by organizations with more complex cloud environments, specific compliance requirements, and a need for advanced security features. The decision to choose a third-party CSPM tool over a cloud provider-native tool depends on an organization's unique security needs, cloud environment complexity, and risk management strategy. Many organizations opt for a combination of both native and third-party CSPM tools to leverage the benefits of each.

Concerns and disadvantages of using a third-party CSPM tool

While third-party CSPM tools offer various benefits, they also come with certain concerns and disadvantages that organizations should consider:

- **Integration challenges**: Integrating a third-party CSPM tool with existing security infrastructure can be complex and time-consuming. Ensuring smooth integration and interoperability with other security solutions may require additional efforts and expertise.

- **Cost**: Third-party CSPM tools often come with additional licensing and subscription costs. Depending on the features and scale required, the expense of implementing and maintaining a third-party tool can be a consideration for organizations with budget constraints.

- **Vendor dependency**: Organizations relying on a third-party CSPM tool may become dependent on the vendor for updates, support, and new feature releases. Any issues with the vendor, such as service disruptions or changes in product offerings, could impact the organization's security operations.

- **Learning curve**: Adopting a new third-party CSPM tool may involve a learning curve for security teams and administrators. Training and familiarization with the new tool may take time, potentially affecting the efficiency of security operations initially.

- **Limited visibility**: Some third-party CSPM tools may provide limited visibility into certain cloud providers or services. This can be a concern for organizations that operate in a multi-cloud environment or have specific cloud services that are not fully supported by the tool.

- **Vendor stability**: The stability and reputation of the third-party CSPM vendor are essential considerations. Organizations need to assess the vendor's track record, financial stability, and ability to provide ongoing support and updates.

- **Data privacy and compliance**: Using a third-party tool involves sharing security data with an external vendor. This could raise data privacy concerns, especially if the data includes sensitive information. Organizations must ensure that the vendor follows appropriate data protection and compliance practices.

- **Security vulnerabilities**: Just like any software, third-party CSPM tools are not immune to security vulnerabilities. Organizations must evaluate the vendor's security practices and be proactive in applying updates and patches to address any potential vulnerabilities.

- **Customization limitations**: While third-party CSPM tools offer more flexibility than cloud provider-native tools, there might still be limitations in customizing the tool to fit specific organizational requirements.

- **Vendor lock-in**: Depending solely on a third-party CSPM tool may lead to vendor lock-in, making it challenging to switch to a different solution in the future.

To mitigate these concerns, vendors should conduct thorough research, evaluate different third-party CSPM vendors, and perform pilot tests before committing to a specific tool. It is essential to ensure that the chosen tool aligns with the organization's security needs, budget, and long-term business strategy. Additionally, a combination of cloud provider-native CSPM tools and third-party solutions might be considered to balance advantages and disadvantages based on the organization's unique security requirements.

Careful considerations for CSPM tools and their capabilities

We will cover all other aspects of tool selection in *Chapter 4*; however, it is important to discuss careful considerations for CSPM tools. The CSPM tool should offer continuous monitoring of cloud resources and conduct automated security checks to identify misconfigurations, vulnerabilities, and compliance violations. It is important to understand CSPM tools' offerings/features before planning to invest in them for several reasons:

- **To ensure the tool meets your organization's specific security needs**: CSPM tools can vary in terms of their features, functionality, and capabilities. By understanding the tool, you can ensure that it provides the specific security capabilities that your organization requires.

- **Coverage of industry-specific compliance needs**: The other significant feature of CSPM tools is their ability to support various industry benchmarks and best practices. These benchmarks are established by reputable organizations and CSPs to define a set of security standards and guidelines. CSPM tools use these benchmarks as a reference to assess the security posture of cloud environments and identify potential vulnerabilities and misconfigurations. Some of the commonly supported industry benchmarks by CSPM tools include the following:

  - **CIS Benchmarks**: CIS provides a series of configuration guidelines for different cloud platforms such as AWS, Azure, GCP, and others. These benchmarks cover a wide range of security settings, ensuring that cloud resources are configured securely and align with industry best practices.

  - **National Institute of Standards and Technology (NIST) framework**: NIST offers comprehensive guidelines, standards, and best practices for cloud security. CSPM tools can map their assessments against NIST guidelines to help organizations comply with NIST security recommendations.

  - **Payment Card Industry Data Security Standard (PCI DSS)**: For organizations handling payment card data, CSPM tools can align their assessments with PCI DSS requirements to ensure proper handling and protection of cardholder information in the cloud.

  - **Health Insurance Portability and Accountability Act (HIPAA)**: CSPM tools can also support HIPAA compliance, ensuring healthcare organizations meet the necessary security and privacy standards for handling **protected health information (PHI)** in the cloud.

  - **General Data Protection Regulation (GDPR)**: CSPM tools may include checks based on GDPR guidelines to help organizations protect personal data and maintain compliance with European Union data protection laws.

  - **International Organization for Standardization (ISO)**: CSPM tools might support ISO/IEC 27001 and other relevant ISO standards, providing a more extensive security framework for cloud environments.

- **To determine the level of automation the tool provides**: CSPM tools are designed to automate security tasks, but the level of automation can vary. Understanding the tool's automation capabilities can help you determine how much of the security process can be automated and how much manual intervention will still be required.

- **To evaluate the tool's ease of use**: A CSPM tool should be easy to use and deploy within your organization. By understanding the tool's user interface and integration capabilities, you can determine whether it is user-friendly and how well it integrates with your organization's existing security tools and processes.

- **To ensure the tool is compatible with your cloud environment**: CSPM tools are designed to work with specific cloud platforms and services. Understanding the tool's compatibility with your organization's cloud environment is critical to ensuring it can effectively monitor and secure your cloud assets.

- **To assess the tool's scalability and future-proofing capabilities**: Your organization's cloud environment will evolve over time, and your CSPM tool should be able to keep up with these changes. Understanding the tool's scalability and future-proofing capabilities can help you assess whether it will be able to support your organization's long-term security needs.

By understanding CSPM tools before investing in them, you can ensure that you select a tool that meets your organization's specific security needs, integrates with your existing security tools and processes, and is capable of monitoring and securing your cloud environment effectively. Now that you understand the importance of knowing about the CSPM tool features, let us understand another critical topic regarding the different versions of CSPM tools: agent-based versus agentless.

Agent-based versus agentless CSPM solutions

Agent-based and agentless CSPM solutions are two different approaches to monitoring and securing cloud environments. Each approach has its advantages and considerations. Let us take a closer look.

Agent-based approach

CSPM tools require the installation of software agents on cloud resources to collect security data and monitor for vulnerabilities. The agents are lightweight software components that run on cloud resources and report data back to the CSPM tool. These tools have the advantage of being able to collect more detailed and granular data about cloud resources, including the operating system, applications, and network configuration. This allows for more precise and accurate detection of security risks. However, agent-based CSPM tools can introduce additional complexity and maintenance overhead since agents need to be installed, configured, and updated on each cloud resource.

Advantages include the following:

- **Granular visibility**: Agents provide detailed insights into individual cloud resources, enabling comprehensive monitoring and security assessment

- **Real-time monitoring**: Agents continuously collect data and report in real time, allowing immediate detection of security issues and rapid response

- **Offline detection**: Agents can function offline and store security data locally, ensuring monitoring continuity even during network disruptions

Considerations include the following:

- **Overhead**: Installing agents on every resource can incur some overhead, especially in large-scale environments with thousands of resources

- **Management**: Managing and updating agents on all resources may require additional effort and coordination

Agentless CSPM approach

On the other hand, an agentless solution does not require installing software agents on cloud resources. Instead, it relies on **Application Programming Interfaces** (**APIs**) and other cloud-native integrations to collect data and monitor for vulnerabilities. This approach is easier to deploy and maintain, as it does not require any additional software to be installed on cloud resources. Additionally, agentless CSPM tools are typically faster to deploy and provide broader coverage of cloud resources. However, agentless CSPM tools may not provide as detailed or granular data as agent-based tools, and they may not be able to detect certain types of security risks.

Advantages include the following:

- **Easy deployment**: Since no agents need to be installed, agentless solutions can be deployed quickly and require minimal configuration

- **Lower overhead**: Without agents, there is no resource overhead associated with managing and maintaining agent software

- **Scalability**: Agentless solutions can scale easily to support a large number of cloud resources

Considerations include the following:

- **Limited visibility**: Agentless solutions may provide broader coverage but could lack granular visibility into individual resources compared to agent-based solutions

- **Delayed reporting**: Data collection through APIs might introduce some latency, leading to slight delays in reporting compared to real-time agent-based solutions

- **API limitations**: Relying on cloud provider APIs means the effectiveness of an agentless solution is dependent on the quality and extent of APIs provided by the cloud provider

Choosing between agent-based and agentless CSPM solutions

Most modern CSPM tools now offer both approaches, although the agentless approach is popular for its advantages, as discussed previously. The choice between agent-based and agentless CSPM depends on your organization's specific requirements and considerations. Here are some factors to consider:

- **Granularity**: If you need granular visibility into individual cloud resources and real-time monitoring, an agent-based solution might be more suitable

- **Scalability**: For large-scale environments with a significant number of resources, an agentless solution might be more manageable and scalable

- **Resource overhead**: Consider the impact of agent deployment on resource overhead, especially if your cloud environment is resource-constrained

- **API support**: Assess the completeness and effectiveness of cloud provider APIs and their integration with the CSPM solution

- **Deployment speed**: Agentless solutions can be quicker to deploy and configure due to their lack of agents

- **Offline capabilities**: If offline detection and data storage during network disruptions are crucial, an agent-based solution might be preferred

Ultimately, the right choice depends on your organization's specific cloud environment, security needs, scalability requirements, and resource constraints. Some organizations opt for a hybrid approach, using both agent-based and agentless solutions to leverage the advantages of each in different parts of their cloud infrastructure. Apart from commercial CSPM tools, whether offered by CSPs or third-party vendors, there are some open source CSPM tools as well, which can also serve the need to some extent. Let us try to understand this.

Open source CSPM tools

Open source CSPM tools are software solutions developed and distributed with an open source license, allowing users to access, use, modify, and distribute the source code freely. These tools are designed to help organizations assess and enhance their security posture in cloud environments, just like commercial CSPM tools. Let's explore the advantages and concerns associated with open source CSPM tools.

These are the advantages of open source CSPM tools:

- **Cost**: One of the most significant advantages of open source CSPM tools is that they are usually free to use. Organizations can download, install, and deploy the tool without incurring licensing or subscription costs, making it a cost-effective choice for smaller businesses or those with budget constraints.

- **Transparency**: Open source tools provide full access to their source code, allowing users to examine how the tool works and verify its security measures. This transparency fosters trust and confidence in the tool's effectiveness.

- **Community contributions**: Open source projects often benefit from a vibrant community of developers, security experts, and users who contribute to the code base. This community-driven development can lead to more frequent updates, bug fixes, and the introduction of new features.

- **Customization**: With access to the source code, organizations can customize the open source CSPM tool to meet their specific security requirements and integrate it with other internal systems.

- **Multi-cloud support**: Some open source CSPM tools are designed to support multiple cloud providers, allowing organizations to manage security across different platforms from a single interface.

Here are some concerns about open source CSPM tools:

- **Security risks**: While the transparency of open source tools can be an advantage, it also means that potential vulnerabilities in the code are visible to attackers. Organizations must ensure they are using the latest versions and follow best practices to mitigate security risks.

- **Support and documentation**: Open source projects might lack official support or dedicated customer service channels, which could be a concern for organizations that require timely assistance or comprehensive documentation.

- **Complexity**: Open source tools may require more significant technical expertise to deploy, configure, and maintain, compared to commercial CSPM tools, which often come with user-friendly interfaces and dedicated customer support.

- **Limited feature set**: Some open source CSPM tools may not offer the same level of features and functionalities as commercial alternatives. This could be a drawback for organizations seeking more comprehensive or specialized security capabilities.

- **Implementation challenges**: Organizations might face challenges during the implementation and integration of open source CSPM tools, especially when dealing with multi-cloud environments or complex infrastructures.

Overall, open source CSPM tools can be a viable option for organizations that prioritize cost-effectiveness, transparency, and customization. However, it's crucial to assess each tool's capabilities, community support, security track record, and how well it aligns with the specific needs and requirements of the organization before deciding. Regularly updating and monitoring the open source tools used in the cloud environment is essential to ensure they remain secure and effective in protecting the infrastructure.

Is it safe to use open source CSPM tools?

In general, open source CSPM tools are safe to use. They are developed by a community of developers and undergo regular testing and updates to ensure their security and reliability. However, as with any software tool, it is important to take precautions to ensure the safety and security of your cloud infrastructure. This includes regularly updating the tool, monitoring its performance, and ensuring it is configured correctly.

Who should avoid using open source CSPM tools?

Not every organization may want to use an open source CSPM tool. Organizations that have strict *compliance or regulatory requirements* should avoid using open source tools as they may not meet specific regulatory standards. In addition, organizations with limited in-house technical expertise may struggle to implement and maintain an open source CSPM tool effectively. In these cases, it is more appropriate to use a commercial CSPM tool designed to meet specific regulatory requirements and backed by dedicated support and maintenance teams.

Now that you understand various CSPM solutions and the value they bring to the table, let us understand the *Gartner Magic Quadrant* and its importance in CSPM tool selection.

Understanding the Gartner Magic Quadrant

The Gartner Magic Quadrant is a research methodology used to evaluate and analyze technology markets, vendors, and products. The Magic Quadrant is a visual representation of the market, divided into four quadrants: Leaders, Challengers, Visionaries, and Niche Players. Each vendor is positioned in the quadrant that best represents their ability to execute their capabilities and showcase their completeness of vision in the market.

In the context of CSPM – or **Cloud Workload Protection Platform** (**CWPP**), as they sometimes go hand in hand – the Magic Quadrant assesses the various vendors that offer CSPM solutions based on their capabilities and performance in the market. Gartner evaluates each vendor based on a variety of criteria, including product features and functionality, vendor strategy, customer experience, and market presence.

Figure 3.1 – Gartner Magic Quadrant (https://www.horangi.com/
blog/a-cisos-take-on-the-gartner-magic-quadrant)

The **Leaders** quadrant would typically include vendors that have a strong market presence, a comprehensive CSPM product portfolio, and a proven record of accomplishment of delivering customer value. The **Challengers** quadrant includes vendors that may have a strong product portfolio but may be lacking in certain areas such as market presence or innovation. The **Visionaries** quadrant includes vendors that have a strong vision for the future of CSPM but may be lacking in execution. The **Niche Players** quadrant includes vendors that have a smaller market presence or a more limited product portfolio.

Overall, the Magic Quadrant provides a valuable resource for organizations looking to evaluate and compare CSPM solutions. It can help organizations identify leading vendors in the market, evaluate their strengths and weaknesses, and select the CSPM tool that best meets their specific needs and requirements.

Gartner Peer Insights

Gartner Peer Insights (`https://www.gartner.com/peer-insights/home`) is an online platform that provides user-generated reviews and ratings of technology products and services. It allows technology buyers to read and compare reviews of products from other users within their industry or organization. Gartner Peer Insights covers a wide range of technology markets, including cloud security, network security, endpoint protection, and many others.

The reviews on Gartner Peer Insights are verified by Gartner to ensure their authenticity and credibility. The platform uses a rigorous process to collect, validate, and moderate reviews, which helps ensure that the reviews are unbiased and reflective of actual user experiences. CSPM product reviews and Gartner insights can be found at Gartner's website: `https://www.gartner.com/reviews/market/cloud-security-posture-management-tools`.

Gartner Review

Gartner Review, on the other hand, is a service provided by Gartner to help organizations evaluate and select technology vendors and products. Gartner analysts provide expert insights and advice based on their research and analysis of the technology market. Gartner Review provides an in-depth analysis of technology vendors and products, including their strengths and weaknesses, market position, and strategic direction. This information can help organizations make informed decisions about which technology products and vendors to select based on their specific needs and requirements.

Let us get started to understand the most popular CSPM tools.

Examples of CSPM tools

There are more than 40 vendors offering CSPM products on the market and all cannot be included. Also, there will be more vendors offering CSPM tools due to the ever-increasing demand.

> ### Declaration – tool selection criteria for this book
>
> The selection of the following tools is based on the author's direct or indirect experience with these tools. With years of working experience in the industry, most of these tools have been personally tested and used by the author. The author has been part of product demos, **Proof of Concept** (**PoC**), implementations, and the selection of tools. In some cases, the author was involved in the core team responsible for the security design and architecture of the product itself. The products listed are not in any specific order from best to worst or worst to best, as software products are continuously evolving, and their effectiveness is subjective and can vary based on changing security concerns and needs. The specific shortcomings of the products are not mentioned as the author recognizes that product shortcomings and missing features may already be addressed by the time you access this book. While the author considered the Gartner Magic Quadrant, Peer Insights, and reviews, the primary assessment is based on their personal experience, and there is no sponsorship from any of the companies mentioned. The next chapter will delve into tool selection procedures, addressing all concerns you might have. It is recommended to refer to the official website of each product for the latest details.

CSPM tools can broadly be categorized into three types based on their source and ownership: cloud provider native, third party, and open source. Let us understand some of them briefly.

Cloud provider-native CSPM tools

As we discussed earlier, cloud provider-native CSPM tools are specifically tailored to work seamlessly with the cloud provider's services. Let's look at some examples.

AWS Config

AWS Config is a robust CSPM tool provided by AWS. It is designed to help organizations monitor and maintain the security and compliance of their AWS resources and configurations. AWS Config focuses on providing continuous monitoring, assessment, and evaluation of AWS resource configurations. It helps organizations ensure that their AWS environment adheres to best security practices, compliance standards, and desired configurations. AWS Config provides a set of predefined and customizable rules to assess the configuration of AWS resources. It continuously monitors the AWS environment and reports compliance against these rules, helping identify potential security risks and ensuring adherence to best practices. For more details on the product, refer to `https://aws.amazon.com/config/`.

Microsoft Defender for Cloud

Microsoft Defender for Cloud (**MDC**) is a cloud-native security solution that provides unified visibility and protection for your cloud resources across multiple cloud platforms such as Azure, AWS, and GCP, and hybrid environments with integrated security from code to cloud. MDC is a unified solution that works as CSPM, CWPP, and **Cloud Native Application Protection** (**CNAPP**). It uses machine learning and behavioral analysis to detect suspicious activities and potential security threats, such as unauthorized access, data exfiltration, and malware infections. MDC also integrates with other Microsoft security products such as Microsoft Sentinel and Microsoft 365 Defender to provide a comprehensive security solution for your cloud environment. With its CSPM capabilities, MDC can help you achieve compliance with various regulatory standards and protect your cloud resources from cyber-attacks. For more details, refer to `https://www.microsoft.com/en-us/security/business/cloud-security/microsoft-defender-cloud`.

Google Cloud Security Command Center

Google Cloud **SCC** is a powerful CSPM tool offered by GCP. It is designed to help organizations monitor, analyze, and improve the security of their cloud resources within the Google Cloud environment. Google Cloud SCC focuses on providing continuous security monitoring, risk assessment, compliance tracking, and threat detection for cloud assets and services on GCP. It helps organizations ensure that their cloud infrastructure follows the best security practices and meets industry standards and regulatory requirements. For more details, refer to `https://cloud.google.com/security-command-center`.

Cloud Guard by Oracle Cloud

Cloud Guard is among the most recent CSPM tools offered by Oracle Cloud. It is designed to help organizations monitor, detect, and respond to security threats and misconfigurations within their **Oracle Cloud Infrastructure** (**OCI**) environment. Oracle Cloud Guard, along with its latest feature, Threat Detector, identifies misconfigurations in resources, insecure activities spanning tenants, and potential malicious threats. The tool equips security administrators with the necessary visibility to prioritize and resolve cloud security concerns effectively. For more details, refer to `https://www.oracle.com/security/cloud-security/cloud-guard/`.

Third-party CSPM tools

As we discussed, third-party CSPM tools are security solutions developed and provided by independent vendors or companies. Let us look at some of the most common tools.

CrowdStrike Falcon

CrowdStrike Falcon is a fast, lightweight, and cloud-native platform that provides comprehensive cloud security and compliance solutions. As a CSPM and a CWPP product, it offers real-time visibility into cloud infrastructure and workloads, along with automated remediation capabilities. With Falcon, organizations can secure their cloud environments by identifying and mitigating risks, enforcing compliance policies, and protecting against advanced threats. CrowdStrike is a reputable name because it has been named a leader in the Gartner Magic Quadrant for its **endpoint detection and response** (**EDR**) several times. For more details, refer to `https://www.crowdstrike.com/products/cloud-security/`.

Orca CSPM

Orca Security CSPM is an agentless cloud-native security platform that provides comprehensive CSPM. Orca was one of the very first tools that offered agentless solutions and is one of the fastest-growing start-ups. It offers a wide range of features to help organizations maintain their cloud security posture, identify and remediate vulnerabilities, and ensure compliance with industry regulations. Orca consolidates cloud workloads, identity and entitlement security, misconfiguration, container security, sensitive data discovery, and detection and response, all in one platform across the entire **Software Development Life Cycle** (**SDLC**). To understand the full context of risks, Orca utilizes this unified data model and recognizes when seemingly unrelated issues can create dangerous attack paths. With these insights, Orca is also able to prioritize risks effectively, reducing alert fatigue and ensuring that security teams stay focused on what matters most. For more details, refer to `https://orca.security/`.

Prisma Cloud

Prisma Cloud is a cloud-native agentless security platform that provides comprehensive CSPM, threat detection, and compliance management for multi-cloud and hybrid cloud environments. It is a product of Palo Alto Networks, a leading cybersecurity company. To give you a little background, *RedLock* was a cloud security and compliance platform developed by RedLock, Inc. that provided security and compliance monitoring capabilities for public cloud infrastructure. Palo Alto Networks acquired RedLock, Inc. in 2018 and merged the RedLock platform with its own cloud security product, Prisma Cloud. The merger of RedLock with Prisma Cloud created a more comprehensive cloud security platform that offers not only CSPM capabilities but also other security capabilities such as **Cloud Workload Protection** (**CWP**), container security, and application security. This allowed the organization to manage and secure its cloud environments holistically from a single platform. For more details, refer to https://www.paloaltonetworks.com/prisma/cloud.

Cloud Guard Dome9

Dome9 Security is a cloud security platform that provides comprehensive CSPM capabilities. It is designed to help organizations secure their cloud infrastructure and applications across multi-cloud environments. Dome9 aims to automate security processes across cloud environments, helping organizations orchestrate security policies and responses. In 2018, Check Point Software Technologies acquired Dome9, which means that Dome9's technology has been integrated into the Cloud Guard suite of products. For more details, refer to https://docs.cloudguard.dome9.com/docs.

Cloud Optix

Cloud Optix CSPM is a cloud-native security solution developed by Sophos, a leading cybersecurity company. It provides organizations with complete visibility and control over their cloud infrastructure to ensure compliance with security best practices and industry regulations. I have been fortunate to be part of the security design and architecture team of Sophos in the past and have deep visibility of this product architecture. Cloud Optix has evolved over time tremendously in terms of feautures and offerings. For more details, refer to https://www.sophos.com/en-us/products/cloud-optix.

Wiz CSPM

Wiz CSPM is a cloud security solution that enables organizations to secure their cloud environments across multiple cloud platforms such as AWS, Azure, and GCP. It provides continuous monitoring, automated compliance, threat detection, and response capabilities, among other features. For more details, refer to https://www.wiz.io/solutions/cspm.

Trend Cloud One – Conformity (previously Deep Security)

Trend Cloud One – Conformity is a CSPM tool that provides continuous monitoring and automated compliance checks for cloud environments. It is designed to help organizations maintain compliance with industry standards and regulations, such as CIS Benchmarks, HIPAA, GDPR, and PCI-DSS. For more details, refer to `https://www.trendmicro.com/en_us/business/products/hybrid-cloud/cloud-one-conformity.html`.

Ermetic CSPM

Ermetic CSPM is a cloud security tool that provides continuous monitoring and management of an organization's cloud environment to identify and address potential security risks. The tool works by analyzing the organization's cloud configuration and usage data and comparing it against industry best practices and security standards. For more details, refer to `https://ermetic.com/solution/more-robust-cloud-security-posture-management-cspm/`.

Lacework CSPM

Lacework is a cloud security platform that provides CSPM capabilities for multi-cloud environments such as AWS, Azure, and GCP. It helps organizations automate cloud security monitoring, threat detection, and compliance management, giving them complete visibility and control over their cloud infrastructure. For more details, refer to `https://www.lacework.com/platform/cloud-security-posture-and-compliance/`.

Now that we have gone through various commercial CSPM tools, let us look at some of the open source CSPM tools too.

Open source CSPM tools

There are several open source CSPM tools available to use; let us get to know some of them next.

Cloud Custodian

This is a rules engine that allows users to define policies to be executed across an AWS, Azure, or GCP account. It helps identify and remediate security risks by automating the enforcement of security policies. Features include automated policy enforcement, real-time monitoring, and integration with popular tools such as Slack and Jira. For more details, refer to `https://cloudcustodian.io/`.

CloudMapper

This is a tool that helps visualize and understand a cloud infrastructure's attack surface. It uses data collected from AWS accounts to create network diagrams, visualize resource relationships, and highlight potential security vulnerabilities. Key features include network mapping, resource discovery, and interactive visualizations. For more details, refer to `https://github.com/duo-labs/cloudmapper`.

Scout Suite

This is a multi-cloud security auditing tool that assesses cloud environments based on CIS Benchmarks and best practices. It provides a comprehensive report of security vulnerabilities and misconfigurations across AWS, Azure, and GCP accounts. Key features are automated security audits, customizable policies, and reporting. For more details, refer to `https://github.com/nccgroup/ScoutSuite`.

OpenSCAP

This is a security compliance framework that enables automated vulnerability scanning, configuration assessment, and policy enforcement for cloud environments. It supports multiple cloud providers, including AWS, Azure, and GCP. Key features include automated compliance scanning, customizable policies, and integration with popular tools such as Ansible and Puppet. For more details, refer to `https://www.open-scap.org/`.

Cloudnosys

This is a cloud security and compliance platform that helps organizations manage cloud risks and automate compliance reporting. It supports multiple cloud providers, including AWS, Azure, and GCP. Key features include continuous monitoring, automated remediation, and compliance reporting. For more details, refer to `https://cloudnosys.com/an-insight-to-the-cloud-security-solutions/`.

Overall, using an open source CSPM tool can be cost-effective and can also offer a greater degree of control and flexibility compared to commercial CSPM solutions. However, it is important to note that open source tools may require additional effort and expertise to set up and maintain, and they may not provide the same level of support or feature set as commercial solutions.

Summary

CSPM tools are essential for organizations to maintain security and compliance in their cloud environments. We learned about various CSPM solution types including cloud provider-native solutions, third-party, and open source CSPM tools. We also carried out a comparative analysis to understand why an organization needs to spend money on third-party CSPM tools. There are some security concerns around using open source CSPM tools, including the risk of vulnerabilities in the code and lack of support compared to commercial solutions. The benefits of using a CSPM tool include reducing the risk of data breaches, improving compliance with regulatory frameworks, and increasing visibility and control over cloud environments.

Leveraging the learning from this chapter, we are going to talk about how to select the right tool based on the organization's needs next. We will also learn how to plan and perform a PoC for the CSPM product.

Further reading

To learn more about the topics covered in this chapter, visit the following links:

- *Microsoft CNAPP*: `https://www.microsoft.com/en-us/security/blog/2023/03/22/the-next-wave-of-multicloud-security-with-microsoft-defender-for-cloud-a-cloud-native-application-protection-platform-cnapp/`

- *Top 28 CSPM tools*: `https://startupstash.com/cloud-security-posture-management-tools/`

4

CSPM Tool Selection

In recent years, cloud computing has become the backbone of modern IT infrastructure, allowing organizations to scale and grow their businesses rapidly. However, this transformation has also introduced new security risks that need to be mitigated. CSPM tools are designed to help organizations identify and remediate security risks in their cloud infrastructure. Selecting a CSPM tool is a critical decision that requires careful consideration of numerous factors, such as the organization's cloud environment, security needs, budget, and vendor offerings.

In this chapter, we will explore the key considerations and best practices for selecting a CSPM tool that meets your organization's unique security requirements. We will also discuss the vendor selection process, **proof of concept** (**POC**) testing, and the stakeholder management involved in the procurement of a CSPM tool. This empowers the stakeholders to focus on key considerations when choosing the tool. If stakeholders are not prepared for their actual needs, they can always fall for marketing gimmicks.

The following main topics will be covered in this chapter:

- Structured thought to choose the right CSPM tool
- Vendor selection process checklists for CSPM
- PoCs for CSPM tools

To choose the right CSPM solution for your organization, you should carefully read this chapter. Let's get started.

Structured thought to choose the right CSPM tool

There are many CSPM solutions available in the market, each with its strengths and weaknesses. To choose the right CSPM solution for your organization, you should follow a structured thought process that considers the following factors.

1. Understand your organization's cloud security needs

Before choosing a CSPM solution, it is important to understand your organization's cloud security requirements. This includes identifying the types of cloud services you are using, the data you are storing in the cloud, and the compliance regulations you need to adhere to. To do this, you should follow a process that involves four steps.

i. Identify your cloud environment

The first step is to understand the cloud services and infrastructure used by your organization. This includes identifying which cloud service providers you are using, the type of data you are storing in the cloud, and which applications and workloads are running in the cloud. For example, let's say your organization uses multiple cloud providers, including **Amazon Web Services** (**AWS**), Microsoft Azure, and **Google Cloud Platform** (**GCP**), where various cloud services, such as virtual machines, storage accounts, databases, and container services are utilized. Furthermore, your organization may have various applications and workloads running in the cloud, such as web applications, mobile applications, and analytics workloads. Your organization may also be storing sensitive data, such as customer information and financial data, in the cloud. By identifying these aspects of your cloud environment, you can develop a better understanding of the security risks and requirements associated with your cloud infrastructure, which will help you select the right CSPM tool to meet your organization's specific security needs.

ii. Define your security requirements

Once you have a clear understanding of your cloud environment, you should define your security requirements. This includes identifying the types of threats you need to protect against, such as data breaches, insider threats, and external attacks. You should also identify the compliance requirements your organization needs to adhere to, such as the **Payment Card Industry Data Security Standard** (**PCI DSS**), **Health Insurance Portability and Accountability** (**HIPAA**), or **General Data Protection Regulation** (**GDPR**). As an example, let's say your organization is a financial institution that provides online banking services to its customers. Your organization is subject to regulatory compliance requirements, such as PCI DSS and the **Gramm-Leach-Bliley Act** (**GLBA**). Furthermore, your organization is concerned about data breaches, ransomware attacks, and insider threats that could compromise customer data and disrupt the availability of online banking services. Based on these security risks and compliance requirements, your organization needs a CSPM tool that provides continuous monitoring, vulnerability management, compliance reporting, and threat detection and response capabilities. Additionally, the CSPM tool must support the compliance requirements of PCI DSS and GLBA, which may include monitoring access controls, encryption, and logging sensitive data.

iii. Identify the risks

This includes assessing the security posture of your cloud infrastructure, identifying vulnerabilities in your cloud configuration, and understanding the risks associated with the data stored in the cloud. For example, let's say your organization uses AWS for hosting its web application, which contains several instances of web servers, database servers, and storage accounts in the cloud. Your organization's web application contains sensitive customer data, such as **personally identifiable information (PII)** and credit card information. After conducting a security assessment, your organization identifies several risks associated with the AWS cloud infrastructure, including configuration issues that could lead to exploitation, misconfigurations of storage accounts that could result in data exposure or loss, lack of encryption of sensitive data at rest and in transit, weak data masking (also known as data obfuscation or data anonymization), and weak tokenization methods. The list could go on and could include weak access controls, such as shared access keys and weak passwords, that could be exploited by attackers to gain unauthorized access to cloud resources, and a lack of monitoring and logging, which could hinder the ability to detect and respond to security incidents.

Based on these risks, your organization needs a CSPM tool that provides vulnerability management, compliance monitoring, configuration management, and threat detection and response capabilities.

iv. Define the scope of the CSPM tool

Based on the risks and security requirements identified previously, you should define the scope of the CSPM tool you need. This includes identifying the features and capabilities that are necessary to address your organization's specific security needs. Based on the risks that have been identified, the bank needs a CSPM tool that provides vulnerability management, compliance monitoring, configuration management, and threat detection and response capabilities. However, the CSPM tool should also be scoped to monitor the AWS cloud services and assets that are critical to the bank's financial operations and comply with regulatory requirements.

Therefore, the *scope of the CSPM tool* would be defined as monitoring EC2 instances, S3 buckets, and RDS instances within the AWS account that hosts the bank's financial systems, applications, and data. This scope would ensure that the CSPM tool is focused on monitoring the most critical cloud services and assets and providing the necessary security controls to protect sensitive financial data and comply with regulatory requirements such as PCI-DSS and **Service Organization Control (SOC)** type 2.

Now that we understand the organization's needs, let's understand the key CSPM features that would be beneficial for any organization in totality.

2. Identify the CSPM features you need

Once you have a clear understanding of your organization's cloud security needs, you should identify the CSPM features you require. This includes asset discovery and inventory, vulnerability management, compliance monitoring, configuration management, threat detection and response, and remediation workflows. The priority matrix can vary from organization to organization. Identifying the CSPM features you need depends on your organization's cloud security needs and requirements. Let's understand what feature you should look for and the reasoning behind this.

Asset discovery and inventory

The asset discovery and inventory feature is important because it allows organizations to gain visibility into their cloud infrastructure and understand the scope of their security risks. In a cloud environment, assets can be created and destroyed rapidly, making it difficult for security teams to keep track of what is in their environment. With this information, organizations can more effectively manage their security risks by identifying misconfigurations, vulnerabilities, and potential attack surfaces. It also plays a crucial role in compliance and audit requirements. Many regulatory frameworks require organizations to maintain an accurate inventory of their assets and track changes that have been made to their configurations. CSPM tools can automate this process, reducing the workload for security teams and ensuring compliance with regulatory requirements.

> **Asset tagging – an important consideration**
>
> Asset tagging is important in cloud environments because it enables organizations to manage and secure their cloud resources more effectively. By tagging resources with metadata such as their purpose, owner, and criticality, organizations can more easily track and manage these resources over time. This information can also be used to set up automated policies that enforce security controls, such as access restrictions or encryption, on specific resources. The asset discovery and inventory feature of a CSPM tool can help organizations identify all their cloud resources, including those that may have been created without proper authorization or are not being used anymore. Once all the resources have been discovered and inventoried, the CSPM tool can then help organizations apply asset tags to these resources so that they can track them more effectively. Together, the asset tagging and asset discovery and inventory features of a CSPM tool help organizations gain a better understanding of their cloud environment, improve resource management, and enhance their overall security posture.

Vulnerability management

Vulnerability management is yet another important feature of CSPM tools because it helps organizations identify and remediate security vulnerabilities in their cloud environment. Like any other environment, vulnerability in clouds can also arise due to misconfigurations, outdated software, or other factors. These vulnerabilities can be exploited by attackers to gain unauthorized access to resources or data, causing significant damage to the organization. CSPM tools can scan cloud assets for known vulnerabilities and generate reports detailing the severity and impact of each vulnerability. This information can help organizations prioritize their remediation efforts, focusing on the vulnerabilities that pose the greatest risk to their environment.

In addition to identifying vulnerabilities, CSPM tools can also help organizations remediate them. Some CSPM tools can automate the remediation process, such as by automatically applying patches or configuration changes to vulnerable resources. This can help organizations reduce the time and effort required to remediate vulnerabilities, improving their overall security posture.

Compliance monitoring

Compliance monitoring is an important feature of a CSPM tool because it helps organizations ensure that they are meeting regulatory and compliance requirements in their cloud environment. Many industries are subject to strict compliance regulations, such as healthcare, finance, and government, and failure to comply with these regulations can result in significant financial penalties and reputational damage. It can continuously monitor the cloud environment for compliance violations and alert administrators if any are found. This includes monitoring for specific regulatory requirements such as HIPAA, PCI-DSS, GDPR, and others. It also includes the **CIS Centre for Internet Security (CIS)** Benchmark, cloud provider-specific benchmarks such as **Microsoft Cloud Security Benchmark (MCSB)**, and best practices.

In addition to identifying compliance issues, a CSPM tool with compliance monitoring features can also generate reports that demonstrate compliance with regulatory requirements. These reports can be used to prove compliance to auditors, regulators, and other stakeholders.

Configuration management

Configuration management helps organizations maintain control over their cloud infrastructure and ensure that it is configured according to best practices and compliance requirements. With cloud environments becoming increasingly complex, configuration management can be a daunting task, especially in large organizations. A CSPM tool with configuration management features can help organizations automate and streamline configuration management tasks. The tool can continuously monitor the cloud environment for configuration changes and alert administrators if any are found. It can also provide automated remediation to bring the infrastructure back into compliance.

In addition to identifying configuration issues, it provides recommendations for best practices and compliance requirements. This includes providing guidance on security configurations, network configurations, **Identity and Access Management (IAM)** configurations, and resource usage.

Threat detection and response

CSPM tool needs to have a threat detection and response feature because it allows organizations to proactively identify and respond to security threats in their cloud environment. With the rise of sophisticated cyberattacks and the increasing complexity of cloud environments, organizations need to have a robust threat detection and response strategy in place. A CSPM tool that leverages this feature can continuously monitor the cloud environment for suspicious activity, such as **unauthorized access** or **data exfiltration**. It can also provide automated alerts and notifications when potential threats are detected.

Usually, CSPM tools can be integrated with SIEM/SOAR tools, which complement threat response features that provide automated incident response capabilities. This includes automated remediation to contain and mitigate security incidents.

Remediation workflows

Remediation workflows refer to the automated processes that help organizations identify and fix security vulnerabilities in their cloud environment. These workflows can be customized based on the specific needs of the organization, and they typically involve a series of steps:

1. **Identification**: The CSPM tool identifies security vulnerabilities in the cloud environment by scanning the environment for known vulnerabilities and misconfigurations.

2. **Prioritization**: The tool prioritizes the vulnerabilities based on their severity and the potential impact on the organization.

3. **Remediation plan**: The tool develops a remediation plan that outlines the steps needed to fix the vulnerabilities, including any configuration changes or updates required.

4. **Execution**: The tool executes the remediation plan by applying the necessary configuration changes or updates to the cloud environment.

5. **Verification**: The tool verifies that the remediation actions were successful and that the vulnerabilities have been resolved.

Remediation workflows are an important feature of a CSPM tool because they help organizations automate the process of identifying and fixing security vulnerabilities in their cloud environment, which can help improve their overall security posture and reduce the risk of data breaches and other security incidents.

Integration with existing security tools

Seamlessly integrating a CSPM tool with other security tools used by an organization, such as SIEM, vulnerability scanners, and other security products is very important. This integration helps centralize security monitoring and management, streamline security workflows, and avoid duplication of effort across multiple security tools. This enables security teams to identify and respond to security threats quickly and effectively. Integration with existing security tools also allows for better collaboration between security and other teams, such as IT and DevOps, who may be responsible for managing different aspects of the organization's cloud infrastructure.

The CSPM solution should integrate with various other tools, but this will depend on the needs of the organization. However, some common security tools that a CSPM solution might integrate with are as follows:

- **Security Information and Event Management (SIEM) tools**: SIEM tools aggregate and analyze security data from across an organization's network and security systems. Integration with a CSPM tool can help provide additional context and visibility into cloud-based threats and incidents.

- **IAM tools**: IAM tools are used to manage user access to an organization's cloud resources. Integration with a CSPM tool can help identify any misconfigurations or policy violations related to IAM, which can help prevent unauthorized access to cloud resources. For example, integrating your identity provider tool, such as AWS IAM or Microsoft Entra, with the CSPM tool will help you identify potential risks such as overly permissive access policies, unused credentials, or insecure configurations. The tool can also help in implementing automated remediation actions. For example, if an IAM policy violation is detected, Prisma Cloud can trigger remediation actions, such as removing excess permissions or disabling compromised credentials.

- **DevOps tools**: DevOps tools are used to manage the deployment of applications and infrastructure. Integration with a CSPM tool can help ensure that security is integrated into the DevOps process by providing security-related feedback and alerts during the development and deployment process.

> **Note**
> CSPM integration with other tools will be discussed in detail in *Chapter 8*.

User-friendly interface

Having a user-friendly interface for a CSPM tool is important for several reasons:

- **Ease of use**: A user-friendly interface makes it easy for security teams to navigate and use the tool, which can save time and reduce errors

- **Adoption**: If the interface is not user-friendly, security teams may be reluctant to adopt the tool, which could result in reduced visibility into cloud security risks

- **Training**: A user-friendly interface can reduce the amount of training required to use the tool effectively

- **Efficiency**: A user-friendly interface can improve the efficiency of security teams by providing easy access to critical information and streamlining workflows

- **Collaboration**: A user-friendly interface can promote collaboration between security teams, enabling them to work together more effectively to address cloud security risks

Overall, a user-friendly interface can help ensure that a CSPM tool is effective and efficient in helping organizations manage their cloud security risks.

Automation capabilities

Automation capabilities refer to the ability of a CSPM tool to automate tasks such as scanning, detection, and remediation of security issues in a cloud environment. It is important for several reasons:

- **Time-saving**: Automation capabilities can save time and reduce the burden on security teams, allowing them to focus on more critical tasks

- **Accuracy**: Automation can improve the accuracy and consistency of security tasks, reducing the risk of human error

- **Speed**: Automation can enable security teams to detect and respond to security issues more quickly, reducing the risk of a security breach

- **Scalability**: Automation can help security teams scale their operations to keep up with the growing demands of cloud environments

- **Cost-saving**: Automation can help organizations save costs by reducing the need for manual labor and minimizing the potential impact of a security breach

Overall, automation capabilities are important for ensuring the efficiency and effectiveness of a CSPM tool in managing cloud security risks.

Ease of generating reports

CSPM tools should provide robust reporting capabilities to effectively communicate the security posture of your cloud environment. This involves the ability to generate comprehensive reports that highlight security issues, compliance violations, and remediation efforts. Here are some key considerations:

- **Customizable reports**: The tool should allow users to customize reports based on specific criteria, time frames, or compliance standards. This flexibility enables organizations to tailor reports to their unique requirements.

- **Scheduled reporting**: Automate the generation and delivery of reports on a regular schedule. This feature ensures that stakeholders receive up-to-date information without manual intervention.

- **Export formats**: Support for various export formats (for example, PDF, CSV, and JSON) enhances the tool's usability. Different stakeholders may prefer different formats, and having options facilitates effective communication.

- **Integration with reporting tools**: Integration capabilities with popular reporting tools (for example, Tableau and Power BI) allow for further customization and visualization of CSPM data.

Customizing CSPM compliance frameworks

Each organization may have its own set of security hardening standards and exceptions based on specific regulatory requirements, internal policies, or industry best practices. Therefore, the ability to customize CSPM compliance frameworks is crucial. Let's take a closer look:

- **Editable compliance policies**: The CSPM tool should allow users to modify and create compliance policies that align with the organization's specific security requirements. This includes adding or removing rules and adjusting severity levels.

- **Customization of rules and exceptions**: The tool should provide the capability to customize individual rules within compliance frameworks. This allows organizations to account for their unique security considerations and exceptions.

- **Version control**: Maintain version control for customized compliance frameworks to track changes and ensure traceability. This is especially important for audit purposes and maintaining a history of security policy modifications.

- **Audit trails**: Track and log changes made to compliance frameworks to provide transparency and facilitate auditing. Knowing who made changes and when is essential for accountability and compliance tracking.

- **Reusable template**: If your organization operates in a multi-cloud environment or has multiple teams with different requirements, the ability to share and reuse customized compliance templates can be beneficial for consistency and efficiency.

Now that we understand the key CSPM features, it is time to understand the vendor evaluation process. However, before that, let's try and find some answers to some important questions that are important for the vendor evaluation process.

What are Gartner's Magic Quadrant, Gartner Peer Insights, and Gartner Reviews, and how do they play an important role in CSPM tool selection?

Gartner's Magic Quadrant, Gartner Peer Insights, and Gartner Reviews are all important resources for organizations looking to select a CSPM tool. Here is how each can be useful in the CSPM tool selection process:

- **Gartner's Magic Quadrant**: Magic Quadrant provides an overview of the CSPM market and helps organizations understand the relative positions of CSPM vendors in terms of their ability to execute and completeness of vision. This can help with selecting a CSPM tool because it allows organizations to compare and evaluate vendors based on their strengths and weaknesses and their ability to meet the organization's specific needs.

- **Gartner Peer Insights**: Peer Insights provides user-generated reviews and ratings of CSPM tools from other users within the industry or organization. This can be valuable because it allows organizations to read about the experiences of other users with similar needs and requirements. It can also help organizations identify any potential issues or limitations of the tool that may not be apparent from the vendor's marketing materials.

- **Gartner Reviews**: Gartner analysts provide expert analysis and advice on CSPM tools, including their strengths and weaknesses, market position, and strategic direction. This can help with evaluating CSPM tools because it provides an independent assessment of the tool's capabilities and limitations, as well as insights into the vendor's strategy and direction. This can help organizations make more informed decisions about which CSPM tool to select.

Overall, each of these resources provides valuable insights into the CSPM market and can help organizations select a CSPM tool that meets their specific needs and requirements. By using a combination of these resources, organizations can get a more complete picture of the CSPM market and make more informed decisions about which tool to select.

Why is it important to understand Gartner's Magic Quadrant, Peer Insights, and Gartner Reviews?

Understanding Gartner's Magic Quadrant, Peer Insights, and Gartner Reviews is important in the vendor evaluation process for CSPM tools because they provide valuable insights into the performance and capabilities of different vendors in the market:

- **Vendor evaluation**: Gartner's Magic Quadrant is a research methodology that evaluates vendors in a specific market based on their completeness of vision and ability to execute. By understanding Magic Quadrant, businesses can evaluate and compare vendors in a specific market and make more informed decisions when selecting vendors for their technology solutions.

- **Product selection**: Peer Insights and Gartner Reviews provide user-generated reviews and ratings of products and vendors. These reviews can provide valuable insights into the strengths and weaknesses of a product or vendor, as well as real-world experiences from other users. This can help businesses make more informed decisions when they're selecting products and vendors for their technology solutions.

- **Market trends**: Gartner's research and analysis can provide insights into market trends, emerging technologies, and industry best practices. By keeping up to date with Gartner's research, businesses can stay ahead of the curve and make more informed decisions about their technology investments.

- **Industry benchmarking**: Gartner's research and analysis can also provide benchmarks for businesses to compare their technology solutions and practices against industry best practices. This can help businesses identify areas for improvement and make more informed decisions about their technology investments.

Overall, understanding Gartner's Magic Quadrant, Peer Insights, and Gartner Reviews is important for businesses to make informed decisions about their technology investments, evaluate vendors and products, and stay up to date with industry trends and best practices.

What are other review organizations other than Gartner?

Several other review organizations provide similar research and analysis to Gartner:

- **Forrester Research**: Forrester is a research and advisory firm that provides insights into technology trends, markets, and best practices. Their research covers a wide range of industries, including technology, healthcare, finance, and more.

- **International Data Corporation (IDC)**: This is another organization known for providing global market intelligence, advisory services, and events for the IT, telecom, and consumer technology markets. Their research focuses on emerging technology trends, industry analysis, and vendor evaluation.

- **451 Research**: 451 Research is a leading provider of technology research and advisory services. Their research covers a range of technology topics, including cloud computing, big data, cybersecurity, and the **Internet of Things (IoT)**.

- **TechValidate**: TechValidate is a software platform that collects and validates customer feedback and transforms it into data-driven content such as case studies, testimonials, and **return on investment (ROI)** analyses.

- **TrustRadius**: TrustRadius is a review platform that collects and verifies customer feedback for B2B technology products. Their reviews cover a range of categories, including marketing, sales, HR, finance, and more.

Overall, these organizations provide valuable insights and analysis on technology trends, markets, and vendors, and can be a valuable resource for businesses when they're evaluating technology solutions.

Who are CSPM tool procurement stakeholders?

Several stakeholders are involved in the procurement of a CSPM tool. Some of these stakeholders are as follows:

- **Information security team**: The information security team is responsible for the overall security of an organization's cloud infrastructure. They are the primary stakeholders in the CSPM tool procurement process as they will be using the tool to monitor, identify, and remediate cloud security risks.

- **Cloud operations team**: The cloud operations team is responsible for managing and maintaining an organization's cloud infrastructure. They will be using the CSPM tool to monitor and maintain the security posture of the cloud infrastructure.

- **Compliance team**: The compliance team is responsible for ensuring that an organization's cloud infrastructure adheres to regulatory requirements and industry standards. They will be using the CSPM tool to monitor and ensure compliance with relevant regulations.

- **Procurement team**: The procurement team is responsible for purchasing the CSPM tool. They will be evaluating vendor proposals, negotiating contracts, and ensuring that the procurement process is compliant with organizational policies and procedures.

- **Executive management**: Executive management oversees the overall direction of the organization and is responsible for approving the purchase of the CSPM tool. They are interested in the tool's ability to meet organizational objectives, ROIs, and alignment with strategic goals.

- **End users**: End users are the individuals who will be using the CSPM tool daily. Their feedback on the tool's usability and functionality is crucial to ensuring it meets the organization's needs.

> **Important note**
>
> Effective communication and collaboration between these stakeholders are essential for successful CSPM tool procurement. Each stakeholder's perspective and requirements need to be considered to ensure that the chosen CSPM tool meets the organization's overall goals and objectives.

Now, let's deep dive into the vendor evaluation process for a CSPM tool.

3. Evaluate the CSPM vendor

The vendor evaluation process for CSPM tools is conducted to assess and compare the capabilities of different vendors that provide CSPM offerings. When evaluating CSPM vendors, it is important to consider their experience in cloud security, their reputation in the industry, and the quality of their customer support.

This process involves several steps:

1. **Define the requirements**: Identify the security requirements specific to your organization and list the essential features you expect from a CSPM tool. We covered this part in the previous section (*point 1*).

2. **Create a shortlist of vendors**: Research the market to identify potential vendors that meet your requirements. Consider factors such as their reputation, customer reviews, and product features.

3. **Send request for proposals (RFPs)**: RFP documents are sent to the shortlisted vendors. These documents outline your requirements and ask vendors to provide information on how their CSPM tool can meet those requirements.

4. **Evaluate vendor proposals**: Evaluate the responses to the RFPs to shortlist vendors for further consideration. You can use an evaluation matrix to compare vendors based on factors such as feature sets, pricing, ease of use, scalability, support, and integration capabilities.

5. **Conduct POC**: After shortlisting the vendors, conduct a POC to assess their CSPM tool's capabilities in your cloud environment. This step allows you to test the tool's effectiveness and identify any issues or challenges.

6. **Check references**: Contact the vendors' references to verify their claims about the product's capabilities, performance, and support.

7. **Finalize the selection**: Evaluate the results of the POC and reference checks to select the vendor that best meets your requirements.

8. **Negotiate and finalize the contract**: After selecting the vendor, negotiate the contract terms and pricing, including licensing, support, and maintenance agreements.

9. **Implementation and deployment**: Work with the vendor to implement and deploy the CSPM tool in your cloud environment.

Overall, the vendor evaluation process for CSPM tools requires careful planning and evaluation to ensure that the selected vendor meets your organization's specific security requirements and delivers effective cloud security solutions.

Let's understand this by considering an example.

Example

Let's say a financial organization needs a CSPM tool to secure its cloud infrastructure. After identifying the organization's security requirements, the organization decides to evaluate two CSPM vendors: **Vendor A** and **Vendor B**.

- **Vendor A**:

  - Offers real-time monitoring of cloud resources, alerting, and threat detection

  - Provides a wide range of compliance checks and can scan for vulnerabilities

  - Has a user-friendly interface and provides actionable insights to remediate security issues

  - Has experience in working with financial organizations and can customize its offerings to meet the organization's specific security requirements

- **Vendor B**:

  - Offers continuous monitoring of cloud resources, alerting, and threat detection

  - Provides a comprehensive set of compliance checks and can scan for vulnerabilities

  - Has robust automation capabilities and can automate remediation of security issues

  - Offers a comprehensive reporting dashboard and provides detailed analytics to track security incidents

Based on the organization's security requirements, the organization should evaluate these vendors based on the following questions:

- Which vendor provides the most comprehensive set of compliance checks that meet the organization's regulatory requirements?

- Which vendor offers the best vulnerability management capabilities to scan for vulnerabilities and remediate them promptly?

- Which vendor provides the most effective real-time monitoring, alerting, and threat detection capabilities to detect and respond to security incidents?

- Which vendor provides the most user-friendly interface and actionable insights to remediate security issues quickly and efficiently?

- Which vendor has experience in working with financial organizations and can customize its offerings to meet the organization's specific security requirements?

- Which vendor offers the best customer support and has a proven record of accomplishment in addressing customer concerns?

By evaluating these factors, the financial organization can choose the CSPM vendor that best meets its security needs and provides the most value for its investment.

4. Consider the ease of use

A CSPM solution should be easy to deploy, configure, and use. Look for a solution that provides a user-friendly interface and a streamlined workflow that can help you quickly identify and remediate security issues. When considering a CSPM tool for your organization, it is important to evaluate the ease of use of the tool. The tool should be intuitive and easy to navigate, with clear instructions and minimal technical expertise required to use it effectively.

Let's consider an example of how to consider the ease of use of a CSPM tool.

Let's say a healthcare organization is evaluating two CSPM tools: **Tool A** and **Tool B**. Both tools offer similar features, including vulnerability scanning, configuration management, and threat detection. However, Tool A is known for its user-friendly interface, while Tool B has a steeper learning curve and requires more technical expertise to use effectively. In this scenario, the healthcare organization should consider the ease of use of each tool. Here are some factors to consider:

- **User interface**:

  - Which tool has the most intuitive and user-friendly interface?

  - Which tool is easy to navigate and provides clear instructions for performing security tasks?

- **Technical expertise required**:

  - Which tool requires less technical expertise to use effectively?

  - Which tool can be used by non-technical staff members, such as compliance officers or auditors?

- **Training and support**:

  - Which tool provider offers the best training and support resources?

  - Which tool provider has a comprehensive knowledge base or customer support team that can assist with technical issues?

Based on these factors, the healthcare organization should choose the CSPM tool that is easiest to use, requires minimal technical expertise, and offers the best training and support resources. In this case, Tool A would be the better choice as it has a user-friendly interface and requires less technical expertise to use effectively. By choosing an easy-to-use CSPM tool, the healthcare organization can ensure that its security tasks are performed efficiently and effectively, without adding unnecessary complexity or technical overhead.

5. Look for automation capabilities

CSPM solutions should have automation capabilities to reduce the manual effort required to manage cloud security. This includes automation of compliance checks, vulnerability scans, and remediation workflows. When evaluating a CSPM tool, it is important to consider the automation capabilities of the tool. Automation can significantly reduce the time and effort required to perform security tasks and can help ensure consistent and thorough coverage of cloud resources. When evaluating a CSPM tool's automation capability, there are some key factors to consider:

- **Policy enforcement automation**: CSPM tools can automatically detect policy violations in your cloud environment and remediate them. Check whether the tool can automate policy enforcement and whether it provides flexible remediation options.

- **Continuous monitoring**: A good CSPM tool should be able to continuously monitor your cloud environment and detect changes that could impact security. The tool should be able to automatically adjust policies based on these changes to maintain security.

- **Remediation automation**: A CSPM tool should not only detect security issues but also provide automated remediation. The tool should be able to remediate issues without manual intervention, such as disabling insecure services or fixing misconfigured security groups.

- **Integration with other tools**: A CSPM tool should be able to integrate with other security tools in your environment, such as vulnerability scanners or incident response platforms. This allows for a more comprehensive and automated security approach across your environment.

- **Customizable automation workflows**: The CSPM tool should provide flexibility in designing automated workflows that align with your organization's specific security needs. You should be able to customize the tool's automation capabilities so that it fits your organization's unique security requirements.

- **Alerting and notification automation**: The CSPM tool should be able to provide automatic alerts and notifications to relevant personnel when security issues are detected. This ensures that security issues are quickly addressed and resolved.

Overall, when evaluating a CSPM tool's automation capabilities, look for a tool that can automate policy enforcement, continuous monitoring, remediation, integration with other tools, customizable workflows, and alerting and notification automation. A CSPM tool with strong automation capabilities will help your organization maintain a high level of security while reducing manual effort and potential errors.

Let's consider an example of how to look for automation capabilities in a CSPM tool.

Example

Let's say a manufacturing company is evaluating two CSPM tools: **Tool A** and **Tool B**. Both tools offer similar features, including vulnerability scanning, configuration management, and threat detection. However, Tool A has robust automation capabilities, while Tool B requires more manual effort to perform security tasks. In this scenario, the manufacturing company should consider the automation capabilities of each tool.

Here are some key factors to consider:

- Which tool offers the most comprehensive automation coverage for security tasks? Which tool can automate most tasks, such as vulnerability scanning, remediation, and policy enforcement?

- Which tool offers the most flexibility in automating security tasks?

- Which tool can be customized to meet the specific needs of the organization, such as integrating with existing automation workflows or customizing remediation actions?

- Which tool offers the best reporting and analytics capabilities for automation tasks?

- Which tool provides clear and actionable insights into security incidents and automation performance?

Based on these factors, the manufacturing company should choose the CSPM tool that offers the most comprehensive automation capabilities, can be customized to meet its specific needs, and provides clear reporting and analytics. In this case, Tool A would be the better choice as it has robust automation capabilities that can significantly reduce the time and effort required to perform security tasks. By choosing a CSPM tool with strong automation capabilities, the manufacturing company can improve the efficiency and effectiveness of its security operations and reduce the risk of security incidents.

6. Evaluate pricing and licensing

CSPM solutions can vary in terms of pricing and licensing models. It is important to evaluate the cost of the solution and whether it aligns with your budget and expected return on investment.

When evaluating a CSPM tool, it is important to consider pricing and licensing. CSPM tools can vary widely in terms of pricing models, licensing options, and **total cost of ownership** (**TCO**). Let's look at an example of how to evaluate pricing and licensing for a CSPM tool.

Let's say a retail company is evaluating two CSPM tools: **Tool A** and **Tool B**. Both tools offer similar features, including vulnerability scanning, configuration management, and threat detection. However, Tool A has a higher upfront cost and a perpetual licensing model, while Tool B has a lower upfront cost and a subscription-based licensing model.

In this scenario, the retail company should consider the pricing and licensing options of each tool. Let's look at some key factors to consider.

Upfront cost

Upfront cost refers to the initial expense that an organization incurs when purchasing a product or service. In the context of a CSPM tool, upfront cost would refer to the initial cost of acquiring the tool, which may include licensing fees, implementation costs, and any associated hardware or software requirements. This cost is typically paid upfront, at the time of purchase, and can be a significant factor in an organization's decision-making process when evaluating CSPM tools.

Here are some key questions that should have clear answers:

- Which tool has a lower upfront cost?
- Which tool fits within the organization's budget constraints?

For example, if a financial services company is considering purchasing a CSPM tool, it should evaluate several options and compare the upfront costs associated with each tool. One tool may have a higher upfront cost than another but may offer more advanced features or better automation capabilities. The financial services company would need to weigh the upfront cost against the value provided by the tool to determine which option is the best fit for its needs and budget.

Licensing model

The licensing model refers to how a software product is licensed to the end user. This typically includes terms and conditions governing the software's use, including the number of users allowed to access it, the duration of the license, and any restrictions on how it can be used or distributed. In the context of a CSPM tool, the licensing model can vary depending on the vendor and the specific product. Some CSPM tools may offer perpetual licenses, which allow the customer to use the software indefinitely after paying an upfront fee. Other tools may offer subscription-based licenses, which require the customer to pay a recurring fee to use the software over a specified time.

Here are some key questions that should have clear answers:

- Which tool offers the most flexible licensing model?
- Which tool provides options for both perpetual and subscription-based licensing?

The licensing model can also impact the level of support and updates provided by the vendor. For example, a subscription-based license may include ongoing updates and technical support, while a perpetual license may require the customer to pay for upgrades or support separately.

Here are some of the key factors to keep in mind while checking the licensing model:

- **License type**: The license type refers to whether the CSPM tool is licensed on a perpetual or subscription basis. Perpetual licenses require an upfront payment and provide the customer with ongoing access to the software, while subscription licenses require ongoing payments for continued use.

- **License duration**: The license duration refers to the length of time for which the license is valid. For subscription licenses, this will be the length of the subscription term, while for perpetual licenses, it may be indefinite or a specified number of years.

- **License scope**: The license scope refers to the number of users, devices, or environments covered by the license. Some CSPM tools may offer per-user licensing, while others may charge based on the number of devices or cloud accounts being monitored.

When evaluating CSPM tools, it is important to consider the licensing model and how it aligns with the organization's needs and budget.

TCO

TCO is a financial calculation that considers all the costs associated with owning and operating a technological solution over its entire life cycle. It is important to consider the TCO over the entire life cycle of the tool. This can help organizations make informed decisions about which licensing model to choose and how to budget for ongoing costs. When evaluating CSPM tools, TCO can be a key factor to consider as it can help organizations understand the true cost of using the tool over time.

Here are some key questions that should have clear answers:

- Which tool has the lowest TCO over the long term?
- Which tool offers the most value for the organization's investment?

TCO can be impacted by several factors, some of which are as follows:

- **Upfront costs**: Upfront costs associated with purchasing perpetual licenses or onboarding subscription licenses can impact the overall TCO of a CSPM tool.

- **Recurring costs**: Ongoing costs associated with subscription-based licensing models can also impact TCO. Organizations must factor in the recurring costs of annual or monthly license renewals.

- **Additional costs**: Additional costs associated with CSPM tools may include consulting fees, training costs, or customization expenses.

In this case, Tool B would be the better choice as it has a lower upfront cost and a flexible subscription-based licensing model. However, the retail company should also consider the long-term TCO of each tool and ensure that the pricing and licensing options are sustainable over the long term. By carefully evaluating pricing and licensing, the retail company can choose a CSPM tool that provides the best value for its investment and fits within its budget constraints.

Other factors to consider for the CSPM licensing model

Here are some other factors to consider:

- **Support and maintenance**: Support and maintenance costs can be a significant component of TCO, especially for perpetual licenses. These costs may include technical support, software updates, and bug fixes.

- **Flexibility**: Some CSPM vendors offer flexible licensing options that allow customers to adjust the license type and scope as their needs change over time. This can be a key factor to consider for organizations with rapidly changing cloud environments or unpredictable usage patterns.

By carefully evaluating these factors, organizations can choose a CSPM tool with a licensing model that meets their needs and provides the best value for their budget.

Vendor selection process checklists for CSPM

Checklists are a useful tool in the vendor selection process as they provide a structured approach to evaluating and comparing vendors. Here is a comprehensive vendor selection checklist for selecting a CSPM tool:

- *Does the CSPM tool meet the security requirements of the organization?* Ensure that the CSPM tool offers the necessary features and capabilities to meet the organization's security needs.

- *Does the CSPM tool support the cloud environment(s) used by the organization?* Ensure that the CSPM tool supports the cloud platform(s) used by the organization, such as AWS, Azure, or GCP.

- *Can the CSPM tool integrate with existing security tools and solutions used by the organization?* Ensure that the CSPM tool can integrate with other security tools, such as SIEM solutions, vulnerability scanners, and firewalls.

- *Is the CSPM tool easy to use and configure?* Ensure that the CSPM tool is easy to use and does not require extensive training or technical expertise.

- *Does the CSPM tool offer automation capabilities, such as automated remediation and incident response?* Ensure that the CSPM tool can automate routine security tasks and reduce the workload of security teams.

- *Can the CSPM tool scale meet the needs of the organization as it grows and expands its cloud environment?* Ensure that the CSPM tool can scale to monitor additional cloud accounts and workloads as needed.

- *Does the CSPM tool offer robust reporting and analytics capabilities?* Ensure that the CSPM tool provides detailed reports and insights into the security posture of the organization's cloud environment.

- *What is the reputation of the CSPM vendor?* Ensure that the CSPM vendor has a track record of delivering quality solutions and providing excellent customer support.

- *Is the CSPM tool priced competitively and does the licensing model fit within the organization's budget?* Ensure that the CSPM tool is priced competitively and offers a licensing model that meets the organization's needs.

- *What level of support and maintenance is provided by the CSPM vendor?* Ensure that the CSPM vendor offers comprehensive technical support and regular updates to the CSPM tool.

Now that we have understood the vendor selection process and some key important questions, let's understand how POCs are conducted.

POC for CSPM tools

POC is a critical step in selecting a CSPM tool. The goal of a POC is to evaluate the capabilities of a CSPM tool and determine if it can meet the organization's specific needs. In this section, we'll cover the comprehensive process for conducting a POC for CSPM tools.

Define objectives

Define the specific objectives of the POC, including the scope of the evaluation, the key use cases, and the expected outcomes. We discussed this in detail previously.

Identify key metrics

Key metrics refer to the measurable values that are used to evaluate and track the performance of a specific process, product, or service. They are used to provide objective data for decision-making and to monitor progress toward achieving goals and objectives. Identify the key metrics that are used to evaluate the CSPM tool. These metrics should be aligned with the objectives of the POC and should be measurable and relevant.

In the context of CSPM tool selection, key metrics may include the following:

- **Accuracy of asset discovery and inventory**: This metric measures the CSPM tool's ability to accurately detect and track cloud assets

- **Vulnerability coverage and remediation rate**: This metric measures the percentage of vulnerabilities detected by the CSPM tool and the rate at which they are remediated

- **Compliance coverage and adherence rate**: This metric measures the percentage of compliance requirements covered by the CSPM tool and the rate at which they are adhered to

- **Threat detection and response time**: This metric measures the time it takes for the CSPM tool to detect and respond to a security threat

- **User satisfaction**: This metric measures the satisfaction level of users with the CSPM tool, including ease of use, effectiveness, and overall value

These metrics can be used to compare different CSPM tools and evaluate their effectiveness in meeting the organization's security needs.

Select a POC team

The POC team for a CSPM tool should consist of individuals responsible for managing the cloud infrastructure and security in the organization. This includes cloud architects, security architects, operations managers, and IT managers. It is important to select a team that has a good understanding of the organization's cloud infrastructure and security requirements and can provide feedback on the tool's effectiveness in meeting those requirements. Additionally, the team should have the technical skills to evaluate the tool's features and functionality and provide feedback on its ease of use and effectiveness. Select a team of stakeholders who will participate in the POC. This team can include IT, security, compliance, and audit personnel.

Select a test environment

When conducting a PoC for a CSPM tool, it is important to select an appropriate test environment. This is a critical step in ensuring that the results that are obtained during the POC are meaningful and applicable to the organization's actual environment. Ideally, the test environment should be representative of the production environment and should have similar cloud service configurations and security policies. This can include creating a replica of the production environment or using a subset of the production environment for testing purposes. The test environment should also be isolated from the production environment to prevent any potential impact on ongoing operations. This can be achieved through dedicated test accounts, separate networks, and restricted access controls.

Install and configure the CSPM tool

Installing and configuring the CSPM tool is a critical step in conducting a PoC to evaluate the tool's effectiveness. The POC team should work with the vendor to install and configure the tool in the test environment. This involves setting up the required infrastructure, including servers, databases, and networks, and installing and configuring the software. During this process, it is important to ensure that the tool is configured to meet the specific requirements and objectives of the POC. This may involve setting up policies, rules, alerts, and reports and integrating the tool with other security tools and systems. It is also important to ensure that the tool is configured to collect and analyze the relevant data, such as log files, system events, and network traffic. This will enable the tool to identify and prioritize security issues and provide actionable insights to improve the organization's security posture.

Perform an initial assessment

Performing an initial assessment is an essential step in conducting a POC for a CSPM tool. It involves evaluating the tool's performance and functionality in a controlled environment to determine if it meets the organization's security needs. During this stage, the POC team should identify the assets they want to protect and use the CSPM tool to perform an initial assessment. This assessment should include an analysis of the asset inventory, risk assessments, compliance checks, and vulnerability scans. The team should document the results and compare them to the objectives and key metrics they identified earlier. This comparison will help the team determine if the CSPM tool is performing as expected and meeting their security needs.

Evaluate the results

Evaluating the results of the CSPM tool POC is an essential step to determine if the tool meets the organization's requirements and if it can be effectively integrated into its existing cloud environment. The POC team should evaluate the CSPM tool's performance against the established key metrics and objectives. During the evaluation process, the team should assess the accuracy of the CSPM tool's asset discovery and inventory, vulnerability management, compliance monitoring, configuration management, and threat detection and response capabilities. They should also evaluate the effectiveness of the remediation workflows and the automation capabilities.

In addition to the tool's technical performance, the POC team should evaluate the tool's user interface and ease of use. The team should also assess the vendor's customer support and responsiveness to issues and concerns.

Test use cases

Test use cases are specific scenarios or situations that are created to test the functionality and performance of a particular system or application. They are designed to ensure that the system or application works as intended and meets the requirements and expectations of the end users.

In the context of CSPM tool selection, test use cases could include scenarios such as the following:

- Simulating a security incident and observing how the CSPM tool detects and responds to the threat
- Testing the asset discovery and inventory feature by adding a new resource to the cloud environment and ensuring that it is properly identified and classified by the tool
- Checking the compliance monitoring capability by verifying that the tool correctly flags any non-compliant resources or configurations
- Testing the automation capabilities by running a remediation workflow and verifying that the tool executes the desired actions correctly

Evaluate the integration

Evaluating the integration is a crucial step in the PoC process for CSPM tool selection. It involves testing the integration of the CSPM tool with existing security tools and infrastructure to determine if it works seamlessly and effectively. This evaluation is important because integration issues can lead to inefficiencies and gaps in security coverage. To evaluate integration, the POC team should identify the security tools and infrastructure that will be integrated with the CSPM tool and test the integration in a controlled environment. This includes testing the flow of data between systems and verifying that the CSPM tool can consume and process data from the integrated systems. The POC team should also evaluate the level of automation provided by the integration. The CSPM tool should be able to automate the ingestion of data from the integrated systems and use it to enrich the CSPM tool's analysis and findings.

Analyze metrics

Analyzing metrics involves analyzing the data that was collected during the POC process. This data can provide insights into the effectiveness of the CSPM tool and its ability to meet the organization's security needs. Metrics can also help in identifying areas for improvement and optimization. The analysis should involve examining the metrics from various perspectives to gain a comprehensive understanding of the CSPM tool's performance. The analysis should include evaluating the tool's ability to detect security risks and vulnerabilities, automate security tasks, and provide actionable insights.

Some of the key metrics that can be used to evaluate the effectiveness of a CSPM tool are as follows:

- **False positive rate**: This measures the number of alerts that are generated by the tool that are not actual security risks. A high false positive rate can lead to alert fatigue and increase the workload for security teams.

- **Time to detect**: This measures the amount of time it takes for the tool to detect a security risk or vulnerability. A shorter time to detect can help in minimizing the impact of security incidents.

- **Time to remediate**: This measures the amount of time it takes to remediate a security risk or vulnerability after it has been detected. A shorter time to remediate can help in minimizing the impact of security incidents.

- **Compliance posture**: This measures the organization's compliance with industry regulations and best practices. The CSPM tool should be able to identify areas where the organization is not compliant and provide recommendations for remediation.

- **Cost savings**: This measures the savings that can be achieved through the CSPM tool. The tool should be able to automate security tasks and reduce the workload for security teams, leading to cost savings for the organization.

Determine ROI

Return on Investment (**ROI**) is a financial metric that's used to measure the profitability of an investment. In the context of CSPM tool selection, determining ROI involves calculating the financial benefits that can be obtained from the tool against its cost. To determine the ROI of a CSPM tool, you need to consider the potential benefits that the tool can provide, such as reducing the cost of security incidents, increasing the efficiency of security operations, and reducing the risk of non-compliance fines. These benefits can be translated into financial figures such as cost savings, increased revenue, and reduced penalties.

Next, you need to calculate the cost of the CSPM tool, which includes the licensing fee, hardware, and software infrastructure, and the cost of implementation, training, and maintenance. Once you have determined the benefits and costs, you can calculate the ROI using the following formula:

ROI = (Net Benefits / Cost of Tool) x 100%

The net benefits are calculated by subtracting the total cost of the tool from the total benefits. If the ROI is positive, it indicates that the CSPM tool is financially viable and will provide a return on investment. If the ROI is negative, it suggests that the tool is not cost-effective, and alternative options should be considered. Calculating the ROI of a CSPM tool is a crucial step in the vendor selection process as it allows organizations to make informed decisions and choose a tool that will provide the most value for their investment.

Document findings

Documenting findings is an essential step in the POC process for a CSPM tool. It involves recording all the observations, feedback, and results gathered during the testing phase. This documentation will help the organization assess whether the CSPM tool is suitable for their needs and compare it with other vendors' tools they are evaluating.

The documentation should be detailed and provide an overview of the CSPM tool's capabilities, strengths, and limitations. It should also include a summary of each use case's results and any issues that were encountered during testing.

Documenting findings should also involve identifying any areas of improvement and making recommendations for the vendor regarding how they can improve the CSPM tool's functionality and usability.

The documentation should be shared with all relevant stakeholders, including the POC team, IT security team, and procurement team, to ensure that everyone is aware of the findings and can make informed decisions about the selection of the CSPM tool.

Make a recommendation

Making a recommendation is the process of presenting a conclusion based on the results of the CSPM tool POC. It involves analyzing the metrics that were collected during the testing phase and comparing them against the objectives that were defined at the beginning of the process. The recommendation should consider factors such as the CSPM tool's functionality, ease of use, performance, cost, and licensing model. Additionally, it should consider the organization's specific needs, goals, and budget. When making a recommendation, it is important to provide a detailed analysis of the CSPM tool's strengths and weaknesses and how they align with the organization's requirements.

The recommendation should also provide a clear justification for why a particular CSPM tool is the best fit for the organization and why other options were not chosen. The recommendation should be presented to key stakeholders, including the IT department, security team, and executive management. It should be accompanied by a detailed report that outlines the findings and metrics that were collected during the POC and a comparison of the different CSPM tools that were evaluated.

What is the key outcome of the CSPM tool's POC?

The outcome of a POC for a CSPM tool is to determine if the tool is suitable for an organization's specific needs. The POC provides the organization with the opportunity to evaluate the capabilities of the CSPM tool in a controlled test environment, identify any limitations or issues, and determine if it can effectively meet the organization's requirements.

The specific outcomes of a CSPM tool POC will depend on the objectives and metrics established by the organization. However, some common outcomes of a successful POC may include the following:

- Identifying misconfigurations, vulnerabilities, and compliance violations in the test environment
- Evaluating the CSPM tool's ease of use and quality of reports generated
- Testing the CSPM tool against specific use cases, such as policy enforcement and incident response
- Evaluating the CSPM tool's integration capabilities with other security tools and workflows
- Analyzing the metrics that were collected during the POC to evaluate the effectiveness of the CSPM tool in meeting the organization's specific needs
- Determining the ROI of the CSPM tool
- A recommendation to either proceed with the purchase and implementation of the CSPM tool or to look for other options

The outcome of a CSPM tool's POC is an essential step in the vendor selection process and helps ensure that the organization chooses the best CSPM tool for their needs.

Summary

Selecting a CSPM tool is a critical decision for organizations to mitigate security risks in their cloud infrastructure. In this chapter, we explored the key considerations for selecting a CSPM tool, including identifying your cloud environment, defining your security requirements, and prioritizing your security needs. We also discussed the vendor selection process, POC testing, and stakeholder management, all of which are involved in the procurement of a CSPM tool. This chapter emphasized the importance of selecting a tool that aligns with organizational goals and objectives, has a user-friendly interface, and provides automation capabilities to reduce the workload of security teams. Finally, we discussed the pricing and licensing model of CSPM tools, and the TCO involved in their procurement. By considering these factors, organizations can select a CSPM tool that meets their unique security requirements and provides effective risk management for their cloud infrastructure.

In the next chapter, we will dive deep into the deployment aspects of CSPM tools.

Further reading

To learn more about the topics that were covered in this chapter, take a look at the following resources:

- *Cloud Security Posture Management (CSPM) Buyers Guide*, by SANS Institute
- *Top Cloud Security Posture Management (CSPM) Tools*, by Gartner
- *Cloud Security Posture Management: How to Select the Right Tool*, by Infosec Institute
- *Cloud Security Posture Management: What You Need to Know*, by Cloud Academy
- *The Role of Automation in Cloud Security Posture Management*, by Dark Reading

Part 2: CSPM Deployment Aspects

This part dives into the pragmatic side of CSPM. From deploying CSPM tools to onboarding cloud accounts and containers, you will explore the hands-on aspects of securing diverse cloud environments. This part will delve into environment settings to refine your understanding of crucial configurations. Tailored for practical insights, this part equips you with actionable knowledge to deploy CSPM tools effectively for robust cloud security.

This part contains the following chapters:

- *Chapter 5, Deploying the CSPM Tool*
- *Chapter 6, Onboarding Cloud Accounts*
- *Chapter 7, Onboarding Containers*
- *Chapter 8, Exploring Environment Settings*

5
Deploying the CSPM Tool

In recent years, cloud computing has become increasingly popular due to its scalability, cost-effectiveness, and flexibility. However, as organizations move more of their data and applications to the cloud, the need for cloud security has become more critical than ever before. CSPM is a security strategy that provides organizations with a comprehensive approach to identifying, assessing, and remediating security risks in their cloud environment. We have understood this through previous chapters.

One of the key components of CSPM is the deployment of a CSPM tool. Deploying a CSPM tool can be a complex process that requires careful planning, coordination, and execution. In this chapter, we will discuss the essential aspects of deploying a CSPM tool. We will explore the key considerations that organizations should follow when selecting a CSPM tool, such as its features, integration capabilities, and compatibility with their cloud environment.

We will also examine the deployment process itself, covering key topics such as tool installation, configuration, and integration with other security tools. We will discuss best practices for testing and validating the tool's functionality and security before going live. Finally, we will explore how organizations can use their CSPM tool to enhance their overall cloud security posture and protect against a wide range of security threats.

By the end of this chapter, you will have a solid understanding of the key steps and considerations involved in deploying a CSPM tool, enabling you to select and implement the right tool for your organization's needs.

In this chapter, we'll cover the following main topics:

- Common deployment model and strategies
- Different deployment methodologies
- Tool deployment best practices

Let's get started!

Deployment model overview

CSPM tools can be deployed in several ways based on the organization's specific requirements, usually termed the deployment model. It consists of various aspects, such as the deployment architecture, hosting location, and management of the CSPM tool. It can broadly be divided into three types: **Software-as-a-Service** (**SaaS**), hybrid, and on-premises. Before we deep dive into the strategies, let's understand the factors to consider for effective deployment strategies.

Key considerations for effective deployment

When selecting a deployment strategy for a CSPM solution, several key factors should be considered. These factors include data privacy and ownership, scalability, accessibility, customization, and control. Let's explore each factor in the context of CSPM deployment:

- **Data privacy and ownership**: Data privacy is a critical consideration when deploying a CSPM solution. It is important to understand how the solution handles and protects sensitive data. Ensure that the CSPM solution adheres to industry-standard security practices and compliance regulations to safeguard your data. Additionally, verify that you retain ownership of your data and have control over how it is used and shared.

- **Scalability**: The scalability of a CSPM solution is crucial as it needs to adapt to the evolving needs of your organization. Consider the ability of the solution to handle increasing workloads and support the growing infrastructure of your cloud environment. Evaluate whether the CSPM solution can scale horizontally by adding more resources or vertically by optimizing existing resources to accommodate your future requirements.

- **Accessibility**: Accessibility refers to the ease of use and availability of the CSPM solution. It should provide a user-friendly interface and intuitive workflows for administrators and security teams. The solution should support integration with various cloud platforms and provide visibility across multiple cloud providers. Consider whether the CSPM solution offers **application programming interfaces** (**APIs**) or integrations with existing security tools to streamline operations.

- **Customization**: Each organization has unique security requirements, and a CSPM solution should offer customization capabilities to align with those needs. Look for a solution that allows you to define custom policies, alerts, and remediation actions based on your specific security policies and compliance standards. The ability to customize the CSPM solution ensures that it can adapt to your organization's specific security posture.

- **Control**: Control is a critical factor in CSPM deployment. Assess the level of control the CSPM solution provides over security configurations and policy enforcement. You should also look for features such as automated remediation, policy drift detection, **role-based access control** (**RBAC**), TAG-based access control, and **attribute-based access control** (**ABAC**) to ensure you have granular control over your cloud environment's security posture.

By considering these key factors in CSPM deployment, you can choose a solution that prioritizes data privacy and ownership, offers scalability, ensures accessibility, allows customization, and provides the desired level of control over your cloud security posture. It is *important* to thoroughly evaluate different CSPM vendors and their offerings to find the best fit for your organization's specific needs and requirements.

Now, let's try to understand the different deployment models, their pros and cons, and a few more things associated with these, starting with the SaaS/cloud-based deployment model.

The SaaS/cloud-based deployment model

In this model, the CSPM tool is provided as a cloud-based service. The organization accesses the tool through a web browser or a dedicated application. The CSPM provider is responsible for hosting, maintaining, and updating the tool, while the organization focuses on utilizing the service and managing its cloud security posture. This model offers convenience, scalability, and easier deployment without the need for infrastructure setup. It also requires minimal hardware and software resources from the organization as the CSPM tool is maintained and updated by the vendor. Cloud-based deployment offers flexibility, scalability, and easy accessibility. However, it also means that the organization is relying on the vendor's infrastructure and security practices, and there may be concerns about data privacy and ownership.

Over time, the popularity of this deployment model has increased considerably for several reasons as more customers have opted for this model and hence vendors have also started offering competitive features and various pricing models for this approach. Let's understand the pros and cons of this approach.

Pros

The pros are as follows:

- **Convenience and accessibility**: SaaS-based CSPM tools are accessible through web browsers, allowing users to access and utilize the tool from anywhere with an internet connection. This enables remote management, collaboration, and easy access to real-time security information.

- **Scalability**: Cloud-based deployment allows for easy scalability as the CSPM tool can adapt to the organization's changing needs. The service provider handles infrastructure scaling, ensuring that resources are available as the organization's cloud environment grows.

- **Lower upfront costs**: With SaaS, organizations typically pay a subscription fee for the CSPM tool, avoiding the need for significant upfront investments in hardware and software infrastructure. This makes it more accessible to organizations with limited resources.

- **Maintenance and updates**: SaaS-based CSPM tools relieve the organization from the burden of maintaining and updating the underlying infrastructure and software. The service provider takes care of maintenance, ensuring that the tool is up to date with the latest security features and patches.

- **Rapid deployment**: SaaS-based CSPM tools can be deployed quickly without the need for complex infrastructure setup. This allows organizations to start using the tool and benefit from its security capabilities without significant delays.

Cons

The cons are as follows:

- **Data privacy and security concerns**: Organizations using SaaS-based CSPM tools must trust the service provider with their data. It is essential to ensure that the provider has robust security measures in place to protect sensitive information. Data privacy and compliance with regulations must be thoroughly assessed.

- **Limited customization**: Cloud-based CSPM tools may have limitations on customization options compared to on-premises deployments. Organizations may need to adapt their processes to fit within the framework provided by the SaaS solution.

- **Dependency on the service provider**: Organizations relying on SaaS-based CSPM tools are dependent on the service provider's infrastructure, performance, and support. Downtime or service disruptions from the provider can impact operations and security monitoring. Organizations should assess the **service-level agreements** (**SLAs**) and reliability of the provider.

- **Connectivity and latency**: The performance and availability of SaaS-based CSPM tools depend on internet connectivity. Organizations need to ensure a stable and robust internet connection to access and utilize the tool effectively. Latency issues can arise if the organization's network or the service provider's infrastructure experiences delays.

- **Limited control**: With a SaaS-based model, organizations have limited control over the underlying infrastructure and the tool's functionality. Customization options may be limited to what the service provider offers, potentially constraining the organization's ability to tailor the tool to specific needs.

> **Important note**
>
> Organizations should carefully consider these pros and cons when evaluating the SaaS/cloud-based deployment model for CSPM tools. It is important to align the organization's requirements, security considerations, and risk tolerance with the benefits and limitations of the chosen deployment model.

What companies/industries should adopt the SaaS/cloud-based model?

The SaaS/cloud-based model for CSPM tools is well-suited for a wide range of companies and industries. Here are a few scenarios where it is most recommended:

- **Small and medium-sized enterprises (SMEs)**: SMEs often have limited IT resources and budgets. This is particularly beneficial for these companies as it eliminates the need for extensive infrastructure investments and reduces upfront costs. It provides SMEs with access to robust CSPM capabilities without the burden of managing and maintaining complex on-premises infrastructure.

- **Start-ups and agile organizations**: Start-ups and agile organizations value speed, scalability, and flexibility. This model aligns well with their business needs by offering rapid deployment, easy scalability, and the ability to adapt quickly to changing cloud environments. It allows these organizations to focus on their core business activities while leveraging the expertise and infrastructure of the CSPM service provider.

- **Remote and distributed teams**: With the increasing prevalence of remote work and distributed teams, the SaaS/cloud-based model provides seamless access to CSPM tools from any location with an internet connection. This makes it ideal for organizations with geographically dispersed teams or remote workforces, enabling collaboration and consistent security monitoring across various locations.

- **Organizations with dynamic workloads**: Industries with dynamic workloads, such as e-commerce, media, or seasonal businesses, can benefit from the scalability of the SaaS/cloud-based model. It allows organizations to scale their CSPM capabilities based on fluctuating demands, ensuring adequate security monitoring during peak periods while avoiding overprovisioning during slower periods.

- **Multi-cloud or hybrid cloud environments**: Organizations that operate across multiple cloud platforms or have hybrid cloud environments can leverage this model effectively. These tools provide a centralized view and management of security across different cloud providers, simplifying monitoring, compliance, and policy enforcement across the complex cloud landscape.

- **Fast-growing and global enterprises**: Fast-growing enterprises that are expanding globally require CSPM solutions that can scale rapidly and support their evolving needs. This model provides the agility and scalability necessary to accommodate growth and easily adapt to new cloud deployments or acquisitions in different regions.

It is important to note that the SaaS/cloud-based model can benefit companies of all sizes and industries. However, these scenarios highlight the specific advantages of this model for certain types of organizations. Each company should evaluate its unique requirements, security considerations, and budget constraints to determine if this model is the most suitable choice for their CSPM deployment.

On-premises deployments

An on-premises deployment for CSPM involves installing and running the CSPM tool within an organization's infrastructure, rather than relying on a cloud-based or managed service model. In this deployment model, the CSPM tool is hosted and managed internally by the organization, allowing for direct control and visibility over the security posture of both on-premises and cloud environments. As organizations are moving to clouds, on-premises deployment has become significantly less common compared to cloud-based or hybrid deployment models. The majority of CSPM solutions in the market are designed to be cloud-native or offered as a managed service. This is because cloud environments often require continuous monitoring and the ability to scale dynamically, making cloud-based solutions more suitable and convenient. It may not be even a smarter idea to deploy a CSPM tool on-premises. However, for on-premises environments, other security and compliance tools serve a similar purpose but are tailored to traditional data centers and local infrastructure. Organizations use tools that fall under the category of **configuration manager database** (**CMDB**) in combination with vulnerability and patch management tools. These tools help organizations ensure that their on-premises infrastructure is configured securely and is free from vulnerabilities. Here are examples of such tools:

- **BMC Helix CMDB**: BMC Helix CMDB manages and tracks configuration items, which include hardware, software, and other components within the IT infrastructure. It provides visualization tools and reporting capabilities to help users understand the current state of the IT infrastructure, dependencies, and trends.

- **Ansible**: Ansible is an open source automation tool that is commonly used for configuration management, application deployment, and task automation. Ansible can be used to define and enforce security policies for on-premises infrastructure by automating configuration changes, ensuring consistency, and detecting and remediating misconfigurations.

- **Tenable Nessus**: Tenable Nessus is a widely used vulnerability management tool that helps organizations identify and assess vulnerabilities in their systems and networks. Nessus can be used to scan and assess the security posture of on-premises servers, network devices, and other infrastructure components. It provides reports on vulnerabilities and helps organizations prioritize and remediate issues.

- **Chef**: Chef is an automation platform that allows you to define and manage the state of your infrastructure as code. Chef can be used for configuration management in on-premises environments. It enables organizations to define and enforce security policies by automating the deployment and configuration of servers and applications.

Now, let's understand the hybrid deployment model.

Hybrid deployment

This deployment strategy combines both cloud-based and on-premises deployment models. The CSPM tool can be hosted in the cloud, but the data collected by the tool can be stored and processed on the organization's servers. This deployment strategy offers the benefits of both cloud-based and on-premises deployment, including flexibility, scalability, control, and customization. This strategy may also involve a combination of agent-based, API-based, and/or proxy-based deployments. For example, you might use agent-based deployment for workloads running in your own data center, API-based deployment for workloads running in a public cloud environment, and proxy-based deployment for workloads running in a private cloud environment. The deployment strategy that's chosen will depend on a variety of factors, such as your organization's cloud environment, security requirements, and resources.

Now, let's understand the pros and cons of this feature.

Pros

Here are its pros:

- **Flexibility**: The hybrid deployment model offers flexibility by allowing organizations to monitor and secure resources across different environments, including on-premises and public cloud. It accommodates organizations with diverse infrastructure setups, such as those transitioning from on-premises to the cloud, or those with specific security or compliance requirements that necessitate certain components to be managed internally.

- **Control**: Hybrid deployment provides organizations with a level of control over their security infrastructure. They can maintain control over sensitive data or critical systems by keeping certain components on-premises while still benefiting from the scalability and agility of cloud-based monitoring and analysis.

- **Data privacy and compliance**: In some cases, certain data or regulatory requirements may necessitate keeping specific resources or information on-premises. This model allows organizations to maintain compliance and data privacy by keeping sensitive data in their private infrastructure while utilizing cloud-based monitoring for non-sensitive components.

- **Customization**: Hybrid deployment allows organizations to customize and tailor the CSPM tool to their specific needs. They can integrate the tool with their existing security infrastructure, policies, and processes, leveraging their on-premises capabilities while benefiting from cloud-based features and scalability.

Cons

Here are its cons:

- **Increased complexity**: Hybrid deployments can introduce complexity due to the integration of on-premises and cloud components. It requires additional planning, configuration, and management efforts to ensure seamless operation and data flow between different environments. It may require expertise in managing both on-premises and cloud-based infrastructure.

- **Integration challenges**: Integrating and synchronizing data and controls between on-premises and cloud environments can be challenging. Organizations need to ensure smooth integration between the hybrid components to avoid data discrepancies, delays, or disruptions in security monitoring and response.

- **Resource allocation**: Hybrid deployments require allocating resources for managing both on-premises infrastructure and cloud-based components. This includes ensuring appropriate staffing, expertise, and maintenance for both environments. Organizations need to consider the cost and effort associated with managing hybrid deployments effectively.

- **Dependencies**: Hybrid deployments may introduce dependencies on both on-premises infrastructure and cloud service providers. Any issues or outages in either environment can impact the overall security monitoring and response capabilities.

> **Important note**
>
> It is important for organizations to carefully assess their specific requirements, security needs, resource availability, and expertise before opting for a hybrid deployment model. The benefits of flexibility, control, and customization should be weighed against the complexity and additional management efforts associated with a hybrid approach.

What companies/industries should adopt a hybrid model?

The hybrid deployment model for CSPM tools can be beneficial for several types of companies and industries, depending on their specific requirements and circumstances. Here are a few scenarios where the hybrid deployment model is recommended:

- **Regulated industries**: Industries with strict regulatory compliance requirements, such as finance, healthcare, or government sectors, may find the hybrid deployment model advantageous. These organizations often have specific data privacy and security requirements that necessitate keeping certain resources on-premises, while still benefiting from the scalability and agility of cloud-based monitoring and analysis.

- **Legacy infrastructure**: Companies with substantial investments in on-premises infrastructure or applications may find the hybrid model suitable. It allows them to leverage their existing infrastructure and security investments while gradually transitioning to cloud-based environments. This gradual migration enables them to maintain control over critical systems and data during the transition period.

- **Data sensitivity**: Organizations with overly sensitive data, intellectual property, or proprietary information may prefer the hybrid deployment model. They can keep their most sensitive data on-premises while utilizing cloud-based monitoring and analysis for less sensitive components. This model provides an additional layer of control and security for critical assets.

- **Scalability and bursting needs**: Companies experiencing fluctuating workloads or seasonal spikes may benefit from the hybrid model. They can maintain their on-premises infrastructure for regular workloads and leverage the cloud for bursting or scaling needs. This allows them to quickly scale their CSPM capabilities up or down based on demand while optimizing costs.

- **Industry-specific requirements**: Certain industries, such as defense or aerospace, may have specific security requirements or regulations that necessitate a hybrid deployment model. These industries often handle classified or sensitive information and may require specific security controls or infrastructure for compliance purposes.

The decision to adopt a hybrid deployment model for CSPM depends on factors such as data sensitivity, compliance requirements, infrastructure investments, and the need for scalability and control. Each organization should assess its unique circumstances and consult with security experts to determine the most suitable deployment model for their specific needs.

Leveraging managed service provider (MSP) support

This is more of a deployment strategy than a deployment model; it is where the organization outsources the management of the CSPM tool to a third-party MSP. The MSP is responsible for hosting, configuring, and maintaining the CSPM tool, and the organization pays a subscription fee for the service. This deployment strategy can reduce the burden on the organization's IT team and provide access to expertise and resources that may not be available in-house. The service provider assumes responsibility for the ongoing monitoring, maintenance, and support of the deployed services, allowing the client organization to focus on its core business activities. However, this also means that the organization is relying on the MSP's security practices and may have limited control over the configuration and customization of the tool. Organizations can decide on the right deployment model (SaaS or hybrid) and can leverage MSP services for the deployment. You can even choose to involve MSPs in the early stages, even if it's just to help you decide on the best deployment model for your organization.

Let's understand the pros and cons of this strategy.

Pros

Here are the pros:

- **Expertise and support**: MSPs are specialized in their respective domains and possess the expertise and experience to efficiently manage and operate the services they offer. They have dedicated teams of professionals who are well-versed in the latest technologies and best practices, ensuring high-quality service delivery. Additionally, MSPs provide 24/7 support, which can be beneficial for organizations that require round-the-clock availability.

- **Cost savings**: Adopting a managed service deployment strategy can lead to cost savings for organizations. Instead of investing in building and maintaining in-house infrastructure, which can be expensive, organizations can leverage the infrastructure and resources of the MSP. This eliminates the need for upfront capital investments and reduces ongoing operational costs, such as hiring and training dedicated IT staff.

- **Scalability and flexibility**: Managed services are designed to be scalable, allowing organizations to easily adjust the scope and scale of services based on their changing requirements. MSPs offer flexible SLAs that can be tailored to meet specific needs. This scalability and flexibility enable organizations to adapt quickly to market demands and business growth without significant disruptions or delays.

- **Enhanced security and compliance**: MSPs prioritize security and compliance in their service offerings. They employ robust security measures, such as encryption, access controls, and regular security audits, to protect data and systems. Additionally, MSPs stay updated with the latest regulations and industry standards, ensuring that the deployed services comply with legal and regulatory requirements. This can be particularly advantageous for organizations operating in highly regulated industries.

Cons

Here are the cons:

- **Dependency on the service provider**: Organizations relying on managed services become dependent on the MSP for the smooth operation of their IT infrastructure and services. Any issues or delays from the MSP's side can impact the organization's operations. It is crucial to choose a reliable and trustworthy MSP with a proven record of accomplishment to minimize the risk of potential disruptions.

- **Limited control**: With managed services, the organization relinquishes a certain degree of control over its IT operations. Since the MSP manages and maintains the services, the organization may have limited control over customization, configuration, and decision-making related to the underlying infrastructure. This lack of control can sometimes hinder the organization's ability to tailor services according to their specific needs.

- **Communication and vendor management**: Effective communication and coordination between the organization and the MSP are vital for successful managed service deployment. Ensuring that goals align, addressing issues promptly, and maintaining a strong working relationship requires ongoing effort from both parties. Organizations must invest time and resources in managing the relationship with the MSP to ensure expectations are met.

- **Data privacy and confidentiality concerns**: When entrusting sensitive data to a third-party provider, there is always a level of risk involved. Organizations need to carefully assess the security measures and data handling practices of the MSP to ensure data privacy and confidentiality. A thorough evaluation of the MSP's policies, procedures, and compliance certifications is necessary to mitigate these concerns.

- **Integration and compatibility**: When adopting managed services, there may be a need for integration with existing systems and applications. Ensuring compatibility between the organization's infrastructure and the MSP's services may require additional investments in terms of customization, configuration, or development.

- **Additional costs**: While there are cost savings associated with leveraging MSPs, it is also true that there can be costs involved in adopting this model. In some cases, MSPs have tie-ups with product companies, and they may offer a great deal when a customer agrees to a certain product and their deployment as a combination of offerings. Regardless, there could be other costs associated with this model and it is important to do a cost analysis versus value added before signing any such agreement. The following could be an additional cost to the company:

  - **Service costs**: MSPs typically charge a fee for their services, which can vary depending on factors such as the scope of services, SLAs, and the complexity of the infrastructure being managed. While these costs can be significant, they should be compared against the expenses associated with training and/or hiring new talents.

  - **Transition costs**: Moving from an in-house IT model to a managed service deployment model may require an initial investment in terms of transitioning systems, migrating data, and training employees.

  - **Vendor lock-in**: Depending heavily on a managed service provider can create a level of vendor lock-in. Switching to a different provider or changing the product before a certain period can involve additional costs and effort.

Overall, the managed service strategies offer numerous benefits, such as access to specialized expertise, cost savings, scalability, and enhanced security. However, organizations should carefully consider their specific needs, risks, and the reputation of the MSP before adopting this model to ensure a successful and mutually beneficial partnership.

> **Important note**
>
> Organizations should carefully evaluate the terms and conditions of the contract to ensure flexibility and options for transitioning if needed. It is important to establish measurable metrics for assessing and ensuring quality-of-service delivery. Penalties and remedies for breaches of SLAs should also be clearly outlined.

Valid concerns associated with managed service strategy

When leveraging a managed service strategy for CSPM deployment, organizations should address several valid concerns to ensure the effectiveness and security of their cloud environments. Here are some key considerations:

- **Data privacy and security**: Organizations should thoroughly assess the MSP's data handling practices, security controls, and compliance certifications. The provider should have robust measures in place to protect sensitive data, including encryption, access controls, and regular security audits. Clear policies and agreements should be established to define data ownership, confidentiality, and breach notification protocols.

- **Compliance and regulatory requirements**: Depending on the industry and geographic location, organizations may have specific compliance obligations. The MSP should have a strong understanding of relevant regulations (such as the **General Data Protection Regulation (GDPR)**, **Health Insurance Portability and Accountability Act (HIPAA)**, or **Payment Card Industry Data Security Standard) (PCI DSS)**) and demonstrate compliance in their service offerings. It is essential to establish clear responsibilities and procedures for meeting compliance requirements within the managed service agreement.

- **Visibility and transparency**: Organizations must have clear visibility into their cloud environment and the actions performed by the MSP. They should establish reporting mechanisms and access controls to monitor the provider's activities, track changes, and verify compliance with policies and security requirements. Regular audits and reports from the provider can help maintain transparency and ensure accountability.

- **Incident response and recovery**: Organizations should define incident response and recovery procedures with the managed service provider. This includes establishing clear communication channels, incident escalation processes, and coordination between the organization's internal security teams and the provider. It is crucial to ensure that the provider has robust incident response capabilities and regularly tests their incident response plans.

- **Vendor assessment and due diligence**: Organizations should conduct a thorough assessment of the MSP's capabilities, experience, and reputation. This assessment should include a review of their security practices, incident response processes, SLAs, and customer references. It is essential to evaluate the provider's expertise in CSPM solutions and their ability to align with the organization's specific security requirements.

- **Integration and compatibility**: The managed service model for CSPM deployment should seamlessly integrate with the organization's existing cloud infrastructure and security tools. Compatibility and interoperability with other cloud services, **Security Information and Event Management (SIEM)** systems, and other relevant tools are crucial. Organizations should assess the provider's ability to integrate and their experience with the organization's chosen cloud platforms and technologies.

- **SLAs**: The SLAs between the organization and the MSP should clearly define the scope of services, expected performance levels, incident response times, and responsibilities of each party. It is important to establish measurable metrics for assessing and ensuring quality-of-service delivery. Penalties and remedies for breaches of SLAs should also be clearly outlined.

Addressing these concerns and establishing a strong partnership with the managed service provider helps organizations effectively manage their cloud security posture while maintaining control, compliance, and transparency in their cloud environment. Regular communication, performance monitoring, and continuous improvement efforts are essential to ensuring a successful CSPM deployment within the managed service model.

What companies/industries should adopt managed service strategies?

The managed service strategy can be beneficial for a wide range of companies and industries. Here are some examples of companies and industries that should adopt the managed service model:

- **SMEs**: SMEs often have limited resources and IT expertise. Adopting a managed service model allows them to leverage the specialized skills and infrastructure of an MSP without the need for significant upfront investments. It enables SMEs to focus on their core business activities while leaving IT management to the experts.

- **Healthcare**: The healthcare industry handles large volumes of sensitive patient data and must adhere to strict regulatory requirements, such as HIPAA. MSPs with expertise in healthcare IT can ensure the security, privacy, and compliance of healthcare organizations' systems and data, allowing them to focus on delivering quality care.

- **Financial services**: The financial services industry, including banks, insurance companies, and investment firms, deals with complex regulatory frameworks and security requirements. MSPs can help manage and secure critical infrastructure, implement strong cybersecurity measures, and ensure compliance with industry regulations, such as PCI DSS, **Financial Industry Regulatory Authority (FINRA)**, **Anti-Money Laundering (AML)**, **Sarbanes-Oxley Act (SOX)**, and Basel III.

- **E-commerce and retail**: Online retailers and e-commerce companies require robust and highly available IT infrastructure to handle high transaction volumes, secure online payment processing, and manage inventory and supply chain systems. MSPs can offer scalable, secure, and reliable infrastructure solutions, as well as assist with monitoring, performance optimization, and disaster recovery.

- **Manufacturing**: Manufacturers increasingly rely on advanced technologies, such as **Internet of Things (IoT)** devices, automation, and data analytics. MSPs can help optimize manufacturing processes, manage and secure IoT deployments, and ensure seamless connectivity across production facilities. They can also assist with predictive maintenance, data analytics, and supply chain management.

These are just a few examples, and the managed service model can be applied to various other industries and companies of varied sizes. The key factor is the need for specialized IT services, expertise, scalability, cost optimization, and compliance management, which can be efficiently addressed through a partnership with a trusted MSP.

Different deployment methodologies

CSPM deployment methodologies refer to the various approaches by which CSPM tools are deployed within an organization's cloud environment to assess and manage its security posture. These methodologies are broadly categorized as *agent-based*, *API-based*, and *proxy-based*, and they determine how the CSPM tool interacts with the cloud resources, collects data, and performs security analysis. When selecting a CSPM tool and deployment methodology, it is essential to consider factors such as the tool's capabilities, integration with the cloud provider's APIs, scalability, ease of deployment and management, and the organization's specific security and compliance objectives.

Let's delve into the details of each CSPM deployment methodology.

Agent-based deployment

This strategy involves installing an agent on each cloud workload that needs to be monitored. The agent can collect data on the workload's security posture and report that data back to the CSPM tool. This approach provides a granular view of each workload's security posture but can also be resource-intensive, especially if you have many workloads. These agents are typically lightweight programs or scripts that run on individual instances or virtual machines. They collect data about the resource configurations, network traffic, system logs, and other relevant information within the cloud environment.

The agent-based deployment model for CSPM solutions has its own set of advantages and disadvantages. Let's look at some of the pros and cons of the agent-based deployment model.

Pros

Here are the pros:

- **Real-time visibility and control**: The agent-based deployment model provides real-time visibility and control over the security posture of individual cloud resources. The agents continuously monitor the resources and send data to the CSPM solution for analysis, which allows for quick identification and remediation of any security risks or compliance issues.

- **Granular data collection**: The agents collect granular data on the security posture of the resources, including configuration details, network traffic, and user activity, which enables more detailed analysis and insights.

- **Offline analysis**: Agent-based deployment allows for offline analysis of the collected data. Even if the agents are not constantly connected to the CSPM tool, they can still capture information and transmit it when they regain connectivity, ensuring continuous monitoring.

Cons

Here are the cons:

- **Operational overhead**: The agent-based deployment model requires the installation and management of software agents on the cloud resources, which can add to the operational overhead and maintenance of the solution. It requires resources and efforts to deploy, update, and maintain the agents across the cloud environment.

- **Performance impact**: The agents can potentially impact the performance of the cloud resources they are installed on, particularly if the agents are resource-intensive or not optimized for the specific workload.

- **Limited coverage**: The agent-based deployment model may not cover all cloud resources, particularly those that are outside the scope of the agents, which can result in blind spots in security posture monitoring.

- **Compatibility issues**: The agents may not be compatible with all types of cloud resources, particularly if the resources are using custom or legacy software.

- **Scalability challenges**: As the cloud environment grows, managing and scaling the deployment of agents across all resources can become complex and resource-intensive.

Organizations that are considering agent-based deployment for CSPM tools should carefully evaluate these pros and cons against their specific requirements, resources, and cloud architecture to determine if this deployment methodology aligns with their needs.

API-based deployment

The API-based deployment model involves directly integrating the CSPM tool with the cloud service provider's APIs. The tool uses the cloud provider's APIs to collect configuration data, access controls, security groups, and other relevant information. Then, it analyzes this data to identify security risks and provide recommendations for improvement. API-based deployment offers scalability and ease of setup since it does not require agents or proxies. However, it relies on the cloud provider's APIs and may have limitations in terms of real-time visibility and monitoring capabilities.

Let's look at some of the pros and cons of the API-based deployment model.

Pros

Here are the pros:

- **Comprehensive coverage**: The API-based deployment model allows the CSPM tool to collect data directly from the cloud service provider's APIs. This provides comprehensive coverage of the cloud environment as APIs typically expose a wide range of information about resource configurations, access controls, security groups, and more.

- **Ease of setup and scalability**: The API-based deployment model does not require installing agents or proxies on individual resources. This simplifies the setup process and makes it easier to scale the CSPM solution across the cloud environment. It offers flexibility in managing and monitoring resources, even as the environment evolves and grows.

- **Real-time or near real-time insights**: By integrating with the cloud provider's APIs, the CSPM tool can gather data on resource configurations and activities in real time or near real time. This enables immediate detection of security risks, misconfigurations, compliance violations, and other potential issues.

- **Reduced resource consumption**: The API-based deployment model eliminates the need for agents running on individual resources, reducing the resource consumption associated with agent-based approaches. This can be particularly beneficial in large-scale cloud environments with numerous resources.

Cons

Here are the cons:

- **Dependency on the cloud provider's APIs**: The API-based deployment model relies on the availability, reliability, and performance of the cloud provider's APIs. Any issues or limitations with the APIs can impact the functionality and effectiveness of the CSPM tool.

- **Delayed or batched data retrieval**: The API-based deployment model may retrieve data from the cloud provider's APIs periodically or in batches. This introduces a potential delay in obtaining the latest information about the cloud environment, resulting in slightly less real-time visibility compared to agent-based or proxy-based approaches.

- **Limited visibility for non-API-accessible resources**: Certain resources or services within the cloud environment may not be accessible through APIs, which can limit the visibility and coverage provided by API-based deployment. This may require supplementing the CSPM tool with additional methodologies or integrations to achieve comprehensive coverage.

- **Lack of offline analysis**: Since data is retrieved from APIs, API-based deployment may not provide offline analysis capabilities. Continuous connectivity to the cloud provider's APIs is necessary to collect and analyze data, which may limit monitoring during network disruptions or outages.

Organizations should consider these pros and cons when evaluating API-based deployment for their CSPM needs. It is essential to assess the compatibility of the CSPM tool with the cloud provider's APIs, evaluate the coverage and real-time capabilities provided, and ensure the cloud environment's dependencies on API availability align with the organization's security requirements.

> **Important note**
>
> It is worth noting that these deployment methodologies are not mutually exclusive, and CSPM tools can incorporate multiple methodologies to provide comprehensive cloud security management. The choice of deployment methodology depends on factors such as the cloud environment's architecture, the desired level of visibility and control, and the organization's security policies and compliance requirements. These deployment methodologies may be used individually or in combination, depending on the CSPM tool's capabilities and the organization's cloud architecture. Additionally, other methodologies might exist, depending on the specific tool or vendor. When selecting a CSPM tool and deployment methodology, it is crucial to consider factors such as the cloud environment's complexity, the desired level of visibility and control, integration capabilities, and the organization's security objectives and compliance requirements.

Now, let's understand another deployment methodology.

Proxy-based deployment

This strategy involves deploying a proxy server between your cloud workloads and the internet. The proxy server can monitor traffic to and from the workloads and report data back to the CSPM tool. This approach can provide a more comprehensive view of your cloud environment's security posture, but it may require additional configuration and maintenance. The proxy-based deployment model for CSPM solutions involves using proxies to monitor and control network traffic between cloud resources and external entities. Here is an overview of how it works:

- **Proxy deployment**: Proxies are deployed between the cloud resources and external entities and act as intermediaries for network communication. The proxies intercept and inspect traffic flowing between the resources and external entities.

- **Traffic analysis**: The proxies analyze network traffic, including protocols, data payloads, and metadata, to identify security risks, compliance violations, and potential threats.

- **Enforcement and remediation**: If any security issues or violations are detected, the proxies can enforce security policies, implement access controls, and initiate remediation actions to mitigate the risks.

Now, let's discuss the pros and cons of the proxy-based deployment model.

Pros

Here are the pros:

- **Centralized control**: The proxy-based deployment model offers centralized control and visibility over network traffic, enabling organizations to implement consistent security policies and enforce them across all communication channels.

- **Deep packet inspection**: Proxies can perform deep packet inspection, allowing for detailed analysis of network traffic content. This enables the identification of specific vulnerabilities, malware, and other security threats that may be missed by other deployment models.

- **Advanced threat detection**: Proxies can employ advanced threat detection mechanisms, such as **Intrusion Detection and Prevention Systems (IDS/IPS)**, to actively monitor network traffic and detect potential malicious activities.

- **Compliance monitoring**: Proxies can enforce compliance policies and monitor traffic for adherence to regulatory requirements, helping organizations meet industry-specific compliance standards.

Cons

Here are the cons:

- **Performance impact**: The proxy-based deployment model can introduce latency and increase network overhead due to the additional processing required for traffic interception, inspection, and redirection. This may impact the performance of cloud resources, particularly in high-traffic environments.

- **Complex configuration**: Implementing proxy-based deployments requires careful configuration and maintenance of the proxies to ensure accurate traffic analysis and appropriate enforcement actions. It may require expertise in configuring and managing proxy technologies.

- **Scalability challenges**: Scaling proxy-based deployments can be complex, especially in large-scale environments, as it requires deploying and managing multiple proxies to handle increased traffic volumes effectively.

- **Single point of failure**: If the proxies themselves become compromised or experience downtime, it can lead to a disruption in network traffic and potential security vulnerabilities. Redundancy and failover mechanisms need to be implemented to mitigate this risk.

The proxy-based deployment model provides centralized control and in-depth traffic analysis but may introduce performance overhead and configuration complexity. Organizations should carefully evaluate the pros and cons of proxy-based deployment, considering factors such as the cloud environment's complexity, the desired level of visibility and control, network infrastructure, and the CSPM tool's compatibility with the cloud provider's APIs. This assessment will help determine if the proxy-based deployment model aligns with the organization's specific security requirements and operational considerations. It is well-suited for organizations that prioritize granular network visibility and control for enhanced security monitoring and compliance enforcement.

Tool deployment best practices

CSPM tools are critical for ensuring the security of cloud environments. To maximize the effectiveness of CSPM tool deployment, it is important to follow best practices. Let's discuss some key CSPM tool deployment best practices in detail:

- **Clearly define objectives and requirements**: Before deploying a CSPM tool, clearly define your organization's objectives and requirements. Identify the specific security goals you want to achieve, such as detecting misconfigurations, ensuring compliance, or managing security risks. This will help you select the right CSPM tool and configure it so that it aligns with your organization's needs.

- **Evaluate and select the right CSPM tool**: Thoroughly evaluate different CSPM tools in the market to find the one that best suits your requirements. Consider factors such as scalability, compatibility with your cloud environment, real-time monitoring capabilities, depth of analysis, reporting capabilities, and ease of integration with existing systems. Choose a tool that offers the features and functionalities that align with your security goals.

- **Align with cloud service provider (CSP) recommendations**: Understand the recommendations and best practices provided by your CSP. They often offer security guidelines and best practices specific to their platforms. Ensure your CSPM tool deployment aligns with these recommendations to optimize security and maximize compatibility with the cloud environment.

- **Plan and prepare for deployment**: Create a deployment plan that outlines the steps involved in deploying the CSPM tool. Assess the impact on your cloud environment, consider any necessary network configuration changes, and plan for any required integrations or permissions with the cloud provider's APIs. Make sure you have the necessary resources, expertise, and support for a successful deployment.

- **Configure proper access controls**: Implement strong access controls for the CSPM tool to ensure only authorized personnel can access and modify its settings and data. Follow the principle of least privilege to grant appropriate access to users based on their roles and responsibilities. Regularly review and update access controls as personnel roles change or when new team members join or leave.

- **Enable continuous monitoring**: Set up the CSPM tool for continuous monitoring of your cloud environment. Enable real-time or near real-time monitoring capabilities to detect security incidents, misconfigurations, or compliance violations as they occur. Continuous monitoring helps you identify and respond to security risks promptly, minimizing potential damage.

- **Integrate with incident response processes**: Integrate the CSPM tool with your organization's incident response processes. Ensure that security alerts and notifications from the CSPM tool are properly integrated into your incident management system. Define clear escalation and response procedures to address security incidents identified by the CSPM tool effectively.

- **Regularly update and maintain the tool**: Keep your CSPM tool up to date with the latest vendor-provided updates, patches, and feature enhancements. Regularly review the configuration settings to ensure they align with your evolving security requirements. Stay informed about new threats, vulnerabilities, and best practices in cloud security, and adjust your tool's settings and policies accordingly.

- **Monitor and analyze tool performance**: Monitor the performance of the CSPM tool itself to ensure it's functioning optimally. Track metrics such as data collection speed, analysis speed, and resource utilization. Analyze the tool's performance over time to identify any potential bottlenecks or areas for optimization.

- **Regularly audit and review results**: Perform regular audits and reviews of the CSPM tool's findings and reports. Validate the accuracy of the tool's assessments by conducting manual checks or utilizing other security assessment mechanisms. Regularly review and refine policies, rules, and configurations based on the tool's results and your organization's evolving security requirements.

By following these best practices, you can ensure the successful deployment and operation of your CSPM tool, enhancing the security and compliance of your cloud environment. *Remember* to adapt these practices to your organization's specific needs and continuously monitor and improve your cloud security posture.

Summary

CSPM tools play a critical role in ensuring cloud infrastructure security and compliance. When selecting a deployment strategy for a CSPM solution, several key factors should be considered. These factors include data privacy and ownership, scalability, accessibility, customization, and control. In this chapter, we explored the diverse deployment strategies, methodologies, and best practices for effective implementation. Cloud-based deployment involves hosting the tool on a cloud provider's infrastructure, offering scalability and easy maintenance. On-premises deployment entails running the tool within an organization's infrastructure, providing greater control but requiring dedicated resources. Hybrid deployment combines both cloud-based and on-premises approaches, catering to specific needs. Managed service deployment involves outsourcing the deployment and management of the CSPM tool to a third-party provider. This chapter also explored different deployment methodologies for CSPM tools. API-based deployment utilizes cloud provider APIs to collect data and analyze the cloud environment for security issues. Agent-based deployment involves installing lightweight agents on cloud instances to monitor and assess their security posture. Proxy-based deployment utilizes a proxy server to intercept and analyze traffic between the organization and the cloud provider, identifying potential security gaps. Finally, we discussed industry best practices involving CSPM deployment.

That concludes this chapter. In the next chapter, we will dive deep into different aspects of onboarding cloud accounts to CSPM.

Further reading

To learn more about the topics that were covered in this chapter, take a look at the following resources:

- *Guideline on Effectively Managing Security Service in the Cloud*, by Cloud Security Alliance: Guideline on Effectively Managing Security Service in the Cloud | CSA (`cloudsecurityalliance.org`)

- *Getting Started with Cloud Security Posture Management*, by Microsoft Azure: Cloud Security Posture Management (CSPM) with Azure Security Center | Microsoft Learn

- *A Guide to CSPM Tools and Strategies*, by Palo Alto Networks: A Guide to CSPM Tools and Strategies – Palo Alto Networks

Onboarding Cloud Accounts

Cloud security posture management (**CSPM**) tools have emerged as essential solutions to help organizations ensure the security and compliance of their multi-cloud deployments. This chapter focuses on the critical process of onboarding multi-cloud accounts to a CSPM tool. Onboarding refers to the initial setup and configuration required to connect and integrate cloud accounts from different providers into the CSPM tool's centralized platform. This process is vital as it lays the foundation for effective cloud security monitoring, compliance assessment, and risk mitigation.

Throughout this chapter, we will delve into the key considerations, best practices, and steps involved in successfully onboarding multi-cloud accounts to a CSPM tool. Additionally, we will address potential challenges and roadblocks that organizations may face during the onboarding process. These challenges may include complexities related to identity and access management, establishing appropriate permissions, dealing with different APIs and authentication mechanisms, and ensuring data security during the transfer. We will discuss strategies to mitigate these challenges and offer practical solutions to overcome them effectively.

In this chapter, we'll cover the following topics:

- Key considerations, steps involved, and best practices
- Account onboarding process
- Challenges and roadblocks during onboarding
- Offboarding cloud accounts

Let us get started!

Key considerations and steps involved

Onboarding cloud accounts to a CSPM tool is a critical step in ensuring the security and compliance of your cloud infrastructure. There are many things to consider before starting to invest effort into a CSPM tool.

> **Note**
>
> Key considerations and steps involved in onboarding accounts are discussed in a generic manner intentionally, as the scope of this book is to have a deep-dive discussion on CSPM technology and not a specific CSPM tool. Organizations should define their specific use cases that fit and align with their cyber security strategy and with the tool chosen. In addition to what is discussed in this chapter, you must follow the vendor documentation and support to cover your specific needs.

Let us dive deep into key considerations to keep in mind when onboarding cloud accounts to a CSPM tool.

Account onboarding key considerations

When onboarding cloud accounts to a CSPM tool, key considerations refer to the crucial factors that should be considered when selecting and implementing the tool. These considerations help ensure a smooth and successful onboarding process. This could vary from CSPM product to product and we have also discussed this topic comprehensively in previous chapters; however, some of the most important considerations are as follows:

- **Cloud provider support**: Ensure that the CSPM tool supports the cloud providers that your organization currently uses or plans to use. Different cloud providers have unique features, APIs, and security configurations, so it is essential to choose a tool that can effectively integrate and manage multiple cloud environments.

- **Integration capabilities**: Consider the integration options provided by the CSPM tool. It should have compatible APIs, agent-based or agentless deployment options, and support for integrating with other existing security tools or frameworks within your organization. Seamless integration enables efficient data collection, monitoring, and reporting across multi-cloud accounts.

- **Scalability and performance**: Evaluate the tool's scalability to handle the increasing number of cloud accounts, resources, and workloads within your multi-cloud environment. It should be capable of efficiently managing and monitoring large-scale deployments while maintaining optimal performance and responsiveness.

- **Customization and flexibility**: Look for a CSPM tool that allows customization of security policies, rules, and alerts to align with your organization's specific requirements. Every organization has unique security policies and compliance standards, so the tool should offer the flexibility to tailor its configurations accordingly.

- **Compliance and governance**: Ensure that the CSPM tool provides comprehensive compliance monitoring and reporting capabilities. It should support industry standards and regulatory requirements relevant to your organization, such as **Center for Internet Security** (**CIS**) **benchmarks**, **General Data Protection Regulation** (**GDPR**), **Health Insurance Portability and Accountability** (**HIPAA**), and data protection regulations, among others. The tool should assist in identifying compliance violations and help enforce governance policies.

- **User interface and user experience**: Evaluate the usability and intuitiveness of the CSPM tool's user interface. A well-designed and user-friendly interface simplifies the onboarding process and enables efficient management and monitoring of multi-cloud accounts.

- **Security and data privacy**: Assess the security measures implemented by the CSPM tool to protect sensitive data, such as cloud account credentials and monitoring data. The tool should adhere to industry best practices for data encryption, access controls, and data privacy.

- **Vendor support and updates**: Consider the vendor's reputation, reliability, and ongoing support for the CSPM tool. Ensure that the vendor provides regular updates, bug fixes, and new features to address emerging security challenges and keep pace with evolving cloud environments.

Environment-specific considerations

When onboarding a cloud account to CSPM, several key considerations come into play, considering different environments such as production, staging, and testing. Here are some important considerations:

- **Environment-specific policies**: Enforce strict security policies in the production environment, focusing on compliance, data protection, and minimal exposure of sensitive information. Adapt policies for staging and testing to allow more flexibility while still maintaining essential security controls. Consider data masking or anonymization in testing environments to protect sensitive data.

- **Identity and access management (IAM)**: Define IAM roles in production with the principle of least privilege. Ensure that only necessary individuals or systems have access to critical resources. In testing environments, allow broader permissions for ease of development and testing. Regularly review and adjust IAM roles based on changing requirements.

- **Continuous compliance monitoring**: Implement continuous compliance monitoring in the production environment to ensure adherence to regulatory standards and organizational policies. Relax some compliance checks in non-production environments to facilitate development and testing processes. However, maintain a baseline level of security to prevent misconfigurations.

- **Resource visibility and inventory**: Keep a comprehensive inventory of production resources, regularly updating and monitoring it for changes. Maintain visibility into staging and testing environments but tolerate more dynamic changes and resource churn.

- **Data encryption**: Enforce strict encryption standards for data in production, both in transit and at rest. Relax encryption requirements in testing environments but maintain encryption for sensitive data. Use self-signed certificates or simplified key management for convenience.

- **Vulnerability management**: Regularly scan production resources for vulnerabilities, prioritizing critical issues for immediate remediation. Integrate vulnerability scanning into the testing process, but allow for more leniency in addressing issues, understanding that it's a dynamic and evolving environment.

- **Network security**: Implement strict network controls in production, utilizing security groups, firewalls, and other measures to restrict access. Allow more permissive network configurations in testing environments to facilitate development but monitor for unusual traffic patterns.

- **Incident response and monitoring**: Establish a robust incident response plan for the production environment, including real-time monitoring and alerting. Adapt incident response practices for testing environments, recognizing that the impact of incidents may be less critical.

- **Automation and integration**: Fully integrate CSPM tools into production CI/CD pipelines, ensuring that security checks are automated and integral to the deployment process. Maintain integration in testing environments but allow for more manual checks during development phases.

- **Environment tagging**: Implement clear tagging standards for resources in production, which will aid in resource management and cost allocation. Use tagging in non-production environments for organizational purposes, understanding that the structure may be more fluid.

- **Resource scaling and cost management**: Implement auto-scaling and resource optimization strategies in production to handle varying workloads efficiently. Allow for more manual resource scaling in testing environments, focusing on cost control and efficiency.

Adapting CSPM practices to the specific needs and risk profiles of each environment helps strike a balance between security, agility, and flexibility across different stages of the development life cycle. Regularly reassess and refine these considerations as the cloud environment evolves and requirements change.

Steps for successful onboarding

Successful onboarding paths may also vary depending on other factors such as deployment models, tools, and API availabilities. However, the generic steps for successful onboarding can be defined as follows:

- **Defined onboarding strategy**: Develop a well-defined strategy and roadmap for onboarding multi-cloud accounts to the CSPM tool. Identify the sequence of cloud providers and accounts to be onboarded based on criticality, complexity, and business priorities.

- **Pre-onboarding preparation**: Gather all the necessary information, credentials, and access permissions required for onboarding. Ensure that you have the necessary administrative rights and privileges for the cloud accounts.

- **Established connectivity**: Configure the required connectivity between the CSPM tool and each cloud provider. This involves setting up API access, configuring credentials, and establishing secure communication channels.

- **Account authentication and authorization**: Define and implement the appropriate authentication and authorization mechanisms for each cloud account within the CSPM tool. This ensures that the tool can access and monitor the relevant resources securely.

- **Resource discovery and mapping**: Initiate the discovery process to identify and map all the cloud resources associated with each onboarded account. This includes virtual machines, storage buckets, databases, and networking components.

- **Policy configuration**: Define and configure security policies within the CSPM tool based on your organization's requirements and compliance standards. This includes defining rules, thresholds, and checks to monitor for security and compliance violations.

- **Testing and validation**: Conduct thorough testing and validation of the onboarding process. Ensure that the CSPM tool accurately detects and reports security vulnerabilities, misconfigurations, and compliance issues within the onboarded cloud accounts.

- **Ongoing management and optimization**: Regularly review and optimize the CSPM tool's configuration, policies, and alerting mechanisms. Stay updated with the latest features and releases of the tool to leverage new capabilities for improved security and compliance management.

Best practices for onboarding of cloud accounts

Successful onboarding of cloud accounts to a CSPM tool involves following best practices to ensure the security and compliance of your cloud infrastructure. Here are some key best practices for a successful onboarding process:

- **Automated onboarding process**: This involves leveraging **infrastructure as code (IaC)** tools such as *Terraform* or *CloudFormation* to streamline and standardize the deployment of infrastructure elements. By encoding onboarding procedures into code, organizations can ensure consistency and repeatability when provisioning resources across various environments. This approach not only accelerates the onboarding of new personnel but also minimizes the risk of errors and discrepancies, as the entire process is automated and can be easily replicated, fostering a more efficient and reliable onboarding experience for admins.

- **Inventory and classification**: Create a comprehensive inventory of all the cloud accounts and resources within your multi-cloud environment. Classify them based on their criticality, sensitivity, and compliance requirements. This helps in prioritizing security controls and monitoring efforts.

- **Audit trail and logging**: Implement robust auditing and logging mechanisms within your cloud environment to track crucial activities such as user account creation, access changes, and login activity. This serves as a fundamental aspect of security monitoring and compliance, providing visibility into the who, what, when, and where of system events.

- **Identity and access management (IAM)**: Establish a centralized IAM strategy that aligns with your organization's security policies. Implement strong access controls, least privilege principles, and multi-factor authentication across all cloud accounts.

- **Cloud configuration monitoring**: Continuously monitor and evaluate the configurations of your cloud resources to identify misconfigurations, deviations from best practices, and security vulnerabilities. Leverage the CSPM tool's automated checks and remediation capabilities to ensure compliance with security standards.

- **Continuous monitoring and alerting**: Implement real-time monitoring and alerting mechanisms to detect and respond to security incidents promptly. Set up alerts for suspicious activities, unauthorized access attempts, or configuration changes that violate security policies.

- **Regular assessments and audits**: Conduct periodic assessments and audits of your multi-cloud environment using the CSPM tool. Review security posture and compliance status, and identify areas for improvement. Regularly update and refine security policies and controls based on the findings.

- **Ticketing integration**: Integrating ticketing systems such as *Jira* or *ServiceNow* into CSPM tools enhances incident response and issue resolution processes. This integration helps streamline communication and collaboration between security teams, DevOps, and other stakeholders. This ensures that critical security issues are addressed promptly, aligning with organizational priorities and compliance requirements.

Now that we understand the key considerations, steps involved in successful onboarding, and best practices, it is time to learn how onboarding cloud accounts works.

Account onboarding steps

The account onboarding process is also known as the account connection process for public clouds. It is the process of establishing a connection between a CSPM account and your CSP account such as Microsoft Azure, AWS, GCP, Oracle Cloud, and so on. When the connection between the CSPM tool and the cloud account is established, CSPM can access your cloud infrastructure and scan it for vulnerabilities and other security issues.

> **Note**
>
> To make the concept easily understandable, the Microsoft Defender for Cloud CSPM tool is taken as a reference wherever it is imperative to explain with an example. This book does not justify one tool over another. The tool is chosen based on the information available publicly. Generic and high-level steps are provided here, which is not enough for onboarding an account. You must follow vendor documentation and support for successful onboarding. It is beyond the scope of this book to dive deep into a particular tool.

Onboarding AWS accounts

Connecting your AWS accounts to Microsoft Defender for Cloud allows you to leverage the security capabilities of Microsoft Defender to protect your AWS resources and workloads. This integration provides centralized visibility, threat detection, and incident response across your AWS infrastructure. Microsoft Defender for Cloud protects workloads in AWS, but you need to set up the connection between them and your Azure subscription.

Every CSPM vendor provides comprehensive documentation and support for successful account onboarding as part of their contract with customers. To connect your AWS account to Microsoft Defender for Cloud, you should follow its documentation and guidance.

Follow this documentation link to connect your AWS accounts to Microsoft Defender for Cloud: `https://learn.microsoft.com/en-us/azure/defender-for-cloud/quickstart-onboard-aws`.

Prerequisites

Before we set up the connection, you'll need to be ready with the following:

- You need a Microsoft Azure subscription. If you do not have an Azure subscription, set one up.

- You must set up your CSPM (Microsoft Defender for Cloud in this case) on your Azure subscription.

- You must have access to an AWS account.

- Ensure you have appropriate permissions and access to manage AWS resources. You need to have **Contributor** permission for the relevant Azure subscription and **Administrator** permission on the AWS account.

Let's begin!

1. **Set up an AWS IAM role:** The first step is to create an IAM role in your AWS account that grants necessary permissions to Microsoft Defender for Cloud. Assign appropriate permissions to the IAM role, such as read-only access to your AWS resources. Make sure to define a trust relationship between the IAM role and the Microsoft Defender for Cloud service principal.

2. **Configure AWS account in Microsoft Defender for Cloud:** Sign in to the Microsoft Defender Security Center. Navigate to **Settings** and select **AWS accounts** or **Add AWS account**. Provide the necessary details such as account name, AWS account ID, and the IAM role **ARN (Amazon Resource Names)** you created. Click on **Add account** to initiate the connection process.

3. **Validate the connection:** Microsoft Defender for Cloud will attempt to establish a connection with the specified AWS account using the provided IAM role. If the connection is successful, you will see the AWS account listed as connected in the Microsoft Defender Security Center.

4. **Enable data collection**: Once the connection is established, you can configure data collection settings for the AWS account. Decide which types of AWS data you want to collect, such as CloudTrail logs, VPC flow logs, or CloudWatch events. Enable the necessary data connectors and configure any required permissions or settings.

5. **Monitor and respond to threats**: Defender for Cloud will start collecting and analyzing the security data from your AWS resources. Monitor the alerts and security recommendations provided by Defender for Cloud and take appropriate actions to remediate any identified threats.

If you follow the documentation steps correctly, you should be able to see that your AWS account has onboarded into the Microsoft Defender for Cloud CSPM tool, as shown in the following screenshot:

Figure 6.1 – Microsoft Defender for Cloud

Now that we have seen how an AWS account can be onboarded to Microsoft Defender for Cloud, let us look at how to onboard the same for Microsoft Azure.

Onboarding Azure accounts

Defender for Cloud offers comprehensive security management and threat protection for your hybrid and multi-cloud workloads. The free features focus on securing your Azure resources specifically, while additional paid plans provide enhanced protection for your on-premises infrastructure and resources across different cloud platforms. With Defender for Cloud, you can achieve unified security and peace of mind across your entire IT environment, regardless of its composition and location.

Follow this link to enable Defender for Cloud for Azure workloads: `https://learn.microsoft.com/en-us/azure/defender-for-cloud/get-started`.

Since Microsoft offers Defender for Cloud through the Microsoft Azure portal, it becomes super-easy to enable it for Azure workloads, and for other cloud environments, the process remains like other CSPM tool processes.

Prerequisites

- You need an active subscription to Microsoft Azure to utilize Microsoft Defender for Cloud.

- Ensure you have appropriate permissions and access to manage Azure resources. You should have an Owner, Contributor, or Reader role assigned for the subscription or for the resource group that the resource is located in.

Enable Defender for Cloud on your Azure subscription

Once you follow the steps mentioned in the preceding link, Defender for Cloud gets enabled on your subscription and you have access to the basic features provided by Defender for Cloud, such as the Foundational CSPM plan, recommendations, access to the asset inventory, workbooks, Secure Score, and regulatory compliance with the Microsoft cloud security benchmark. The other important links are provided at the end of the chapter under the *Further reading* section.

Let us now understand how to onboard GCP accounts to Microsoft Defender for Cloud.

Onboarding GCP accounts

Microsoft Defender for Cloud provides robust protection for workloads hosted on **Google Cloud Platform (GCP)**. However, it is necessary to establish a connection between your Azure subscription and GCP to leverage these security services effectively.

Follow this link to enable Defender for Cloud for GCP projects: `https://learn.microsoft.com/en-us/azure/defender-for-cloud/quickstart-onboard-gcp#connect-your-gcp-project`.

Prerequisites

- You need a Microsoft Azure subscription as Microsoft offers the Defender for Cloud service through the Azure portal.

- Microsoft Defender for Cloud on your Azure subscription must be enabled.

- You need access to a GCP project.

- You need to have a Contributor role on the relevant Azure subscription and an Owner role on the GCP organization or project.

- It is possible to connect your GCP projects to Microsoft Defender for Cloud on the project level and also connect multiple projects to one Azure subscription. You can connect multiple projects to multiple Azure subscriptions as well.

Steps to onboard GCP accounts

Once you follow the steps mentioned in the preceding link, you will be able to establish a connection between your GCP project and Defender for Cloud and then a scan starts on your GCP environment. New recommendations will appear in Defender for Cloud after up to six hours. When auto-provisioning is enabled, Azure Arc and any enabled extensions are automatically installed for each newly detected resource.

Let us now look at some important points related to other environments.

Onboarding other clouds

Every CSPM vendor is on a journey to bring new features every day. It is part of the vendor assessment process to make sure that the vendor you are choosing has the capabilities to support all other cloud environments your organization is using. For example, as of today while writing this chapter, Microsoft Defender for Cloud supports Azure DevOps and GitHub environment (in preview) but no other cloud environments, such as **Oracle Cloud Infrastructure** (**OCI**) or Alibaba Cloud. However, you can still onboard your SQL servers, Windows servers, or any other workloads by installing Microsoft Defender for Endpoint agents to the workloads. Defender for Cloud can monitor the security posture of non-Azure computers, but first, you need to connect them to Azure.

The following are some links that you can refer to when onboarding non-Azure workloads to Microsoft Defender for Cloud:

- *Connect on-premises machines by using Azure Arc*: `https://learn.microsoft.com/en-us/azure/defender-for-cloud/quickstart-onboard-machines#connect-on-premises-machines-using-azure-arc`

- *Connect on-premises machines by using the Azure portal*: `https://learn.microsoft.com/en-us/azure/defender-for-cloud/quickstart-onboard-machines#connect-on-premises-machines-using-the-azure-portal`

- *Onboard your Windows server*: `https://learn.microsoft.com/en-us/azure/defender-for-cloud/quickstart-onboard-machines#onboard-your-windows-server`

- *Onboard your Linux server*: `https://learn.microsoft.com/en-us/azure/defender-for-cloud/quickstart-onboard-machines#onboard-your-linux-servers`

Please refer to the *Further reading* section of this chapter to learn more about cloud account onboarding.

Let us now look at challenges and roadblocks that may arise during onboarding.

Onboarding roadblocks and mitigation best practices

During the onboarding process of cloud accounts to a CSPM tool, organizations may encounter several roadblocks. Let us understand these roadblocks one by one, along with mitigation best practices.

Roadblock #1 – Lack of necessary permissions

Obtaining the required permissions and credentials to connect cloud accounts can be challenging, especially in larger organizations.

Best practices are as follows:

- Work closely with your cloud service providers to grant the necessary access
- Clearly define and communicate the required permissions to relevant stakeholders
- Use **role-based access control (RBAC)** to manage access more effectively

Roadblock #2 – Complex cloud environments

Multi-cloud or hybrid environments can be complex, with different configurations and security practices across platforms.

Best practices are as follows:

- Develop a standardized approach for security policies and practices
- Ensure your CSPM tool can support multiple cloud platforms
- Create a comprehensive inventory of all cloud assets

Roadblock #3 – Resistance to change

Resistance from IT or development teams when introducing a CSPM tool can be a roadblock.

Best practices are as follows:

- Communicate the benefits of the CSPM tool, such as improved security and compliance
- Collaborate with teams to address their concerns and involve them in the onboarding process
- Provide training to ensure that teams can use the tool effectively

Roadblock #4 – Policy complexity

Defining and configuring complex security policies can be time-consuming and prone to misconfigurations.

Best practices are as follows:

- Start with foundational security policies and gradually add complexity as needed
- Leverage industry-standard templates for common policies
- Use automation to simplify policy creation and enforcement

Roadblock #5 – Alert fatigue

Overwhelming numbers of alerts can lead to alert fatigue, where important alerts may be overlooked.

Best practices are as follows:

- Customize alert thresholds and priorities based on the severity and business impact
- Implement intelligent alerting that correlates multiple events to reduce noise
- Use automated remediation to address common, low-level issues without generating alerts

Roadblock #6 – Integration complexity

Integrating the CSPM tool with existing security and operations tools can be complex.

Best practices are as follows:

- Use pre-built integrations where available
- Develop clear integration strategies and roadmaps
- Engage with the CSPM tool vendor or consult with experts to facilitate integration

Roadblock #7 – Monitoring and alerting configuration

Configuring the monitoring and alerting features of the CSPM tool correctly can be daunting.

Best practices are as follows:

- Consult with CSPM tool documentation and vendor support for guidance
- Start with a small set of critical alerts and expand gradually
- Conduct regular testing and validation to ensure alerts are functioning as expected

Roadblock #8 – Data privacy and security

Handling sensitive data collected by the CSPM tool can pose privacy and security concerns.

Best practices are as follows:

- Implement data protection measures, including encryption and access controls
- Comply with data privacy regulations (e.g., GDPR) and data retention policies
- Conduct regular security assessments of the CSPM tool itself

Roadblock #9 – Compliance variability

Different cloud platforms may have variations in compliance standards and terminology.

Best practices are as follows:

- Ensure that the CSPM tool can handle these variations and offer consistent reporting
- Collaborate with compliance experts to align your policies and practices

Roadblock #10 – Scalability

The CSPM tool should be able to scale with your growing cloud infrastructure.

Best practices are as follows:

- Choose a CSPM tool that can handle increased volumes of cloud accounts and resources
- Regularly assess the performance and capacity of the tool to plan for scaling

Addressing these roadblocks and implementing the recommended best practices will help ensure a smooth onboarding process and effective use of a CSPM tool in securing your cloud accounts and resources.

Offboarding cloud accounts

Offboarding cloud accounts from a CSPM solution is an essential process to ensure the secure removal of cloud resources and associated monitoring from the CSPM platform. Every tool offers different ways to achieve this. Let us look at some scenarios that show why it is important to offboard the cloud accounts.

Importance of offboarding cloud accounts from CSPM

Offboarding cloud accounts from a CSPM tool is an important process that should not be overlooked for several reasons. Here are some key reasons why offboarding is important:

- **Security and compliance**: When an organization no longer requires the monitoring and management of specific cloud accounts, it is crucial to remove them from the CSPM solution to avoid potential security risks and maintain compliance with relevant regulations.

- **Resource optimization**: Offboarding cloud accounts helps optimize the resources utilized by the CSPM solution, reducing unnecessary costs and overhead.

- **Access control**: By removing the cloud accounts from the CSPM platform, you ensure that only authorized personnel can access and manage those accounts, improving overall security.

- **Cost optimization**: Many CSPM tools are subscription-based or incur costs based on the number of cloud accounts or resources they monitor. Failing to offboard unused or decommissioned accounts can result in unnecessary subscription fees or resource consumption, leading to increased costs.

- **Auditing and accountability**: Organizations may be subject to audits or compliance checks, where they are required to demonstrate that inactive or decommissioned cloud accounts are properly managed and offboarded from the CSPM tool. Non-compliance can result in penalties or regulatory issues.

To ensure the ongoing effectiveness of your CSPM tool and maintain a strong security and compliance posture, it's crucial to prioritize the offboarding of cloud accounts when they are no longer in use or relevant to your organization's operations.

Process for offboarding cloud accounts from CSPM

The process for offboarding cloud accounts from a CSPM tool is an essential step in maintaining the security and compliance of your cloud infrastructure. Here is a general process for offboarding cloud accounts:

- **Identify inactive or decommissioned cloud accounts**: Determine which cloud accounts are no longer in use, have been decommissioned, or are otherwise no longer relevant to your organization's operations. This can be based on input from IT and operations teams, account status, or business requirements.

- **Review account dependencies**: Before offboarding a cloud account, assess its dependencies within the CSPM solution. Identify any connected resources, configurations, or associated data that may require migration or backup.

- **Plan the offboarding process**: Create a clear plan outlining the steps involved in offboarding the cloud accounts. Include considerations such as data backup, resource migration, and access revocation.

- **Backup or transfer data**: If there is any relevant data associated with the offboarding cloud accounts in the CSPM solution, ensure it is properly backed up or transferred to a suitable location for future reference or auditing purposes.

- **Terminate monitoring and alerting**: Disable monitoring and alerting for the specific cloud accounts within the CSPM solution. This ensures that the CSPM platform no longer collects data or generates alerts for those accounts.

- **Revoke access and permissions**: Remove the CSPM solution's access and permissions to the offboarding cloud accounts, ensuring that the solution can no longer access or manage the resources within those accounts.

- **Update documentation and processes**: Update any relevant documentation, procedures, or workflows to reflect the offboarding of the cloud accounts from the CSPM solution. Ensure that stakeholders are informed of the changes and any alternative monitoring mechanisms, if applicable.

- **Validate and verify offboarding**: After completing the offboarding process, perform validation checks to ensure that the cloud accounts are successfully removed from the CSPM solution and that monitoring and management have ceased.

- **Decommission resources** (if applicable): If there are any resources associated with the offboarding cloud accounts that are no longer needed, follow proper decommissioning processes to remove or delete those resources securely.

Remember that the specific steps for offboarding cloud accounts from a CSPM solution may vary depending on the solution itself and the cloud provider involved. Always consult the documentation and guidelines provided by the CSPM solution and the respective cloud provider for the most accurate and up-to-date offboarding procedures.

Summary

In this chapter, we explored the best practices and steps involved in onboarding cloud accounts to a CSPM solution. We discussed the importance of automating the onboarding process to streamline and expedite account setup. Additionally, we examined the deployment architecture for onboarding multi-cloud environments, considering the complexities and unique requirements of each cloud provider. We also delved into the challenges that can arise during the onboarding process and provided mitigations to address them. We explored the topic of offboarding cloud accounts from the CSPM solution and its significance.

The next chapter is focused on containers onboarding to CSPM tool. As containers are complex and vast in themselves, their onboarding aspects are discussed separately.

Further reading

To learn more about the topics that were covered in this chapter, take a look at the following resources:

- *Connect your AWS account to Microsoft Defender for Cloud*: `https://learn.microsoft.com/en-us/azure/defender-for-cloud/quickstart-onboard-aws?pivots=env-settings`

- *Connect your GCP project to Microsoft Defender for Cloud*: `https://learn.microsoft.com/en-us/azure/defender-for-cloud/quickstart-onboard-gcp?pivots=env-settings`

- *Using Terraform, onboard your AWS/GCP environment to Microsoft Defender for Cloud with Terraform*: `https://techcommunity.microsoft.com/t5/microsoft-defender-for-cloud/onboarding-your-aws-gcp-environment-to-microsoft-defender-for/ba-p/3798664`

7

Onboarding Containers

Organizations are increasingly adopting cloud-native architectures to enhance scalability, agility, and cost-effectiveness as a result of the rapidly evolving digital landscape. They are leveraging containerization to enhance their application deployment processes. Containers offer portability, scalability, and agility, allowing businesses to accelerate software development and delivery. However, they introduce unique security challenges that must be addressed to maintain a strong security posture. With increased complexity comes the need for robust security measures to protect containerized environments from potential vulnerabilities and threats. Onboarding containers to a CSPM tool is a vital step in this process, enabling organizations to extend their security capabilities to containerized workloads and effectively mitigate risks.

In this chapter, we will delve into the intricacies of onboarding containers to a CSPM tool, equipping security professionals, cloud architects, and DevOps teams with the knowledge and skills needed to bolster container security within their cloud environments. Throughout this chapter, you will gain valuable insights and skills to effectively onboard containers to a CSPM tool.

Here are the main topics we'll be looking at:

- Containerization overview and its benefits
- Understanding container security challenges
- Onboarding containers to CSPM tools
- Onboarding roadblocks and mitigation best practices
- Most recent trends and advancements in container security in the context of CSPM

Let's get started!

Containerization overview and its benefits

Containerization is a method of lightweight virtualization that involves the isolated packaging of an application and its dependencies into a self-contained unit called a container. Containers provide an isolated and consistent runtime environment, allowing applications to be easily deployed and executed across different computing environments, such as development machines, servers, and cloud platforms.

Benefits of containerization

Containerization has revolutionized the way applications are developed, deployed, and managed. Some key advantages include the following:

- **Portability**: Containers possess remarkable portability, facilitating the consistent execution of applications across various operating systems, cloud platforms, and infrastructure environments. This inherent mobility effectively eliminates the pervasive issue of "works on my machine" and simplifies the deployment process.

- **Scalability**: Containers facilitate the easy scaling of applications. They can be quickly replicated and distributed across multiple instances, allowing organizations to handle increased workloads efficiently. With container orchestration platforms such as Kubernetes, scaling applications becomes seamless and automated.

- **Resource efficiency**: Containers are lightweight, consuming minimal resources compared to traditional **virtual machines** (**VMs**). They share the host operating system kernel, reducing the overhead associated with full OS virtualization. This efficiency enables higher density and optimal utilization of infrastructure resources.

- **Faster deployment**: Containers provide rapid application deployment and release cycles. By encapsulating all dependencies within the container image, applications can be deployed consistently and quickly. This agility is particularly beneficial in modern DevOps and continuous delivery practices.

- **Isolation and security**: Containers offer process-level isolation, ensuring that applications and their dependencies run independently of one another. This isolation provides enhanced security by mitigating the impact of potential vulnerabilities or exploits in one container or many. Container security measures, such as sandboxing and restricted access, further strengthen the overall security posture.

- **DevOps collaboration**: Containerization fosters collaboration between development and operations teams. By providing a standardized environment, developers can package their applications with all required dependencies, ensuring consistent behavior throughout the development life cycle. Operations teams can then deploy these containers seamlessly across various environments.

- **Microservices architecture**: Containers align well with microservices-based architectures. They enable the decomposition of complex applications into smaller, independently deployable, and scalable services. This modular approach enhances agility and fault isolation, and facilitates easier maintenance and updates.

Now that you understand what containers are and the benefits they bring, let us now understand the importance of security in a containerized environment.

Understanding container security challenges

Security in containerized environments is of paramount importance due to the unique challenges posed by containerization. While containerization provides many benefits in terms of agility, scalability, and portability, it also introduces unique security challenges that need to be addressed.

Let us now look at common security risks and threats in containerized environments:

- **Isolation and vulnerability management**: Containers rely on a shared host kernel, and if one container is compromised, it can potentially impact other containers and the underlying host. Therefore, ensuring strong isolation between containers and proactive vulnerability management is crucial to prevent lateral movement of threats and unauthorized access.

- **Container image security**: Containers are built from images that contain the application and its dependencies. These images must be regularly scanned for vulnerabilities and validated to ensure they do not include any malicious or outdated components. Failure to secure container images can lead to the exploitation of known vulnerabilities and compromise the integrity of the entire containerized environment.

- **Runtime threats and monitoring**: Monitoring container runtime is essential to detect and respond to security incidents in real time. It involves tracking container behavior, network traffic, and application activity to identify anomalies or malicious activities. Continuous monitoring helps in the timely detection of runtime threats, such as unauthorized access attempts, abnormal resource usage, or malicious code execution.

- **Compliance and regulatory requirements**: Organizations working in regulated industries need to ensure their containerized environments comply with industry-specific security standards and regulatory frameworks. Failure to meet these requirements can lead to severe legal and financial consequences. Proper security measures, such as access controls, data encryption, and audit logs, must be implemented to maintain compliance.

- **Orchestration and configuration security**: Container orchestration platforms such as Kubernetes introduce additional security considerations. Securing the orchestration layer, managing access controls, and enforcing secure configuration practices are vital to protecting the underlying infrastructure and preventing unauthorized access or manipulation of containers.

- **Complex networking**: Containers are often dynamic, and their IP addresses may change frequently. Service discovery becomes challenging in a dynamic and distributed environment. Managing networking for containers can be complex, especially when dealing with multiple containers on different hosts that need to communicate with each other.

- **Resource overhead**: Container orchestration tools, such as Kubernetes or Docker Swarm, introduce additional resource overhead to manage and coordinate container deployment, scaling, and load balancing. Running multiple containers on a host can lead to resource contention, such as container density requiring careful resource allocation to ensure optimal performance.

- **Monitoring**: Monitoring containers poses challenges due to their ephemeral nature. Traditional monitoring tools may struggle to provide real-time insights into the state of containers. Containers require specific monitoring tools that understand container orchestration platforms and can track metrics such as container health, resource usage, and application performance.

- **Logging management and aggregation**: Containerized applications generate a large volume of logs, and managing and analyzing these logs becomes challenging. Centralized log management solutions are crucial but can be complex to set up. Aggregating logs from multiple containers and services requires a comprehensive strategy to ensure that logs are accessible for debugging and auditing purposes.

- **Secure deployment pipelines**: Security should be integrated into the entire container deployment pipeline. From the development stage to production deployment, each step should include security checks and measures to ensure that containers are free from vulnerabilities and adhere to security best practices. Implementing secure container registries, automated security testing, and secure image signing are critical aspects of a secure deployment pipeline.

- **Container escape and privilege escalation**: Container escape vulnerabilities, though rare, have the potential to compromise the entire host system. Proper security measures, such as user namespace remapping, seccomp, and AppArmor, must be implemented to mitigate the risk of container escape and privilege escalation attacks.

> **What is container escape?**
>
> **Container escape** is an exploitative technique in which an unauthorized individual gains entry to the underlying host operating system from inside a container. This illicit access enables them to breach the container's isolated environment and potentially manipulate or access resources on the host system. If container escape is successfully executed, it can jeopardize the security of other containers residing on the same host and potentially compromise the entire infrastructure.

Despite these challenges, containerization remains a popular and valuable technology. Many of these issues can be addressed with careful planning, proper tooling, and ongoing management practices. To address these security challenges, organizations use various tools and practices, including container security scanners, CSPM solutions, runtime protection tools, network security policies, access controls, and security best practices tailored to containers.

How does CSPM address these unique security challenges?

CSPM addresses the unique security challenges introduced by containers through its holistic approach. It provides complete visibility into containerized environments, constantly monitors for misconfigurations, compliance violations, and vulnerabilities, and automatically enforces security policies. This proactive stance ensures that dynamic, short-lived containers are always configured securely. Additionally, CSPM integrates seamlessly with DevOps, promoting security throughout the development and deployment process, thus mitigating issues early. It offers real-time alerts and automates incident response, enabling quick reactions to security threats within containers. This combination of continuous monitoring, proactive configuration management, and integration into the development life cycle allows CSPM to effectively tackle the challenges of container security.

Now that we understand the unique security challenges of a containerized environment and how CSPM addresses these concerns, let us explore the onboarding aspects of containers to a CSPM tool.

Onboarding containers to CSPM tools

Onboarding containers to a CSPM tool refers to the process of integrating containers into the CSPM tool for enhanced security monitoring and management. The onboarding process involves configuring the CSPM tool to scan, assess, and protect containers against security risks and compliance violations.

> **Note**
>
> To make the concept easily understandable, the Microsoft Defender for Containers feature of the Microsoft Defender for Cloud tool is taken as a reference wherever it is imperative to explain with an example. There are many other tools available on the market that offer container security posture management features as well. The example chosen here is purely based on publicly accessible information.

Understanding Microsoft Defender for Containers features

Microsoft Defender for Containers is a cloud-based solution designed to safeguard your containerized environments. It protects your clusters whether they're running in **Azure Kubernetes Service** (**AKS**), **Amazon Elastic Kubernetes Service** (**EKS**) in a connected **Amazon Web Services** (**AWS**) account, **Google Kubernetes Engine** (**GKE**) in a connected **Google Cloud Platform** (**GCP**) project, or other Kubernetes distributions (using Azure Arc-enabled Kubernetes). Defender for Containers brings with it the three core aspects of container security, which are as follows:

- **Environment hardening**: As stated previously, Defender for Containers safeguards your Kubernetes clusters regardless of whether they are operating on Azure Kubernetes Service, on-premises or **infrastructure as a service** (**IaaS**) Kubernetes, or Amazon EKS. Container Sentry offers ongoing assessments of clusters, delivering enhanced visibility into misconfigurations and supported with actionable guidelines to mitigate identified threats.

- **Vulnerability assessment**: It also supplies vulnerability assessment for images stored in Azure Container Registry and **Elastic Container Registry (ECR)**.

- **Runtime nodes and clusters protection**: Alerts are generated by the threat protection system for both clusters and nodes, signaling potential threats and suspicious activities.

Let us now understand the Defender for Containers architecture diagram.

Defender for Containers architecture diagram

Defender for Containers is developed differently for each Kubernetes environment. The links in this section give you the detailed and updated architecture diagram for each Kubernetes environment.

Azure Kubernetes Service (AKS)

When safeguarding a cluster hosted in AKS, Defender for Cloud ensures a seamless and effortless process for collecting audit log data without the need for an agent. The deployment of the Defender profile on each node enables runtime protections and helps the collection of signals. For more comprehensive information, please consult the Microsoft documentation (`https://learn.microsoft.com/en-us/azure/defender-for-cloud/defender-for-containers-architecture?tabs=defender-for-container-arch-aks#architecture-diagram-of-defender-for-cloud-and-aks-clusters`).

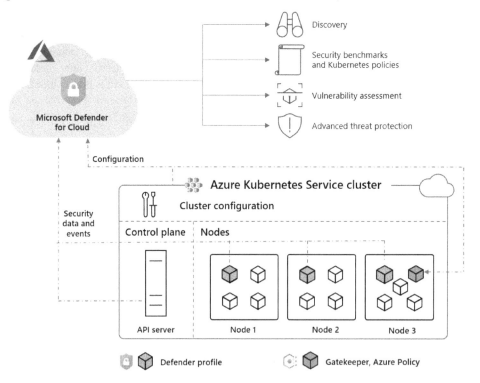

Figure 7.1 – Architecture diagram of Defender for Cloud and AKS cluster (source: Microsoft)

Arc-enabled Kubernetes clusters

When a non-Azure container is integrated with Azure through Arc, the Arc extension collects Kubernetes audit logs from every control plane node within the cluster. Subsequently, the extension transmits the log data to the Microsoft Defender for Cloud backend in the cloud, enabling comprehensive analysis. Although the extension is associated with a Log Analytics workspace used as a data pipeline, the audit log data itself is not stored within the Log Analytics workspace.

For more details and updated information on this, refer to your chosen CSPM vendor documentation or, in this case, the Microsoft documentation (`https://learn.microsoft.com/en-us/azure/defender-for-cloud/defender-for-containers-architecture?tabs=defender-for-container-arch-eks#architecture-diagram-of-defender-for-cloud-and-eks-clusters`).

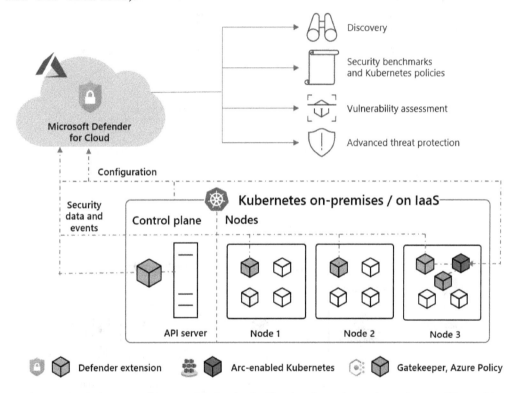

Figure 7.2 – Architecture diagram of Defender for Cloud and non-Azure cluster (source: Microsoft)

Amazon EKS clusters

At the time of writing this chapter, Defender for Containers support for Amazon EKS clusters is a preview feature. To receive the full protection offered by Microsoft Defender for Containers, the following components are needed:

- Kubernetes audit logs
- Azure Arc-enabled Kubernetes
- The Defender extension
- The Azure Policy extension

To understand the full concepts and updated information, read the Microsoft documentation (`https://learn.microsoft.com/en-us/azure/defender-for-cloud/defender-for-containers-architecture?tabs=defender-for-container-arch-eks#architecture-diagram-of-defender-for-cloud-and-eks-clusters`).

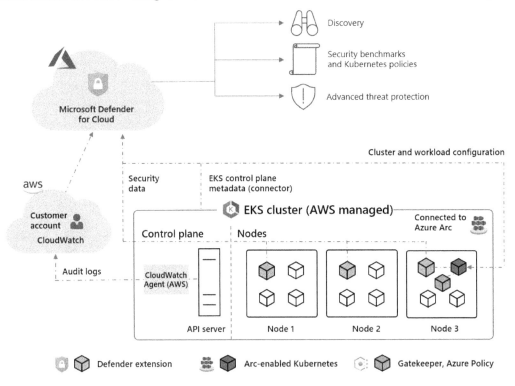

Figure 7.3 – Architecture diagram of Defender for Cloud and Amazon EKS cluster (source: Microsoft)

Google Cloud GKE cluster

At the time of writing this chapter, Defender for Containers support for GKE in a connected GCP project cluster is a preview feature. To receive the full protection offered by Microsoft Defender for Containers, the following components are needed:

- Kubernetes audit logs
- Azure Arc-enabled Kubernetes
- The Defender extension
- The Azure Policy extension

To understand the full concepts and updated information, read the Microsoft documentation (`https://learn.microsoft.com/en-us/azure/defender-for-cloud/defender-for-containers-architecture?tabs=defender-for-container-arch-eks#architecture-diagram-of-defender-for-cloud-and-eks-clusters`).

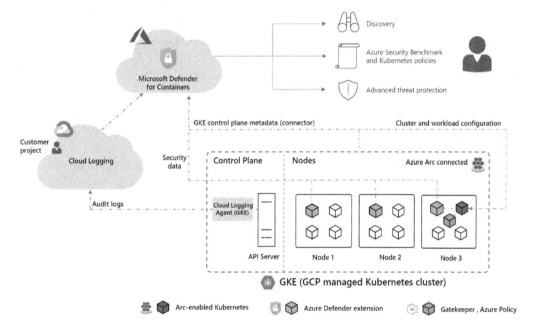

Figure 7.4 – Architecture diagram of Defender for Cloud and GKE cluster (source: Microsoft)

Once containers are onboarded, Defender for Containers receives and analyzes the following information to protect Kubernetes containers:

- Audit logs and security events from the API server
- Cluster configuration information from the control plane
- Workload configuration from Azure Policy
- Security signals and events from the node level

Now that you understand the architecture diagram of Kubernetes clusters along with Microsoft Defender for Containers, let us now understand how the onboarding of Kubernetes clusters works.

Enabling Microsoft Defender for Containers for Kubernetes clusters

Microsoft Defender for Containers is a feature bundled with cloud-native solutions through Microsoft Defender for Cloud for securing your Kubernetes clusters.

Let us now understand how it works in the case of Azure Kubernetes clusters.

Azure Kubernetes Service (AKS)

AKS is a managed service for developing, deploying, and managing containerized applications offered by Microsoft. To onboard AKS to Microsoft Defender for Cloud, the following provides important steps to take and the relevant documentation from Microsoft:

1. **Network requirement**: It is important to note that by default, AKS clusters have unrestricted outbound (egress) internet access. To understand more about outbound network rules and FQDNs for AKS clusters, refer to the Microsoft documentation (`https://learn.microsoft.com/en-us/azure/aks/outbound-rules-control-egress#required-outbound-network-rules-and-fqdns-for-aks-clusters`).

2. **Enable the Defender plan**: To follow the steps to enable the Defender plans for containers, refer to the Microsoft documentation (`https://learn.microsoft.com/en-us/azure/defender-for-cloud/defender-for-containers-enable?tabs=aks-deploy-portal%2Ck8s-deploy-asc%2Ck8s-verify-asc%2Ck8s-remove-arc%2Caks-removeprofile-api&pivots=defender-for-container-aks#enable-the-plan`).

3. **Deploy the Defender profile**: You can enable the Defender for Containers plan and deploy all of the relevant components from the Azure portal, the REST API, or with a Resource Manager template. A default workspace is automatically assigned once the Defender profile is deployed. It is also possible to assign a custom workspace in place of the default workspace through Azure Policy, which is a helpful feature for collecting logs in one centralized workspace. To learn

more about the detailed and updated steps, follow the Microsoft documentation (`https://learn.microsoft.com/en-us/azure/defender-for-cloud/defender-for-containers-enable?tabs=aks-deploy-portal%2Ck8s-deploy-asc%2Ck8s-verify-asc%2Ck8s-remove-arc%2Caks-removeprofile-api&pivots=defender-for-container-aks#deploy-the-defender-profile`).

4. **View scan results**: After vulnerability scanning is enabled and configured, Microsoft Defender for Cloud will automatically scan the registry images based on the specified settings. You can view the scan results in the Azure portal. Navigate to the Container Registry and select **Vulnerabilities** in the **Security** section to see the scan results and any identified vulnerabilities.

5. **Take remediation actions**: If any vulnerabilities are detected, review the details provided by Microsoft Defender for Cloud and take the necessary remediation actions. This may involve updating the vulnerable images, applying patches, or implementing other security measures.

Similar to the preceding example, you can follow CSPM documentation and in this case, Microsoft documentation, for onboarding Kubernetes clusters hosted in another environment. Refer to the following document to understand the onboarding process for on-premises/IaaS (Arc), Amazon EKS, and GKE clusters: `https://learn.microsoft.com/en-us/azure/defender-for-cloud/defender-for-containers-enable?tabs=aks-deploy-portal%2Ck8s-deploy-asc%2Ck8s-verify-asc%2Ck8s-remove-arc%2Caks-removeprofile-api&pivots=defender-for-container-aks#deploy-the-defender-extension`.

Now you understand the process of onboarding containers to the CSPM tool with the help of an example using Microsoft Defender for Cloud. Let us now understand the challenges and issues that may arise while onboarding Kubernetes clusters to the CSPM tool.

Onboarding roadblocks and mitigation tips

When onboarding containers to a CSPM tool, you may encounter several roadblocks. These roadblocks can impede the smooth integration of container security into your cloud environment. Here are some common roadblocks and mitigation best practices:

*   **Lack of container visibility**: Containers are highly dynamic, and it can be challenging to maintain visibility into their activities and configurations.

    Mitigation tips: Utilize container orchestration tools such as Kubernetes to provide better visibility into containers. Integrate with container runtime security solutions for real-time monitoring. Ensure your CSPM tool has the capability to discover and track containers in real time.

*   **Complex container orchestration platforms**: The complexity of container orchestration platforms, such as Kubernetes, can make integration with CSPM tools challenging.

    Mitigation tips: Choose a CSPM tool that provides native support for common container orchestration platforms. Invest in training and expertise to ensure proper configuration and integration with the chosen container orchestration solution.

- **Container image scanning**: Scanning container images for vulnerabilities can be time-consuming and may delay deployment.

  Mitigation tips: Integrate container image scanning into your CI/CD pipeline to identify vulnerabilities early. Use automation to schedule and perform regular image scans. Select a CSPM tool that supports image scanning and vulnerability assessment.

- **Security misconfigurations**: Misconfigurations in container security settings can lead to vulnerabilities.

  Mitigation tips: Implement IaC and version control to ensure consistent and auditable configurations. Use automated configuration checks within the CSPM tool to detect misconfigurations.

- **Compliance monitoring**: Ensuring containers adhere to security and compliance policies can be a complex task.

  Mitigation tips: Define compliance policies within your CSPM tool and set up continuous monitoring to track and alert compliance violations. Regularly review and update compliance policies as regulations change.

- **Rapid scaling and dynamic nature**: Containers can scale rapidly and are short-lived, making it challenging to maintain security controls.

  Mitigation tips: Implement automation for security controls and scaling policies, adapting to container scaling in real time. Use CSPM tools that can handle rapid changes in the environment.

- **Integrating with container orchestration platforms**: Different container orchestration platforms require specific integration for security monitoring.

  Mitigation tips: Select a CSPM tool that supports your container orchestration platform or can be extended through APIs. Work closely with your container orchestration vendor to ensure a seamless integration.

- **Multi-cloud environments**: Managing containers across multiple cloud providers can introduce complexity.

  Mitigation tips: Choose a CSPM tool that supports multi-cloud environments. Standardize your security policies and configurations to work consistently across various cloud providers.

- **Access control and permissions**: Managing access controls for containers and underlying infrastructure can be complex.

  Mitigation tips: Implement strong access control policies, utilizing **role-based access control** (**RBAC**) where possible. Regularly audit and review access permissions and monitor for unauthorized access using CSPM tools.

- **User training**: Ensuring your security and operations teams are well-trained in using the CSPM tool can be a challenge.

  Mitigation tips: Invest in training and awareness programs to ensure teams understand container security best practices and the proper use of CSPM tools.

Addressing these roadblocks requires a combination of technology, process improvements, and ongoing diligence. Regularly reviewing and updating your container security strategy will help you adapt to evolving threats and best practices in the ever-changing world of container security.

Latest trends and advancements in container security

Container security and CSPM are areas that continue to evolve and advance as technology progresses. Here are some of the most recent trends and future advancements to watch for in container security and CSPM:

- **Enhanced container image security**: There has been an increased focus on improving container image security by integrating advanced scanning techniques, machine learning, and **artificial intelligence (AI)**. This will help identify even more complex vulnerabilities, malware, and supply chain attacks.

- **Runtime protection and behavioral analysis**: Container runtime protection will evolve to include more advanced behavioral analysis and anomaly detection capabilities. This will enable the detection of suspicious activities and real-time mitigation of threats during container runtime.

- **Kubernetes-native security solutions**: As Kubernetes remains the dominant container orchestration platform, there will be a rise in Kubernetes-native security solutions. These solutions will provide tighter integration with Kubernetes, offering enhanced visibility, configuration management, and automated remediation for Kubernetes-specific security risks.

- **Immutable infrastructure**: The concept of immutable infrastructure, where containers are treated as disposable and immutable, will gain more traction. This approach simplifies security management by minimizing the attack surface and reducing the impact of security incidents.

- **Compliance automation**: CSPM tools will increasingly automate compliance monitoring and reporting processes. This will help organizations align with various regulatory frameworks by continuously assessing the security posture of their container environments and generating compliance reports.

- **Integration with DevSecOps**: Container security and CSPM solutions have seamlessly integrated with DevSecOps practices and toolchains. This integration enables security to be embedded throughout the software development life cycle, ensuring security and compliance from the initial stages of application development.

- **Zero trust architecture**: Zero trust architecture, which assumes no implicit trust for any user or container, will be adopted more widely. Container security solutions and CSPM tools will incorporate zero trust principles to enforce strict access controls, authentication, and authorization mechanisms.

- **Serverless security**: As serverless computing gains popularity, container security solutions and CSPM tools will adapt to address the unique security challenges of serverless environments. This includes securing serverless functions, managing access rights, and monitoring functions for vulnerabilities or misconfigurations.

- **Threat intelligence and threat hunting**: Container security solutions and CSPM tools will leverage threat intelligence feeds and advanced threat hunting techniques to proactively identify emerging threats and indicators of compromise. This proactive approach will help organizations stay ahead of potential attacks.

- **Continuous integration and continuous delivery** (**CI/CD**): Container security and CSPM solutions will integrate more seamlessly with CI/CD pipelines to enable automated security testing, vulnerability scanning, and configuration checks during the application build and deployment stages.

Staying current with the latest developments in container security is essential to maintaining the security of containerized applications and infrastructure.

Summary

In this chapter, we understood containerization and explored its benefits in the context of CSPM by explaining the concept of containerization, which involves encapsulating an application and its dependencies into a portable and isolated unit called a container. We also discussed unique container security challenges, onboarding containers to CSPM tools, particularly in the context of Microsoft Defender for Cloud, and challenges that may arise in the onboarding process. We also delved into security best practices for containers and the most recent trends and advancements in container security in the context of CSPM.

In the next chapter, we will discuss CSPM tool environment settings and integration with other IT tools.

Further reading

To learn more about the topics that were covered in this chapter, take a look at the following resources:

- *Secure Your Containers with Confidence*: `https://start.paloaltonetworks.com/container-security-101-understanding-the-basics-of-securing-containers`

- *Scan registry images with Microsoft Defender for Cloud*: `https://learn.microsoft.com/en-us/azure/container-registry/scan-images-defender?source=recommendations`

- *Containers support matrix in Defender for Cloud*: `https://learn.microsoft.com/en-us/azure/defender-for-cloud/support-matrix-defender-for-containers`

8

Exploring Environment Settings

As organizations increasingly rely on cloud services, it becomes paramount to ensure the security and compliance of their cloud environments. A robust **cloud security posture management (CSPM)** tool is a key component in achieving this goal, and the effective environment setting of the CSPM tool forms the foundation for its success. This chapter focuses on CSPM environment settings, which play a critical role in establishing a robust security posture for cloud-based infrastructures. We discuss the integration of CSPM tools with other tools such as **single sign-on (SSO)**, ticketing tools, setting up the right configurations, scheduling reports, and accounts management. We delve into the significance of environment settings in a CSPM tool.

Throughout this chapter, we provide practical examples and expert recommendations to help you develop a comprehensive understanding of the CSPM environment setting. By the end of this chapter, you will have the knowledge and insights necessary to configure your CSPM tool effectively, optimize your cloud security posture, and ensure a robust defense against potential threats.

In this chapter, we'll cover the following topics:

- Environment settings overview
- Managing users and permissions
- CSPM integrations with other tools
- Setting up an effective reporting environment
- Activity logging

Let us get started!

Environment settings overview

Environment settings typically refer to configurations and parameters that are specific to the environment in which the CSPM tool is deployed. This allows you to customize the CSPM tool to fit the specific requirements and characteristics of your cloud environment. Every organization's cloud setup is unique, and these settings enable you to adapt the tool to your infrastructure, compliance standards, and security policies. Also, every CSPM tool is different, and hence no one explanation fits for every tool.

> **Note**
>
> There are dozens of CSPM tools on the market; for example, Prisma Cloud by Palo Alto Networks, Wiz, Orca, Microsoft Defender for Cloud, **Amazon Web Services** (**AWS**) Security Hub, Google Cloud Security Command Center, and Dome9, to name a few. Some of them are discussed in *Chapter 3* at a very high level. Every tool comes with a distinct set of integration features and different ways of communicating with cloud environments and other tools. Some of the most critical aspects associated with setting up or fine-tuning CSPM tools are discussed in a generic manner without going into many details about a particular CSPM tool, deliberately.

Let us explore the various aspects of environment settings:

- **Cloud provider-specific settings**: These settings are specific to the cloud provider you are using, and they configure how the CSPM tool interacts with and retrieves information from your cloud environment. For example, to connect to your AWS environment, you would need to configure the CSPM tool with AWS access keys or **identity and access management** (**IAM**) roles.

- **Compliance standards**: CSPM tools often allow you to specify the compliance standards or frameworks that your organization needs to adhere to, such as the **Center for Internet Security** (**CIS**) benchmarks, the **National Institute of Standards and Technology** (**NIST**), the **Health Insurance Portability and Accountability Act** (**HIPAA**), or the **General Data Protection Regulation** (**GDPR**). For example, you can set your CSPM tool to check for the CIS AWS Foundations Benchmark or **Payment Card Industry Data Security Standard** (**PCI DSS**) compliance and configure the desired compliance level.

- **Notification and alerting settings**: You can configure how the CSPM tool notifies you about security issues or policy violations. This includes email notifications, integrations with **incident management** (**IM**) tools, or other alerting mechanisms. For example, you can specify which email addresses or IM systems should receive notifications when a security issue is detected.

- **Scanning schedule**: You can define/customize how often the CSPM tool should scan your cloud environment for security issues. This involves setting up regular scans, immediate scans after specific events, or custom schedules based on your organization's requirements; for example, daily scans during off-peak hours or real-time scans triggered by specific cloud events.

- **Policy definitions**: You can define and customize security policies or rules that the CSPM tool should enforce in your environment. These policies cover aspects such as proper data encryption, access control, network configurations, and more. For example, you can create custom policies to ensure that your resources are configured in alignment with your organization's specific security requirements.

- **Remediation actions**: CSPM tools often include automated remediation capabilities, allowing you to specify actions to be taken automatically when a security violation is detected. For example, the tool might automatically close a security group rule that is deemed too permissive or set up automated actions, such as closing unused security groups or rotating access keys, when violations are found.

Environment settings in a CSPM tool allow you to tailor the tool's behavior to your specific cloud environment and security needs, ensuring that it effectively monitors, reports, and helps remediate security issues in your cloud infrastructure. Let us now explore those key aspects one by one, starting with **user access management (UAM)**.

Managing users and permissions

A *user* is a member of your organization whom you would like to grant access to your CSPM tool. Usually, you can invite a user from the CSPM tool with specific permissions to define the scope of their activities and create groups consisting of multiple users with a single set of permissions, and you can also create custom roles defining specific user permissions. User and group permissions settings refer to the configuration and management of user accounts, groups, and their associated access permissions within the CSPM environment. These settings play a crucial role in maintaining a secure and well-controlled access control framework. Let us now understand how user management works in most CSPM tools.

User management

User management involves the management of individual user accounts within the CSPM environment. This includes creating user accounts, assigning unique identifiers (such as usernames or email addresses), and defining authentication mechanisms (for example, passwords or **multi-factor authentication (MFA)**). Managing users' permissions in CSPM tools involves configuring and controlling access to the tool's functionalities and resources. Let us look at the process involved in managing users' permissions in CSPM tools:

- **User account creation**: The first step in managing users is creating user accounts within the CSPM tool. This typically involves providing necessary details such as usernames, email addresses, and authentication credentials. CSPM tools also integrate with existing identity management systems, allowing administrators to synchronize user accounts or authenticate users through SSO mechanisms.

- **Role assignment**: After user accounts are created, roles are assigned to determine the level of access and permissions for each user. Roles typically correspond to predefined sets of permissions within the CSPM tool. Common roles include super-admins, administrators, viewers, security analysts, compliance managers, and resource owners. The selection of roles depends on the tool's capabilities and the organization's requirements.

- **Permission configuration**: Once roles are assigned to users, administrators configure permissions associated with each role. Permissions define the actions and operations a user can perform within the CSPM tool. This includes accessing specific features, viewing security findings, generating reports, modifying settings, and managing resources. Permission configuration ensures that users have appropriate access levels based on their responsibilities and requirements.

- **Access control management (ACM)**: Managing access control involves defining rules and policies to control user access to the CSPM tool and its resources. This includes configuring MFA requirements, password policies, and session timeouts. Access control settings help ensure secure user authentication and prevent unauthorized access to sensitive information within the CSPM tool.

- **User life cycle management**: Over time, the user landscape may change within an organization. Managing users also includes handling tasks such as user onboarding, offboarding, and role changes. When a user joins a security team, and their responsibility includes working on the CSPM tool, their account is created and assigned appropriate roles and permissions. When a user leaves or moves to another department, their account is disabled or removed to prevent unauthorized access. Role changes may also occur as users' responsibilities evolve, requiring adjustments to their permissions.

- **Auditing and monitoring**: CSPM tools often provide auditing and monitoring capabilities to track user activities and permission changes. Auditing logs can help identify any suspicious or unauthorized actions within the tool. Regular monitoring of user accounts and permissions helps maintain the integrity and security of the CSPM environment.

- **Regular access reviews and updates**: It is important to conduct periodic access reviews of user accounts and permissions to ensure they remain aligned with the organization's evolving needs and security requirements. This includes removing unnecessary access, adjusting permissions based on role changes, and identifying potential security gaps or excessive privileges.

Managing users' permissions in CSPM tools is a crucial aspect of maintaining an effective and secure cloud security posture. Let us understand how user group management works.

User group management

User group management is a process of organizing and managing users into coherent groups or roles within a CSPM tool. Grouping users provides organizations with a streamlined approach to **access management** (**AM**) and the ability to collectively assign permissions. Administrators can create groups, allocate users to these groups, and manage group membership. This simplifies administration by enabling permissions to be granted to the entire group, eliminating the need to individually assign permissions to each user. You can use groups to give multiple users a single set of permissions. This is the preferred method for assigning the same uniform permissions to many users. Making a user group consists of the following:

1. **Creating a new group**: The group acts as a container for adding users with a single set of permissions.

2. **Setting group permissions**: Choose what permissions you would like the group to have.

3. **Adding users to the group**: When users are added to the group, they will all receive the same permissions and account accesses.

Most CSPM tools are already equipped with built-in user roles that serve the distinct set of permissions that an organization mostly uses to function. Let us look at some built-in roles.

Built-in user roles

As with any other **Software-as-a-Service** (**SaaS**) tools, built-in user roles in CSPM are predefined roles that come with the tool's default configuration. These roles are designed to provide distinct levels of access and permissions to users based on their responsibilities and tasks within the CSPM environment. Next are common built-in user roles you may find in CSPM tools:

*   **Super-admin/administrator/owner**: The administrator or owner role typically has the highest level of access and control over the CSPM tool. Administrators have complete administrative privileges, allowing them to configure settings, manage user accounts, define permissions, and access all features and functionalities of the tool. They have the authority to make changes, create and modify policies, and oversee the overall operation of the CSPM tool.

*   **Auditor/viewer/read-only**: The auditor, viewer, or read-only role is for users who need read access to the CSPM tool without making any modifications. Users with this role can view security findings, reports, dashboards, and other relevant information but do not have the authority to change settings, configure policies, or modify user permissions. This role is suitable for stakeholders who need visibility into the security posture and compliance status of the cloud environment.

*   **Security analyst/operator**: Security analysts or operators play an active role in investigating security findings, triaging alerts, and taking appropriate actions within the CSPM tool. They have permissions to interact with security data, manage remediation workflows, communicate with other team members, and access specific features related to security analysis and **incident response** (**IR**). However, they may not have administrative capabilities or access to sensitive configuration settings.

*   **Compliance manager**: Compliance managers have specialized roles focused on ensuring adherence to regulatory requirements and internal policies. They have access to compliance-related features within the CSPM tool, such as defining compliance rules, benchmarks, and requirements. Compliance managers can generate compliance reports, track the organization's compliance posture, and oversee remediation activities related to compliance violations.

- **Cloud account/resource owner**: Some CSPM tools offer roles specific to individual cloud accounts or resource owners. These roles provide users with permissions to view and manage security findings, configurations, and compliance posture for their owned cloud resources. Resource owners can monitor and take actions related to the security of their specific cloud accounts or resources while maintaining segregation from other areas of the organization. For example, in the Orca CSPM tool, you can group the onboarded cloud accounts into **business units** (**BUs**) and provision access to the responsible team.

- **Custom roles**: Custom roles and additional permissions are also offered by every CSPM tool to cater to specific requirements or to provide more granular access control within the tool.

These built-in user roles provide a foundation for managing access and permissions in CSPM tools. They offer predefined levels of access and authority, aligning with common organizational roles and responsibilities. However, it is important to note that the specific user roles available may vary depending on the CSPM tool. Organizations can assign these built-in user roles based on the user's responsibilities and the **principle of least privilege** (**PoLP**), ensuring that users have the necessary access required to perform their tasks while minimizing the risk of unauthorized actions or data breaches.

Let us now understand another important topic: managing API tokens.

Managing API tokens

Managing API tokens involves the administration and control of access tokens used to authenticate and authorize API-based interactions between the CSPM tool and **cloud service providers** (**CSPs**) or other external systems. API tokens serve as credentials to establish secure communication and enable the tool to gather security-related information, analyze cloud configurations, and assess the security posture of the cloud environment.

Let us understand how managing API tokens works in most CSPM tools:

- **Token generation and configuration**: In CSPM, you can generate more than one API token and use them for different purposes. For example, you can create API tokens that are used in different automations to request different data from the CSPM tool. After generating API tokens, administrators define access control policies and permissions associated with each token. This determines the level of access the CSPM tool has to various cloud resources and services. Access control ensures that the tool only accesses the necessary information and resources required for security assessments and monitoring.

- **Token usage**: Once you have configured the API token, you can use it for integration with other applications. You can make requests from your application to the CSPM tool API to receive data on alerts, assets, vulnerabilities, and other objects. The API tokens can be used in CSPM automations. When you create an automation, you can select the API token created for your application in the tool integrations; for example, with the integration of the CSPM tool with the **security information and event management** (**SIEM**)/**security orchestration, automation and response** (**SOAR**) section.

- **Token life cycle management**: Managing API tokens involves handling their life cycle, including creation, rotation, and revocation. Periodic token rotation is recommended as a *security best practice* to minimize the risk of compromised tokens. When a token is no longer needed or if there are concerns about its security, administrators should promptly revoke or disable the token to prevent unauthorized access.

- **Secure storage**: API tokens should be stored securely within the CSPM tool's infrastructure. Proper measures such as encryption and access controls should be implemented to protect tokens from unauthorized access or accidental exposure. Additionally, it is crucial to follow security best practices for securing the storage system that holds the tokens, such as strong access controls, monitoring, and auditing.

- **Token usage tracking and auditing**: Administrators should track and audit the usage of API tokens within the CSPM tool. This helps identify any suspicious or unauthorized activities associated with tokens. By monitoring token usage, administrators can detect potential security incidents or misuse of privileges, enabling timely response and mitigation.

- **Integration with IAM**: CSPM tools often integrate with IAM systems or cloud provider IAM services. This integration enables the seamless management and synchronization of API tokens with existing user accounts and access control policies. It ensures that the tokens align with the organization's broader IAM framework and security policies.

Effective management of API tokens in CSPM tool management helps ensure secure and controlled access to cloud resources and enables accurate security assessments.

Key challenges in permission management

Managing users, groups, and API permissions in CSPM tools comes with several challenges and requires adherence to best practices to ensure effective access control and security. Let us look at some usual challenges in permissions management in CSPM tools:

- **Complexity and scale**: CSPM tools often deal with complex and dynamic cloud environments, involving multiple cloud platforms, numerous resources, and many users. Managing users and their permissions across such a dynamic landscape can become challenging, especially when considering frequent changes, onboarding/offboarding users, and evolving cloud resources.

- **Role and permission creep**: This refers to the gradual accumulation of excessive privileges or permissions assigned to user roles over time. This occurs when users accumulate excessive privileges or are granted permissions beyond what is necessary for their role, leading to increased security risks and potential misuse of privileges.

- **Granularity and fine-grained access control**: CSPM tools may require fine-grained access control to ensure that users have appropriate access to specific features, resources, or data. Implementing and managing granular access control can be challenging, as it requires a careful balance between granting sufficient access for users to perform their tasks while limiting unnecessary privileges.

Best practices to overcome permission-related challenges

Organizations can effectively manage permissions in CSPM tools, reduce security risks, maintain compliance, and ensure the integrity of their cloud security posture. Let us understand the best practices to overcome the challenges discussed previously:

- **Centralized IAM**: Integrate CSPM tools with centralized IAM systems to leverage existing user directories and authentication mechanisms. Centralized IAM provides a **single source of truth** (**SSOT**) for user management and simplifies access control across multiple systems and applications.

- **PoLP**: Adhering to PoLP is crucial in CSPM user management. Users should be granted the minimum privileges necessary to perform their specific tasks, reducing the risk of unauthorized access or misuse of privileges. Regular reviews of user permissions should be conducted to ensure permissions align with job responsibilities.

- **Role-based access control (RBAC)**: Implement RBAC to simplify and streamline user management. Define roles based on job functions, responsibilities, and access requirements. Assign users to appropriate roles rather than individually assigning permissions. This allows for easier administration, scalability, and consistent access control across the organization.

- **Standardize attributes and use attribute-based access control (ABAC)**: Standardize attributes to ensure consistency across your cloud environment. This simplifies the management of permissions and reduces the potential for misconfiguration. ABAC enables precise, context-aware access decisions, reducing over-privileging and the risk of unauthorized access. It provides a more precise and versatile alternative to traditional access control models such as RBAC.

- **Utilize tag-based access control (TBAC)**: Utilize tags and TBAC effectively because it provides a dynamic and fine-grained approach to access control in complex and dynamic environments.

- **Regular access reviews and audits**: Conduct periodic reviews and audits of user accounts and permissions to ensure they remain accurate, up to date, and aligned with organizational requirements. Review user access privileges, remove unnecessary access, and identify any anomalies or deviations from established access controls.

- **Segregation of duties (SoD)**: Implement SoD to prevent conflicts of interest and reduce the risk of fraudulent activities. Ensure that critical tasks, such as configuration changes or approving access requests, require multiple individuals with distinct roles and responsibilities to prevent **single points of failure** (**SPOFs**) or potential security breaches.

- **Streamlined user onboarding and offboarding processes**: Establish well-defined processes for user onboarding and offboarding. This includes ensuring proper user provisioning and deprovisioning procedures, including the creation, modification, or deletion of user accounts and associated permissions. Promptly remove access for users who leave the organization or change roles to prevent unauthorized access.

- **Training and awareness**: Provide training and awareness programs to educate users about the importance of security, appropriate use of privileges, and adherence to organizational security policies. Users should be aware of their responsibilities, the potential risks of inappropriate access or actions, and the importance of reporting any security concerns.

- **Regular backup and disaster recovery (DR)**: Implement regular backups of user and permission configurations within the CSPM tool. This ensures that user management settings can be restored in case of accidental deletion, system failure, or other unforeseen circumstances.

Effective cost management using TBAC, showbacks, and chargebacks

Cost management in cloud environments is crucial to optimizing expenditure and ensuring efficient resource allocation. TBAC can play a vital role in controlling costs by allowing organizations to categorize and manage resources based on their attributes. By tagging resources with attributes such as `department`, `project`, or `environment`, it becomes easier to track costs associated with each category. This enables more accurate showback and chargeback practices, where the costs of cloud resources are transparently attributed to specific departments or teams. Showback allows you to provide insights to various stakeholders on their resource consumption, while chargeback enables you to bill the respective departments or teams for their resource usage. Implementing TBAC alongside showback and chargeback concepts ensures that cost management is both effective and transparent, facilitating better decision-making and cost optimization.

Regular access reviews, adherence to PoLP, and robust processes for user life cycle management are essential for maintaining a secure and well-managed CSPM environment. Let us now understand another important aspect of environment setting, which is the integration of CSPM tools with other tools.

CSPM integrations with other tools

Most CSPM tools offer integration with other tools to improve overall security management processes. Integration is nothing but the process of connecting and combining the functionalities of different software tools or systems to achieve enhanced functionality, streamlined workflows, and improved data exchange. Integration allows tools to work together seamlessly, leveraging each other's capabilities and data to create a more comprehensive and efficient solution.

Tool integration provides several benefits, including the following:

- **Streamlined workflows**: Integration reduces manual effort, improves data accuracy, and streamlines processes by enabling data and actions to flow seamlessly between tools. This enhances productivity and reduces the potential for errors.

- **Enhanced functionality**: By combining the capabilities of different tools, integration extends the functionality and effectiveness of each individual tool. This allows organizations to leverage the strengths of multiple tools and create a more comprehensive solution.

- **Data synchronization**: Integration ensures that data remains consistent and up to date across different systems. For example, integrating a CSPM tool with a **configuration management database** (**CMDB**) ensures that security assessments are based on the most accurate and recent configuration data.

- **Automation and efficiency**: Integration enables automated workflows and actions triggered by events or conditions in one tool. This reduces manual intervention, improves response times, and increases overall operational efficiency.

Implementing tool integrations requires understanding APIs, protocols, or interfaces provided by the tools involved and configuring them to work together. Integration capabilities can vary depending on the tools and the availability of pre-built connectors or APIs for integration purposes.

> **Important note**
>
> It is important for organizations to make sure the various tools (SIEM, ticketing, SSO, and so on) used within the organization are also part of the tools offered by CSPM vendors. CSPM vendors also must provide comprehensive guidance and support for the integration type they offer.

Let us now understand the most common integrations offered by CSPM tools.

SSO integration

SSO integration enables users to access the CSPM tool using their existing login credentials from a central IM system. This integration eliminates the need for separate login credentials, simplifies user management, and improves the user experience. Most CSPM tools are leveraged to integrate with industry-wide **identity providers** (**IDPs**) such as Okta, OneLogin, **Azure Active Directory** (**AAD**), AWS, SSO, Google Workspace, JumpCloud, Auth0, Ping Identity, and more. CSPM vendors usually also provide generic integration features for SSO integrations that are not offered directly by them.

SSO integration is a crucial step for modern security concepts such as **zero-trust architecture** (**ZTA**). Let us now understand another important topic, which is CSPM integration with ticketing tools.

Ticketing system integration

Integration with a ticketing or IM system allows the CSPM tool to automatically generate tickets or incidents when security findings or alerts are detected. This integration streamlines IR processes, ensures proper tracking and resolution of security issues, and provides a centralized view of security events. An effective CSPM tool should be able to integrate with a commonly used and wide range of ticketing tools such as BMC Remedy and ServiceNow, and agile tools such as Jira and Azure DevOps.

Ticketing tool integration is a crucial step for the remediation of security issues such as misconfigurations in the cloud environment. Let us now understand the integration of CSPM tools with communications tools.

Collaboration and communication (notifications) integrations

Integration with collaboration and communication platforms, such as Slack or Microsoft Teams, allows the CSPM tool to send real-time notifications, alerts, or reports to designated channels or individuals. This integration ensures that stakeholders are promptly informed about security events and can collaborate effectively to address them. Some of the most common notification integrations offered by CSPM tools are Slack, Microsoft Teams, PagerDuty, Opsgenie, **Google Cloud Platform (GCP) Publish/Subscribe (Pub/Sub)**, **Amazon Simple Queue Service (Amazon SQS)**, and **Amazon Simple Notification Service (Amazon SNS)**.

By leveraging Webhook integration, you can automate the transmission of alerts to external applications. This functionality is particularly useful in **client-side object model (CSOM)** automations, where alerts from the CSPM tool can be seamlessly pushed to your application when specific automation conditions are fulfilled. Typically, CSPM tools send alert data to a designated Webhook endpoint through a POST HTTP request in JSON format. Webhook integrations offer distinct advantages over API token-based integrations as they are event-driven, triggering actions as opposed to scheduled API requests.

The integration of CSPM tools with communications tools is a very important step for the remediation of severe security issues as it enables us to inform the right stakeholders at runtime. Let us now understand the integration of CSPM tools that enrich reporting capabilities.

Reporting and analytics integration

Integration with reporting and analytics platforms enables the CSPM tool to generate comprehensive security reports, visualizations, and insights. This integration allows security teams to analyze trends, track compliance status, and present the organization's security posture to stakeholders effectively. Integration can be with Microsoft Power BI and Grafana, which are the most common tools used in the industry. Using a wide range of API offerings by CSPM tools, it becomes possible to integrate these with reporting. We will discuss reporting in detail in the next section of this chapter. Let us now understand CSPM tool integration with SIEM/SOAR tools.

Monitoring (SIEM/SOAR) tool integration

Integrating SIEM and SOAR tools with CSPM solutions is a crucial part of monitoring the security of cloud infrastructure. This integration helps you centralize and automate security monitoring, incident detection, and response in your cloud environment. Let's take a closer look at this:

- **SIEM integration**: Integration between a CSPM tool and an SIEM system allows the exchange of security-related data and events. CSPM tools can feed security findings, alerts, and configuration data to the SIEM system, enriching overall security event monitoring and analysis. SIEM integration provides a broader context to CSPM data, enabling correlation with other security events across the infrastructure and enhancing threat detection capabilities.

- **SOAR integration**: CSPM tools can integrate with SOAR platforms to automate IR workflows. By exchanging data and alerts between the CSPM tool and the SOAR platform, security teams can automate response actions based on predefined playbooks or workflows. This integration streamlines IR, enables the rapid containment and remediation of security incidents, and enhances overall operational efficiency.

Using CSPM data in your applications is a key reason for configuring integration with the CSPM tool. Once the CSPM tool is integrated with your application, you can receive data from it, including data on alerts, assets, and other objects. This data can be utilized for diverse purposes such as in-depth analysis, storage, ticket creation, and more.

You can integrate your application with CSPM tools using the API and Webhooks:

- **Using API integration**: The API functionality of the CSPM tool enables you to retrieve data and perform actions within the tool, such as initiating asset scans or verifying alerts. To utilize the API, you need to set up an API token within the tool. Once the API token is configured, you can send API requests from your application to interact with the CSPM tool, accessing the desired data or triggering specific actions.

- **Using Webhook integration**: Webhooks enable the real-time pushing of alert data from the CSPM tool to your system as soon as specific alerts are identified. By incorporating Webhooks into notification integrations, you can promptly send messages or emails when critical alerts are detected, requiring immediate response actions. This ensures timely awareness and enables swift IM.

An effective CSPM tool should be able to integrate with a commonly used and wide range of SIEM/SOAR tools such as Splunk, Microsoft Sentinel, Sumo Logic, IBM QRadar, Cribl, JupiterOne, Vulcan, Chronicle, Swimlane, and more.

Storage integrations

A CSPM tool can also be integrated with the storage systems of different CSPs to enable the transmission of security-related alerts and notifications. This integration enhances the overall monitoring and IR capabilities of the CSPM tool by extending the reach of alerting mechanisms to include the storage environment. When the storage systems are integrated with the CSPM tool, you can configure sending data of the regular alert and asset reports from the tool to these storage systems for easy and convenient storing, searching, and auditing:

- **Integrating with an Amazon Simple Storage Service (S3) bucket**: Amazon S3 is a highly scalable and secure object storage solution provided by AWS. It offers reliable data availability and performance and the ability to store and retrieve data of any size. With Amazon S3, you can effectively organize your data and manage access control through S3 buckets. When integrating Amazon S3 buckets with a CSPM tool, you can configure the seamless transfer of regular alert and asset report data to the S3 buckets. This integration simplifies the auditing process by providing a convenient and centralized location for storing and accessing these reports.

- **Integrating with Azure blobs**: Azure Blob Storage is a cloud-based object storage solution provided by Microsoft. It is designed to efficiently store large volumes of unstructured data. Access to the objects stored in Blob Storage is enabled through the HTTP/HTTPS protocols. When integrating Azure Blob Storage with a CSPM tool, you gain the ability to configure the transfer of regular alert and asset report data to Blob Storage. This integration allows for multiple configurations, enabling the sending of various reports to distinct storage containers within Azure Blob Storage.

- **Integrating with a GCP bucket**: GCP buckets serve as fundamental containers for storing data in cloud storage. All data stored in the cloud storage environment must be organized within buckets. Buckets provide a means to organize and manage your data while controlling access to it. When integrating GCP buckets with your CSPM tool, you gain the ability to configure the transfer of regular alert and asset report data to GCP buckets. This integration enables the seamless and automated delivery of important reports to designated GCP buckets within your cloud storage environment.

Storage integration makes it possible to bring different sorts of logs into one bucket, and you can then decide to build cases based on requirements. Let us understand key integration challenges and the best practices to tackle them.

Key integration challenges

Integrating a CSPM tool with other tools or systems can bring several challenges. However, by following best practices, organizations can overcome these challenges and ensure successful integration. Let us look at the challenges when integrating a CSPM tool with other tools.

Data quality

Integrating a CSPM tool with other tools can introduce several **data quality** (**DQ**) challenges. These challenges can impact the accuracy and reliability of the data used by the CSPM tool and other security and compliance tools. Let us look at some DQ challenges:

- **Data inconsistencies**: Different tools and systems use varying data formats and structures. Integrating them may lead to data inconsistencies, making it challenging to correlate and analyze the data accurately.

- **Data duplication**: Integration processes can sometimes inadvertently duplicate data, leading to issues with data accuracy and complicating data management.

- **Data silos**: If data is not effectively shared between integrated tools, it may lead to data silos, where certain tools have access to only a subset of the data, potentially resulting in incomplete or inaccurate insights.

- **Data mapping and transformation**: Mapping and transforming data from one format to another during integration can introduce errors or data loss if not done correctly, affecting DQ.

- **Data validation and cleansing**: If data validation and cleansing processes are omitted or inadequately implemented during integration, it may lead to inaccuracies, inconsistencies, and missing data.

- **Data latency**: Delays in data transmission between integrated tools can result in data that is not up to date, which can impact the accuracy of security and compliance assessments.

- **Data governance alignment**: Ensuring that DQ standards and governance policies are maintained during integration can be challenging, leading to potential DQ issues.

- **Data source reliability**: The reliability and trustworthiness of data sources used by integrated tools may vary, affecting the overall DQ.

Mitigating DQ challenges requires careful planning and adherence to best practices. Some mitigation strategies include the following:

- Standardizing data formats and structures across integrated tools

- Implementing data validation and cleansing processes to detect and rectify DQ issues

- Developing a data governance framework that encompasses DQ standards and policies

- Ensuring data mapping and transformation processes are accurate and comprehensive

- Implementing data integration platforms or middleware solutions that can normalize and synchronize data efficiently

- Monitoring and auditing DQ continuously and addressing issues as they arise

- Establishing clear data ownership and stewardship responsibilities

Handling scalability, performance, and maintenance requirements can be challenging, requiring careful planning and resource allocation.

Data governance

Integrating a CSPM tool with other tools can introduce various data governance challenges. Data governance is essential for ensuring DQ, security, and compliance, and these challenges can impact the overall effectiveness of the integration. Let us take a look at some common data governance challenges:

- **Data ownership**: Determining data ownership responsibilities for data used by integrated tools can be complex, leading to ambiguities regarding who is accountable for DQ and data security.

- **Data privacy and compliance**: Maintaining data privacy and compliance with data protection regulations is critical. Integrating tools may expose sensitive data, increasing the risk of non-compliance and privacy breaches.

- **Data access control**: Coordinating and enforcing consistent data access control policies across integrated tools can be challenging, potentially leading to unauthorized access or data leakage.

- **Metadata management**: Creating and maintaining a comprehensive metadata management system to track data sources, definitions, lineage, and attributes across integrated tools can be resource-intensive.

- **Data lineage**: Ensuring data lineage is tracked accurately and consistently as data flows between integrated tools can be difficult, making it challenging to trace the origin and transformations of data.

- **Data governance policies**: Integrating tools may require adapting or aligning data governance policies across different systems, which can result in conflicts or gaps in policy enforcement.

- **Compatibility**: Ensuring compatibility between the CSPM tool and the target tool or system can be challenging. Differences in data formats, APIs, authentication mechanisms, or protocols may require additional configuration or customization for seamless integration.

- **Data collection**: Collecting data from various cloud services, such as **virtual machines (VMs)**, storage accounts, databases, and containers, can be complex due to differences in data formats, access controls, and logging mechanisms across providers.

- **Data synchronization**: Keeping data synchronized and up to date between the CSPM tool and other tools can be a challenge. Changes or updates made in one system may need to be reflected in the integrated systems in a timely and accurate manner.

- **Security and access control**: Integrating multiple tools introduces potential security risks, such as exposing sensitive data or creating new attack vectors. Ensuring proper access controls, secure data transmission, and encryption measures is crucial to maintaining a secure integration environment.

- **Complexity and scalability**: Managing integrations between multiple tools can become complex, especially as the number of integrated systems increases.

Mitigating data governance challenges during the integration of CSPM tools with other tools involves the following best practices:

- Establish clear data ownership roles and responsibilities to ensure accountability for DQ and data security

- Implement robust data privacy and compliance measures to protect sensitive data, such as encryption, access controls, and data masking

- Create a centralized data catalog and metadata management system to document data sources, definitions, lineage, and attributes

- Implement data access controls consistently across integrated tools to prevent unauthorized access

- Maintain data lineage tracking to ensure that the path of data is clearly understood and documented

- Review and adapt data governance policies and standards to align with integrated tools while maintaining DQ and data security

- Monitor and audit data governance practices continuously, ensuring adherence to policies and standards

Leveraging AI to build proactive DQ and data governance processes

DQ and data governance are reactive processes; however, with recent advancements in **artificial intelligence** (**AI**), a proactive process can be developed for early detection and remediation of these DQ and data governance issues. Let's break down the key aspects of this approach:

- **Automated configuration monitoring**: A CSPM tool leveraged with AI-enhanced anomaly detection algorithms can continuously monitor cloud configurations, looking for anomalies or deviations from established security and governance policies. By understanding normal configuration patterns, AI can quickly identify potential issues. AI can be programmed to perform DQ checks directly within cloud configurations, ensuring that data storage, access controls, and encryption settings align with governance and quality standards.

- **Continuous compliance monitoring**: AI-driven policy enforcement can assist in enforcing data governance policies by continuously monitoring cloud resources for compliance with industry standards and regulations. This proactive approach helps identify non-compliant configurations that may impact DQ. AI algorithms can analyze configurations and access patterns to identify potential governance violations, such as unauthorized access or data usage, triggering alerts for prompt remediation at a very early stage proactively.

- **Threat detection and IR**: AI-powered behavioral analytics can be employed to analyze user and entity behavior within the cloud environment. This helps in the early detection of suspicious activities that may pose threats to both security and DQ. AI can be integrated into IR mechanisms to align with data governance policies, ensuring a coordinated approach to addressing security incidents that may impact data integrity.

- **Vulnerability management**: AI can analyze data from vulnerability scanners and other security tools to identify potential vulnerabilities in cloud infrastructure. This proactive identification allows organizations to remediate vulnerabilities before they can be exploited. AI can assess the potential impact of vulnerabilities on DQ, helping prioritize remediation efforts based on the criticality of the affected data.

- **Automated IR**: Develop IR playbooks with AI-driven automation to expedite the remediation of security incidents. This ensures a rapid and consistent response to incidents that may have implications for DQ and governance.

- **Collaboration with data governance**: Integrate AI-driven CSPM with data governance processes to create a unified strategy. This involves aligning security policies with data governance requirements to ensure comprehensive protection for both security and DQ. AI can facilitate cross-domain analysis, assessing how changes in security configurations may impact DQ and governance, providing a holistic view of the potential risks and their remediation.

Leveraging AI for CSPM to build a proactive DQ and data governance process involves incorporating AI capabilities into security practices to detect and remediate issues that may impact the integrity, availability, and compliance of data stored in the cloud. This integrated approach can ensure a robust and proactive stance toward managing both security and data governance in cloud environments. Let us now dive deep into the best practices involved in overcoming integration challenges.

Best practices to overcome integration challenges

As mentioned, integrating a CSPM tool with your organization's infrastructure ecosystem can lead to various challenges. To overcome these challenges and ensure a successful integration, consider the following mitigation best practices:

- **Clearly define integration objectives**: Clearly define the objectives and expected outcomes of the integration. Identify specific use cases and requirements that the integration should address. This helps ensure that the integration efforts are focused and aligned with the organization's goals.

- **Thoroughly assess integration compatibility**: Conduct a thorough assessment of the compatibility between the CSPM tool and the target tools or systems. Verify data formats, APIs, authentication mechanisms, and protocols to identify any potential compatibility issues in advance.

- **Utilize standard protocols and APIs**: Whenever possible, use standard protocols and APIs for integration. Standardization simplifies integration efforts, reduces complexity, and promotes interoperability between systems.

- **Implement secure communication**: Implement secure communication channels and encryption mechanisms when transferring data between systems. Secure data transmission protects sensitive information and mitigates the risk of data breaches during integration.

- **Follow security best practices**: Apply security best practices throughout the integration process. Implement appropriate access controls, authentication mechanisms, and authorization mechanisms to ensure that only authorized users and systems can access integrated data.

- **Monitor and test the integration**: Regularly monitor and test the integration to ensure its proper functioning. Monitor data synchronization, error handling, and system performance to identify and address any issues promptly.

- **Establish documentation and support**: Document the integration process, including configuration settings, data mappings, and troubleshooting guidelines. Provide support and training to users or administrators who interact with the integrated systems to ensure smooth operation and effective utilization of the integration.

- **Regularly review and update integrations**: Conduct periodic reviews of integrations to assess their effectiveness and address any evolving requirements or changes. Stay updated with new releases, patches, or updates from both the CSPM tool and the integrated systems to maintain compatibility and security.

By adhering to these best practices, organizations can successfully integrate their CSPM tool with other systems, enhance overall security and compliance capabilities, streamline operations, and leverage the combined functionalities of multiple tools for improved **cloud security management** (**CSM**).

Let us now understand how to set up effective reporting in a CSPM tool.

Setting up an effective reporting environment

Setting up effective reporting in a CSPM tool involves careful planning and configuration to ensure that the reports generated provide valuable insights into your cloud security posture. Here is a general guide to help you set up the reporting environment as per industry best practices:

- **Identify reporting requirements**: Clearly define the objectives of your reporting. Identify key stakeholders who will be consuming the reports and understand their specific requirements. Determine the frequency, scope, and depth of the reports based on these requirements.

  For example, determine reporting requirements for compliance. It is crucial to understand the compliance frameworks or regulations applicable to your organization.

- **Identify relevant metrics**: Identify key metrics and security controls that are critical to monitor and report on. These metrics can include factors such as misconfigurations, compliance violations, access controls, network security, data encryption, and more.

  For example, ensure that the selected metrics align with your organization's security policies, compliance frameworks, and industry best practices.

- **Select report types**: Determine the types of reports you need to generate. In addition to compliance reports, you may also require vulnerability reports, risk assessment reports, asset inventory reports, or any other reports relevant to your CSM objectives; for example, management reports about the overall improvement of the vulnerability posture over time.

- **Define report templates**: Create or customize report templates that align with your reporting requirements. These templates should include sections and placeholders for the required data, metrics, visualizations, and any compliance-related information.

- **Identify data sources**: Identify data sources that provide the necessary information for generating reports. This includes integration with CSP APIs, CMDBs, vulnerability assessment tools, or other relevant systems that capture the required data for the reports.

- **Configure data collection**: Configure the CSPM tool to collect the relevant data for report generation. Specify the data collection settings, such as the frequency of data collection, specific metrics, or events to be captured, and any filters or criteria to apply during data collection.

- **Data processing and analysis**: Once the data is collected, the CSPM tool processes and analyzes it to generate insights, compliance status, and other relevant information. This involves applying compliance frameworks, risk algorithms, or custom rulesets to assess the security posture and compliance levels.

- **Report generation and customization**: Utilize report templates and processed data to generate reports. The CSPM tool should provide functionality or reporting modules to customize reports based on your specific requirements. Customize data visualizations, including summary statistics, graphs, tables, and charts, and ensure the report layout meets your needs.

- **Schedule report generation**: Set up a schedule for automatic report generation based on the desired frequency (for example, daily, weekly, or monthly). Configure the CSPM tool to generate compliance reports and other reports at specified intervals.

- **Distribution and delivery**: Determine recipients or stakeholders who should receive the reports. Configure the CSPM tool to automatically distribute generated reports to the designated recipients via email, file-sharing platforms, or other delivery methods. Ensure proper access controls and encryption measures are in place to protect the confidentiality and integrity of reports during transmission. You can also consider building a unified dashboard for different stakeholders using tools such as Microsoft Power BI or Grafana.

- **Monitoring and maintenance**: Regularly monitor the reporting environment to ensure that reports are generated correctly, data sources are up to date, and delivery mechanisms are functioning properly. Perform periodic checks and updates to report templates, data collection settings, and distribution settings as needed.

- **Continuous improvement and feedback**: It is important to seek feedback from report recipients to understand their needs and preferences. Continuously improve the reporting process by incorporating feedback, refining report templates, and enhancing data analysis techniques.

You can overcome challenges and establish an effective reporting environment within the CSPM tool. This enables informed decision-making, improved compliance monitoring, and enhanced visibility into the security posture of the cloud environment. Let us now understand another component of environment settings, which is activity logging.

Activity logging

Activity logging refers to the process of recording and tracking activities and events within the CSPM environment. It involves capturing relevant information about user actions, system activities, and security events to maintain an audit trail for monitoring, analysis, and compliance purposes. These activities also include changes to configurations, user access and permissions, network traffic, system events, and more. The *purpose* of activity logging is to provide a comprehensive audit trail and visibility into actions and behaviors within the cloud infrastructure, helping organizations monitor, detect, and respond to security threats and compliance issues. Let us now understand the key elements associated with activity logging.

User activities

Activity logging records user actions within the CSPM tool, such as user logins, changes to user permissions, configuration modifications, and execution of various operations or tasks. These actions include the following:

- **User authentication and authorization**: Logging user logins, successful and failed authentication attempts, and authorization decisions (for example, granting or revoking user access)

- **Resource provisioning and management**: Tracking actions such as creating, modifying, or deleting cloud resources such as VMs, databases, storage buckets, network configurations, and so on

- **Configuration changes**: Recording modifications made to the configuration settings of cloud services, such as firewall rules, access controls, encryption settings, or any other parameters that affect security and compliance

- **Data access and manipulation**: Logging when users access or modify data stored within the cloud environment, including reading, writing, or deleting files, databases, or other sensitive information

- **Account and identity management**: Tracking changes related to user accounts, such as user creation and deletion, password resets, or changes to user roles and permissions such as privilege escalation

---

Vendor access to customer CSPM environment – benefits, risks, and best practices

Benefits: It is quite common for vendor-side engineers to have access to your CSPM environment in the deployment phase. Usually, vendors provide support for the smooth deployment of the tool, and it is quite beneficial and time-saving for customers. Sometimes, it is also beneficial to extend permissions to the vendor side when a customer needs help with investigations into abnormal behavior of tools or with some exceptional cases. These situations continue to grow and are not rare.

Risks: Having vendor access to your environment introduces risks such as exposure to security loopholes, data infiltrations, data theft, and more. Organizations need to be aware of these situations and should introduce certain measures to mitigate those risks.

Best practices: The first and most important action is to have a **non-disclosure agreement** (**NDA**) signed by the vendor that is legally binding and establishes a confidential relationship. This makes the vendor agree that sensitive information they may obtain will not be made available to others. There must not be default and forever access to the vendor. If needed, the CSPM admin should provide time-bound access to the tool and must revoke access as soon as the support task is completed. During this period, a complete activities log *must* be tracked, stored, and reviewed. It is also important to understand that most CSPM tools are offered as SaaS versions, and hence as a CSPM customer, you do not have visibility of the inline infrastructure of the tool. However, on the application front, the customer must have complete visibility and control of the user's activities.

System activities

System activities refer to events and actions related to the underlying cloud infrastructure of CSPM tools and their components. Some examples include IT captures, system-level activities, including system startup and shutdown, data synchronization processes, data backups, and system health monitoring.

> **Note**
>
> As mentioned previously, most modern CSPM tools are offered as a SaaS version, and hence, as a customer, you are not responsible for the health of the inline infrastructure of the CSPM tool. It is the CSPM vendor's responsibility to maintain and secure online infrastructure such as system activities. Based on mutual agreement or for transparency, vendors *can* and *should* share the high-level penetration testing report or **System and Organizations Controls 2 (SOC 2)**-type report of their infrastructure. However, read on to understand the full context.

Let's look at this in more detail:

- **System startup and shutdown**: Recording when cloud services, VMs, or containers start or stop running

- **Resource allocation and deallocation**: Logging events related to the allocation and deallocation of computing resources, such as VM instances, storage volumes, or network resources

- **Network traffic and communication**: Capturing network-related activities, including incoming and outgoing traffic, communication between different cloud resources, and network security events such as port scanning or suspicious network connections

- **Performance monitoring**: Tracking system performance metrics such as CPU utilization, memory usage, disk I/O, or network latency to identify potential bottlenecks, resource constraints, or anomalies

Security events

Security events represent activities or incidents that have potential security implications or indicate a breach or violation. It also monitors and logs security-related events and incidents, such as policy violations, unauthorized access attempts, potential breaches, or changes to security configurations. Let's look at some examples:

- **Intrusion attempts**: Logging activities such as failed login attempts, brute-force attacks, or unauthorized access attempts to systems or applications

- **Malware or virus detection**: Recording events related to the detection or quarantine of malware, viruses, or other malicious software within the cloud environment

- **Security policy violations**: Capturing events that indicate violations of security policies, such as attempts to bypass security controls, unauthorized changes to configurations, or non-compliance with regulatory requirements

- **Anomalies and suspicious behavior**: Logging activities that deviate from normal patterns or behavior, such as unusual login times, repeated failed authentication attempts, or abnormal resource usage

- **Security IR**: Documenting actions taken during IR, including alerts triggered, investigations conducted, containment measures implemented, and remediation steps performed

Challenges in activity logging

Let's look at some challenges:

- **Log volume and storage**: CSPM tools generate a significant volume of log data, especially in large-scale environments. Managing and storing this data can be a challenge, requiring adequate storage capacity and efficient log management practices.

- **Log integrity and protection**: Ensuring the integrity and protection of log data is essential. Unauthorized access or tampering with logs can undermine the reliability and accuracy of the audit trail.

- **Log retention and compliance**: Compliance requirements may dictate specific log retention periods. Managing long retention policies and ensuring compliance with regulatory guidelines can be challenging, especially in complex or highly regulated environments.

Best practices for activity logging

Here are a few best practices:

- **Log aggregation and centralization**: Aggregate logs from various sources within the CSPM environment into a centralized logging system. Centralized logging simplifies log management, analysis, and correlation.

- **Log format standardization**: Standardize log formats and structures to facilitate log analysis and correlation across different CSPM tools and systems. Adhering to common log formats simplifies log management and enables better interoperability with log analysis tools.

- **Secure log storage**: Implement secure log storage mechanisms to protect log data from unauthorized access or tampering. Encrypt log data at rest and in transit and restrict access to logs based on PoLP.

- **Log retention and rotation**: Define and adhere to log retention policies based on compliance requirements. Implement log rotation practices to manage log volume and ensure optimal storage utilization.

- **Log analysis and monitoring**: Establish processes and tools for log analysis and real-time monitoring. Proactively analyze log data for anomalies, security incidents, or policy violations to identify potential threats or vulnerabilities.

- **Integration with SIEM/log management systems**: Integrate the CSPM tool's activity logs with SIEM or log management systems. This integration enhances the correlation and analysis of log data with other security events across the infrastructure.

- **Regular log reviews and audits**: Conduct regular log reviews and audits to detect any suspicious activities, identify patterns, and ensure compliance with security policies and regulatory requirements.

- **IR and forensics**: Leverage activity logs for IR and forensic investigations. Detailed logs can provide critical information for **root cause analysis** (**RCA**), impact assessment, and identifying remediation actions.

By carefully considering the aforementioned challenges and best practices, you can gain valuable insights into the cloud environment, identify potential security threats or compliance issues, and respond effectively to incidents or breaches. These logs are essential for security monitoring, IR, forensic investigations, and overall cloud infrastructure governance.

Summary

Setting the CSPM environment is a crucial procedure for tools as it establishes the foundation for effective CSM. In this chapter, we delved into crucial topics such as user management, permissions settings, integrations with other tools, reporting capabilities, challenges, and best practices to overcome challenges. In the next chapter, we will deep dive into cloud asset inventory.

Further reading

To learn more about the topics that were covered in this chapter, take a look at the following resources:

- *Key requirements of a modern CSPM* (`https://www.wiz.io/academy/what-are-the-key-requirements-of-a-modern-cspm`)

- *How Gartner Defines CSPM and 3 Tips for Success* (`https://www.aquasec.com/cloud-native-academy/cspm/gartner-cspm/`)

Part 3: Security Posture Enhancement

In this part, you will delve into the operational dimensions of CSPM. It is specially designed for those seeking to enhance the security posture of their cloud footprints. You will explore cloud asset inventory and review CSPM dashboards to gain crucial insights into your cloud environment. The chapters in this part address major configuration risks, investigating risks with attack path analysis, vulnerability and patch management, compliance management and governance, and the intricacies of security alerts and monitoring. This part provides a comprehensive approach to deepen your practical understanding of the operational aspects of CSPM, ensuring the development of a robust CSPM strategy for your cloud infrastructure.

This part contains the following chapters:

- *Chapter 9, Exploring Cloud Asset Inventory*
- *Chapter 10, Reviewing CSPM Dashboards*
- *Chapter 11, Major Configuration Risks*
- *Chapter 12, Investigating Threats with Query Explorer and KQL*
- *Chapter 13, Vulnerability and Patch Management*
- *Chapter 14, Compliance Management and Governance*
- *Chapter 15, Security Alerts and Monitoring*

9

Exploring Cloud Asset Inventory

As organizations harness the benefits of cloud infrastructure, they must also grapple with the inherent challenges of ensuring robust security measures across their cloud environments. This chapter delves into asset inventory, which is the crucial component of a CSPM. We will explore the intricacies of effectively managing and securing cloud assets, providing a comprehensive overview of the tools, techniques, and best practices involved. By conducting thorough asset inventory management, we'll delve into the vital components of maintaining a strong cloud security posture. Join us as we navigate the complex landscape of cloud security and unveil the strategies and methodologies necessary to safeguard organizations' valuable digital assets in an ever-evolving threat landscape.

In this chapter, we'll cover the following topics:

- Understanding the cloud asset inventory landscape
- Asset categorization and classifications
- Key challenges in asset inventory management
- Best practices for asset inventory management
- Other tools and techniques for asset discovery

Let's get started!

Understanding the cloud asset inventory landscape

Inventory refers to all the assets in your cloud environment. Assets are the objects of cloud infrastructure. Inventory landscape refers to recognizing and comprehending the various asset types that exist within a cloud environment. These assets encompass a range of digital resources and components essential for operating in the cloud. CSPM tools scan the assets for any abnormal behavior, vulnerabilities, or malware attacks. Analyzing both the impacted asset and its interconnected assets is essential to comprehend the potential spread of an attack across the network. This analysis helps in understanding the attack vectors and identifying vulnerabilities or weak links in the system. CSPM tools offer a comprehensive set of features and information for conducting asset and alert analysis, empowering organizations to gain deep insights into their cloud security posture. We will deep dive into alert investigations later; for now, we'll focus on the core aspects of cloud assets.

Cloud assets overview

Assets are the objects of cloud infrastructure that are protected by CSPM tools. These assets can include virtual machines, databases, applications, files, configurations, and other types of digital information that are hosted and managed in the cloud. The following figure shows the inventory dashboard of the Microsoft Defender for Cloud CSPM tool. At a very high level, you can see the total resources onboarded to the CSPM tool, the number of unhealthy resources, the number of unmanaged resources, and the number of unregistered cloud accounts. Dashboards are customizable and vary by CSPM tool. You also get the option to download the inventory in the form of a CSV report, open a query on the inventory, and more. We will dive deep into dashboards in *Chapter 10*:

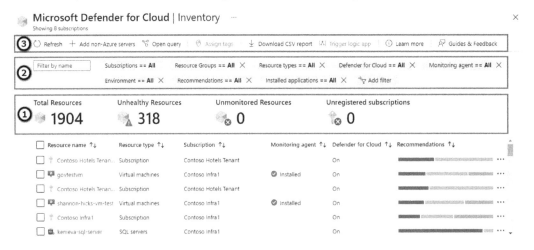

Figure 9.1 – CSPM inventory dashboard (source: https://learn.microsoft.com/en-us/azure/defender-for-cloud/asset-inventory)

Let's understand some important properties of assets that can help us uniquely identify and manage their security posture.

Asset properties

Assets can be super complex with multiple properties, and it can be incredibly challenging to manage them for an organization that has a huge footprint in a multi-cloud environment. The key properties of an asset are as follows:

- **Asset name**: The asset's (a virtual machine, database, or network) instance name.

- **Asset type**: This refers to whether the instance is a virtual machine, Kubernetes instance, or something else.

- **Cloud account**: This provides the name of the cloud provider that the asset originally belonged to.

- **Tags**: Tags are crucial properties to import from a cloud environment to CSPM tools as they provide additional context for the asset. This can include the asset owner, asset department, or any other specific details about the assets. Tags are helpful for security teams to easily recognize the asset owner and reach out in case of any critical situations.

- **Asset status**: Status indicates the operational status of the asset. This is dependent on the asset's type. For example, if the asset is a virtual machine instance, then this option dictates whether it is currently *running* or *stopped*. If the asset belongs to databases, users, accounts, or serverless functions, its status can be *enabled* or *disabled*.

- **Exposure**: This property helps determine whether an asset can be accessed from the internet, after which its level of exposure can be assessed. This provides insights into the potential security risks and vulnerabilities associated with the asset.

- **Asset category/group**: This is a logical set of assets that you can use to easily find all database instances. For example, all instances of databases, buckets, container registries, filesystems, and other similar asset types can be grouped under these names.

- **Attack path**: An attack path serves as a visual representation of how an adversary can exploit a discovered vulnerability, outlining the sequence of steps from the initial point of entry to the ultimate target. It highlights the vulnerabilities present on the selected asset and demonstrates how they can be exploited either directly on that asset or through lateral movement to reach more critical assets, often referred to as *crown jewel* assets.

- **Recommendations**: While other CSPM tools also provide similar features, recommendations are exclusive to Microsoft Defender for Cloud. It provides the assets with violating policies that you have applied to it.

Asset properties provide essential information about these assets, which is valuable for tracking, managing, and securing them. Now, let's understand how assets can be classified.

Cloud asset classification

Assets are organized into categories and subcategories based on their similarities and shared properties. These predefined categories and subcategories provide a structured framework for managing assets within a CSPM system. Cloud assets can vary in their importance and sensitivity to an organization. By classifying assets properly, organizations can prioritize their security efforts and allocate appropriate resources. For example, critical assets such as customer databases or financial systems may require stricter security controls compared to less critical assets such as development environments.

Purpose-based classifications (categories and groups)

Assets can be classified based on their intended purpose within the organization's cloud infrastructure. This classification considers the specific role or function of the asset and how it contributes to business operations. By applying filters based on categories and subcategories, you can narrow down your search and focus on specific groups of assets based on the purpose they serve. Let's look at the different asset classifications that most CSPM tools use:

- **Compute services**: These are virtualized instances of computing resources, such as servers, operating systems, and applications. Virtual machines provide the foundation for running software and processing data in the cloud. Compute services can further be sub-categorized as follows:

  - **Virtual instances**: Examples include Amazon EC2 instances, Azure Virtual Machines, and Google Compute Engines

  - **Containers**: Examples include Azure Container Instances and Amazon Fargate

  - **Serverless**: Examples include **Amazon Web Services** (**AWS**) Lambda Functions, Azure Functions, Azure Functions app, and Google Cloud Functions

  - **Image**: Examples include **Azure Container Registry** (**ACR**) images, Amazon **Elastic Container Registry** (**ECR**) images, and **Google Container Registry** (**GCR**) images

- **Data storage**: Cloud databases store, organize, and manage structured and unstructured data. They offer scalable storage and retrieval capabilities, facilitating data-driven applications and analytics. Along with other cloud resources, CSPM tools fetch data storage and sub-categorize it into different logical groupings based on the common features that the data storage shares. Let's look at some common groupings:

  - **Database**: Examples include Amazon DynamoDB instances, Amazon Kafka cluster, Amazon **Relational Database Service** (**RDS**) instances, Azure Cosmos DB, Azure Data Factory, Azure MySQL DB, and Google Redis Instances

  - **Storage buckets**: Examples include AWS S3 buckets, Azure File Share, Azure Blob Storage, Google Storage buckets, and an Azure storage account

- **Filesystem**: Examples include Azure Disk, Amazon **Elastic File System** (**EFS**), Azure Snapshot, Google VM Snapshot, and Amazon **Elastic Block Store** (**EBS**)

- **Messaging and queue**: Examples include Azure Storage Queue, Amazon **Simple Queue Service** (**SQS**), and Azure Service Bus

- **Container registry**: Examples Cloud include Amazon ECR Repository, Azure Container Registry, and Google Cloud Artifact Registry

- **Networks**: Cloud networks enable communication between various cloud resources, such as virtual machines, databases, and containers. They facilitate secure data transfer and connectivity within the cloud infrastructure. Let's understand what assets fall under the Networks category and how they are usually categorized:

  - **Load balancers**: Examples include AWS ELB, Amazon EC2 load balancers, Azure load balancers, Azure HTTP Listener, Azure Application Gateways, and GCP load balancers

  - **Domain name system** (**DNS**): Examples include AWS Route 53 Domain, AWS Route 53 Host Zone, Azure DNS Hosted Zone, Domain, and GCP DNS Managed Zone

  - **Content delivery network** (**CDN**): Examples include AWS CloudFront, Azure Front Door, and Google Cloud CDN

  - **Public exposure**: Examples include domains and IP addresses

  - **API endpoints**: An example is cloud-managed endpoints

  - **Network segmentation and security**: Examples include Azure **Network Security Group** (**NSG**), Amazon EC2 security groups, Amazon **Virtual Private Network** (**VPN**) Gateway, network interfaces, AWS Subnet, AWS **Virtual Private Cloud** (**VPC**), cloud-native firewalls and **Web Application Firewalls** (**WAFs**), Azure Public IP, Azure Subnet, API Gateways, and Azure Virtual Network

- **Encryption and secrets**: These provide a comprehensive record of the encryption status and management of sensitive information within an organization's assets. It encompasses identifying assets that store or process sensitive data, tracking their encryption levels, and managing encryption keys and secrets associated with those assets. Let's understand how assets associated with encryption are categorized:

  - **Encryption keys**: Examples include AWS Cloud **Hardware Security Module** (**HSM**), AWS **Key Management Services** (**KMS**), Azure Key Vault, Google Cloud KMS, and **customer-managed keys** (**CMKs**)

  - **Secrets**: Examples include Azure Key Vault secrets, auth tokens, customer secret keys, and API keys

  - **Certificates**: Examples include AWS certificates, Azure Key Vault certificates, and Google Cloud SSL certificates

- **Kubernetes**: This refers to the comprehensive record of the Kubernetes resources and configurations that have been deployed within an organization's Kubernetes clusters. It encompasses identifying, tracking, and managing the various assets within the Kubernetes environment. Let's understand how Kubernetes assets are usually categorized, which can be super helpful for further management:

  - **Kubernetes clusters**: Examples include AWS EKS clusters, Azure AKS clusters, GKE clusters, and self-managed clusters

  - **Kubernetes controller**: Examples include Kubernetes config maps, Kubernetes daemon sets, Kubernetes services, and Kubernetes deployments

  - **Kubernetes network**: Examples include Kubernetes endpoints and Kubernetes network policies

  - **Kubernetes compute**: Examples include Kubernetes namespaces and Kubernetes nodes

Furthermore, recognizing the distinctions between **Infrastructure-as-a-Service** (**IaaS**), **Platform-as-a-Service** (**PaaS**), and **Software-as-a-Service** (**SaaS**) assets is essential. In IaaS, organizations have more control over the underlying infrastructure, including virtual machines and networks. PaaS provides a higher level of abstraction, offering a platform for developing and deploying applications without worrying about the infrastructure details. SaaS delivers complete software applications hosted and managed by the cloud provider. Refer to *Chapter 1* to understand the cloud security responsibility matrix in detail. By discerning the service model associated with each asset, organizations can determine the level of control and responsibility they have in managing and securing those assets.

This understanding is crucial for effective cloud security posture management as it allows for accurate asset identification, tracking, and the ability to implement the appropriate security controls for each asset type. We will dive deep into this later.

Criticality-based classification

Assets are classified based on their criticality to the organization's operations. This classification considers the potential impact on the organization if the asset becomes unavailable or compromised. Let's look at some examples:

- **Mission-critical assets**: Assets that are vital for the organization's core operations. The loss or compromise of these assets could significantly impact business continuity.

- **High-value assets**: Assets that are important but not as critical as mission-critical assets. Their compromise or unavailability can cause disruptions but may not result in severe consequences.

- **Non-critical assets**: Assets that are less essential for immediate operations. Their compromise or unavailability may have minimal impact on business continuity.

- **Development/test environments**: Assets that are used for software development, testing, and staging purposes.

- **Backup and recovery systems**: Assets that are dedicated to storing backup copies of data or disaster recovery.

Sensitivity-based classification

Assets/resources can be classified based on the sensitivity of the information they handle or process. This classification considers the level of sensitivity of the data stored, transmitted, or processed by the asset. Here are some examples:

- **Personally identifiable information (PII) assets**: Assets that handle sensitive personal information, such as customer data, social security numbers, or medical records.

- **Intellectual property (IP) assets**: Assets that store or process proprietary or confidential information, such as trade secrets, patents, or research data.

- **Public information assets**: Assets that handle non-sensitive information intended for public access, such as publicly available web pages or marketing collateral.

- **Protected health information (PHI) assets**: PHI is a specific category of sensitive and confidential information related to an individual's medical or healthcare records, as defined by the **Health Insurance Portability and Accountability Act (HIPAA)** in the United States.

- **Payment card industry (PCI) assets**: PCI assets are subject to PCI, which is a set of security standards designed to protect cardholder data and ensure the secure handling of payment card transactions. PCI assets include various hardware, software, and systems that are involved in credit card payment processing.

By categorizing cloud assets based on their purpose, criticality, and sensitivity, organizations can allocate appropriate security measures and resources. For example, mission-critical assets with sensitive data may require stricter access controls, regular monitoring, and additional security layers. On the other hand, non-critical assets may have less stringent security requirements.

Tagging concepts and asset classification

Tagging is a system of labeling or categorizing assets and resources within an organization using descriptive labels, or "tags," to make them easier to organize, track, and manage. Tags are short descriptions or keywords that can be attached to assets to provide information about their attributes, purpose, location, asset owner, or security contact. Tagging assets is crucial because it provides a structured and efficient way to categorize, organize, and manage resources, especially for organizations with complex infrastructure. Let's understand tagging by considering a use case.

One common use case for tagging is in cloud computing and infrastructure management. Cloud service providers allow users to tag various cloud resources, such as virtual machines, storage buckets, or databases. These tags are helpful for the following purposes:

- **Cost allocation and budgeting**: By tagging cloud resources with attributes such as a project name, department, or environment (for example, production or development), organizations can allocate costs and track expenses more accurately. This is crucial for budgeting and understanding how resources are being utilized by different teams or projects.

- **Security incident contacts**: By tagging resources as owned-by or managed-by, you can easily reach out to the owner if there are security events/incidents or breaches. This is crucial when an asset is under attack or your security system generates critical alerts where every second is paramount.

- **Resource management**: Tags make it easier to organize and manage a large number of cloud resources. For example, by tagging resources with the `Environment: Production` label, administrators can quickly identify and manage critical production systems and apply specific policies and access controls.

- **Security and access control**: Tags can be used to define security and access policies. For instance, resources tagged as *confidential* can have stricter access controls in place to protect sensitive data.

- **Resource life cycle**: Tags can indicate the stage of the resource life cycle, making it clear whether a resource is in active use, pending decommissioning, or part of a testing environment.

- **Automation**: Tags can be used to trigger automation actions. For instance, when a resource is tagged with `Backup: Daily`, an automated process can be initiated to schedule daily backups for that resource.

By using tagging in cloud computing, organizations can efficiently manage, allocate costs, and maintain control over their cloud resources, improving both the operational and financial aspects of cloud infrastructure management.

How to manage tags effectively

Tagging can be a lifesaver if utilized properly. However, if you do not manage the tags themselves effectively, then you may lose the whole purpose of using them. Let's look at some effective ways we can manage tags:

- **Consistency**: Define a consistent set of tags and ensure that they are used uniformly across the organization. Consistency makes it easier for everyone to understand and apply tags correctly.

- **Taxonomy**: Organize tags into a logical hierarchy or taxonomy that makes sense for your organization. This helps in categorizing and searching for assets more efficiently.

- **Training and education**: Train your team on the use and importance of tags. Ensure that they understand how to assign, modify, and interpret tags correctly.

- **Regular review**: Periodically review and update tags to adapt to changes in your organization's asset inventory. As assets change or new ones are added, your tags may need to be modified to stay relevant.

- **Governance**: Establish a governance process for managing tags. This may include defining policies and procedures for creating, modifying, and retiring tags, as well as assigning responsibility for tag management.

Using tags to manage assets simplifies asset organization and access control, enhances visibility and compliance, and streamlines asset management processes, ultimately contributing to improved efficiency and better control over your organization's resources.

This classification helps organizations prioritize their security efforts, focus on protecting high-value assets, allocate resources effectively, and tailor security controls based on the specific classification of each asset. It ensures that security measures align with the importance and sensitivity of the assets, enhancing the overall security posture of the cloud infrastructure.

Key challenges in asset inventory management

As we've discussed, asset inventory management is a critical aspect of cybersecurity, and CSPM tools are designed to help organizations monitor and manage their cloud infrastructure for security risks and compliance. However, managing asset inventory effectively can present several challenges:

- **The dynamic nature of cloud assets**: One of the primary challenges in gaining visibility into cloud assets is their dynamic nature. Cloud environments are highly agile, allowing assets to be provisioned, modified, or decommissioned rapidly. This dynamic nature makes it challenging to keep track of the current state of assets, their configurations, and their relationships with other resources. CSPM tools need to continuously discover and track assets across multiple cloud providers, regions, and accounts.

- **Multi-cloud, hybrid cloud environments, and colocation (COLO)**: Many organizations utilize multiple cloud service providers, maintain a hybrid cloud, or utilize COLO. Managing asset inventory across diverse environments adds complexity as each provider or infrastructure has different APIs, access controls, and discovery mechanisms. CSPM tools should support a wide range of cloud platforms and provide comprehensive asset visibility.

> COLO
>
> **Colocation**, or **COLO**, is a facility where organizations can rent space, power, cooling, and network connectivity to house their own server and networking equipment. Organizations own and maintain their hardware and equipment, while the COLO facility provides the physical environment. It's a cost-effective solution for organizations that want control over their hardware and infrastructure without the upfront capital investment of building their data centers.

- **Shadow IT and unauthorized assets**: Shadow IT refers to employees utilizing cloud services or resources without the knowledge or approval of the IT department. It involves the unauthorized adoption of technology outside the purview of IT governance and can pose various security and compliance risks. These unauthorized assets can introduce security risks and compliance violations. CSPM tools must have mechanisms in place to detect and identify shadow IT resources and include them in the asset inventory.

- **Lack of standardized tagging and naming conventions**: Cloud resources are often provisioned with different naming conventions and tags, which can vary across teams, projects, and cloud platforms. Inconsistent or missing tags and naming conventions make it difficult to group and categorize assets accurately. Effective CSPM tools support intelligent tagging mechanisms and provide options to normalize and enforce consistent naming conventions.

- **Scale and volume of assets**: Large organizations and cloud-native applications can have many assets, including virtual machines, storage buckets, databases, and containers. Managing and tracking these assets manually becomes impractical and error-prone. CSPM tools should offer automated asset discovery and inventory capabilities, including periodic scans and integration with cloud provider APIs to scale efficiently.

- **Asset visibility in shared environments**: In multi-tenant cloud environments, organizations share underlying infrastructure with other tenants. This shared infrastructure can make it challenging to gain full visibility into assets and understand their interdependencies. CSPM tools need to provide comprehensive visibility into shared resources and ensure assets are attributed to the appropriate tenant with accuracy.

- **Continuous monitoring and updates**: Asset inventory management is not a one-time activity but an ongoing process. Assets change over time, and new assets are provisioned regularly. CSPM tools must provide continuous monitoring and update mechanisms to track changes in the asset inventory, detect unauthorized or misconfigured assets, and generate alerts for potential security issues.

Addressing these challenges requires a combination of robust technology, automation, and integration capabilities within CSPM tools. Now, let's understand the best practices to overcome these challenges.

Best practices for asset inventory management

To establish robust asset inventory management within the context of CSPM, it is essential to follow best practices that ensure accuracy, completeness, and efficiency. Here are some key practices to consider:

- **Automated asset discovery**: Leverage automated tools and capabilities provided by the CSPM solution to discover assets across your cloud infrastructure. These tools should regularly scan the environment, identify new assets, and update the inventory accordingly. Automation reduces manual effort, ensures timeliness, and minimizes the risk of overlooking assets.

- **Tagging and metadata management**: Implement a consistent tagging and metadata strategy for your assets. Establish standard naming conventions and tags that align with your organizational structure, project hierarchy, and compliance requirements. This practice enhances the searchability, grouping, and categorization of assets. The CSPM tool should support tagging mechanisms and provide options to enforce standardized tagging practices.

- **Integration with cloud provider APIs**: Integrate the CSPM tool with the APIs of your cloud service providers. This integration allows for seamless asset discovery, visibility, and synchronization with the provider's infrastructure. It ensures accurate and up-to-date inventory management across multi-cloud and hybrid cloud environments.

- **Continuous monitoring and alerting**: Enable continuous monitoring of your asset inventory. The CSPM tool should actively track changes, configurations, and vulnerabilities associated with assets. Set up alerts and notifications to promptly address any deviations or potential security risks. Continuous monitoring helps maintain the accuracy and security of your asset inventory.

- **Asset life cycle management**: Incorporate asset life cycle management practices into your inventory management process. Track the entire life cycle of assets, from provisioning to decommissioning. Regularly review and retire unused or obsolete assets to minimize security risks and optimize resource utilization. The CSPM tool should provide visibility into the life cycle stages and enable proactive management.

- **Integration with configuration management database (CMDB) or IT asset management (ITAM) systems**: Integrate your CSPM tool with your CMDB or ITAM system, if applicable. This integration ensures consistency and alignment between your asset inventory and broader IT management processes. It allows for better asset tracking, change management, and overall visibility.

- **Regular reconciliation and validation**: Conduct periodic asset reconciliation and validation exercises to ensure the accuracy and completeness of your inventory. Compare the inventory data from the CSPM tool with other sources of truth, such as billing records or CMDBs, to identify discrepancies or missing assets. Address any inconsistencies promptly to maintain data integrity.

- **Role-based access control (RBAC)**: Implement RBAC within the CSPM tool to control access to the asset inventory. Define roles and permissions based on job responsibilities and the need-to-know principle. This practice ensures that only authorized personnel can view, modify, or manage the asset inventory, enhancing security and accountability.

- **Attribute-based access control (ABAC)**: Identify the relevant attributes for assets, such as type, location, and sensitivity. For users, including roles and departments, you can create precise policies that dictate who can access, modify, or interact with assets under specific conditions. ABAC enables dynamic access control, meaning access decisions can change in real time based on changing attributes, offering fine-grained control over asset management. This approach not only enhances security but also ensures assets are handled as per regulatory and compliance requirements, leading to a more organized and secure asset inventory management process.

- **TAG-based access control (TAGBAC)**: TAGBAC involves categorizing assets with tags or labels to enhance control and organization. It simplifies asset tracking and access control, offering a more organized and efficient way to manage inventory. When combined with monitoring and reporting, TAGBAC helps organizations maintain control over their assets, ensuring that the right individuals have appropriate access while improving visibility and compliance with asset management policies.

- **Documentation and documentation management**: Maintain comprehensive documentation of your asset inventory management processes, including procedures, policies, and guidelines. Document any exceptions, deviations, or change management processes. Regularly update and review the documentation to reflect changes in your environment and ensure consistency in asset management practices.

By following these best practices, organizations can establish a robust asset inventory management process within the context of CSPM. This approach enables improved visibility, enhanced security posture, and effective risk management across their cloud infrastructure. Now that we have discussed the challenges and best practices, let's understand how an organization should maintain asset inventory in the absence of CSPM tools.

Other tools and techniques for asset management

In the absence of dedicated CSPM tools, there are several compensating tools and techniques that organizations can employ to enhance their cloud security posture. When conducting cloud asset inventory, organizations can utilize various tools and techniques to discover and track their assets accurately. These tools and techniques help address the gaps and provide alternative approaches for managing and improving security in the cloud. Here are some compensating tools and techniques:

- **Cloud security monitoring and incident response**: Implementing cloud security monitoring tools, such as **Security Information and Event Management (SIEM)** systems or cloud-native security monitoring solutions, enables real-time detection of security incidents and threats. These tools collect and analyze logs and events from cloud resources, allowing organizations to respond promptly to security incidents and mitigate risks. For example, when investigating a security incident, cloud security monitoring tools can provide insights into unauthorized or suspicious activities related to specific assets.

- **Infrastructure as Code (IaC) security**: IaC can be utilized for asset inventory by incorporating asset tracking and management as part of the infrastructure provisioning process. By including asset inventory in the IaC workflow, organizations can maintain an accurate and up-to-date record of their cloud resources. Here are some tools and techniques that can be used for asset inventory within an IaC approach:

  - **Terraform**: Terraform can be extended to capture asset information during infrastructure provisioning. Custom scripts or modules can be created to gather asset details and store them in a centralized location such as a database or file. This allows organizations to maintain an inventory of provisioned resources alongside their associated metadata.

    Example: With Terraform, a custom script can be developed to retrieve information about provisioned resources (for example, virtual machine instances, databases, and storage buckets) and store it in a separate file or database. This provides a comprehensive inventory of assets with associated attributes, such as resource names, types, and configurations.

- **AWS CloudFormation stack outputs**: AWS CloudFormation allows outputs to be defined within the infrastructure template. These outputs can include asset-related information that is automatically generated during stack creation or updates. The outputs can be retrieved and stored in a centralized system for asset inventory purposes.

  Example: In an AWS CloudFormation template, outputs can be defined to capture details such as resource IDs, IP addresses, or endpoint URLs. These outputs can be extracted and stored in a database or file, creating a centralized asset inventory with relevant information.

- **Azure Resource Manager (ARM) template outputs**: Like AWS CloudFormation, ARM templates support outputs that can be used to capture asset information during provisioning. By defining outputs in the template, asset metadata can be collected and stored in a dedicated system for inventory management.

  Example: In an ARM template, outputs can be defined to extract details such as resource IDs, connection strings, or access keys. These outputs can be extracted and stored in a central repository, enabling effective asset inventory management.

- **Custom scripts and API integrations**: Organizations can develop custom scripts or leverage APIs provided by cloud service providers to gather asset information. By integrating these scripts or APIs into the IaC workflow, asset details can be retrieved during the infrastructure provisioning process and stored in a centralized system.

  Example: Custom scripts can be written to call cloud provider APIs and retrieve asset metadata, such as resource names, sizes, or configurations. The scripts can then store this information in a database or file, creating an asset inventory that reflects the provisioned resources.

- **Policy as Code (PaC)**: If the organization has clear and comprehensive asset management policies that cover areas such as asset identification, access control, and data protection, then they can translate these policies into machine-readable code or configuration files using a PaC framework such as Terraform or AWS CloudFormation. This code represents the rules and standards that assets must adhere to.

- **Cloud access security brokers (CASBs)**: While CASB and CSPM tools have overlapping functionalities, their primary focus areas differ. CASBs primarily concentrate on data protection, user and entity behavior monitoring, and policy enforcement, while CSPM tools specialize in assessing and managing the security posture of cloud environments, including asset inventory. However, CASBs can complement CSPM tools for asset inventory purposes in the following ways:

  - **Shadow IT discovery**: CASBs can identify and track cloud services and applications that are used within the organization, even those not sanctioned or known by the IT department. By discovering shadow IT, CASBs help identify additional assets that might not be covered by the CSPM tools' native asset discovery capabilities. This enhances the completeness and accuracy of the asset inventory.

- **Cloud service coverage**: CASBs can provide visibility and control across various cloud services, including SaaS, IaaS, and PaaS. They can discover assets within each service type and provide information on their usage and configurations. This complements CSPM tools, which primarily focus on the infrastructure layer, by extending asset inventory coverage to cloud services and applications.

- **User and data visibility**: CASBs monitor user activity and data flows within cloud services, providing insights into the usage of assets and associated data. By integrating with CSPM tools, CASBs can provide additional context to the asset inventory by associating user activities with specific assets and enriching the inventory with data-related attributes, such as data sensitivity or ownership.

- **Data loss prevention (DLP) capabilities**: CASBs offer DLP features that help identify and classify sensitive data within cloud services. By analyzing data flows, CASBs can detect instances where sensitive information may be at risk. Integrating CASBs with CSPM tools can enhance the asset inventory by including data-centric attributes, such as data classification and exposure risk, alongside asset information.

- **Unified policy enforcement**: CASBs provide policy enforcement capabilities that can be used to enforce security policies across various cloud services. By integrating CASBs and CSPM tools, organizations can ensure that policy violations identified by CASBs, such as unauthorized access or data sharing, are reflected in the asset inventory. This helps maintain a comprehensive and accurate view of assets and their compliance status.

- **Vulnerability scanning and management**: Vulnerability management tools can also be used to supplement asset inventory management in the absence of a dedicated CSPM tool. While its primary focus is on identifying and addressing vulnerabilities, a vulnerability management tool can provide valuable insights into asset discovery and inventory. Let's look at some examples:

  - **Example tool 1 – Qualys Vulnerability Management**: Qualys Vulnerability Management is a widely used vulnerability management tool that helps organizations identify, assess, and remediate vulnerabilities across their IT infrastructure, including cloud assets. While its primary purpose is vulnerability management, it can provide asset inventory capabilities as well. OpenVAS can contribute to asset inventory for the following capabilities:

    - Network scanning and asset discovery

    - Asset identification and categorization

    - Asset attribute collection

    - Asset dependency mapping

    - Asset tracking and changes

- **Example tool 2 – Open Vulnerability Assessment System (OpenVAS)**: OpenVAS is an open source vulnerability management tool that can be utilized to enhance asset inventory management. Although its primary purpose is vulnerability scanning and assessment, it offers features that aid in asset discovery and inventory. While its primary purpose is vulnerability management, it can provide asset inventory capabilities as well:

  - Asset discovery

  - Asset classification

  - Vulnerability assessment

  - Continuous monitoring

  - Integration with cloud platforms

  By leveraging the asset discovery and vulnerability assessment features of tools such as Qualys and OpenVAS, or any other existing vulnerability management tool, you can compensate for asset discovery and inventory management. Organizations can enhance their understanding of the assets within their cloud environment and maintain an up-to-date inventory of vulnerabilities associated with those assets.

- **Compliance and configuration auditing**: Organizations can utilize existing compliance auditing tools, such as open source solutions or cloud provider-specific auditing services, to verify their adherence to regulatory requirements and security best practices. These tools check cloud configurations, access controls, and policies against established standards, highlighting areas of non-compliance and suggesting remediation steps. While these tools primarily focus on ensuring compliance and assessing configurations, they can provide asset discovery and inventory management capabilities.

- **Cloud governance frameworks and policies**: Implementing cloud governance frameworks, such as the **Cloud Security Alliance** (**CSA**) Cloud Controls Matrix or **National Institute of Standards and Technology** (**NIST**) Cloud Computing Security Reference Architecture, helps define and enforce cloud security policies and practices. These frameworks provide guidelines and best practices for securing cloud assets and can act as compensating measures in the absence of dedicated CSPM tools.

While compensating tools and techniques can enhance cloud security, it is important to note that dedicated CSPM tools offer comprehensive capabilities specifically designed for managing and improving the security posture of cloud environments. Organizations should consider investing in CSPM tools when feasible to gain the full range of benefits and efficiencies they provide.

Summary

In this chapter, we explored the importance of maintaining an accurate and up-to-date inventory of assets within cloud environments. We discussed how a dedicated CSPM tool can play a crucial role in effectively managing and securing cloud assets. CSPM tools provide comprehensive capabilities for asset discovery, classification, and monitoring, enabling organizations to gain visibility into their cloud resources. These tools offer features such as automated asset scanning, configuration assessment, and continuous monitoring to identify misconfigurations, vulnerabilities, and compliance issues. We also examined various aspects related to cloud asset inventory, including understanding the cloud asset landscape, categorizing assets based on their purpose and criticality, and utilizing tools and techniques for asset discovery and inventory management.

In the next chapter, we will dive deep into the CSPM dashboard.

Further reading

To learn more about the topics that were covered in this chapter, take a look at the following resources:

- *Introduction to Cloud Asset Inventory*: `https://cloud.google.com/asset-inventory/docs/overview`

- *Use asset inventory to manage your resources' security posture*: `https://learn.microsoft.com/en-us/azure/defender-for-cloud/asset-inventory`

- *Prisma Cloud Asset Inventory*: `https://docs.paloaltonetworks.com/prisma/prisma-cloud/prisma-cloud-admin/prisma-cloud-dashboards/asset-inventory`

10

Reviewing CSPM Dashboards

The CSPM dashboard acts as a central command center, consolidating critical information from various cloud platforms and presenting it in a user-friendly manner. It serves as a single source of truth for security administrators, enabling them to monitor, assess, and remediate security risks across their cloud infrastructure. This chapter aims to equip you with a solid understanding of how the dashboard functions, its key features, and its role in enhancing cloud security. You will gain insights into the primary objectives of the dashboard and how it facilitates comprehensive security management, the core features and components of the CSPM tool, customization and configuration possibilities, data visualization, and reporting. You will also explore different dashboards, such as the compliance dashboard, identity dashboard, vulnerability dashboard, and reporting dashboard.

By the end of this chapter, you will have gained a comprehensive understanding of the purpose of CSPM dashboards, their key features, and their role in bolstering cloud security.

We'll be covering the following main topics:

- General dashboard overview
- Custom dashboards
- Exporting dashboards
- Best practices for effectively using CSPM dashboards

Let's get started!

Reviewing general dashboard types

The CSPM dashboard is a centralized user interface that provides a comprehensive view of an organization's cloud security posture and allows security administrators to monitor and manage security risks across their cloud environments. The primary *purpose* of the CSPM dashboard is to enhance cloud security management by offering real-time visibility into potential vulnerabilities, misconfigurations, and compliance gaps within the cloud infrastructure. It serves as a command center for security teams, enabling them to assess risks, enforce security policies, and take proactive measures to protect sensitive data. The specific design and layout of a CSPM dashboard vary depending on the provider or tool being used. A wide range of dashboards will be discussed in this chapter in the form of use cases. It is not necessary to find all these dashboards under one tool. Some of them are more common, while some can be created using the dashboard customization feature provided by vendors. The following screenshot provides a glimpse of what the dashboard of a CSPM tool looks like. Typically, it includes the overall secure score, risk summary, and recommendations:

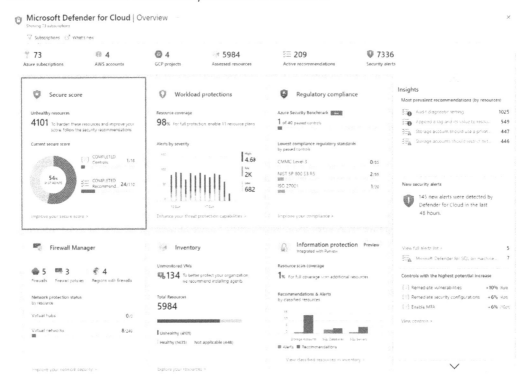

Figure 10.1 – Microsoft Defender for Cloud dashboard overview (source: https://
learn.microsoft.com/en-us/azure/defender-for-cloud/overview-page)

> **Note**
> The figures in this chapter provide a visual understanding of various dashboard types based on their availability.

The type of CSPM dashboard you choose can depend on factors such as the cloud service providers you use, the complexity of your cloud environment, and your organization's security needs. Let's look at some common types of CSPM dashboards.

Risk dashboards

The risk dashboard of a CSPM tool is a visual representation of the security risks associated with an organization's cloud infrastructure. It provides a consolidated overview of vulnerabilities, misconfigurations, and other security issues that could potentially lead to breaches, data leaks, or compliance violations. The primary purpose of a risk dashboard is to help security teams identify, prioritize, and address these risks effectively. The following screenshot provides a glimpse of what the risk dashboard of the Orca CSPM tool looks like. Typically, it includes the overall secure score, risk summary, and more:

Figure 10.2 – Orca CSPM risk dashboard (source: https://orca.
security/resources/blog/orca-cloud-security-score/)

Here's a breakdown of its key components and features:

- **Risk scores and severity levels**: The dashboard assigns risk scores or severity levels to different cloud resources or configurations based on the potential impact and likelihood of exploitation. These scores help prioritize which issues require immediate attention.

- **Risk mapping and visualization**: Risk dashboards often use visual elements such as charts, graphs, heatmaps, and color-coding to represent the distribution of risks across various cloud providers, regions, categories, resource types, or severity levels. This aids in identifying risk hotspots and prioritizing risk mitigation efforts in terms of quickly assessing the overall risk landscape.

- **Risk aggregation**: The dashboard aggregates individual risk scores of workloads to provide an overall risk assessment for the entire cloud infrastructure. This helps in understanding the collective security risk and identifying critical areas that require immediate attention.

- **Top risks**: The dashboard highlights the most critical and high-impact risks at the top. This allows security teams to address the most severe vulnerabilities first, reducing the organization's exposure to potential threats.

- **Filtering and sorting**: Users can usually filter and sort risks based on parameters such as risk score, resource type, severity, or compliance standard. This functionality helps users focus on specific areas of concern.

- **Detailed risk descriptions**: Each identified risk is accompanied by a detailed description of the issue, including information about the misconfiguration, the potential impact, and recommended remediation steps.

- **Historical data and trend analysis**: A risk dashboard may/should display historical data to show trends in risk mitigation efforts over time. This enables organizations to track improvements and the effectiveness of their risk management strategies.

- **Alerts and notifications**: The dashboard can generate alerts and notifications for new or existing risks. This ensures that security teams stay informed about the latest developments.

- **Remediation guidance/recommendations**: For each risk, the dashboard typically provides guidance on how to remediate the issue. This guidance can include step-by-step instructions, links to relevant documentation, or recommended configuration changes.

- **Compliance mapping**: The dashboard also indicates how identified risks align with specific compliance standards or frameworks, making it easier for organizations to meet their regulatory requirements.

- **Customizable risk policies**: Organizations can often customize risk policies so that they can align the risk assessment process with their specific security requirements and risk tolerance levels.

- **Collaboration features**: In some cases, the dashboard enables collaboration among different teams by allowing them to annotate risks, discuss remediation strategies, and track progress collectively. For example, in the Orca CSPM tool, you can group all resources of a particular team within the organization (in Orca, it is called a business unit) and invite the responsible stakeholders by business units so that they can discuss their security scores and help them improve their security posture.

Before we look at the next dashboard type, let's explore the significance of the risk acceptance and exception management features offered by CSPM vendors in the risk dashboard.

Risk acceptance and exception management

Risk acceptance and exception management are important features that are offered under the risk dashboard. These features allow security teams to assess and document security risks that they or the business have decided to *accept* rather than *mitigate*.

Here's what risk acceptance and exceptions mean to the user and how these features typically work in CSPM dashboards:

- **Risk acceptance**: Risk acceptance is the process of acknowledging and allowing certain security risks to exist within your cloud environment. It's a conscious decision that's made by an organization to accept a level of risk for specific reasons, such as operational necessity or cost-effectiveness.

  Why does it matter?

  In the cloud, achieving absolute security can be challenging, and there might be situations where mitigating a particular risk is either *too costly* or *disrupts essential business operations*. Risk acceptance allows organizations to balance security with business needs. CSPM dashboards typically include a feature that enables users to identify and document specific risks they have decided to accept. This documentation is important for compliance and auditing purposes.

- **Exceptions/deviations management**: Exceptions refer to situations where an organization has decided to deviate from standard security policies or practices due to a legitimate reason. Exceptions are typically granted on a *case-by-case* basis and are *temporary*.

  Why does it matter?

  There could be scenarios where strict security policies or configurations might not be feasible or appropriate for a specific application or business unit. Exceptions provide a mechanism for allowing these deviations while maintaining overall security. CSPM tools offer a feature for managing exceptions. Businesses can request exceptions and specify the reasons, and the security team can approve, record, and track the status of these exceptions within the dashboard.

Here's what these features mean to the users of CSPM dashboards:

- **Visibility and accountability**: Users can use the dashboard to document their risk acceptance decisions and exceptions. This provides transparency and accountability within the organization, ensuring that responsible parties are aware of the associated risks.

- **Compliance and auditing**: Risk acceptance and exception management help organizations maintain compliance with industry standards and regulations. By documenting these decisions, users can demonstrate to auditors that they have considered the risks and have valid reasons for accepting them.

- **Balancing security and business needs**: These features help users strike a balance between maintaining a secure cloud environment and accommodating the operational and business needs of the organization. It allows for more flexible security policies without compromising overall security.

- **Security governance**: Users can demonstrate that risk acceptance and exception processes are part of their security governance framework. This is essential for ensuring that deviations from standard security practices are controlled, monitored, and temporary.

- **Tracking and reporting**: CSPM dashboards often offer reporting and tracking capabilities to monitor the status of accepted risks and granted exceptions. Users can assess the ongoing impact of these decisions.

To summarize, risk acceptance and exception management features allow organizations to make informed decisions about accepting security risks and granting exceptions to security policies. These features are essential for aligning security practices with business requirements while maintaining transparency, compliance, and accountability.

A well-designed risk dashboard is a valuable tool for organizations to make informed decisions, prioritize risk mitigation efforts, and ensure that risks are managed effectively. It provides a centralized view of the organization's risk profile and fosters a proactive approach to risk management. Now, let's look at compliance dashboards.

Compliance dashboards

Compliance dashboards focus on monitoring and ensuring compliance with various industry standards and regulatory requirements, such as the **General Data Protection Regulation** (**GDPR**), **Health Insurance Portability and Accountability Act** (**HIPAA**), and **Payment Card Industry Data Security Standard** (**PCI DSS**) benchmarks, Azure Security Benchmark, and **Amazon Web Services** (**AWS**) security benchmarks. They provide visibility into the compliance status of cloud resources and identify potential violations. In some tools, compliance dashboards may also show historical data, trends, and progress toward achieving and maintaining compliance. Compliance dashboards play a crucial role in demonstrating adherence to security and privacy requirements, reducing the risk of fines and penalties, and maintaining a trustworthy image with customers and partners. The following screenshot shows the compliance dashboard of Microsoft Defender for Cloud:

Figure 10.3 – Microsoft Defender for Cloud compliance dashboard (source: https://learn. microsoft.com/en-us/azure/defender-for-cloud/regulatory-compliance-dashboard)

Here are the key features and functionalities of compliance dashboards:

- **Regulatory mapping**: Compliance dashboards map specific compliance requirements to cloud resources and configurations. They help identify gaps between the organization's current state and the requirements of relevant regulations, such as GDPR, HIPAA, PCI DSS, ISO 27001, and others.

- **Policy monitoring**: The dashboard continuously monitors cloud resources and services to ensure that they comply with internal security policies and best practices defined by the organization. It checks for configuration drift and policy violations.

- **Audit trails and reporting**: Compliance dashboards maintain comprehensive audit trails of activities within the cloud environment. They generate reports that can be used for internal audits and regulatory compliance reporting.

- **Automated compliance checks**: These dashboards automate compliance checks against the specified regulations and policies. Automated checks ensure that compliance is continuously assessed, reducing the risk of oversights and manual errors.

- **Compliance score**: Some compliance dashboards provide a compliance score or rating that quantifies the organization's level of adherence to various regulatory requirements and internal policies. This score helps measure progress and identify areas that need improvement.

- **Violation alerts**: The dashboard can generate alerts and notifications when compliance violations are detected. This enables security teams to respond promptly and remediate issues before they escalate.

- **Remediation guidance**: When compliance violations are identified, the dashboard may offer remediation guidance, recommending specific actions to address the non-compliant areas effectively.

- **Evidence collection**: Compliance dashboards often facilitate evidence collection to demonstrate compliance to auditors or regulators. This evidence can include logs, reports, configurations, and other artifacts that validate adherence to security controls.

- **Integration with compliance tools**: These dashboards can integrate with third-party compliance tools and frameworks, making it easier for organizations to consolidate and manage their compliance efforts.

- **Data privacy management**: For regulations such as GDPR that involve data privacy requirements, compliance dashboards assist in managing data processing activities, consent management, and data subject rights.

Organizations can proactively monitor their cloud environment's compliance status, identify potential violations, and take appropriate actions to align with security standards and regulations by effectively using the compliance dashboard. This helps organizations build trust with customers, partners, and regulators and ensures they meet the necessary security and privacy standards in their cloud operations.

Now, let's look at inventory dashboards.

Inventory dashboards

An inventory dashboard provides a comprehensive view of all the cloud workloads deployed within your organization's cloud environment. It serves as a central hub where you can gather and visualize information about various cloud resources, configurations, and metadata. The primary purpose of an inventory dashboard is to offer you real-time visibility into your cloud infrastructure, facilitating effective management, monitoring, and security of your cloud assets. The following screenshot shows the inventory dashboard of Microsoft Defender for Cloud. This figure has been chosen based on it being available for public use:

Figure 10.4 – Microsoft Defender for Cloud dashboard overview (https://learn. microsoft.com/en-us/azure/defender-for-cloud/asset-inventory)

Chapter 9 covers all other aspects of cloud asset inventory. Let's take a closer look at the key features of an inventory dashboard:

- **Resource overview**: The inventory dashboard presents a comprehensive list of all your cloud resources in a structured manner, including virtual machines, databases, storage, load balancers, networking components, security groups, and more.

- **Resource details**: For each resource, the dashboard provides detailed information, such as names, IDs, creation dates, associated tags, metadata, and configuration settings. This allows you to quickly identify specific resources and understand their attributes.

- **Resource relationships:** The dashboard often illustrates relationships between different resources, showing how they are interconnected. For instance, it might display which security groups are linked to specific virtual machines or which virtual machines are part of a load balancer pool. This helps with quickly navigating from one resource to another to find the relevant information.

- **Visibility across cloud providers**: If an organization uses multiple cloud providers, the inventory dashboard should consolidate information from all providers into a unified view. This cross-cloud visibility is crucial for managing complex multi-cloud environments.

- **Categorization and tagging**: CSPM usually imports resource tags, along with other details, when you onboard resources. You can also categorize resources and assign tags to group them based on projects, departments, owners, criticality (crown jewels), or other custom criteria using the CSPM tool. This makes resource management and identification more organized.

- **Frequent dashboard updates**: The dashboard may update in near real-time or frequent intervals as cloud resources are created, modified, or deleted. This ensures you always have the latest information about your cloud infrastructure.

- **Configuration verification**: The inventory dashboard allows you to verify the configurations of your cloud resources, helping you ensure that they adhere to security best practices and compliance requirements.

- **Optimal resource utilization**: Some inventory dashboards provide insights into resource utilization metrics such as CPU usage, memory usage, disk space, and network bandwidth. This helps you optimize resource allocation and cost optimization and identify performance issues.

- **Resource life cycle management**: You can track the life cycle of resources, from creation to retirement, and ensure proper management throughout their existence.

- **Bulk actions**: To streamline resource management tasks, the user can perform bulk actions, such as applying security policies, configuring access controls, or making configuration changes across multiple resources simultaneously.

- **Dependency mapping**: In complex cloud environments, certain resources may depend on others. An advanced dashboard should provide a visual map or diagram illustrating these dependencies, helping users understand the impact of changes.

- **Customizable views**: Depending on your needs, some tools allow you to be able to customize the way resources are displayed, categorized, and sorted on the dashboard.

- **Troubleshooting**: The dashboard aids in troubleshooting by giving you an overview of resource availability, configurations, and relationships. This can assist you in identifying the root cause of issues.

An inventory dashboard in a CSPM tool empowers you with a holistic understanding of your cloud environment. By leveraging this dashboard, you can efficiently manage cloud resources, troubleshoot problems, ensure proper configurations, and enhance security measures. It contributes to maintaining a well-organized, optimized, and secure cloud infrastructure. Next, we'll look at identity dashboards.

Identity dashboards

The identity dashboard of a CSPM tool is a component that's designed to provide insights and oversight into the **Identity and Access Management (IAM)** aspects of an organization's cloud environment. It focuses on managing user identities, access permissions, authentication, and authorization within cloud services. The goal of an identity dashboard is to enhance security by ensuring that only authorized users have appropriate access to cloud resources. The following screenshot depicts the identity risk dashboard of the Orca CSPM tool:

Figure 10.5 – Orca CSPM identity risk dashboard (source: https://orca.security/resources/ blog/ciem-cloud-identity-entitlements-management-beyond-identity-hygiene-risks/)

> **Note**
>
> Many security companies offer identity-specific services under separate product lines such as **Cloud Infrastructure Entitlement Management (CIEM)**, which allows you to track your cloud platforms' users, roles, groups, and policies in one place. In the most recent trend, due to competition and other reasons, it is observed that various features are combined into one product and hence some CSPM vendors have already started offering CIEM features under their CSPM products.

Here is an explanation of the key features and functionalities of an identity dashboard:

- **User and group management**: The identity dashboard displays a list of all users and groups that have access to the cloud environment. It allows administrators to view, add, modify, or remove user accounts and groups.

- **Access permissions**: For each user or group, the dashboard shows their assigned roles, permissions, and access levels across various cloud resources. This helps administrators ensure that permissions are aligned with the principle of least privilege.

- **Role-based access control (RBAC)**: The dashboard highlights the roles defined within the cloud environment and shows which users or groups are associated with each role. It ensures that users have appropriate access based on their roles and responsibilities.

- **Authentication methods**: The dashboard provides an overview of the authentication methods being used, such as passwords, **multi-factor authentication (MFA)**, or **single sign-on (SSO)**. It allows administrators to monitor and enforce strong authentication practices.

- **Access policies**: Organizations often define access policies to control user access to resources. The identity dashboard may display these policies and their associated users, helping administrators verify that access is compliant with policies.

- **Privileged users**: The dashboard may/should highlight privileged users with elevated access levels and showcase their activities and permissions. This is crucial for ensuring oversight and accountability.

- **Access reviews**: An identity dashboard may include a feature for conducting access reviews. This involves periodically assessing and verifying that users' access permissions are still necessary and appropriate.

- **User activity monitoring**: Some dashboards include logs of user activities, showing what actions users have performed and which resources they accessed. This information aids in detecting unauthorized or suspicious activities.

- **Integration with identity providers**: If an organization uses external identity providers for authentication and SSO, the dashboard might display integrations and configurations related to these providers.

- **Compliance auditing**: The dashboard includes features to assist with compliance audits. It helps administrators demonstrate that access controls are managed effectively and align with regulatory requirements.

- **User onboarding and offboarding**: The dashboard may streamline the process of adding or removing users by providing templates for common roles and permissions during onboarding and offboarding procedures.

- **API access management**: For cloud services that offer APIs, the identity dashboard displays information about API keys, tokens, and their associated permissions.

- **Access anomaly detection**: Advanced IAM dashboards may employ machine learning algorithms to detect anomalous access patterns, such as unusual login locations or unauthorized role changes. This helps with identifying potential security incidents.

In summary, an identity dashboard within a CSPM tool focuses on managing and monitoring user identities and their access to cloud resources. By providing visibility into identity-related aspects and ensuring that access permissions are correctly configured and regularly reviewed, the dashboard contributes to maintaining a secure and well-governed cloud environment. Now, let's look at network security dashboards.

Network security dashboards

The network security dashboard of a CSPM tool offers an overview of an organization's cloud network infrastructure and its associated security posture. This dashboard focuses on monitoring and managing the security aspects of network configurations, traffic flows, and connectivity within the cloud environment. The following screenshot provides a glimpse of the network security dashboard of Microsoft Defender for Cloud:

Figure 10.6 – Microsoft Defender for Cloud – the Firewall Manager dashboard
(source: Microsoft Defender for Cloud CSPM dashboard)

Here is an explanation of the key components and functionalities of a network security dashboard:

- **Network topology visualization**: The dashboard provides a visual representation of the cloud network topology, including **virtual networks** (**VNets**), subnets, gateways, load balancers, and other network components. This helps administrators understand the layout of the network infrastructure.

- **Security groups and firewall rules**: It displays firewall rules and security group configurations that control inbound and outbound traffic to and from resources. Administrators can assess whether rules are properly configured and aligned with security policies.

- **Virtual private cloud** (**VPC**) **configuration**: For cloud providers that use the concept of a VPC (for example, AWS), the dashboard provides a comprehensive view of VPC configurations. It includes details such as IP address ranges, subnets, route tables, and internet gateways. Administrators can review and manage VPC settings to ensure secure network architecture.

- **Network segmentation**: The dashboard shows how resources are segmented within the network. This is crucial for isolating sensitive workloads and reducing the attack surface. If some critical component is missing, it also provides recommendations. For example, the dashboard can provide a list of Azure subnets that are not attached to a **network security group** (**NSG**) or VNet without an NSG. This helps you quickly find out the critical areas where immediate attention is required.

- **Traffic flow analysis**: It provides insights into network traffic patterns, showing the volume and types of traffic flowing between different resources. This helps with identifying anomalies and potential security threats.

- **Security group analysis**: The dashboard highlights security groups and their associated rules, helping administrators identify overly permissive rules or misconfigurations that might expose resources to risks.

- **Access control lists** (**ACLs**): It displays ACLs that control traffic at the subnet level, allowing administrators to verify that traffic between subnets is properly controlled.

- **Network encryption**: The dashboard might provide information about encryption protocols used for data in transit within the network, ensuring that sensitive data is adequately protected.

- **Virtual private network** (**VPN**) **and peering connections**: For hybrid cloud environments, the dashboard could show VPN and peering connections between on-premises infrastructure and the cloud.

- **Public and private connectivity**: It highlights public-facing and private-facing resources, helping administrators confirm that public resources are appropriately exposed and that private resources are not inadvertently accessible.

- **Network anomalies**: Dashboards also bring anomaly detection capabilities that flag unusual or unexpected network behavior, indicating potential security breaches or misconfigurations. Misconfigurations will be discussed separately in *Chapter 11*.

- **Integration with threat intelligence**: The dashboard may integrate with threat intelligence feeds to provide information about known malicious IP addresses or domains attempting to access resources. Threat intelligence tools such as *Mandiant* and *CrowdStrike* are integrated in many cases. Next-generation CSPM tools are also trying to bring threat intelligence feeds directly into the tool itself.

- **Network compliance**: It helps assess whether network configurations comply with industry standards, best practices, and regulatory requirements.

- **Alerts and notifications**: The dashboard can generate alerts and notifications for security incidents, policy violations, or suspicious network activities.

- **Integration with remediation**: Some tools are also equipped with remediation capabilities. The dashboard might allow administrators to take immediate action to modify firewall rules, adjust security group settings, or isolate compromised resources. This may require additional permissions from the tools so that you can make changes to your cloud environment.

- **Historical network data**: The dashboard might display historical network data and trends to help administrators understand changes and improvements over time.

- **User access control**: Just like other dashboards, the network security dashboard supports RBAC to ensure that only authorized individuals can view and manage network-related configurations.

The network security dashboard in a CSPM tool focuses on visualizing and managing the security aspects of an organization's cloud network infrastructure. By providing insights into network configurations, traffic flows, and connectivity, administrators can identify vulnerabilities, misconfigurations, and potential security risks, allowing them to take proactive measures to maintain a secure cloud environment. Now, let's look at another important dashboard.

Vulnerability dashboards

The vulnerability dashboard of a CSPM tool focuses specifically on monitoring and managing vulnerabilities within an organization's cloud environment. It is a key component of a CSPM platform, providing real-time insights into security weaknesses and potential risks associated with cloud resources and configurations. The following screenshot provides a glimpse of a vulnerable resources dashboard in Microsoft Defender for Cloud under the **Workload protections** offering:

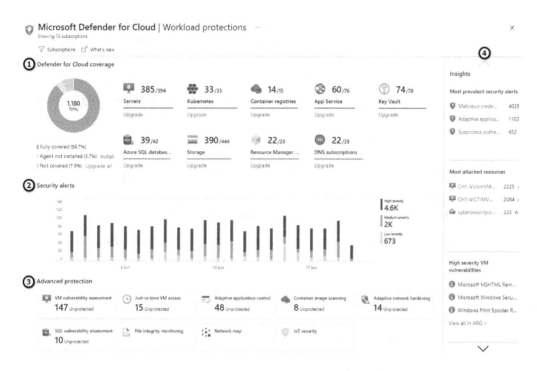

Figure 10.7 – Microsoft Defender for Cloud – the Workload protections
dashboard (Source: Microsoft Defender for Cloud CSPM dashboard)

Here are the key aspects and functionalities of a vulnerability dashboard within a CSPM tool:

- **Vulnerability scanning**: The vulnerability dashboard in a CSPM tool leverages vulnerability scanners or agents to conduct regular scans across the cloud infrastructure. These scans detect vulnerabilities, misconfigurations, and security weaknesses in cloud resources and services.

- **Cloud resource visibility**: The dashboard provides an aggregated view of all cloud resources and their respective vulnerabilities. This includes virtual machines, containers, storage buckets, databases, load balancers, and more.

- **Vulnerability prioritization**: Vulnerabilities are categorized and prioritized based on their severity levels, such as *critical*, *high*, *medium*, and *low*. The dashboard highlights critical vulnerabilities that require immediate attention.

- **Compliance mapping**: The dashboard may map identified vulnerabilities to specific compliance standards, industry best practices, and security benchmarks. This helps ensure that the cloud environment meets relevant security and compliance requirements.

- **Frequent dashboard updates**: The vulnerability dashboard in a CSPM tool continuously updates as new scans are performed or as configurations change, providing up-to-date information on the security posture of the cloud infrastructure.

- **Risk scoring**: Some CSPM platforms assign risk scores to vulnerabilities based on factors such as potential impact, exploitability, and resource criticality based on tags (crown jewels) and affected resources. This helps in prioritizing remediation efforts effectively.

- **Integration with remediation tools**: The vulnerability dashboard can integrate with various cloud orchestration and automation tools to facilitate remediation actions. Security teams can take immediate actions from the dashboard to address identified vulnerabilities.

- **Remediation recommendations**: This is another important feature that brings all relevant remediations, guideline information, and best practices together to fix vulnerabilities efficiently. These recommendations assist security teams in resolving issues effectively.

- **Customizable policies**: Organizations can often customize vulnerability scanning policies so that they align with their specific security requirements and compliance standards.

- **Historical data and trends**: In some cases, the dashboard may maintain historical data and vulnerability trends, enabling organizations to track progress, analyze patterns, and assess security improvements over time.

The vulnerability dashboard aids in optimizing the security posture, reducing the attack surface, and mitigating potential security risks effectively. It allows security teams to stay ahead of cyber threats and ensure the integrity and confidentiality of cloud resources and data.

Alerts and incident dashboards

An alert and incident dashboard is a crucial component that helps organizations monitor, manage, and respond to security alerts and incidents within their cloud environments. This dashboard provides a centralized view of security events, vulnerabilities, misconfigurations, and other potential threats detected by the CSPM tool. It enables security teams to stay informed, take prompt action, and maintain a strong security posture. While companies might have centralized incident management tools, integrating the specialized cloud-focused insights from the CSPM tool's dashboard can enhance incident response effectiveness, especially for cloud-related incidents. The key is to ensure that both tools work in harmony, enabling a comprehensive and well-coordinated incident response across the entire organizational landscape:

> **Note**
>
> Many CSPM tools perform scans periodically, which might not align with the traditional definition of "real-time" monitoring. However, the term "real-time" in the context of CSPM dashboards refers to the immediacy of alerting and response once the scans are conducted and potential issues are detected. While the scans themselves might occur daily or at scheduled intervals, the alerting and incident management process that follows can still be considered real time due to the swift response and actions taken by security teams. Once the CSPM tool completes its scan and identifies potential security issues, misconfigurations, vulnerabilities, or compliance violations, it generates alerts. These alerts are often categorized by severity levels, and the most critical ones are escalated for immediate attention.

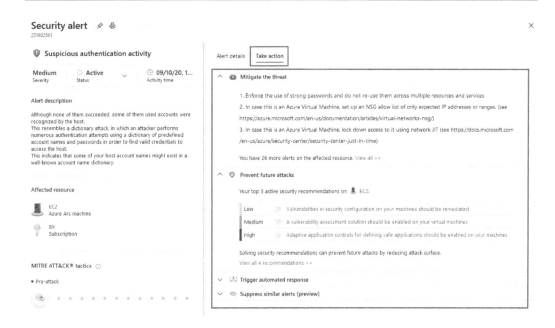

Figure 10.8 – Microsoft Defender for Cloud – Security alert (Source: https://learn.
microsoft.com/en-us/azure/defender-for-cloud/tutorial-security-incident)

Here are the key features and functionalities of an alert and incident dashboard:

- **Real-time monitoring**: The dashboard provides real-time visibility into security events and incidents, allowing security teams to promptly respond to emerging threats.

- **Alert aggregation**: It aggregates alerts from various sources within the cloud environment, such as configuration checks, security scans, anomaly detection, and user activity logs.

- **Severity levels**: Alerts are categorized by severity levels, such as *high*, *medium*, or *low*. This categorization helps prioritize responses based on the potential impact of the threat.

- **Alert types**: Alerts can encompass a wide range of issues, including misconfigurations, unauthorized access attempts, data breaches, vulnerabilities, compliance violations, and more.

- **Incident tracking**: The dashboard allows security teams to track ongoing incidents and investigations, as well as the progress of remediation efforts.

- **Detailed information**: Each alert or incident entry typically includes detailed information about the issue, including affected resources, risk assessment, recommendations, and a timeline of events.

- **Drill-down capabilities**: Security teams can drill down into specific alerts to gather more information and context about the incident.

- **Automated responses**: Some CSPM tools integrate with automation frameworks to enable automatic responses to certain types of alerts. For instance, the system might automatically isolate compromised resources.

- **Playbooks and workflows**: The dashboard might include predefined incident response playbooks or workflows that guide security teams through the steps needed to mitigate and resolve incidents.

- **Integration with remediation**: Security teams can often initiate remediation actions directly from the dashboard, such as adjusting configurations, applying patches, or isolating resources.

- **Collaboration and communication**: The dashboard might include features for collaboration and communication among security team members, facilitating coordination during incident response.

- **Alert workflow management**: Security teams can manage the life cycle of alerts, from detection to resolution, ensuring proper documentation and follow-up.

An alert and incident dashboard is a critical tool for maintaining cloud security by providing a consolidated view of security events, vulnerabilities, and incidents. It empowers security teams to respond effectively, minimize risks, and maintain a secure and well-managed cloud environment.

Custom dashboards

A custom dashboard is a feature offered by every CSPM tool that enables users to create personalized and tailor-made dashboards to visualize and manage the security and compliance aspects of their cloud environments. This type of dashboard allows users to select, arrange, and display specific metrics, data points, visualizations, and other elements that are most relevant to their organization's unique needs and goals. Here is a more detailed explanation of the key components and functionalities of a custom dashboard:

- **Widget selection**: Users can choose from a variety of pre-designed widgets, which are components that display specific data or visualizations. Widgets might include charts, graphs, lists, tables, and more.

- **Drag-and-drop interface**: The custom dashboard typically employs a user-friendly drag-and-drop interface, allowing users to easily add, arrange, and organize widgets on the dashboard canvas.

- **Data sources**: Users can select the data sources from which the dashboard will pull information. These sources may include cloud service APIs, configuration checks, security scans, user activity logs, and more.

- **Metric customization**: Users can define the specific metrics, **key performance indicators (KPIs)**, and compliance standards they want to track and visualize on the dashboard.

- **Visualizations**: Users can choose the appropriate visualization types for the selected metrics and data points. This might include bar charts, pie charts, line graphs, heat maps, and more.

- **Filters and time ranges**: Users can apply filters to focus on specific subsets of data, such as a particular time period, resource type, region, or other parameters.

- **Grouping and segmentation**: Custom dashboards often allow users to group data based on different criteria, such as resource categories, compliance levels, or risk severity.

- **Interactive elements**: Some recent CSPM dashboards support interactive elements, enabling users to drill down into specific data points for more detailed insights or analysis.

- **Color schemes and themes**: Users may have the option to choose color schemes and themes that align with their organization's branding or visual preferences.

- **Multiple dashboards**: Many CSPM tools enable users to create multiple custom dashboards, each tailored to different audiences, projects, or areas of focus.

- **Sharing and collaboration**: Custom dashboards can usually be shared with colleagues, teams, or management to facilitate collaboration and decision-making.

- **Responsive design**: Ideally, the custom dashboard supports responsive design, ensuring that it remains usable and visually appealing on various devices and screen sizes.

- **User access control**: As with other dashboard types, custom dashboards support RBAC to ensure authorized individuals can view, modify, or create dashboards.

Custom dashboards empower users to create a highly personalized and tailored visualization tool for monitoring and managing their cloud security and compliance. This flexibility allows organizations to focus on the metrics and insights that matter most to them, promoting a proactive approach to maintaining a strong security posture.

Exporting dashboards

Exporting CSPM dashboards to external reporting tools is a valuable feature that allows organizations to integrate their CSPM data with other reporting and analysis platforms such as Grafana, Power BI, and more. This integration enhances data analysis, sharing, and presentation, and can contribute to a more comprehensive understanding of an organization's cloud security and compliance posture. The following screenshot shows an example of a vulnerability dashboard that's been exported to Grafana from a CSPM tool:

Figure 10.9 – Sample Grafana dashboard generated from a CSPM tool

Here's how the process works:

- **Data integration**: CSPM tools collect and store data related to cloud security configurations, compliance status, vulnerabilities, and more. These tools typically provide built-in dashboards for visualizing this data within the CSPM platform.

- **Exporting data**: To export dashboard data to external reporting tools, the CSPM tool provides options for exporting the data in a compatible format. This could involve exporting to common formats such as CSV, Excel, JSON, or XML.

- **Integration with reporting tools**: External reporting tools could include **Business Intelligence** (**BI**) platforms such as Tableau, Power BI, or specialized security and compliance reporting tools. These tools offer advanced data visualization, reporting, and analysis capabilities.

- **Data transformation**: Once the data has been exported, it must be transformed or formatted so that it aligns with the data structure that the external reporting tool expects. This involves mapping data fields, cleaning up data, or transforming it into the required format.

- **Importing data**. The external reporting tool then imports the exported data. This is done through manual data upload or automated data integration pipelines.

- **Dashboard design**: Within the external reporting tool, users can design and customize their dashboards or reports using the imported CSPM data. They can choose different visualization types, combine data from multiple sources, and create interactive dashboards (as shown in the preceding screenshot).

- **Advanced analysis**: External reporting tools often provide more advanced analytical capabilities than CSPM platforms alone. Users can perform complex data analysis, build predictive models, and uncover insights that might not be easily achievable within the CSPM tool.

- **Sharing and collaboration**: With external reporting tools, organizations can create reports that are easily shareable with stakeholders, management, compliance teams, or auditors. Reports can be exported, saved, scheduled for automatic generation, or shared via secure links.

- **Customization**: External reporting tools offer more customization options for visualizing data. Users can choose from a wider range of visualization types, create interactive dashboards, and apply branding or styling.

- **Comprehensive insights**: By integrating CSPM data with other data sources in the organization, such as user behavior analytics or threat intelligence feeds, organizations can gain a more comprehensive and holistic view of their security posture.

- **Automation**: Some reporting tools allow data updates to be automated, ensuring that the reports are always based on the most recent CSPM data without manual intervention. Some security companies have announced that they are going to integrate generative AI and predictive analytics features into CSPM and other BI tools for generating reports. One such example is Microsoft Copilot. For more details, refer to Power BI Copilot (`microsoft.com`).

In summary, exporting CSPM dashboards to external reporting tools allows organizations to extend the value of their CSPM data by integrating it with advanced reporting and analysis platforms. This integration enhances data analysis, visualization, and sharing capabilities, helping organizations make more informed decisions and maintain a robust cloud security posture.

Best practices for effectively using CSPM dashboards

Effectively using a CSPM dashboard is crucial for maintaining a robust security posture and ensuring compliance in your cloud environment. Here are some best practices so that you can make the most of your CSPM dashboard:

- **Regular monitoring and review**: Regularly monitor the dashboard to stay updated on the security and compliance status of your cloud infrastructure. Review the data, alerts, and reports provided by the dashboard to identify potential security risks and vulnerabilities.

- **Configure real-time alerts**: Set up real-time alerts for critical security events or policy violations. This allows you to respond quickly to security incidents and address issues as they arise.

- **Prioritize critical risks**: Focus on addressing high-severity risks and vulnerabilities first. Prioritize remediation efforts based on the potential impact on your cloud resources and data.

- **Automate remediation**: Integrate the CSPM dashboard with cloud orchestration and automation tools to automate remediation tasks. This helps streamline the process and reduces the time it takes to address security issues.

- **Customize policies**: Customize the CSPM dashboard's policies so that they align with your organization's specific security requirements, compliance standards, and risk tolerance levels.

- **Drill down into details**: Utilize the dashboard's drill-down capabilities to investigate and analyze specific cloud resources and configurations in detail. This will help you understand the root cause of security issues.

- **Share insights with stakeholders**: Share the dashboard insights and reports with relevant stakeholders, including IT teams, security teams, compliance officers, and management. Effective communication ensures everyone is on the same page regarding security risks and compliance status.

- **Implement security best practices**: Follow security best practices recommended by your CSPM provider and cloud service providers to optimize your cloud security posture.

- **Educate and train teams**: Ensure that your IT and security teams are familiar with the CSPM dashboard and its features. Provide training to maximize its effectiveness and empower them to use it efficiently.

- **Periodic reviews and updates**: Periodically review and update your CSPM policies, configurations, and alerts so that you can adapt to changes in your cloud infrastructure and security requirements.

- **Integrate with other security tools**: Integrate the CSPM dashboard with other security tools, such as **Security Information and Event Management** (**SIEM**) systems and threat intelligence platforms, to enhance your overall security capabilities.

- **Continuous improvement**: Continuously analyze the data and trends provided by the dashboard to identify areas of improvement in your security practices. Use these insights to implement proactive measures and continuously enhance your security posture.

By following these best practices, organizations can effectively leverage their CSPM dashboards to identify and address security risks, maintain compliance, and strengthen the overall security posture of their cloud environment. These dashboards become powerful tools for proactive security management and ensuring the confidentiality, integrity, and availability of cloud resources and data.

Summary

CSPM dashboards serve as visual interfaces that provide insights into an organization's cloud security and compliance posture. This chapter delved into different types of dashboards, including risk dashboards, inventory dashboards, identity dashboards, network security dashboards, and reporting dashboards. Each dashboard type has unique features tailored to specific aspects of cloud security and management. This chapter emphasized the importance of visualizing data related to risks, vulnerabilities, misconfigurations, user identities, network infrastructure, and compliance statuses. It also touched on the value of exporting CSPM dashboard data to external reporting tools, enabling comprehensive analysis, sharing, and collaboration across different departments and stakeholders.

In the next chapter, we will dive deeper into major configuration risks.

Further reading

To learn more about the topics that were covered in this chapter, take a look at the following resources:

- *Simplifying Your Multi-Cloud Security Strategy*: `https://www.paloaltonetworks.com/blog/2019/03/simplifying-multi-cloud-security-strategy/`

- *Manage & prioritize vulnerabilities across your entire cloud estate*: `https://orca.security/platform/vulnerability-management/`

- *CSPM Executive Dashboard*: `https://help.accuknox.com/saas/cspm-executive-dashboard/`

11
Major Configuration Risks

Major configuration risk refers to vulnerabilities or weaknesses in the configuration of cloud resources that could lead to the unintentional hosting, spread, or propagation of malware within a cloud environment. Cloud assets, such as virtual machines, containers, storage systems, and other resources, can become carriers or hosts for malware if they are not properly configured and secured. A report states that more than 99% of cloud breaches happen due to misconfiguration on the cloud user's side. The main reason this occurs could be due to a combination of factors related to the complexity of cloud infrastructure, the speed of deployment, human error, and lack of understanding of cloud security best practices. It is important to understand those areas where extra attention is needed.

CSPM provides visibility into those areas in cloud environments where proper configuration is not set right. This chapter highlights the areas where things are not set right so that they can be remediated wherever possible through automation or other recommended ways.

We'll cover the following main topics in this chapter:

- Workload misconfigurations overview
- Understanding malware, vulnerabilities, and misconfiguration
- Network misconfigurations
- IAM misconfigurations
- Lateral movement, data protection, and other security risks
- Critical, suspicious, and malicious activities
- Best practices and lessons learned

Let's get started!

Workload misconfigurations overview

Major configuration risk involves critical misconfigurations that can potentially lead to data breaches, unauthorized access, or other security incidents. These risks usually stem from deviations from recommended security guidelines and practices set forth by the **cloud service providers** (**CSPs**) or industry standards such as the **Center for Internet Security** (**CIS**) benchmarks. They can be broadly grouped as network security misconfigurations, misconfigured host operating systems, and IAM-related misconfigurations. Before we dive deep into this topic, let's understand misconfigurations, malware, and vulnerabilities.

Malware, misconfigurations, and vulnerabilities and their correlations

Malware, misconfigurations, and vulnerabilities are interconnected factors that contribute to security risks and potential breaches.

Malware

Malware is malicious software designed to infiltrate, damage, or compromise computer systems. It can affect virtual machines, containers, or cloud infrastructure components and can be introduced through infected files, compromised applications, or vulnerabilities in the cloud environment. Malware can spread across cloud resources and networks, leading to data breaches, data theft, or service disruption. Attackers use malware to gain unauthorized access to cloud instances, exfiltrate sensitive information, or launch further attacks within the cloud environment.

Example: A type of malware known as "ransomware" gains access to the organization's network through a vulnerability in an outdated component of an application running on their on-premises servers. Once inside the network, the ransomware spreads to cloud-based virtual machines and any containers that are interconnected. The malware encrypts critical data across both on-premises and cloud environments and demands a ransom for its decryption.

Misconfigurations

Misconfigurations refers to errors in the setup and configuration of cloud services, resources, and security settings. These mistakes can lead to unintended exposure of data or resources, making them vulnerable to unauthorized access or attacks.

Example: Misconfigured access controls, leaving default credentials unchanged, or improperly configured network settings can leave resources exploitable. Misconfigurations can be the result of human error, lack of understanding of the cloud platform, or even the complexity of managing various cloud services.

Vulnerabilities

Vulnerabilities are weaknesses or flaws in workloads in software, applications, or systems that can be exploited by attackers to gain unauthorized access or perform malicious actions. These vulnerabilities can occur from coding errors, outdated software, or insecure configurations. In cloud environments, vulnerabilities can exist in the underlying infrastructure, virtualization software, applications, and more. Attackers actively search for and exploit these vulnerabilities to gain access to cloud resources. Vulnerabilities in cloud services or platforms can have far-reaching consequences, potentially affecting multiple users and customers who rely on the same infrastructure.

Example: Customers rely on various operating systems to run virtual machines or containers in cloud environments. It is the customer's responsibility to apply patches to these operating systems. If the operating system is not promptly and consistently patched to address known vulnerabilities, attackers may exploit those vulnerabilities to compromise the system. Failure to apply operating system patches promptly can leave cloud instances exposed to security threats that have already been addressed by the software updates. Attackers may take advantage of unpatched vulnerabilities to gain unauthorized access, launch attacks, or compromise the integrity and confidentiality of data. Since vulnerability and patch management is a large and complex topic, it will be discussed in great detail in *Chapter 13*.

Correlation

To establish a *correlation*, it can be stated that misconfigurations and vulnerabilities can create opportunities for malware to infiltrate and propagate within cloud environments. Once inside the cloud environment, malware can propagate, exploit further vulnerabilities, or compromise resources. Malware, in turn, can exploit misconfigurations and vulnerabilities to cause damage or steal sensitive data. Incorrectly configured security settings can introduce vulnerabilities. For example, failing to properly configure firewall rules might expose a database to unauthorized access. Security vulnerabilities in cloud services, applications, or infrastructure can provide entry points for malware. Attackers can exploit these weaknesses to inject malicious code or scripts into cloud instances.

The risks associated with malware and its vulnerabilities

Malware and vulnerabilities related to misconfigurations can lead to severe security risks. Here are some common malware and vulnerability-related misconfigurations to be aware of:

- **Outdated software and patch management**: Failing to regularly update and patch cloud resources, leaving them vulnerable to known exploits.

  Risk: Outdated software can be targeted by attackers who exploit known vulnerabilities to gain unauthorized access.

- **Unsecured storage and databases**: Failing to apply proper access controls or encryption to storage and databases.

  Risk: Unsecured storage and databases can become targets for data breaches or malware injection.

- **Poor container security**: Not properly securing containers by using vulnerable images, misconfigured permissions, or outdated components.

  Risk: Poor container security can lead to malware propagation within containerized environments.

- **Inadequate malware scanning**: Not implementing regular malware scanning of files and attachments in storage or email services.

  Risk: Undetected malware can be uploaded or spread through cloud resources, causing data loss or system compromise.

CSPM tools help detect these malware and vulnerability-related misconfigurations by continuously scanning cloud environments, comparing configurations against best practices, and providing recommendations for remediation. Vulnerability and patch management is a very vast topic and very much the core function of any CSPM tool; we'll discuss it in more detail in *Chapter 15*. Now, let's dive deep into the most critical misconfigurations and their impacts (associated risks), starting with identity misconfigurations.

Identity misconfigurations

Identity and Access Management (**IAM**) misconfigurations are among the most critical issues to address for a hybrid multi-cloud environment. IAM controls who can access what resources and perform what actions within your cloud environment. Misconfigurations in IAM can lead to unauthorized access, data breaches, and other security incidents. Here are some of the most important IAM misconfigurations to be aware of:

- **Excessive permissions**: Assigning overly permissive IAM roles or policies that grant more privileges than necessary to users, groups, or services. This happens when you rely on default roles/policies as you end up assigning a similar set of permissions or roles to a large group, which may sometimes be overly permissive for some users.

  Risk: This can lead to the principle of least privilege being violated, enabling attackers who compromise an account to access and modify resources beyond their intended scope.

- **Unused or stale IAM users and roles**: Not regularly reviewing and deactivating or deleting unused IAM users, roles, and permissions. It is quite easy to assign an admin role to some users, but keeping track of that access isn't easy to manage and has always remained a challenge.

  Risk: Dormant accounts can become attractive targets for attackers, who might exploit these accounts to gain unauthorized access.

- **Missing multi-factor authentication** (**MFA**): Not requiring MFA for sensitive actions, such as accessing administrative consoles or modifying critical resources.

  Risk: In cases where passwords are stolen, MFA provides an extra barrier, making it more difficult for attackers to use compromised credentials. Without MFA, the organization has a limited means of preventing unauthorized access, even if they are aware that credentials have been compromised.

- **Shared credentials and API keys**: Sharing credentials and API keys among users or resources instead of using individualized identities.

  Risk: Shared credentials make it difficult to track who is responsible for actions and can lead to unauthorized access if the credentials are compromised.

- **Privilege escalation opportunities**: Failing to mitigate privilege escalation opportunities, where attackers exploit lower-privileged accounts to gain higher-level access.

  Risk: Privilege escalation allows attackers to move laterally through the environment and access more sensitive resources.

- **Unmonitored IAM activities**: Not setting up proper monitoring and alerting for IAM activities, including changes to roles, permissions, and user accounts.

  Risk: Without monitoring, malicious or unauthorized changes to IAM settings can go unnoticed, allowing attackers to maintain persistence.

- **Inadequate role segregation**: Not enforcing strict separation of duties, allowing a single user to have conflicting roles that could lead to abuse or unauthorized actions.

  Risk: Role separation is crucial to prevent abuse of privileges and ensure accountability.

- **Default privileges**: Not modifying or disabling default IAM roles, permissions, or policies that may come with cloud services.

  Risk: Attackers can exploit these default settings to gain access to resources that are not intended to be publicly accessible.

CSPM tools play a vital role in identifying these IAM misconfigurations by continuously monitoring IAM settings, providing visibility into access permissions, and suggesting best practices for maintaining a secure IAM environment.

Now, let's understand another critical misconfiguration area: network security misconfiguration.

Network security misconfigurations

Network security misconfigurations refer to errors, oversights, or improper settings related to the networking infrastructure within a cloud setup involving multiple cloud service providers. These misconfigurations can result in security vulnerabilities, data exposure, and operational inefficiencies. Network misconfigurations can occur at various levels, including virtual networks, subnets, security groups, firewalls, and communication channels between cloud resources. Several important network misconfigurations can lead to security vulnerabilities and breaches. Here are some of the most important network misconfigurations to watch out for:

- **Unrestricted inbound access**: Allowing unrestricted network access (that is, `0.0.0.0/0`) to critical resources such as databases, APIs, or storage buckets.

  Risk: This can expose sensitive data and services to the public internet, making them susceptible to unauthorized access, data breaches, and cyberattacks.

- **Inadequate network segmentation**: Failing to implement proper network segmentation and security groups/firewalls between different tiers of your application.

  Risk: Without proper segmentation, attackers who gain access to one part of your infrastructure can potentially move laterally to other sensitive components, increasing the impact of a breach.

- **Weak network access control lists (ACLs)/firewall rules**: Incorrectly configured network ACLs or firewall rules that permit excessive or unnecessary traffic.

  Risk: Attackers can exploit these misconfigurations to bypass network security controls, perform reconnaissance, or launch attacks.

Network reconnaissance

Reconnaissance or network reconnaissance refers to the initial phase of a cyber attack or hacking where an attacker gathers information about a target system or network. This phase is also commonly known as information gathering or footprinting. The primary goal of reconnaissance is to collect as much relevant information as possible about the target, enabling the attacker to plan and launch subsequent stages of the attack more effectively.

- **Unused security groups and rules**: Leaving unused security groups and rules in place that could provide unintended access paths.

  Risk: Attackers could manipulate these unused rules to gain unauthorized access to resources or services that were not meant to be exposed.

- **Lack of encryption in transit**: Not enforcing encryption (for example, SSL/TLS) for data transmitted between resources within your cloud environment.

  Risk: Attackers can intercept sensitive information transmitted in clear text, leading to data leaks or unauthorized access to data in transit.

- **Missing or misconfigured network monitoring and logging**: Failing to set up proper network monitoring, intrusion detection, and logging for network activities.

  Risk: Without adequate monitoring, it is challenging to detect and respond to suspicious activities or security breaches promptly.

- **Improper virtual private network (VPN) configuration**: Incorrectly configuring VPNs between on-premises infrastructure and cloud resources.

  Risk: Misconfigurations in VPNs can expose your internal network to potential attackers or create unintentional data leakage paths.

- **Neglecting hybrid cloud security**: Overlooking security configurations when integrating on-premises infrastructure with multi-cloud environments.

  Risk: Improper integration can create vulnerabilities that attackers can exploit to compromise both cloud and on-premises resources.

- **Overlooking Domain Name System (DNS) configuration**: Not properly securing DNS settings, leading to DNS spoofing, cache poisoning, or unauthorized domain hijacking.

  Risk: DNS vulnerabilities can redirect legitimate traffic to malicious sites, leading to data exfiltration or service disruption.

Network misconfigurations can lead to serious security incidents, data breaches, and operational disruptions. In a multi-cloud environment, where the complexity is heightened by the presence of multiple cloud providers, these misconfigurations can compound the risks.

Now, let's understand some misconfigurations that can be serious security concerns, such as lateral movement and data leakage.

Lateral movement misconfigurations

Lateral movement refers to the ability of an attacker to move horizontally from one compromised resource or system to another within the same environment. Misconfigurations that allow for lateral movement can lead to the rapid spread of attacks and greater compromise of resources across your cloud environment. Here are some common lateral movement-related misconfigurations to be aware of:

- **Weak network segmentation**: Not properly segmenting network resources and failing to establish appropriate network controls.

  Risk: Weak network segmentation allows attackers who gain access to one resource to easily move laterally and access other resources.

- **Excessive trust between resources**: Overly permissive access policies or trust relationships between resources, allowing unauthorized lateral movement.

  Risk: Excessive trust enables attackers to leverage compromised credentials to access additional resources without detection.

- **Shared privileges across resources**: Assigning identical or similar permissions to multiple resources, facilitating lateral movement.

  Risk: Shared privileges make it easier for attackers to move laterally once they compromise a single resource.

- **Unrestricted inter-resource communication**: Allowing unrestricted communication between resources, even those that do not require direct interaction.

  Risk: Unrestricted communication paths create opportunities for attackers to traverse the environment and escalate their attacks.

- **Misconfigured IAM roles and permissions**: Allowing roles or permissions that are not properly scoped, enabling unauthorized lateral movement.

  Risk: Misconfigured IAM settings can grant attackers broader access than necessary, facilitating lateral movement and privilege escalation.

- **Unpatched or vulnerable resources**: Not regularly updating and patching resources, leaving them vulnerable to exploitation and lateral movement.

  Risk: Attackers can exploit known vulnerabilities to compromise resources and move laterally within the environment.

- **Missing network monitoring and intrusion detection**: Failing to implement proper network monitoring and intrusion detection systems.

  Risk: Without monitoring, attackers can move laterally undetected, making it difficult to respond promptly.

- **Inadequate logging and auditing**: Not enabling comprehensive logging and auditing of resource activities.

  Risk: Insufficient logging makes it challenging to track and trace lateral movement activities.

- **Unsecured remote access**: Not securing remote access to resources, such as SSH or RDP, with strong authentication and encryption.

  Risk: Attackers can use compromised credentials to access resources remotely and move laterally.

- **Undiscovered malware or persistence mechanisms**: Failing to detect and remove malware or persistence mechanisms from compromised resources.

  Risk: Malware and persistence mechanisms enable attackers to maintain access and move laterally within the environment.

CSPM tools help identify these lateral movement-related misconfigurations by continuously assessing access controls, network configurations, and resource behaviors. Let's dive more deeply into another crucial security concern: data protection.

Data protection misconfigurations

Data protection-related misconfigurations can lead to significant security and compliance risks. These misconfigurations can result in data exposure, unauthorized access, and information breaches. Here are some common data protection-related misconfigurations to be aware of:

- **Unencrypted data**: Storing sensitive data, such as customer information or financial records, without proper encryption.

  Risk: Unencrypted data is vulnerable to interception during transmission or storage, potentially leading to data breaches.

- **Insecure storage settings**: Misconfiguring permissions or access controls on storage buckets or databases, allowing unauthorized users to access or modify data.

  Risk: Improperly secured storage resources can lead to data exposure, data leakage, and unauthorized data modification.

- **Missing data classification**: Failing to classify data based on its sensitivity and importance, resulting in inconsistent security controls.

  Risk: Without proper classification, sensitive data may not receive the appropriate level of protection, leading to compliance violations and data breaches.

- **Misconfigured data retention**: Not properly configuring data retention policies, leading to excessive data storage or unintentional data deletion.

  Risk: Inadequate data retention can result in unnecessary data exposure and potential loss of critical information.

- **Exposed credentials and secrets**: Storing sensitive credentials, API keys, or secrets in plain text within the code or configuration files.

  Risk: Exposed credentials can be exploited by attackers to gain unauthorized access to cloud resources and data.

- **Unprotected backups**: Failing to secure backups with appropriate access controls or encryption makes them susceptible to unauthorized access.

  Risk: Unprotected backups can be a target for attackers looking to access sensitive data or disrupt services.

- **Data leakage prevention**: Neglecting to implement mechanisms to prevent accidental or intentional data leakage through outbound traffic.

  Risk: Data leakage can occur when sensitive information is transmitted outside the organization without proper authorization.

- **Lack of logging and monitoring**: Not setting up comprehensive logging and monitoring for data access and modifications.

  Risk: Without proper monitoring, unauthorized or suspicious data access may go undetected, increasing the risk of data breaches.

- **Misconfigured database access control**: Incorrectly configuring access controls for databases, allowing unauthorized users to query or modify data.

  Risk: Misconfigured database access can lead to data manipulation, unauthorized data retrieval, or even data deletion.

- **Data residency and compliance**: Storing data in regions or jurisdictions that do not comply with relevant data protection regulations.

  Risk: Violating data residency requirements can lead to legal and regulatory consequences.

Regular audits, compliance checks, and security training are essential to maintaining a strong data protection posture in a multi-cloud environment. An effective CSPM tool should help identify these data protection-related misconfigurations by continuously scanning cloud environments and providing recommendations for remediation. Now, let's learn more about suspicious and malicious activities.

Suspicious and malicious activities

In multi-cloud environments, detecting suspicious and malicious activity is crucial to maintaining the security of your cloud resources. Here are some common examples of suspicious and malicious activities that a CSPM tool should help detect or can also work in tandem with other existing security tools to detect:

- **Anomalous access patterns**: Unusual patterns of accessing resources, such as logging in from unfamiliar locations or devices, or accessing resources at odd hours. These are also referred to as *impossible travel activities*. These patterns could indicate compromised accounts or unauthorized access attempts.

- **Brute-force attacks**: A brute-force attack is a method that's used in computer security and cryptography to gain unauthorized access to a system, account, or encrypted data by systematically trying all combinations of passwords, encryption keys, or other credentials until the correct one is found.

- **Account takeover attempts**: The goal of an account takeover is to gain control of the targeted account and potentially use it for malicious purposes, steal sensitive information, or perform unauthorized actions. This can be noticed by intelligent systems as they closely monitor sudden changes in user behavior, such as accessing resources they typically do not, changing settings, or escalating privileges. These activities may indicate an ongoing account takeover attempt by an attacker who has gained access to a legitimate user's credentials.

- **Unusual data access or exfiltration**: Large-scale downloads or transfers of sensitive data, especially if the data is being sent to unfamiliar external locations. This activity could indicate data exfiltration, where an attacker is stealing sensitive information.

- **Suspicious API calls**: Unusual or unauthorized API calls, such as those not typically associated with the application or service. These calls might represent attempts to exploit vulnerabilities or gain unauthorized access to resources. It is recommended to use strong authentication and authorization mechanisms to ensure that only authorized users or applications can access the API and its resources.

- **Resource configuration changes**: Changes to critical resource configurations, security groups, firewall rules, or access policies. Unexpected changes could indicate that an attacker is trying to open pathways for unauthorized access or data manipulation. In a cloud environment, resource configuration changes may involve modifying the size of virtual machines, adjusting storage allocations, changing network configurations, or altering auto-scaling thresholds.

- **Privilege escalation**: Privilege escalation can allow attackers to gain broader access to resources, increasing the potential impact of a breach. These are activities that suggest users or entities are attempting to escalate their privileges within the cloud environment. Privilege escalation can be divided into two types – *vertical* and *horizontal*:

  - In **vertical privilege escalation**, an attacker with lower-level access tries to gain higher-level privileges – for example, a regular user attempting to gain administrative or root-level access to a system.

  - In **horizontal privilege escalation**, an attacker with a certain level of access tries to gain the same level of access for a different user or account. This might involve impersonating another user or exploiting vulnerabilities in account management systems.

- **Suspicious network traffic**: Unusual or unexpected network traffic patterns that might indicate communication with known malicious IP addresses or domains. This could indicate a compromised resource or an ongoing attack.

- **Service or instance hijacking**: Unauthorized provisioning, termination, or modification of cloud resources. Attackers might attempt to hijack or take control of cloud instances or services to conduct malicious activities. This can lead to serious consequences for organizations, including data breaches, disruptions, and malware distribution. Attackers can access and steal sensitive information, potentially leading to financial losses and reputational damage.

- **Data manipulation or injection**: Attempts to modify, delete, or inject malicious data into databases or storage systems. These activities could lead to data corruption, unauthorized access, or data breaches.

Promptly detecting and responding to such activities is essential to mitigating potential security breaches and minimizing the impact on your multi-cloud environment.

Best practices and lessons learned

It is crucial for every organization that relies on hybrid and multi-cloud environments, be it small or large-scale, to have a *security-first* mindset. Organizations need to follow recommended guidelines and insights to prevent, detect, and address misconfigurations that can lead to security vulnerabilities and breaches in their cloud infrastructure. The following best practices are based on experiences and lessons drawn from real-world incidents and challenges related to misconfigurations in the cloud. Let's start with best practices for network security misconfigurations.

Best practices to mitigate network security misconfigurations

Mitigating network misconfigurations involves a combination of careful planning, implementation of security measures, and ongoing monitoring. Here is a comprehensive set of best practices to mitigate network misconfigurations:

- **Unrestricted inbound access**: The best practice to mitigate the risk of unrestricted inbound access is to implement strict network access controls and follow the principle of least privilege:

  - **Apply specific IP whitelisting**: Configure network security settings to allow access only from specific IP addresses or ranges that are trusted and necessary for the resource's operation.

  - **Limit open ports and protocols**: Open only the ports and protocols required for the resource's intended functionality. Close all unnecessary ports to minimize exposure.

  - **Inadequate network segmentation**: The risk associated with inadequate network segmentation can be mitigated by establishing robust network segmentation and access controls between different tiers of your application.

  - **Define logical segments**: Clearly define and segment your network into logical zones or tiers based on the sensitivity and functionality of resources. Examples include web, application, and database tiers.

  - **Isolate sensitive resources**: Place sensitive resources in private segments inaccessible from less secure segments. Limit access to authorized users or applications.

  - **Limit cross-tier communication**: Restrict communication between different tiers to the minimum required. For instance, allow only essential traffic from the application tier to the database tier.

- **Weak network ACLs/firewall rules**: The best practice to mitigate the risk of weak network ACLs or firewall rules is to ensure the proper configuration of access controls and firewall rules while following the principle of least privilege. Here is how to address this effectively:

  - **Apply least privilege**: Assign the minimum necessary permissions for each rule. Avoid overly permissive rules that could expose your resources to unnecessary risk.

  - **Deny by default**: Follow a default-deny approach where all traffic is denied by default, and only explicitly allowed traffic is permitted.

  - **Centralize management**: If possible, centralize the management of network ACLs and firewall rules to ensure consistency and prevent misconfigurations.

  - **Limit outbound traffic**: Control outbound traffic as rigorously as inbound traffic. This prevents potential data exfiltration in case of a compromise.

- **Unused security groups and rules**: The best practices to mitigate the misconfiguration of unused security groups and rules involve regular cleanup and auditing of security groups and rules to ensure that only necessary and intended access paths remain. Here is how to address this effectively:

  - **Regularly review and remove unused groups and rules**: Conduct routine audits to identify and eliminate any security groups and rules that are no longer required. Remove anything that does not have a valid purpose.

  - **Implement a naming convention**: Establish a consistent naming convention for security groups and rules. This makes it easier to identify their purpose and ownership.

  - **Automate the security group life cycle**: Use automation tools to manage the life cycle of security groups, including their creation, modification, and removal.

- **Lack of encryption in transit**: The best practice to mitigate the risk of lack of encryption in transit is to enforce strong encryption mechanisms, such as SSL/TLS, for all data transmitted between resources within your cloud environment. Here is how to address this effectively:

  - **Implement SSL/TLS encryption**: Use SSL/TLS protocols to encrypt data in transit between resources. Ensure that encryption is enabled for all communication channels, including APIs, databases, and communication between services.

  - **Disable insecure protocols**: Disable deprecated or insecure encryption protocols (for example, SSLv2 and SSLv3) and use modern, secure versions of **Transport Layer Security (TLS)** (TLS 1.2 or higher).

  - **Use strong cipher suites**: Configure your SSL/TLS settings to use strong cipher suites that provide robust encryption and authentication.

  - **Employ Perfect Forward Secrecy (PFS)**: Implement PFS, which generates a unique key for each session, enhancing the security of encrypted communication.

  - **Monitor SSL/TLS certificates**: Regularly monitor and update SSL/TLS certificates to ensure they are valid and up to date. Expired or compromised certificates can compromise encryption.

  - **Use HTTPS for web traffic**: Utilize HTTPS for websites and web applications to secure user interactions and prevent the interception of sensitive data.

  - **Encrypt data streams between services**: Apply encryption to data streams between microservices and other components of your application to protect data flow.

- **Missing or misconfigured network monitoring and logging**: The best practices to mitigate the risk of missing or misconfigured network monitoring and logging involve implementing comprehensive network monitoring, intrusion detection, and logging mechanisms:

  - **Implement centralized logging**: Centralize logs from various sources, including network devices, servers, and applications, for easier analysis and correlation.

  - **Define logging and monitoring policies**: Clearly define what events and activities should be logged and monitored. This ensures consistent coverage across the network.

  - **Monitor network traffic**: Deploy **network intrusion detection systems (NIDSs)** to monitor network traffic for suspicious patterns or anomalies.

  - **Use intrusion detection/prevention system (IDS/IPS) solutions**: Implement IDS/IPS solutions to detect and respond to potential security threats and attacks in real time.

  - **Monitor critical resources**: Prioritize monitoring for critical resources, such as authentication systems, databases, and key servers.

  - **Use real-time alerts**: Configure real-time alerts to notify IT teams of suspicious activities, enabling swift response and mitigation.

  - **Ensure data retention and compliance**: Ensure that logs are retained for an appropriate duration to meet regulatory requirements and support forensic investigations.

  - **Encrypt log data**: Encrypt log data to ensure the confidentiality and integrity of the information collected.

- **Improper VPN or Direct Connect configuration**: Apart from what we mentioned previously, it is also recommended to limit access points. Reduce the number of access points for VPN and Direct Connect connections to minimize the potential attack surface.

Now, let's learn about some generic best practices for effectively addressing the misconfigurations associated with identity and other security risks that we mentioned earlier:

- **Define baselines**: Establish baseline behavior for your network and systems. Deviations from these baselines should indicate potential security incidents.

- **Implement a strong IAM strategy**: Misconfigured IAM settings can lead to unauthorized access, so proper IAM management is crucial. Follow the *principle of least privilege*, regularly review and revoke unused permissions, and enforce MFA for all users and services.

- **Regularly review network security**: Weak network security can lead to *lateral movement* and data breaches, so continuous monitoring and adjustments are essential.

- **Enforce encryption**: Enable encryption for data at rest, in transit, and, wherever possible, in use while any application uses it. Use encryption key management services to control access to encryption keys.

- **Follow secure coding practices**: Exposed credentials can lead to unauthorized access and data breaches, so proper credential management is critical. Avoid hardcoding sensitive credentials in code or configuration files. Use secret management tools to store and retrieve credentials securely.

- **Regularly update and patch resources**: Outdated software is a prime target for attacks, so staying current with patches is vital. Organizations should implement a robust patch management process to keep all software and resources up to date. Monitor vulnerability databases for relevant patches.

- **Regularly assess and audit configurations**: Use CSPM tools to regularly scan and assess your cloud environment against best practices and industry standards. Regular audits help catch misconfigurations and vulnerabilities before they can be exploited.

- **Implement proper data classification and retention**: Mismanaged data can lead to compliance violations and increased risk of data breaches. Classify data based on its sensitivity and apply appropriate access controls. Establish data retention policies and regularly review and delete unnecessary data.

- **Practice incident response and recovery**: Preparedness is key to minimizing the impact of security incidents. Develop and test incident response plans to ensure a swift and coordinated response to security incidents. Regularly simulate and update your response procedures.

- **Conduct regular threat hunting**: Proactively search for signs of threats or vulnerabilities within your network by conducting regular threat-hunting exercises.

- **Provide ongoing security training**: Human errors contribute to many misconfigurations, so ongoing education is essential. Educate your IT teams about the importance of proper VPN and Direct Connect configuration and the potential risks of misconfigurations.

These best practices are essential for organizations to establish a strong security foundation in their cloud environments, mitigate the risks of misconfigurations, and ensure the confidentiality, integrity, and availability of their data and resources. It is not an easy task to follow all these best practices without an effective and efficient tool. Some of these best practices are discussed in detail throughout this book to establish a quick correlation between risks and remediation for better understanding.

Lesson learned and its implementation

Lessons learned and *retrospective plans* are related concepts in Agile methodologies, both of which are aimed at continuous improvement and optimizing processes. In the context of cloud environments, lessons learned from misconfigurations are the valuable takeaways that organizations derive from previous instances where misconfigurations led to security vulnerabilities, breaches, downtime, or other negative outcomes. These insights should be documented to provide valuable knowledge for future decision-making and to avoid repeating the same errors. In the realm of cloud security, where responsibilities are shared and divided, lessons learned are key takeaways from incidents or situations that help teams make informed adjustments and improvements to their processes:

- **The importance of lessons learned**: Lessons learned play a crucial role in improving processes, decision-making, and overall security posture. They help organizations do the following:

  - **Prevent recurrence**: Lessons learned provide insights into what went wrong and why. This knowledge helps prevent the same misconfigurations from occurring again.

  - **Optimize practices**: Organizations can fine-tune their security practices based on lessons learned, ensuring they are better prepared to address challenges.

  - **Enhance awareness**: Sharing lessons learned raises awareness among teams about potential pitfalls, fostering a culture of continuous improvement.

  - **Mitigate risks**: Applying lessons learned minimizes the likelihood of security incidents, reducing the risk of data breaches and service disruptions.

- **Examples of lessons learned from misconfigurations**: There is no fixed rule on how to maintain and practice the implementation of lessons learned. However, as a security manager, you can decide to use an Excel sheet, restricted SharePoint site, or any other documentation solutions that organizations use. Make sure this repository is protected as it contains sensitive information about the organization's cloud posture. Let's see what a lessons-learned practice should look like:

Misconfigurations	Lesson Learned	Action Taken
Access control oversight	Our data breach occurred due to inadequate access controls on a cloud storage bucket. We did not restrict public access to the bucket.	Implemented strict access controls, reviewed, and secured existing buckets, and conducted regular audits.
Overprivileged roles	An unauthorized user gained access to critical resources due to an overprivileged IAM role we assigned.	Adopted the principle of least privilege, reviewed and modified role permissions, and implemented continuous monitoring.
Lack of encryption	Sensitive data was compromised because we did not encrypt data in transit and at rest.	Enabled encryption for data in transit and at rest, utilized secure communication protocols, and educated teams on encryption best practices.
Misconfigured network security	An external attacker exploited a misconfigured security group rule, gaining unauthorized access to our cloud instances.	Conducted thorough security group reviews, tightened ingress and egress rules, and implemented regular rule audits.

Misconfigurations	Lesson Learned	Action Taken
Inadequate monitoring	We did not have proper monitoring and alerting in place, resulting in delayed detection of suspicious activities.	Implemented robust monitoring and alerts, integrated SIEM solutions, and conducted incident response drills.

This is too generic an example to get you started brainstorming and developing your own version of lessons learned documentation. You can also add other key details, such as impacted resources, environmental details, incident ticket details, stakeholders' details, deviation path and exception followed, and more.

- **Implementing lessons learned**: To effectively implement lessons learned, organizations should follow these practices:

  - **Document lessons**: Record incidents and misconfigurations, documenting the causes, impacts, and actions taken.

  - **Share knowledge**: Communicate lessons across teams, fostering a culture of learning and improving collective awareness.

  - **Update policies**: Integrate lessons into security policies, guidelines, and practices.

  - **Regular reviews**: Continuously review and assess past incidents to ensure sustained improvements.

  - **Train and educate**: Provide training to staff on the identified lessons and best practices. Promote an environment where teams are always seeking ways to become more efficient, effective, and resilient.

By actively embracing and applying the lessons learned from past misconfigurations, organizations can bolster their cloud security efforts, minimize risks, and enhance the overall resilience of their cloud environments.

Summary

This chapter delved into the critical realm of mitigating misconfigurations in multi-cloud environments through the lens of CSPM. Misconfigurations can lead to severe vulnerabilities, unauthorized access, data breaches, and even the introduction of malware. The chapter also outlines key misconfiguration categories, including network, IAM, data protection, lateral movement, vulnerabilities, and malware. Each category was accompanied by an explanation of potential misconfigurations and their associated risks. To counter these risks, this chapter provided comprehensive insights into best practices and lessons learned.

In the next chapter, we will dive deeper into the query explorer feature of CSPM using **Kusto Query Language (KQL)**.

Further reading

To learn more about the topics that were covered in this chapter, take a look at the following resources:

- *Centre for Internet Security*: `https://www.cisecurity.org/`

- *8 common cloud misconfiguration types (and how to avoid them)*: `https://vulcan.io/blog/cloud-misconfiguration/`

- *What Are the Most Common Misconfigurations on the Cloud?*: `https://www.wiz.io/academy/what-are-the-most-common-misconfigurations-on-the-cloud`

12

Investigating Threats with Query Explorers and KQL

As organizations adopt multi-cloud and hybrid cloud architectures, they must equip themselves with advanced tools and methodologies that enable them to proactively identify vulnerabilities, enforce security policies, and swiftly respond to potential threats. One of the foremost difficulties of security teams today is the sheer volume of security issues that emerge on a daily basis. A multitude of security challenges demand resolution, and the resources available are consistently insufficient to tackle them comprehensively. The query explorers offered by most CSPM tools serve as a powerful means by which security professionals can gain deep insights into their cloud configurations, activities, and interactions. Query explorers are extremely useful in threat-hunting activities to investigate and uncover security threats within an organization's digital environment. In this chapter, we will focus on a comprehensive exploration of the roles that query explorers and threat hunting play in the CSPM landscape. We will also explore graph explorers and one of the most popular query languages, **Kusto Query Language** (**KQL**).

This chapter will cover the following:

- Query explorer and attack paths overview

- KQL basics in the context of CSPM tools

- Best practices for effective investigation

- Lessons learned from threat investigation

Let's get started!

Query explorer and attack paths overview

The query explorer or a cloud security explorer feature of a CSPM tool allows users to create, customize, and execute queries to assess the security posture of their cloud infrastructure. CSPM tools are designed to help organizations identify and address security risks, misconfigurations, and compliance issues within their cloud environments. The query explorer enhances these capabilities by providing an interactive interface for constructing and running queries against cloud resources.

> **Note**
> Not to be confused with the terms "Cloud Security Explorer," "Query Explorer," and "Security Explorer". They share the common theme of exploring and investigating security loopholes using a query mechanism to keep your cloud environment secure. CSPM vendors use different names to represent this feature in their interface. The terms are used interchangeably to make you aware of different terminology for similar concepts.

Understanding the security explorer mechanism

A query explorer mechanism refers to the methodology and capabilities provided by CSPM tools for querying and analyzing cloud configuration data, resource settings, and activities within an organization's cloud infrastructure. The goal of a security explorer in a CSPM tool is to help security teams identify misconfigurations, vulnerabilities, and potential security risks within their cloud environment.

Let us understand the core components of query tools in the context of CSPM tools:

- **Cloud security explorer**: CSPM tools offer a query language such as KQL, GraphQL, or SONAR in the form of a user interface that enables security analysts to create custom queries to interrogate the cloud environment's configuration data and resource settings.

- **Data source integration**: At this stage, the CSPM tool has already pulled in data related to cloud resources, configurations, and activities. This data includes information about virtual machines, storage buckets, databases, networking settings, security groups, access controls, and more. The query explorer leverages this data to produce the desired output.

- **Query repository**: CSPM tools also provide a repository or library where security analysts can save, organize, and share commonly used queries. This repository promotes collaboration and allows analysts to reuse queries for continuous monitoring and assessment.

- **Query execution**: Once a query is formulated using the query language or interface, it is executed against the cloud configuration data collected by the CSPM tool. The tool scans through the data, evaluates the query conditions, and identifies resources that match the specified criteria.

- **Result presentation**: Query results are presented to security analysts through the CSPM tool's user interface. The results highlight cloud resources that meet the query conditions, showcasing misconfigurations, security policy violations, and potential vulnerabilities.

- **Visualization**: CSPM tools may offer visualization features, such as graphs, diagrams, and dashboards, to help analysts understand the relationships between different cloud resources and configurations. These visuals make it easier to spot patterns and anomalies.

- **Alerting and notification**: In cases where specific query conditions indicate critical security issues, CSPM tools can be set up to generate alerts and notifications. This enables security teams to take immediate action to address potential threats or vulnerabilities.

- **Continuous monitoring**: CSPM tools also support continuous monitoring by allowing analysts to schedule queries to run at specified intervals. This ongoing monitoring helps organizations maintain a consistent security posture and detect changes or deviations over time.

- **Integration with workflows**: CSPM tools can integrate with other security and IT workflows, enabling automatic responses based on query results. For instance, certain queries could trigger the adjustment of security settings or the initiation of incident response processes.

Overall, the query mechanism empowers security teams to analyze cloud environment data interactively and proactively for misconfigurations, vulnerabilities, and security risks.

Let us now learn about the importance of the query explorer function in the field of threat hunting.

The importance of the security explorer in threat hunting

Threat hunting involves proactively searching for security threats or potential vulnerabilities within an organization's cloud infrastructure by using custom queries and analysis. Let us see how the query explorer plays a crucial role in threat hunting for several reasons:

- **Data gathering**: Threat hunters begin their activities by using query explorer tools and languages to gather data related to the cloud environment's security configuration, activities, and logs. This data includes information about user access, resource configurations, network traffic, and more.

- **Custom queries**: Threat hunters create custom queries using the query explorer to search through the collected data for **indicators of compromise** (**IoCs**), unusual patterns, and security anomalies. These queries are tailored to the specific threat scenarios or behaviors they are investigating.

- **Behavioral analysis**: The query explorer allows threat hunters to perform behavioral analysis on data. They can look for deviations from normal system behavior, identify unauthorized access or unusual data transfers, and pinpoint potentially malicious activities.

- **Incident detection**: By using custom queries and continuous monitoring with the query explorer, threat hunters can potentially identify security incidents or vulnerabilities that may not have been detected by automated security measures. This proactive approach is crucial for detecting sophisticated or novel threats.

- **Response and mitigation**: When suspicious activities or threats are identified through the query explorer, threat hunters can take immediate action to respond and mitigate the security risks. This may involve isolating compromised resources, altering access controls, and initiating incident response procedures.

- **Iterative process**: Threat hunting is an iterative process. As new threats emerge and the threat landscape evolves, threat hunters continually refine their custom queries within the query explorer to adapt to changing circumstances and enhance the organization's security posture.

The security explorer plays a pivotal role in threat hunting within the context of cloud security. It empowers security teams to proactively investigate their cloud environment's data, configurations, and activities, enabling them to detect and respond to potential security threats and vulnerabilities before they can escalate into significant incidents.

What is a cloud security graph?

A CSPM tool incorporates a graph-based context engine known as a security graph. This engine is designed to collect data from various sources within your multi-cloud environment. This includes information such as the inventory of cloud assets, connections and potential lateral movements between resources, internet exposure, permissions, network connections, vulnerabilities, and more. The gathered data is utilized to construct a comprehensive graph that reflects the structure of your multi-cloud environment. Subsequently, the CSPM tool employs this graph to conduct an attack path analysis, identifying and prioritizing issues with the highest risk in your environment. Additionally, users can interact with the graph through the security explorer for querying purposes.

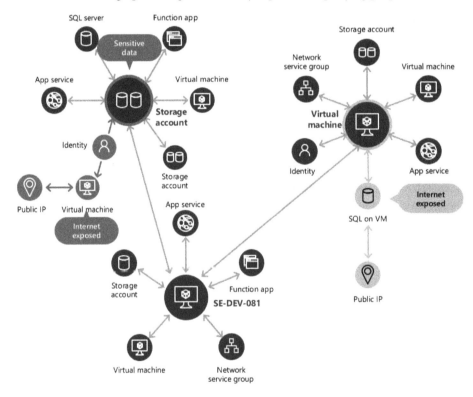

Figure 12.1 – Cloud security graph (https://learn.microsoft.com/en-us/azure/
defender-for-cloud/concept-attack-path#what-is-cloud-security-explorer)

> **What are attack paths?**
>
> Attack path analysis involves a graph-based algorithm that scans the cloud security graph. The scans expose exploitable paths that attackers might use to breach your environment to reach your high-impact assets. Attack path analysis exposes attack paths and suggests recommendations as to how best to remediate issues that will break the attack path and prevent a successful breach. When you take your environment's contextual information into account, attack path analysis identifies issues that might lead to a breach of your environment and helps you to remediate the highest risk ones first – for example, risks to do with exposure to the internet, permissions, and lateral movement.

How does the cloud security explorer feature work?

The CSPM tool collects data about your cloud environment from cloud provider APIs and additional sources, modeling the environment as a graph, and allows you to identify security risks across cloud platforms. Let us understand how the cloud security explorer feature works by using the **Microsoft Defender for Cloud** CSPM tool as an example.

> **Note**
>
> All CSPM tools have similar features, which means you can explore CSPM with whatever tool is accessible to you. If you do not have access to any tool, then you can always sign up for Microsoft Azure and get the Microsoft Defender for Cloud CSPM tool for a 30-day free trial.

Building queries with Cloud Security Explorer

The advanced security capabilities of Defender for Cloud play a crucial role in mitigating the risk of significant breaches. Leveraging contextual information, Defender for Cloud conducts a thorough risk assessment of security issues, pinpointing the most significant risks and distinguishing them from less significant concerns.

In Defender for Cloud, you can utilize **Cloud Security Explorer** to proactively identify potential security risks within your cloud environment. By executing graph-based queries on your cloud security graph, you can tailor your focus to your security team's priorities while considering your organization's unique context and standards. With **Cloud Security Explorer**, you gain the ability to query all security issues and environmental context factors, including asset inventory, internet exposure, permissions, and lateral movement across resources and multiple cloud platforms (Azure, AWS, and GCP).

Let us look at some of the key components of the feature and explore how this feature can be used to gain valuable insights. The functionality of **Cloud Security Explorer** empowers you to construct queries that actively seek out security risks in your environments through dynamic and effective features, such as these:

- **Multi-cloud and multi-resource queries**: The entity selection control filters are organized into logical control categories, allowing you to build queries simultaneously across cloud environments and resources.

- **Custom search**: Utilize drop-down menus to apply filters and construct your query according to specific criteria.

- **Query templates**: Efficiently build your query by selecting from a range of prebuilt query templates.

- **Share query link**: Copy and share a link to your query, allowing collaboration with others by providing easy access to your query parameters.

Remember to refer to the latest documentation of Microsoft Defender for Cloud from official sites. Let us now understand the steps to build a query.

Steps to build a query

To build a query using Microsoft Defender for Cloud, you would start from the Azure Portal. Here are general steps that you can follow:

1. Sign into the Azure portal (`https://portal.azure.com/`).

2. Navigate to **Microsoft Defender for Cloud > Cloud Security Explorer**.

Figure 12.2 – Cloud Security Explorer Dashboard view of Microsoft Defender for Cloud CSPM

3.   Search for and select a resource from the drop-down menu.

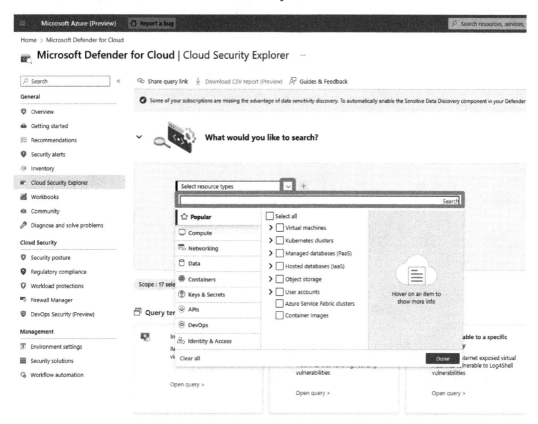

Figure 12.3 – Cloud Security Explorer Dashboard view of Microsoft Defender for cloud

4.   Select + to add other filters to your query.

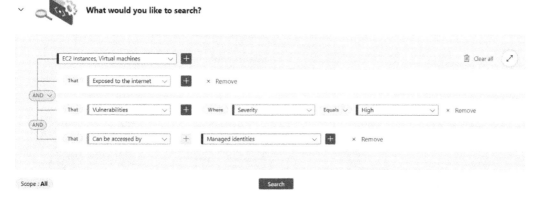

Figure 12.4 – Cloud Security Explorer Dashboard view

5. Add sub-filters as needed.

6. After building your query, click on **Search** to run the query.

Figure 12.5 – Cloud Security Explorer – applying filters

You can also click on the **Download CSV report (Preview)** button to save a copy of your search results as a CSV file if you want to save a copy of your results locally.

Figure 12.6 – Cloud Security Explorer Dashboard – download CSV report

Remember that the steps and features may evolve over time, so it's crucial to refer to the latest documentation provided by Microsoft for Microsoft Defender for Cloud. Let us now explore built-in query templates.

Exploring built-in query templates

Query templates consist of preformatted searches employing commonly used filters. Choose one of the available query templates located at the bottom of the page by selecting **Open query**.

Figure 12.7 – Cloud Security Explorer – query templates

You can also modify any template to search for specific results by changing the query and selecting **Search**. This is super helpful. Let us look at some of the examples and their functions:

- **Internet-exposed VMs**: Returns all the internet-exposed VMs in your cloud environment

- **Internet-exposed VMs with high severity vulnerabilities**: Returns all internet-exposed VMs that have high-severity vulnerabilities

- **Internet-exposed SQL servers with managed identity**: Returns all internet-exposed SQL servers with managed identity assigned

- **Key Vault keys and secrets without any expiration period**: Returns all Azure key vaults where expiration is not set for secrets or keys

- **User accounts without MFA and with permissions to storage accounts**: Returns all user accounts that do not have MFA enabled and have permissions on a storage account

- **Kubernetes Pods running images with high-severity vulnerabilities**: Returns all Kubernetes Pods running an image with a vulnerability severity of high or above

- **VMs with the Log4Shell vulnerability that have permissions to storage accounts**: Returns all VMs that are vulnerable to the Log4Shell vulnerability and have an identity attached with permissions to a storage account

- **VMs with plaintext secrets that can authenticate to a storage account**: Returns all VMs with plaintext secrets that can access object storage

- **Internet-exposed repositories with secrets**: Returns all internet-exposed repositories with secrets

- **Cloud resources provisioned by IaC templates with high-severity misconfigurations**: Returns all cloud resources provisioned by IaC templates with high severity misconfigurations

- **Container images running in production pushed by repositories with high severity vulnerabilities**: Returns all container images running in production pushed by repositories with high-severity vulnerabilities

- **Internet-exposed storage account containers with sensitive data that allow public access**: Returns all storage account containers with sensitive data that are exposed to the internet and allow public access

- **Internet-exposed S3 buckets with sensitive data that allow public access**: Returns all S3 buckets that contain sensitive data that are exposed to the internet and allow public access

- **Internet-exposed API endpoints with sensitive data**: Returns all API collections with internet-exposed API endpoints carrying sensitive data

- **APIs communicating over unencrypted protocols with unauthenticated API endpoints**: Returns all internet-exposed API endpoints that are unauthenticated and communicating over unencrypted protocols

- **External users with permission to SQL VMs allowing code execution on the host**: Returns all the users with permissions to SQL VMs that can run scripts on the host

The number of built-in queries is always growing, and they are very helpful for quickly locating vulnerable resources.

Sharing a query

You can also use the query link to share a query with other people. After creating a query, select **Share query link**. The link is then copied to your clipboard.

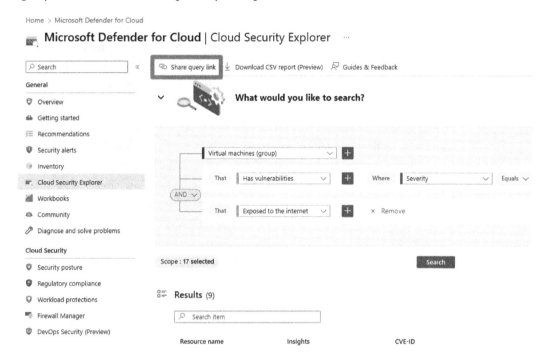

Figure 12.8 – Cloud Security Explorer – sharing a query link

Now that we understand the explorer feature of CSPM tools, let us now learn the basics of one of the most popular query languages, KQL. **Kusto Query Language (KQL)** is a query language that plays a significant role in the effective use of CSPM tools, especially those that utilize KQL for querying and analysis.

> **Note**
>
> To keep the focus of this book's title, KQL is not discussed in detail, but all the important information about KQL is available in the relevant sections and at the end of this chapter under the *Further reading* section.

KQL basics

KQL is a powerful read-only query language used to process data and return results; it was developed by Microsoft. Requests are written in plain text format, using a data-flow model that is easy to read and automate; it does not write any data. Kusto queries are written using one or more query statements. It was originally designed for the Azure Data Explorer service (formerly known as Kusto). KQL has gained popularity for its flexibility and efficiency in handling large volumes of structured and semi-structured data. It is commonly used for log and event data analysis, making it a valuable tool for security, monitoring, and data exploration tasks. Microsoft now uses KQL to write queries in Azure Data Explorer, Azure Sentinel, Azure Monitor Log Analytics, and many more places. Let us learn about some important components of KQL. Here are the basics of KQL:

- **Syntax**: KQL uses a combination of SQL-like syntax and functional programming constructs. Statements are written declaratively, making it easy to express complex data analysis tasks.

- **Query statements**: User query statements can be categorized into three kinds: tabular expression statements, `let` statements, and `set` statements. KQL query statements are always separated by a semicolon (`;`) and only affect the query at hand.

- **Data sources**: KQL is used to query data from various sources, including log files, databases, and more. It is commonly used to analyze time-series data, making it well suited to monitoring and performance analysis.

- **Tabular data model**: KQL treats data as tables with rows and columns. You can perform operations such as those in SQL, including filtering, sorting, grouping, and aggregation.

- **Query components**: Here are the core components of KQL constructs:

  - `SELECT`: Specifies the columns to be included in the query result

  - `FROM`: Specifies the data source or table to be queried

  - `WHERE`: Filters data based on specified conditions

  - `GROUP BY`: Groups data based on one or more columns

  - `SUMMARIZE`: Aggregates data and performs calculations

  - `JOIN`: Combines data from multiple tables using common columns

  - `ORDER BY`: Specifies the sorting order of the query result

  - `PROJECT`: Creates new columns or calculates expressions

  - `EXTEND`: Adds new columns based on existing columns or expressions

  - `PARSE`: Converts strings to structured data using a defined schema

  - `UNION`: Combines the results of multiple queries

- **Functions**: KQL provides a wide range of built-in functions for manipulating and analyzing data. These include string manipulation, date and time functions, statistical and aggregation functions, and more.

- **Time-based queries**: KQL supports time-based queries, allowing you to aggregate, filter, and group data over specified time intervals.

- **Charting and visualization**: KQL is often used with visualization tools to create charts, graphs, and dashboards to better understand and present data insights.

KQL is a versatile and efficient tool for data analysis, particularly when dealing with large and complex datasets. Its ability to handle real-time and historical data makes it valuable for a wide range of use cases. Let us now learn about KQL statement structure.

KQL statement structure

A KQL query is composed of a series of query statements, with at least one statement being a tabular expression that generates data organized in a table-like structure of columns and rows. These tabular expressions are responsible for the query's results. KQL statements utilize a syntax where tabular data flows through a sequence of tabular query operators, starting from the data source and passing through a chain of data transformation operators, all interconnected by the pipe (|) delimiter.

For example, the following query has a single statement, which is a tabular expression statement.

```
SecurityEvent  |  where  EventID  ==  "4626"  |  summarize  count()  by  Account  |  limit  10
```

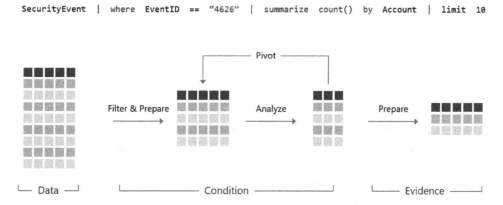

Figure 12.9 – KQL statement structure (Understand the Kusto Query
Language statement structure - Training | Microsoft Learn)

The statement starts with a table called **Security Event**. The **EventID** column's value filters the data (rows) and then the results are summarized by creating a new column for **count() by Account**. Next, in the *Prepare* phase, the results are then limited to 10 rows.

> **Note**
>
> KQL is case-sensitive for table names, table column names, operators, functions, and so on – in short, it is case-sensitive for everything. It is essential to understand how the results flow through the pipe, |. Everything on the left of the pipe is processed and then passed to the right of the pipe.

KQL practice environment

Microsoft provides access to an environment to practice writing KQL statements. The only requirement is to have an account to log in to Azure. There are no charges to your Azure account to access this environment. You can execute the KQL statements in this module in the demo environment. You can access the demo environment at `https://aka.ms/lademo`.

Figure 12.10 – Log Analytics demo environment (https://learn.microsoft.com/en-gb/training/modules/
construct-kusto-query-language-statements/2-understand-kusto-query-language-statement-structure)

The Log Analytics demo database is a dynamic environment. The events recorded in the tables in that environment are continuously updated with different security events. This is similar to what you would experience in a real-world security operation setting. As a result, finite queries in this training may show no results depending on the demo database's state when it is run. For example, a query on the `SecurityEvent` table for `discardEventID = 4688` within the last day may show no results if that event last took place three days ago. Therefore, you may need to adjust variables in the scripts listed in the environment on an ad hoc basis, depending on what data is in the demo database when you run the script, for the query to show results. These script adjustments are similar to what you would perform in the real world and should help you learn how the specific parts of the script function.

The query window has three primary sections:

- The left area is a reference list of the tables in the environment

- The middle top area is the query editor

- The bottom area is for the query results

Before running a query, adjust the time range to scope the data. To change the result columns displayed, select the **Columns** box and choose the required columns.

Additionally, you can also learn KQL by gamified experience through Kusto Detective Agency (`https://detective.kusto.io/`). The following figure shows its interface:

Figure 12.11 – Kusto Detective Agency (https://detective.kusto.io/)

Let us know dive deep into built-in KQL queries and its applicability.

Built-in KQL in the query explorer

The query explorer function within CSPM tools is leveraged with built-in and ready-to-use query features. It includes a set of pre-defined and pre-configured queries that are provided by the tool to help organizations assess and monitor the security posture of their cloud infrastructure. These queries are designed to check for common security misconfigurations, compliance violations, and potential vulnerabilities, making them valuable for organizations looking to quickly identify and address security issues within their cloud environment. The following figure shows how a built-in query looks in a Log Analytics workspace.

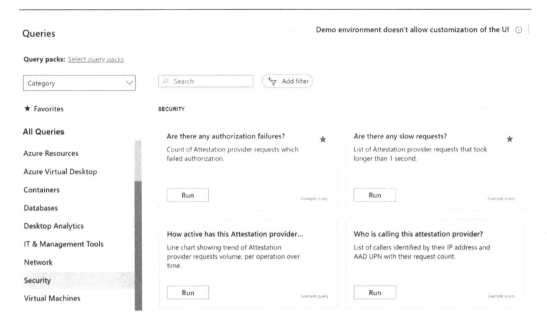

Figure 12.12 – Built-in KQL

You can access the environment by visiting aka.ms/1ademo; you just need an Azure account. Let us look at the use cases of built-in queries:

- They can help organizations quickly identify and address common security misconfigurations and vulnerabilities

- Built-in queries are aligned with industry standards and best practices, making them valuable for compliance assessments

- Built-in queries serve as a starting point for security assessments, especially for users who are new to the CSPM tool or cloud security in general

These are the benefits of using built-in queries:

- **Efficiency**: Built-in queries save time and effort by providing pre-configured assessments for common security concerns

- **Compliance**: Many built-in queries are designed to check compliance with specific regulatory standards, such as **General Data Protection Regulation (GDPR)**, **Health Insurance Portability and Accountability (HIPPA)**, and **Center for Internet Security (CIS)** benchmarks

- **Education**: Queries can be educational tools for users who want to understand essential cloud security considerations

Built-in query examples

Let us take a look at some examples of built-in queries:

- **Malicious blobs per storage account**: The following built-in query will fetch a list of all storage blobs with malicious scan results and group the results by storage account name:

```
StorageMalwareScanningResults
| where ScanResultType == "Malicious"
| summarize BlobUris = make_list(BlobUri), count() by
StorageAccountName
```

- **All attack paths by specific risk level**: The following built-in query will get all attack paths with a specific risk level, such as "critical," and will only show the top 100 outcomes:

```
SecurityAttackPathData
| where RiskLevel == "Critical"
| limit 100
```

- **All firewall decisions**: The following query will display all decisions taken by the firewall, which includes hits on network, application, and NAT rules, as well as threat intelligence hits and IDPS signature hits; it will display the top 100 results:

```
AZFWNetworkRule
| union AZFWApplicationRule, AZFWNatRule, AZFWThreatIntel,
AZFWIdpsSignature
| take 100
```

Built-in KQL comes with many benefits and can be helpful in many ways. However, it cannot serve all your needs. That is why the CSPM analyst/admin should learn as much as possible in order to be able to construct queries that fulfill specific needs. Let us learn more about that.

Custom queries in the query explorer

Custom queries allow users to create their own tailored queries based on their own unique requirements and security concerns. These queries are highly customizable and can be fine-tuned to address specific aspects of cloud security. Custom queries are ideal for organizations with unique security policies or compliance requirements that cannot be fully addressed by pre-built queries. They can be used to investigate specific incidents or areas of concern within the cloud environment. Custom queries are beneficial when you need to monitor and assess specific resource types, configurations, or behaviors that are not covered by built-in queries.

These are the benefits of using custom queries:

- **Flexibility**: Custom queries offer the flexibility to address a wide range of security scenarios and use cases

- **Tailored assessments**: Organizations can align custom queries with their specific security and compliance needs

- **Incident investigation**: Custom queries are valuable for in-depth investigations when suspicious activities or vulnerabilities are detected

Custom query – simple examples

Let us try to understand custom queries by using simple examples:

- **List all security groups with insecure rules**: The following query lists security groups with insecure rules, allowing traffic from any source on any port:

```
SecurityGroup
| where SecurityGroupType == "Ingress" and RuleType == "Allow"
and RulePort == "0-65535" and RuleSource == "0.0.0.0/0"
| project SecurityGroupName, RuleDescription, ResourceName,
ResourceLocation
```

- **Find exposed storage buckets**: The following query identifies storage buckets exposed to the public:

```
StorageBucket
| where ExposedToPublic == true
| project StorageBucketName, ResourceName, ResourceLocation
```

- **Identify unused VMs**: The following query will find VMs that are running but not sending heartbeats, possibly indicating unused or compromised instances:

```
VirtualMachine
| where ResourceStatus == "Running" and HeartbeatStatus == "No
Heartbeat"
| project VMName, ResourceName, ResourceLocation
```

Let us now understand another query with a specific use case below.

Custom query use case scenario and example

Let us understand more about custom queries by using a scenario and a suitable example. This example involves multiple data sources and advanced querying in KQL, and it focuses on identifying potential lateral movement paths in a multi-cloud environment using data from different sources. Let us name this query *Potential Lateral Movement Paths Analysis*. The query would be helpful in a scenario where security teams want to proactively identify and assess potential threats related to lateral movement within a multi-cloud environment.

Scenario

An organization operates in a multi-cloud environment with resources distributed across various cloud providers (e.g., Azure, AWS, and GCP). The security team is responsible for monitoring and securing the cloud infrastructure to prevent unauthorized access and lateral movement between resources.

Objective

The security team wants to identify potential paths that an attacker might exploit to move laterally within the environment. Lateral movement refers to the technique used by attackers to navigate from one compromised system to another to achieve their objectives.

Use case for the query

The query workflow is as follows:

- **Data sources**: The organization's CSPM tool collects security events and logs related to network traffic, including allowed outbound and denied inbound traffic

- **Query execution**: The security team executes the *Potential Lateral Movement Paths Analysis* query on the collected data

The query combines information on allowed outbound traffic and denied inbound traffic to identify potential paths where traffic is allowed to leave a source but denied upon arrival at another destination:

```
let allowedOutboundTraffic = SecurityEvent
| where ActionType == "Allow" and Direction == "Outbound"
| summarize allowedDestinations = make_set(DestinationAddress) by
SourceAddress, TimeGenerated;
let deniedInboundTraffic = SecurityEvent
| where ActionType == "Deny" and Direction == "Inbound"
| summarize deniedSources = make_set(SourceAddress) by
DestinationAddress, TimeGenerated;
let potentialLateralMovementPaths = allowedOutboundTraffic
| join kind=inner (
    deniedInboundTraffic
) on DestinationAddress
| project SourceAddress, DestinationAddress, allowedDestinations,
deniedSources
| extend potentialLateralMovements = set_
difference(allowedDestinations, deniedSources)
| where array_length(potentialLateralMovements) > 0;
potentialLateralMovementPaths
| project SourceAddress, DestinationAddress, potentialLateralMovements
```

The preceding code for the query can be understood as follows:

- **Data preparation**: The query starts by preparing two datasets: `allowedOutboundTraffic` and `deniedInboundTraffic`. These datasets contain information about allowed outbound traffic and denied inbound traffic.

- **Joining datasets**: The query performs an inner join on the `DestinationAddress` field to identify instances where outbound traffic was allowed, and inbound traffic was denied.

- **Identifying potential lateral movement**: The query then projects relevant fields and uses the `set_difference` function to identify potential lateral movement paths by subtracting denied sources from allowed destinations.

- **Filtering results**: Finally, the query filters the results to include only instances where potential lateral movements are detected.

- **Identification of potential threats**: The results of the query provide insights into potential lateral movement paths, highlighting instances where outbound traffic is allowed but inbound traffic to the same destination is denied. These patterns may indicate suspicious or unauthorized attempts at lateral movement within the multi-cloud environment.

- **Mitigation and investigation**: Armed with this information, the security team can proactively investigate and mitigate potential threats. They may focus on securing specific connections, tightening access controls, and addressing vulnerabilities in the identified paths.

- **Enhanced security posture**: By identifying and addressing potential lateral movement paths early on, the organization enhances its overall security posture and reduces the risk of unauthorized access and lateral movement within the multi-cloud environment.

In summary, this query is valuable for security teams aiming to stay ahead of potential threats by identifying and addressing possible lateral movement paths within their multi-cloud infrastructure. It supports a proactive and targeted approach to security monitoring and response.

Let us now learn about the best practices associated with using built-in queries.

Best practices for effective investigation

With a query explorer, users can search through extensive cloud data logs and resources, identify security vulnerabilities, detect compliance violations, and discover potential threats. It offers the flexibility to craft tailored queries for specific security concerns while also including built-in queries aligned with industry standards and best practices, streamlining security assessments, and ensuring robust cloud security. Here are some best practices for when using KQL within the context of cloud security and threat hunting:

- **Understand the data sources**: Before diving into querying and threat hunting, it is crucial to have a deep understanding of the data sources and logs available in your cloud environment. Each platform (e.g., AWS, Azure, and Google Cloud) has its own set of logs and data types. Familiarize yourself with these data sources to make informed queries.

- **Start with basic queries**: Begin your threat-hunting journey with straightforward and broad queries. Gradually refine your queries based on the results. This iterative approach helps you narrow down your focus and find potential threats more effectively.

- **Use KQL functions wisely**: KQL provides a variety of functions for data manipulation and analysis. Use these functions wisely to aggregate, filter, and transform data as needed.

- **Leverage time-based queries**: Time-based queries are invaluable in threat hunting. Analyzing data over specific time ranges can help you spot patterns and anomalies. Experiment with different time intervals to identify trends.

- **Parameterize queries**: Make your queries adaptable by parameterizing them. This allows you to reuse queries with different values, making it easier to investigate various aspects of your cloud environment.

- **Documentation and collaboration**: Document your queries and findings comprehensively. This helps in knowledge sharing and collaboration within your security team. Encourage team members to annotate queries and share insights.

- **Limited Integration**: While KQL is commonly associated with Microsoft's Azure platform, its integration with other security tools and platforms might be limited. This can be a drawback for organizations using a diverse set of security solutions. Alternatively, every CSPM tool offers a query explorer feature that you can utilize for security investigations.

Now that we understand the best practices, here are some lessons learned.

Lessons learned from threat investigation

Based on understanding acquired through years of experiences, failure, and learning from mistakes in this domain, here are some lessons learned that can be applied to write better queries for threat hunting:

- **Start early**: Do not wait for a security incident to start using the query explorer and KQL. Proactive threat hunting is more effective when you are familiar with the tools and techniques beforehand.

- **Regular updates**: Cloud environments change frequently due to new deployments and updates. Ensure that your queries and threat-hunting practices evolve to accommodate these changes.

- **Context matters**: While KQL is a powerful tool, it is essential to consider the context of your cloud environment. Anomalies that might be benign in one context could be significant threats in another. Understanding your specific use case is crucial.

- **Data retention policies**: Be aware of data retention policies in your cloud environment. Querying historical data can be critical for threat hunting, so make sure you have access to the relevant logs.

- **Alerting and automation**: Once you have identified potential threats, consider automating alerting and response processes. This can significantly reduce response times and improve security posture.

- **Continuous learning**: The threat landscape is constantly evolving. Regularly update your knowledge of KQL and the query explorer to stay ahead of emerging threats and vulnerabilities.

- **Limited graphic interface:** KQL lacks extensive graphical query builders or visual design tools, requiring users to compose queries through a command-line interface or text-based editors. This design choice emphasizes the scripting nature of KQL, providing fine-grained control but potentially requiring users to be familiar with the language's syntax. Visualizations of KQL results often occur in external tools with more robust graphical interfaces.

- **Limited visualization:** While KQL supports extracting and manipulating data, the actual visualization of query results is often performed using external tools like Power BI or other data visualization platforms. KQL itself does provide very limited visualizations (table, pie chart, etc.), and users must rely on third-party tools to represent query output in a visually appealing manner.

- **Data volume challenges:** As datasets grow, querying and processing massive amounts of information using KQL may lead to performance issues, increased query execution times, and **resource intensiveness**. Optimizing queries, leveraging appropriate indexes, and considering data partitioning strategies are essential to address challenges related to the scale and volume of data when working with KQL.

- **Dependency on log formats:** KQL relies on a well-defined schema to interpret and analyze data. Inconsistent or poorly formatted log data may pose challenges in constructing accurate and meaningful queries. Organizations using KQL need to ensure that their log formats align with the expectations of the language to achieve reliable and efficient data analysis.

Mastering the query explorer using KQL or any other supported query language for threat hunting is an ongoing process and a critical skill for cloud security professionals. By following these best practices and learning from past experiences, security professionals can enhance their ability to detect and respond to security threats effectively within cloud environments.

Summary

The query explorer is a vital function for CSPM analysts to navigate through extensive cloud infrastructure data, allowing them to discover potential security threats and vulnerabilities. KQL is introduced as the key language for constructing precise queries that can help in identifying security issues within cloud environments. Throughout the chapter, you gained insights into the practical use of query explorers and KQL. You learned about the syntax, structure, and various operators and functions associated with KQL queries, finding out how to filter, aggregate, and analyze cloud-related data effectively. The chapter provided practical examples and best practices for leveraging query explorers and KQL to enhance threat detection and response within cloud environments.

In the next chapter, we will discuss another core feature of CSPM tools: vulnerability and patch management.

Further reading

To learn more about the topics that were covered in this chapter, take a look at the following resources:

- *KQL Online Course: The Basics of Kusto Query Language | Pluralsight*: `https://www.pluralsight.com/courses/kusto-query-language-kql-from-scratch`

- *Advanced KQL Framework Workbook - Empowering you to become KQL-savvy - Microsoft Community Hub*: `https://techcommunity.microsoft.com/t5/microsoft-sentinel-blog/advanced-kql-framework-workbook-empowering-you-to-become-kql/ba-p/3033766`

- *Collection of KQL queries (reprise99 on github.com)*: `https://github.com/reprise99/Sentinel-Queries`

- *Kusto Query Language (KQL) overview – Azure Data Explorer | Microsoft Learn*: `https://learn.microsoft.com/en-us/azure/data-explorer/kusto/query/`

- *Analyze monitoring data with Kusto Query Language - Training | Microsoft Learn*: `https://learn.microsoft.com/en-us/training/paths/kusto-query-language/`

13
Vulnerability and Patch Management

As organizations continue to harness the power of cloud services, they are also exposed to many vulnerabilities that can compromise their data and systems. The cloud infrastructure, while offering unprecedented flexibility and scalability, presents a unique set of challenges when it comes to safeguarding against threats. In this chapter, we'll delve deep into vulnerability and patch management – a fundamental pillar of any comprehensive CSPM strategy. Vulnerability management not only safeguards an organization's digital assets but also contributes to its overall compliance and risk management efforts, hence why understanding how to identify, assess, and mitigate vulnerabilities becomes crucial. We will explore vulnerabilities that emerge within cloud environments, emphasizing the dynamic nature of the cloud and how it necessitates a proactive approach to security. We will also explore one of the key elements of this chapter: the role of **Cyber Threat Intelligence (CTI)** in enhancing vulnerability management.

Furthermore, by delving into the foundations of vulnerability management and patching, we'll equip you with case studies and real-world examples illustrating the consequences of inadequate vulnerability and patch management.

This chapter will cover the following topics:

- Vulnerability management overview
- Effective vulnerability management and CSPM tools
- Challenges and complexities of managing vulnerabilities in cloud environments
- Best practices for vulnerability assessment and prioritization
- The importance of timely and efficient patch management
- Insights into automated vulnerability scanning and remediation
- The role of CTI in vulnerability management
- Case studies and real-world examples

This chapter will empower you to navigate the complex landscape of vulnerabilities and patches within the cloud. By the end of this exploration, you will be well equipped to proactively implement robust vulnerability and patch management practices, safeguarding your cloud infrastructure in an ever-changing threat landscape.

Vulnerability and patch management overview

Vulnerability management is a critical component of cybersecurity that focuses on identifying, assessing, prioritizing, mitigating, and monitoring security vulnerabilities within an organization's IT infrastructure. Vulnerability management is a complex field with various terminologies and concepts.

Important terminologies

Let's understand some basic but extremely important terminologies associated with vulnerability and patch management:

- **Vulnerability**: A vulnerability is a weakness or flaw in a system, software, or configuration that can be exploited by attackers to compromise security. Vulnerability assessment is the process of identifying, categorizing, and prioritizing vulnerabilities within an organization's IT infrastructure. It involves automated scanning tools and manual testing.

- **Patch**: A patch is a software update provided by a vendor to fix or mitigate a known vulnerability. Applying patches is a common method of mitigating vulnerabilities as they are designed to close the security loophole. Patch management is the practice of planning, testing, and deploying security patches and updates to address vulnerabilities in a controlled and systematic manner.

- **Exploit**: An exploit is a piece of code or an attack technique that takes advantage of a vulnerability to compromise a system or gain unauthorized access.

- **Zero-day vulnerability**: A zero-day vulnerability is a security flaw or weakness in software, hardware, or a system that is actively exploited by attackers before the vendor or developers are aware of it. It is called "zero-day" because there are zero days of protection against it when it is first discovered.

- **Penetration testing**: Penetration testing, or ethical hacking, involves simulating real-world attacks to discover vulnerabilities in a controlled environment. It helps organizations identify security weaknesses before malicious actors can exploit them.

- **Threat intelligence**: Threat intelligence refers to information about current threats and vulnerabilities in the cybersecurity landscape. It helps organizations stay informed about emerging risks.

- **Asset management**: Asset management involves maintaining an inventory of all hardware, software, and network resources within an organization. It is crucial for identifying and tracking vulnerabilities.

- **Remediation**: Remediation is the process of addressing and mitigating vulnerabilities. It can involve applying patches, reconfiguring systems, or implementing security controls to reduce risk.

- **Risk assessment**: Risk assessment involves evaluating vulnerabilities to determine their potential impact on an organization's security and operations. It helps prioritize which vulnerabilities should be addressed first.

- **Scan report**: A scan report is a document that's generated after a vulnerability scan that details the vulnerabilities discovered, their severity, and recommendations for mitigation.

- **False positive**: A false positive occurs when a vulnerability scanner incorrectly identifies a non-existent vulnerability. It can lead to wasted resources if not effectively managed.

- **Common Vulnerability Scoring System (CVSS) score**: The CVSS score is a numeric value that's assigned to a vulnerability to quantify its severity based on a range of factors, such as impact and exploitability.

- **Common Vulnerabilities and Exposures (CVE)**: CVE is a standardized identifier for a specific security vulnerability or exposure, providing a unique reference point for vulnerabilities. A CVE identifier is a unique reference number that's assigned to a specific vulnerability, allowing for consistent tracking and reference.

- **Software End-of-Life (EOL) or End-of-Support (EOS)**: EOL/EOS refers to the point in time when a software product or version is no longer supported by the vendor, making it susceptible to unpatched vulnerabilities.

- **Security baseline**: A security baseline is a set of security settings or configurations that represent a secure starting point for a system or application.

- **Compliance**: Compliance refers to adhering to industry regulations, standards, and internal security policies. Vulnerability management plays a crucial role in maintaining compliance.

These terminologies are fundamental to understanding and implementing effective vulnerability management practices in an organization's cybersecurity strategy. Now, let's learn more about CVE and CVSS.

The importance and usability of CVE and CVSS

CVE and CVSS are two important cybersecurity standards that are used to identify and assess vulnerabilities in software, hardware, and other systems. They play a crucial role in providing a common language and framework for describing and quantifying security vulnerabilities. Let's try to understand them further:

- **CVE**: CVE is a standardized identifier for a specific security vulnerability or exposure. Each CVE entry is a unique, publicly disclosed vulnerability or issue that has been assigned a unique CVE identifier. CVE is used to provide a common reference point for vulnerabilities, making it easier for security professionals, researchers, vendors, and organizations to share information about vulnerabilities consistently and unambiguously. CVE helps in tracking and managing vulnerabilities, streamlining vulnerability reporting and communication, and facilitating coordination among various stakeholders in the cybersecurity community:

- **Structure**: A CVE entry consists of a CVE identifier (for example, CVE-2023-12345) and a description of the vulnerability, including details about affected software or systems, the severity of the issue, and any relevant references or links.

- **Assignment**: CVE entries are assigned and maintained by the MITRE Corporation (`https://cve.mitre.org`), a nonprofit organization that operates the CVE program. Security researchers and organizations can request CVE identifiers for newly discovered vulnerabilities.

> **Note**
> The CVE database is being migrated to a new portal: `https://cve.org`.

- **CVSS**: CVSS is a standardized system for assessing the severity of security vulnerabilities. It provides a numeric score, known as the CVSS score, that quantifies the risk associated with a vulnerability. CVSS helps organizations prioritize their efforts in addressing vulnerabilities by quantifying the potential impact and exploitability of each vulnerability:

  - **Components**: The CVSS score is composed of several components, including Base, Temporal, and Environmental metrics. The Base score represents the intrinsic qualities of the vulnerability, while the Temporal and Environmental metrics provide additional context based on the specific circumstances of the vulnerability in a given environment.

  - **Base metrics**: The Base score is calculated using various factors, including the impact on confidentiality, integrity, and availability; the complexity of the attack required; and the privileges required by the attacker.

  - **Scoring range**: The CVSS Base score typically ranges from 0.0 to 10.0, with higher scores indicating greater severity. The Temporal and Environmental scores can also contribute to the overall score. CVSS scores are widely used by organizations to prioritize and categorize vulnerabilities so that they can make informed decisions about which vulnerabilities require immediate attention and which can be addressed later.

  - **Updates**: CVSS is periodically updated to reflect changes in the threat landscape and to improve its accuracy in assessing vulnerabilities. CVSS is managed and maintained by a consortium of organizations, primarily coordinated by the **Forum of Incident Response and Security Teams (FIRST)**. FIRST (`https://first.org/cvss`) is a global nonprofit organization that focuses on improving the incident response and security practices of its members and the broader cybersecurity community.

CVE and CVSS are essential tools in cybersecurity. CVE provides a standardized way to reference and identify vulnerabilities, while CVSS offers a standardized method for quantifying the severity of those vulnerabilities. Together, these standards help security professionals and organizations effectively manage and respond to security threats.

Now, let's take a brief look at an effective vulnerability management life cycle.

Vulnerability management life cycle

Vulnerability management is a continuous process that's designed to proactively identify, assess, prioritize, remediate, and monitor vulnerabilities in an organization's information systems. The goal of vulnerability management is to reduce an organization's exposure to potential security threats and attacks. The vulnerability management process life cycle consists of several key stages:

- **Identification**: This is the first step in vulnerability management. It involves discovering potential vulnerabilities within an organization's assets. Vulnerabilities can include software bugs, misconfigurations, outdated software, weak passwords, and more. Various tools and techniques, such as vulnerability scanning and penetration testing, are used to identify these weaknesses.

- **Assessment**: Once vulnerabilities have been identified, they need to be assessed for their severity and potential impact on the organization's security. This involves analyzing factors such as their ease of exploitation, the potential damage or data loss, and the criticality of the affected system.

- **Prioritization**: Not all vulnerabilities are equally important or pose the same level of risk. Prioritization involves assigning a risk rating or score to each vulnerability based on its severity. This helps organizations focus their efforts on addressing the most critical vulnerabilities first. Prioritization is crucial; effective prioritization will be discussed in the next section of this chapter.

- **Mitigation**: After prioritization, organizations develop a plan to remediate or mitigate the vulnerabilities. This involves applying security patches, reconfiguring systems, changing passwords, or implementing security controls to reduce the risk associated with the vulnerabilities.

- **Verification**: Once mitigations have been implemented, it is crucial to verify that they were successful in addressing the vulnerabilities. This involves retesting or re-scanning the affected systems to confirm that the vulnerabilities have been properly remediated.

- **Monitoring and maintenance**: Vulnerability management is an ongoing process. Organizations should continuously monitor their IT environment for new vulnerabilities and apply patches and updates as necessary. Regular vulnerability assessments and scans are to be conducted to keep the infrastructure secure.

- **Reporting and documentation**: It is important to maintain a record of all identified vulnerabilities and their assessments, mitigations, and verification results. Comprehensive documentation helps in audit compliance and provides a historical reference for future assessments.

- **Risk management**: Vulnerability management is closely tied to an organization's risk management strategy. It helps organizations make informed decisions about which vulnerabilities to address based on their potential impact on the business and the resources available for mitigation.

- **Compliance and regulations**: Many industries and regions have specific compliance requirements related to vulnerability management. Organizations must ensure that their vulnerability management practices align with these regulations and standards.

- **Security awareness and training**: Employees play a crucial role in vulnerability management. Regular security awareness training can help employees identify and report potential vulnerabilities, reducing the organization's attack surface.

To summarize, vulnerability management is a proactive approach to cybersecurity that helps organizations identify, assess, prioritize, and mitigate security vulnerabilities to reduce the risk of security breaches and data loss. It requires a combination of technology, processes, and a commitment to ongoing security efforts to be effective in today's rapidly evolving threat landscape.

Effective strategies to prioritize vulnerabilities

Prioritizing vulnerabilities is a critical aspect of effective cybersecurity management. The prioritization process should consider various factors to ensure that limited resources are allocated to address the most critical and impactful vulnerabilities first. Here's a step-by-step guide on how to prioritize vulnerabilities:

- **Understand your assets**: Begin by having a comprehensive understanding of your organization's assets. This includes both external and internal assets. External assets are systems and services that are accessible from the internet, while internal assets are those within your organization's network.

- **Asset criticality**: Assess the criticality of each asset in your environment. Not all assets are of equal importance. Consider factors such as the asset's role in business operations, the data it handles, and its impact on business continuity. This criticality assessment helps in prioritizing vulnerabilities in assets that are more vital to your organization.

- **CVSS score**: Use CVSS to assign a numerical score to each vulnerability. CVSS provides a standardized method for assessing the severity of vulnerabilities based on factors such as exploitability, impact, and complexity. Prioritize vulnerabilities with higher CVSS scores as they are generally considered more severe.

- **Asset context**: Consider the context in which each asset is used. Not all vulnerabilities with the same CVSS score have an equal impact on different assets. As an example, a CVSS 10 vulnerability on a staging server may have less impact than the same vulnerability on a production server. Assess the use, implementation, and environment of each asset to understand its true risk.

- **Asset inventory or Configuration Management Database (CMDB)**: Leverage your organization's asset inventory or CMDB to understand the attributes of each asset. This information, such as the asset's purpose, the data it processes, and its environment (staging versus production), helps in contextualizing vulnerabilities and prioritizing them accordingly.

- **Consider exploitation potential**: Evaluate the likelihood of a vulnerability being exploited. Some vulnerabilities may have a high CVSS score but a low likelihood of exploitation due to specific conditions required for an exploit. Prioritize vulnerabilities that are not only severe but also have a higher likelihood of being exploited.

- **Patch availability**: Check whether patches or mitigations are available for the identified vulnerabilities. Prioritize vulnerabilities for which patches are readily available, as these can be quickly remediated to reduce the risk of exploitation.

- **Regulatory and compliance requirements**: Consider any regulatory or compliance requirements that mandate addressing specific vulnerabilities. Prioritize vulnerabilities that, if exploited, could lead to non-compliance with industry regulations or legal requirements.

- **Continuous monitoring**: Implement continuous monitoring to detect new vulnerabilities and changes in the threat landscape. Prioritize the assessment and remediation of newly identified vulnerabilities to stay ahead of emerging threats.

- **Risk acceptance and mitigation**: In cases where immediate remediation is not feasible, consider risk acceptance and implement compensating controls or mitigation strategies to reduce the risk until a patch can be applied.

In short, prioritizing vulnerabilities should be a nuanced process that considers the criticality of assets, CVSS scores, asset context, and other relevant factors. It's essential to tailor the prioritization strategy to the specific needs and risk tolerance of your organization. Regularly reassess and update your vulnerability management strategy to adapt to changes in your environment and the evolving threat landscape.

Now that we understand how to prioritize vulnerabilities, let's understand vulnerability and patch management in the context of a hybrid cloud environment.

Effective vulnerability management and CSPM tools

As we have already discussed, vulnerability and patch management are some of the core features of major CSPM tools. A CSPM tool can play a crucial role in effective vulnerability management by helping you identify and remediate vulnerabilities in your cloud environment. But here is a point to ponder – an organization may already have vulnerability management tools such as *Qualys*, *OpenVAS*, and *Tenable Nessus* for managing vulnerabilities of their traditional data center and on-premises infrastructure. *Why do they need a CSPM tool for vulnerability management in their cloud infrastructure? Is it worth spending additional cost on a CSPM tool for this purpose? What are the advantages of a CSPM tool over a traditional tool?*

Let's understand how vulnerabilities are different in cloud environments and why they need extra attention.

Cloud vulnerabilities and CSPM tool relevance in the hybrid cloud

You must be wondering, what difference does it make for vulnerabilities regarding whether they are associated with on-premises resources or cloud resources? Right? A vulnerability is a vulnerability, no matter where it's found. You are correct in thinking this. Vulnerabilities represent weaknesses or flaws in systems or software that can potentially be exploited by attackers, and the fundamental nature of these vulnerabilities remains consistent whether they are associated with on-premises resources or cloud resources. However, there are important contextual differences that arise when dealing with vulnerabilities in on-premises versus cloud environments:

- **Exposure and attack surface**: The attack surface for cloud resources can be vastly different from on-premises resources. Cloud environments are often internet-facing, and misconfigurations or vulnerabilities can be more accessible to attackers. This makes it critical to identify and address cloud-specific issues, such as exposed S3 buckets or unsecured API endpoints.

- **Dynamic nature of cloud environments**: Cloud environments are highly dynamic, with resources being provisioned and decommissioned on demand. This rapid change introduces a unique set of challenges for vulnerability management as traditional on-premises tools may struggle to keep up with the pace of change.

- **Cloud-specific vulnerabilities and misconfigurations**: While the core concept of a vulnerability remains the same, cloud environments introduce new types of vulnerabilities and misconfigurations that may not exist in traditional on-premises infrastructure. These include issues such as overly permissive IAM roles, unencrypted storage, and cloud-specific service misconfigurations.

- **Visibility and control**: Visibility and control in cloud environments can be different from on-premises environments. Organizations need specialized tools to gain deep visibility into cloud resources, monitor configuration changes, and enforce security policies.

- **Compliance and regulatory requirements**: Compliance requirements and regulations often differ for on-premises and cloud environments. CSPM tools are designed to help organizations maintain compliance in the cloud by identifying vulnerabilities and misconfigurations that could lead to compliance violations.

- **Elasticity and scalability**: Cloud environments offer greater elasticity and scalability, which means that vulnerabilities can have a more significant and rapid impact. Tools in the cloud need to adapt to these characteristics.

While the concept of a vulnerability remains consistent, the context in which vulnerabilities exist can vary significantly between on-premises and cloud environments. This contextual difference necessitates specialized tools such as CSPM tools to effectively identify, prioritize, and remediate vulnerabilities in cloud resources. On-premises vulnerability management tools are effective for traditional IT environments, while CSPM tools are essential for cloud-specific vulnerability management due to the unique characteristics, risks, and requirements of cloud environments. They provide the necessary adaptability, scalability, and automation to effectively manage vulnerabilities in the cloud while ensuring security and compliance. However, in many cases, a combination of both on-premises and cloud-specific VM tools may be necessary to cover the full range of an organization's infrastructure.

Now that we understand the vulnerabilities, their impact, and the importance of modern CSPM tools over traditional vulnerability management tools, let's understand patch management in the context of a hybrid cloud environment.

Effective patch management and CSPM tools

Patch management is a critical component of cybersecurity and IT management that involves identifying, applying, and managing software patches and updates to address vulnerabilities and improve the security and stability of software systems, operating systems, and applications. The primary goals of patch management are to mitigate security vulnerabilities and ensure software reliability and compliance.

Patch management for cloud environments differs from its on-premises counterpart because of all the reasons explained previously.

The importance of timely and efficient patch management

As we've discussed, patch management is a critical component of cybersecurity and IT operations that focuses on the timely and efficient application of software updates, patches, and fixes to address known vulnerabilities in software, operating systems, applications, and hardware. The importance of timely and efficient patch management cannot be overstated as it directly contributes to the overall security and stability of an organization's IT infrastructure. In multi-cloud and hybrid environments, where you are using multiple cloud service providers and potentially integrating various services and applications, the importance of patch management becomes even more pronounced.

Here are some key reasons why timely and efficient patch management is essential in a multi-cloud environment:

- **Vulnerability mitigation**: The primary purpose of patch management is to address vulnerabilities that could be exploited by cybercriminals or malicious actors. Timely application of patches closes security holes, reducing the risk of attacks.

- **Compliance**: Many industries have strict regulatory requirements for data protection and security. Efficient patch management helps ensure that your multi-cloud environment complies with these regulations. Failure to do so can result in legal and financial penalties.

- **Data protection**: Timely patching reduces the risk of data breaches. In a multi-cloud environment, data may be distributed across various platforms and services, making it critical to protect data at every point. Patching vulnerabilities helps safeguard sensitive information.

- **Operational stability**: Patching is not just about security; it also addresses stability and performance issues. Outdated software can cause system crashes, slowdowns, and other operational problems. Efficient patch management minimizes these disruptions, ensuring that your multi-cloud environment runs smoothly.

- **Cost savings**: Proactive patch management can save you money in the long run. It is typically less expensive to prevent security incidents and address issues promptly than it is to deal with the aftermath of a breach or downtime.

- **Business continuity**: In a multi-cloud environment, various interconnected services and applications may rely on each other. A vulnerability in one component can affect the entire system. Timely patching helps maintain business continuity by reducing the chances of widespread failures.

- **Reputation management**: Security breaches and service disruptions can harm your organization's reputation. Customers and partners expect their data to be protected, and they rely on the availability of your services. Efficient patch management helps you maintain trust with stakeholders.

- **Agility and scalability**: A well-patched multi-cloud environment is more agile and scalable. You can confidently adopt new cloud services and technologies, knowing that you have a strong security foundation in place.

Timely and efficient patch management is a cornerstone of cybersecurity and risk management. It helps organizations stay ahead of cyber threats, maintain compliance, protect sensitive data, and ensure the reliability of IT systems. Neglecting patch management can leave an organization vulnerable to a wide range of security threats and their associated consequences. Therefore, a proactive and well-structured approach to patch management is essential for modern businesses and institutions. Now, let's dive deep into effective patch management processes.

Effective patch management process

Patch management in a multi-cloud environment is a critical component and requires a well-structured and comprehensive process that addresses the unique challenges presented by the dynamic and distributed nature of multi-cloud deployments. Let's understand the patch management process:

- **Define your patch management policy**: Establish clear policies and procedures for patch management, including roles and responsibilities. Determine the severity levels for patches (for example, critical, important, and optional) and prioritize accordingly.

- **Inventory and assessment**: Create an inventory of all systems, software, and hardware in your environment. Regularly scan for vulnerabilities and assess their impact.

- **Vulnerability identification**: Subscribe to vulnerability databases, such as the **National Vulnerability Database** (**NVD**), to stay informed about new vulnerabilities. Use vulnerability scanning tools to identify vulnerabilities in your systems and applications.

- **Patch testing**: Set up a test environment that mirrors your production environment. Test patches in this environment to ensure they do not disrupt critical operations or cause compatibility issues.

- **Patch deployment**: Develop a deployment plan that outlines the order and timeline for applying patches. Use automation tools, such as patch management software, to streamline the deployment process. Schedule patching during maintenance windows to minimize disruption.

- **Monitoring and reporting**: Continuously monitor the health and security of your systems after patch deployment. Implement monitoring tools to detect anomalies or issues related to patches. Generate reports to track the status of patches and compliance with patch management policies.

- **Rollback plan**: Develop a rollback plan in case a patch causes critical issues. Ensure that you can quickly revert to a previous state if necessary.

- **Documentation**: Maintain detailed records of all patch-related activities, including testing, deployment, and rollback. Document any exceptions or delays in patching.

- **Continuous improvement**: Regularly review and update your patch management process to adapt to new threats and technologies. Learn from past incidents and apply lessons learned to enhance your patch management strategy.

Keep in mind that patch management is an ongoing process, and regular updates are crucial to staying ahead of emerging threats. Effective patch management requires a well-defined process, dedicated resources, and a commitment to staying informed about emerging threats and vulnerabilities. It is a critical component of cybersecurity hygiene and plays a crucial role in maintaining the security and reliability of IT systems and networks.

Patch management tools for hybrid and multi-cloud environments

Patch management tools help organizations keep their software and systems up to date with the latest security updates and patches. In hybrid and multi-cloud environments, these tools need to be versatile and adaptable to different platforms and providers. Here is a list of the most common patch management tools for such environments:

- **Microsoft System Center Configuration Manager (SCCM)**: SCCM is a robust on-premises patch management tool that can also manage updates for Windows-based VMs in the cloud. It supports both Windows and Linux systems and can be extended to manage Azure VMs.

- **AWS Systems Manager**: AWS Systems Manager provides capabilities for managing and automating patch updates for EC2 instances, whether they are in AWS or on-premises. It supports both Windows and Linux environments.

- **VMware vCenter Update Manager**: If you are running VMware on-premises and in the cloud, vCenter Update Manager can be used to patch and update VMware virtual infrastructure, including cloud-hosted VMware environments.

- **Third-party patch management tools**: There are third-party solutions such as Ivanti, ManageEngine, and Qualys that offer hybrid and multi-cloud patch management capabilities. These tools often support a wide range of operating systems and cloud providers.

Is a CSPM tool enough for effective patch management?

CSPM tools primarily focus on identifying and addressing security misconfigurations and vulnerabilities in cloud environments. While CSPM tools play a crucial role in securing cloud infrastructure, they are not typically designed for traditional patch management. The latest CSPM tools have started introducing patch management features. For example, the Orca CSPM tool has introduced patch management as one of its core features and I am sure other vendors will also follow this path. However, CSPM alone may not be enough for patch management. Here's why:

- **Limited patching capabilities**: CSPM tools are primarily designed to detect misconfigurations and vulnerabilities within cloud services. They are not equipped to deploy operating systems or software patches on servers, which is a key function of traditional patch management tools.

- **Operating system and application patches**: Patch management involves keeping operating systems, software applications, and libraries up to date with security patches. CSPM tools are more focused on cloud-specific configurations and permissions.

- **Hybrid environments**: CSPM tools are better suited for assessing the security posture of cloud resources. In hybrid environments, where on-premises systems are involved, you need a dedicated patch management tool that can cover both on-premises and cloud-based resources.

How patch management and CSPM can work best together

To effectively manage patching in hybrid and multi-cloud environments, it is advisable to use both patch management tools and CSPM tools in conjunction:

- **Use patch management tools**: Employ dedicated patch management tools to manage the patching of on-premises servers and cloud-based VMs, ensuring all systems are up to date.

- **Use CSPM tools**: A CSPM tool is instrumental in effective patch management for multi-cloud environments. It provides comprehensive visibility, continuous monitoring, and automated remediation capabilities across all cloud providers, allowing organizations to prioritize and enforce patching policies consistently. CSPM tools integrate with existing patch management processes, ensuring that missing patches and vulnerabilities are promptly identified and addressed. Let's look at the key roles that are played by these tools in the patch management process:

  - **Patch compliance assessment**: CSPM tools can assess the compliance your cloud resources have with your patch management policies and industry standards (for example, CIS Benchmarks). They can flag resources that are not in compliance with patching requirements.

- **Automated remediation**: Many CSPM tools offer automated remediation capabilities. When a vulnerability or missing patch is detected, the CSPM tool can automatically trigger the deployment of the necessary patches or configuration changes to bring resources into compliance.

- **Prioritize patching**: CSPM tools can help you prioritize patching efforts by assessing the severity of vulnerabilities and their potential impact on your multi-cloud environment. This ensures that critical vulnerabilities are addressed first.

- **Policy enforcement**: CSPM tools can enforce security policies, including patch management policies, across all your cloud providers. This consistency is crucial for maintaining a secure and compliant multi-cloud environment.

- **Integration with patch management**: CSPM tools can integrate with your existing patch management processes and tools. This integration streamlines the identification of patch-related issues and ensures that patches are applied consistently.

- **Integrate and automate**: Whenever possible, integrate your patch management and CSPM solutions to automate actions based on CSPM findings. For example, if a CSPM tool identifies a vulnerability related to an unpatched system, it can trigger the patch management tool to initiate the patching process.

CSPM tools and patch management tools serve different but complementary purposes in hybrid and multi-cloud environments. While CSPM tools focus on cloud security posture and vulnerability assessment, patch management tools are essential for keeping operating systems and software up to date. To maximize security, organizations should leverage both types of tools and establish automation and integration between them for a comprehensive security strategy.

Now that we have understood the role of CSPM in patch management, it is time to dive deep into the role of CTI in vulnerability and patch management.

CTI and vulnerability management

In the ever-evolving landscape of cybersecurity, organizations are constantly facing new and sophisticated threats that challenge their ability to protect their digital assets. Cyberattacks are no longer limited to opportunistic hackers; they have become the domain of well-funded and highly skilled adversaries, including nation states and organized criminal groups. To effectively defend against these threats, organizations must adopt a proactive and intelligence-driven approach.

But before we dive deep into this topic, let's understand some fundamental concepts around it.

What is CTI and its key aspects?

CTI is the process of collecting, analyzing, and sharing information about cybersecurity threats and vulnerabilities. CTI is a critical component of cybersecurity efforts and is used to help organizations understand and mitigate cyber threats more effectively. Here are some key aspects of CTI:

- **Data collection**: CTI involves gathering data from a variety of sources, including network logs, security incidents, malware analysis, and information shared by other organizations, government agencies, and cybersecurity researchers. This data can include **Indicators of Compromise (IoCs)**, attack patterns, and vulnerabilities.

- **Analysis**: Once the data has been collected, it is analyzed to identify trends, patterns, and potential threats. Analysts use various techniques to assess the severity and credibility of threats, such as determining the motives of threat actors and evaluating the potential impact of an attack.

- **Classification**: Threat intelligence is often classified into different categories, such as *tactical*, *operational*, and *strategic intelligence*, based on its relevance and scope. Tactical intelligence focuses on immediate threats and helps with incident response. Operational intelligence provides insights into ongoing cyber threats and vulnerabilities, while strategic intelligence helps organizations plan long-term cybersecurity strategies.

- **Sharing**: One of the key aspects of CTI is sharing threat intelligence with trusted parties. This can include sharing information within an organization, with industry peers, or with government agencies. Sharing helps organizations collectively defend against cyber threats and build a more comprehensive understanding of the threat landscape.

- **Integration**: CTI is often integrated into an organization's security infrastructure, including **Security Information and Event Management (SIEM)** systems, **Intrusion Detection/Prevention Systems (IDS/IPS)**, and firewalls. This integration allows for real-time threat detection and automated responses to threats.

- **IoCs**: IoCs are specific pieces of information that indicate a potential cybersecurity threat. These can include IP addresses, domain names, file hashes, and patterns of suspicious behavior. CTI analysts use IoCs to detect and respond to threats.

- **Vulnerability intelligence**: CTI also includes information about software vulnerabilities and patches. This helps organizations prioritize their patch management efforts to protect against known vulnerabilities that can be exploited by threat actors.

- **Attribution**: CTI analysts may attempt to attribute cyberattacks to specific threat actors or groups based on past events. Attribution can be challenging but can provide valuable insights into the motives and tactics of adversaries.

- **Actionable intelligence**: The goal of CTI is to provide actionable intelligence that organizations can use to enhance their cybersecurity posture. This involves implementing new security controls, updating policies and procedures, or enhancing employee training.

Overall, CTI plays a crucial role in helping organizations proactively defend against cyber threats, respond to incidents effectively, and make informed decisions to strengthen their cybersecurity defenses.

The role of CTI in vulnerability and patch management

CTI plays a significant role in vulnerability and patch management by providing crucial insights and information that help organizations prioritize, address, and mitigate vulnerabilities effectively. Here's how CTI contributes to vulnerability and patch management:

- **Early detection of vulnerabilities**: CTI sources, such as threat feeds and intelligence reports, provide information about newly discovered vulnerabilities and their potential impact. This early warning allows organizations to proactively identify vulnerabilities that could be exploited by threat actors.

- **Prioritization of vulnerabilities**: Not all vulnerabilities are equally critical or pose the same level of risk to an organization. CTI helps organizations assess the severity of vulnerabilities by providing context on the likelihood of exploitation, the tactics used by threat actors, and the potential impact on business operations. This information enables organizations to prioritize patching efforts based on the most significant threats.

- **Customized threat intelligence feeds**: Organizations can subscribe to CTI feeds that are specific to their industry, technology stack, or business environment. This customization ensures that the vulnerability information that's received is highly relevant to their infrastructure, reducing noise and improving the accuracy of prioritization.

- **Threat actor tactics**: CTI often includes details about threat actors and their **Tactics, Techniques, and Procedures (TTPs)**. This information helps organizations understand how specific threat actors may attempt to exploit vulnerabilities. It guides the development of mitigation strategies and the application of patches that address the tactics used by these actors.

- **Patch testing and deployment**: CTI can inform organizations about the availability of patches and updates from software vendors. It provides information about which patches are critical for addressing known vulnerabilities. Security teams can use this data to schedule and plan patch testing and deployment, ensuring that critical vulnerabilities are addressed promptly while minimizing disruptions.

- **Exploitation trends**: CTI can highlight trends in vulnerability exploitation, such as the emergence of new exploitation techniques or specific types of software being targeted. This information can help organizations anticipate and defend against evolving threats.

- **Vulnerability scanning and assessment**: CTI can be integrated into CSPM tools. These tools can use threat intelligence data to focus their scans on known vulnerabilities that are actively being targeted by threat actors, saving time and resources.

- **Incident response**: If a vulnerability is exploited before it can be patched, CTI can provide guidance on how to respond effectively to the incident. It can include information on detection methods, IoCs, and recommended mitigation steps.

- **Policy and configuration adjustments**: CTI can inform organizations about broader security policy and configuration adjustments that can reduce vulnerability exposure. This may include implementing network segmentation, access controls, and security best practices.

By integrating CTI into vulnerability and patch management processes or CSPM tools, organizations can make more informed decisions, reduce the window of vulnerability, and enhance their overall cybersecurity posture. It enables them to stay ahead of evolving threats and respond effectively to known vulnerabilities before they can be exploited by malicious actors. CTI serves as a valuable resource for organizations to proactively identify vulnerabilities, prioritize patch management efforts, and ultimately reduce their attack surface. Let's delve into each aspect.

Identifying vulnerabilities through threat intelligence

One of the most valuable aspects of CTI in vulnerability management is its ability to identify vulnerabilities that may otherwise go unnoticed. Threat intelligence provides a proactive approach to vulnerability identification by keeping organizations informed about emerging threats and vulnerabilities. Here's how CTI aids in this process:

- **Threat actor insights**: CTI provides organizations with information about threat actors and their TTPs. By monitoring threat actor activities, organizations can gain insights into potential vulnerabilities they may exploit.

- **Zero-day vulnerabilities**: CTI helps in identifying zero-day vulnerabilities by monitoring the dark web, forums, and other sources where threat actors may disclose or discuss newly discovered vulnerabilities before they become widely known. This early warning can be critical in mitigating such vulnerabilities.

- **Vulnerability scanning and correlation**: CTI can be used to correlate threat intelligence data with vulnerability scanning results. This allows organizations to identify vulnerabilities that are actively being targeted by threat actors, enabling them to prioritize these for patching.

By identifying vulnerabilities early, organizations can take proactive steps to mitigate them before cybercriminals can exploit them.

Patch management and vulnerability prioritization

Once vulnerabilities have been identified through CTI, the next critical step is patch management and prioritization. Not all vulnerabilities are equal, and organizations must prioritize their efforts to address the most critical ones efficiently. Here's how CTI assists in this process:

- **Risk-based prioritization**: CTI helps with prioritizing vulnerabilities based on the perceived risk to the organization. For example, if CTI indicates that a vulnerability is being actively exploited in the wild, it can be classified as high-risk and prioritized for immediate patching.

- **Contextual information**: CTI provides context around vulnerabilities, such as the types of threats that may exploit them and the potential impact on the organization. This information assists in making informed decisions about which vulnerabilities should be addressed first.

- **Patch testing**: Before applying patches, organizations often perform testing to ensure they do not disrupt critical systems. CTI can guide these efforts by highlighting vulnerabilities that are actively exploited or those for which proof-of-concept code is available, making them higher priorities for testing and patching.

Reducing the attack surface with CTI

Reducing the attack surface is a fundamental goal in cybersecurity. CTI contributes significantly to this by enabling organizations to make informed decisions regarding their digital assets and configurations:

- **Proactive defense**: CTI enables organizations to take a proactive approach to reducing their attack surface. By monitoring emerging threats and vulnerabilities, organizations can implement preventive measures and security controls before an attack occurs.

- **Threat mitigation strategies**: CTI can inform organizations about specific threats and adversaries targeting their industry or sector. With this knowledge, organizations can tailor their patch management strategies to address vulnerabilities that are most likely to be exploited by these threat actors.

- **Threat modeling**: Organizations can use CTI to develop threat models that consider the evolving threat landscape. This helps in designing security architectures that minimize the exposure of critical assets to known vulnerabilities.

- **Application whitelisting**: CTI can help identify approved and unapproved applications in the environment, allowing organizations to enforce application whitelisting policies to reduce the risk of unauthorized software running on their systems.

- **Vulnerability mitigation**: By rapidly addressing vulnerabilities identified through CTI, organizations reduce the potential entry points for attackers and strengthen their overall security posture.

- **Security awareness training**: CTI can also inform security awareness training programs, ensuring that employees are educated about current threats and vulnerabilities, reducing the likelihood of social engineering attacks.

CTI is an indispensable practice/tool that plays a significant role in effective vulnerability management, offering organizations the ability to identify vulnerabilities, prioritize patches, and ultimately reduce their attack surface. By integrating CTI into their CSPM tool strategies, organizations can proactively defend against cyber threats and minimize the risk of security breaches.

CTI integration/feeds into CSPM tools

Not every CSPM tool integrates with CTI tools, nor do they provide intelligence feeds automatically. Some of the latest CSPM tools, such as Microsoft Defender for Cloud, can accept custom threat intelligence feeds (refer to `https://learn.microsoft.com/en-us/graph/api/resources/security-threatintelligence-overview?view=graph-rest-beta`). However, more research and increasing demand will lead to enhanced CSPM tools in this domain as well. Integrating CTI with CSPM tools allows organizations to proactively identify and mitigate threats in their cloud environments based on real-time threat intelligence data. Let's look at an example of how CTI can be integrated with a CSPM tool.

Scenario: An organization uses a CSPM tool to monitor and secure its cloud infrastructure on platforms such as AWS, Azure, or Google Cloud. They want to enhance their security posture by integrating CTI feeds into their CSPM tool to identify and respond to emerging threats quickly.

We can use the following integration steps:

1. **Select CTI sources**: The organization may already have CTI tools such as Mandiant onboard or be able to identify reputable CTI sources, such as threat feeds, threat intelligence platforms, and government agencies (for example, DHS and CERTs). These sources provide information on known threats, vulnerabilities, and malicious actors.

2. **Data ingestion**: The CSPM tool is configured to ingest data from selected CTI sources. This data could include IoCs, threat reports, malware signatures, and known attack patterns.

3. **Normalization**: The CTI data is normalized and enriched within the CSPM tool to make it actionable. This involves converting data into a common format, mapping it to cloud-specific resources, and correlating it with existing security policies and configurations.

4. **Alerting and prioritization**: The CSPM tool analyzes the integrated CTI data alongside the current cloud environment's configuration and activity. It generates alerts and prioritizes them based on the relevance and severity of the threats identified in the CTI feeds.

5. **Automated actions**: Depending on the severity of the threats, the CSPM tool can trigger automated actions to remediate or mitigate them. For example, it might automatically adjust security group rules, revoke access permissions, or isolate compromised resources.

6. **Human intervention**: Some threats may require human intervention. The CSPM tool can provide security analysts with detailed information from CTI sources to facilitate investigation and response.

Let's look at an example.

Example use case

Let's say an organization has integrated CTI feeds into their CSPM tool. A new threat intelligence report is received, indicating that a specific IP address is associated with a known botnet involved in DDoS attacks. The CSPM tool, using this CTI data, cross-references the IP address with the organization's cloud environment.

If the IP address is found within their cloud infrastructure, the CSPM tool can automatically take actions such as the following:

- Blocking incoming and outgoing traffic to/from the IP address

- Generating an alert for the security team to investigate further

- Logging the incident for compliance and auditing purposes

This integration enables the organization to proactively respond to threats identified through CTI, helping them maintain a strong security posture in their cloud environment. It is important to understand that this process is a generic example, so the specific implementation and capabilities of CTI and CSPM tools may vary. Due to this, organizations should carefully select tools and feeds that align with their security needs and objectives.

Case studies and real-world examples

Inadequate vulnerability and patch management can have severe consequences, leading to security breaches, data leaks, and significant financial and reputational damage. Here are some real-world examples and case studies that highlight the impact of insufficient vulnerability and patch management:

- **Equifax data breach (2017)**: Equifax, one of the major credit reporting agencies in the United States, suffered a massive data breach in 2017.

  Consequences: The breach exposed the personal information of nearly 147 million people. It occurred because Equifax failed to patch a known vulnerability in the Apache Struts framework. Hackers exploited this vulnerability to gain unauthorized access to sensitive data, leading to significant legal and financial repercussions for Equifax, including fines, lawsuits, and a tarnished reputation. Refer to `https://en.wikipedia.org/wiki/2017_Equifax_data_breach` for more details.

- **WannaCry ransomware attack (2017)**: The WannaCry ransomware attack affected organizations worldwide in 2017, causing widespread disruption.

  Consequences: The ransomware exploited a vulnerability in Microsoft Windows called EternalBlue, for which a security patch had been available for several months before the attack. Organizations that had not applied the patch fell victim to the ransomware, leading to data loss, financial losses, and operational downtime. The attack also highlighted the importance of timely patch management to prevent large-scale cyber incidents. Refer to `https://en.wikipedia.org/wiki/WannaCry_ransomware_attack` for more details.

- **NotPetya/Petya/ExPetr ransomware attack (2017)**: The NotPetya ransomware attack targeted organizations globally, with Ukraine being heavily affected.

  Consequences: The ransomware used a modified version of the EternalBlue exploit, which was responsible for its rapid spread. Again, organizations that had not applied security patches promptly fell prey to the attack. NotPetya caused extensive damage, disrupting critical infrastructure, businesses, and even government operations. The attack resulted in substantial financial losses and demonstrated the need for comprehensive patch management practices. Refer to `https://www.theguardian.com/technology/2017/dec/30/wannacry-petya-notpetya-ransomware` for more details.

- **SolarWinds supply chain attack (2020)**: The SolarWinds supply chain attack was a sophisticated cyberattack that compromised the software supply chain of SolarWinds, a widely used IT management software provider.

  Consequences: Attackers inserted malicious code into SolarWinds' software updates, which were then distributed to thousands of SolarWinds customers, including government agencies and corporations. The breach went undetected for months, leading to unauthorized access to sensitive data. In this case, inadequate supply chain security and patch management played a significant role in the breach's success, with severe consequences for national security and corporate security worldwide. Refer to `https://www.cisecurity.org/solarwinds` for more details.

- **Log4Shell vulnerability (2021)**: The Log4Shell vulnerability (CVE-2021-44228) impacted the widely used Apache Log4j library, which is commonly used in web applications and services.

  Consequences: Organizations worldwide rushed to patch their systems when Log4Shell was disclosed because it allowed attackers to execute arbitrary code remotely. The incident highlighted the importance of promptly addressing vulnerabilities in widely used open source libraries. Organizations that delayed patching faced a higher risk of exploitation and potential breaches. Refer to `https://en.wikipedia.org/wiki/Log4Shell` for more details.

These real-world examples demonstrate the far-reaching consequences of inadequate vulnerability and patch management. They emphasize the critical importance of staying vigilant, proactively applying patches, and continuously monitoring for vulnerabilities to protect against cybersecurity threats and their potentially devastating impacts.

Now, let's understand some of the most crucial operational challenges and how CSPM tools can be a good fit to effectively handle them.

Operational challenges

Operational challenges in the context of vulnerability and patch management can be numerous and complex. These challenges often stem from the dynamic nature of IT environments, the sheer volume of vulnerabilities, and the need for efficient, scalable, and automated solutions. CSPM tools can be instrumental in addressing these challenges.

Let's look at some common operational challenges and how CSPM tools can help:

- **Asset discovery and inventory management**: Maintaining an accurate inventory of assets, especially in large and dynamic cloud environments, can be difficult. Assets come and go as cloud resources scale.

  CSPM solution: CSPM tools can continuously discover and inventory cloud assets. They provide visibility into VMs, containers, storage, and network configurations, helping organizations maintain an up-to-date asset inventory.

- **Vulnerability scanning at scale**: Traditional vulnerability scanners may struggle to scan many cloud assets efficiently and comprehensively, leading to incomplete assessments.

  CSPM solution: CSPM solutions are designed to scan cloud environments at scale. They leverage cloud-native APIs and automation to perform thorough vulnerability assessments across all assets, regardless of the environment's size.

- **Prioritization and risk assessment**: Determining which vulnerabilities to address first can be challenging. Organizations need to consider severity, asset criticality, and potential business impact.

  CSPM solution: CSPM tools often integrate with vulnerability databases and risk assessment frameworks. They provide prioritization mechanisms based on factors such as the CVSS score, asset criticality, and exploitability. This helps organizations focus on the most critical vulnerabilities.

- **Patch management and remediation**: Applying patches promptly can be complex, especially in large-scale, multi-cloud environments. Patching may require coordination across teams and careful planning to minimize service disruptions.

  CSPM solution: CSPM tools can automate patch management and remediation workflows. They can initiate patching processes, apply patches, and orchestrate remediation tasks, reducing manual effort and ensuring consistency across the environment.

- **Compliance and reporting**: Demonstrating compliance with industry regulations and internal security policies requires continuous monitoring and reporting.

  CSPM solution: CSPM tools often provide compliance, monitoring, and reporting features. They assess cloud configurations against predefined benchmarks and generate compliance reports, streamlining audit and compliance efforts.

- **Integration with DevOps practices**: In modern cloud environments, DevOps practices emphasize rapid development and deployment. Integrating security into these workflows is essential but can be challenging.

  CSPM solution: CSPM solutions are designed to integrate seamlessly with DevOps pipelines. They provide APIs and integrations with popular CI/CD tools, allowing organizations to incorporate vulnerability assessments and patch management into their DevOps processes.

- **Automation and scalability**: Manually managing vulnerabilities and patches in large and dynamic cloud environments is impractical and error-prone.

  CSPM solution: CSPM tools leverage automation and scalability to address these challenges. They can automate vulnerability scanning, patching, and remediation tasks, ensuring that security measures can keep pace with the dynamic nature of cloud environments.

CSPM tools play a crucial role in addressing operational challenges related to vulnerability and patch management in cloud environments. They offer automation, scalability, visibility, and integration capabilities that are essential for maintaining a secure and compliant cloud posture while effectively managing vulnerabilities and patches.

Summary

In this chapter, we explored the critical realm of vulnerability and patch management within the context of cloud security. We delved into the challenges and complexities organizations face in identifying, prioritizing, and remedying vulnerabilities in dynamic and ever-evolving cloud environments. From real-world examples showcasing the dire consequences of inadequate vulnerability and patch management to the importance of continuous monitoring and compliance adherence, we underscored the vital role these practices play in safeguarding an organization's data, reputation, and financial stability. We also emphasized the significance of automated vulnerability scanning and remediation, highlighting how CSPM tools can streamline and strengthen these processes. CSPM tools offer a scalable, efficient, and integrated approach to vulnerability and patch management, empowering organizations to proactively protect their cloud environment. This chapter underscored the critical importance of effective vulnerability and patch management as a cornerstone of cloud security, offering insights, best practices, and real-world lessons to guide organizations toward a more secure and resilient cloud posture.

In the next chapter, we will discuss compliance and governance in the context of CSPM.

Further reading

To learn more about the topics that were covered in this chapter, take a look at the following resources:

- *Automated enterprise patch management software*: `https://encr.pw/OP8OX`

- *What is Cyber Threat Intelligence?*: `https://www.crowdstrike.com/cybersecurity-101/threat-intelligence/`

14

Compliance Management and Governance

The cloud, with its unparalleled scalability and flexibility, offers a wide range of opportunities for innovation and growth. Yet, it also presents unique challenges related to data privacy, security, and regulatory compliance. Ensuring that cloud deployments align with industry-specific regulations, international standards, and internal governance policies is a multifaceted task that demands diligence and expertise. Throughout this chapter, we will delve into the concepts of compliance and governance, illustrate the significance of maintaining data integrity and trust, examine various regulatory frameworks and standards pertinent to cloud security, including the **General Data Protection Regulation (GDPR)**, the **Health Insurance Portability and Accountability Act (HIPAA)**, **System and Organizations Controls 2 (SOC 2)**, and others, and understand their implications for cloud operations. We will further investigate the unique challenges and complexities organizations face when striving to maintain compliance in dynamic and shared cloud environments and highlight how **Cloud Security Posture Management (CSPM)** tools offer comprehensive solutions for automating compliance assessments. This chapter also emphasizes the importance of reporting in demonstrating compliance and governance adherence, with a focus on real-time insights. In the end, it showcases some real-world examples and case studies of organizations successfully leveraging CSPM for compliance and governance.

This chapter will help you with insights and strategies to proactively manage compliance and governance in the cloud. You will be equipped to harness the capabilities of CSPM to maintain regulatory compliance, strengthen governance practices, and secure the trust of your cloud stakeholders.

In this chapter, we'll cover the following main topics:

- Compliance management and governance overview
- Regulatory frameworks and compliance standards
- Cloud governance frameworks
- Adapting cloud governance to the organization's need
- Use cases, scenarios, and examples
- Challenges, CSPM roles, and future trends

Let's get started!

Compliance management and governance overview

Compliance management and governance are interconnected concepts that play crucial roles in the effective and ethical operation of organizations. They involve various associated terms and principles that help ensure an organization's adherence to laws, regulations, and ethical standards while promoting responsible decision-making and accountability. Let's delve deeper into these aspects.

Compliance management

Compliance management refers to the systematic approach and set of processes that organizations adopt to ensure that they adhere to relevant laws, regulations, industry standards, internal policies, and best practices. In the context of cloud security, compliance management involves the implementation of measures to ensure that the organization's cloud infrastructure and operations align with various compliance requirements and standards. This includes data protection regulations such as GDPR or HIPAA, industry-specific standards, and internal security policies.

Key components of compliance management in cloud security include:

- **Policy development**: Creating comprehensive security policies and guidelines that outline the specific requirements and controls needed to achieve compliance. These policies should cover data handling, access controls, encryption, **incident response** (**IR**), and more. The CSPM tool offers an in-built policy that can be leveraged directly or can be customized as per organizational needs.

- **Risk assessment**: Identifying and assessing risks associated with cloud deployments, taking into consideration the potential impact on data security, privacy, and compliance.

- **Continuous monitoring**: Implementing tools and processes for continuous monitoring of cloud environments to detect and report any deviations from established compliance standards.

- **Audit and reporting**: Conducting regular audits and generating compliance reports that demonstrate adherence to relevant regulations and standards.

- **Remediation**: Developing processes to address and rectify non-compliance issues, including misconfigurations, vulnerabilities, or policy violations.

Let us now try to understand governance in the context of cloud security and how compliance and governance are related.

Governance

Governance, in the context of cloud security, refers to the framework of policies, processes, and controls that guide an organization's decision-making and actions regarding its cloud infrastructure and services. Cloud governance aims to ensure that cloud resources are used efficiently, securely, and in alignment with the organization's objectives and compliance requirements. Key elements of cloud governance include:

- **Policy framework**: Establishing a set of policies that define how cloud resources should be provisioned, configured, and managed. These policies cover aspects such as access control, data protection, resource allocation, and cost management.

- **Decision-making**: Implementing processes for making informed decisions about cloud adoption, resource provisioning, and security measures. Governance ensures that decisions align with the organization's strategic goals and **risk tolerance (RT)**.

- **Resource management**: Defining procedures for resource provisioning, monitoring, and decommissioning. Governance ensures that resources are used optimally and securely throughout their life cycle.

- **Compliance oversight**: Integrating compliance requirements into the governance framework, ensuring that cloud activities adhere to relevant regulations, industry standards, and internal policies.

- **Risk management**: Identifying and managing risks associated with cloud adoption, including security vulnerabilities, data breaches, and operational disruptions.

Let us now understand the relationship between compliance management and governance and how they complement each other.

Compliance versus governance – Distinctions and interconnections

Compliance primarily focuses on meeting external regulatory and industry standards. It is about ensuring that an organization follows specific rules and guidelines to protect sensitive data and meet legal requirements. *Governance*, on the other hand, is a broader concept, encompassing not only compliance but also internal policies, best practices, resource management, and decision-making processes. It provides the overarching structure that guides an organization's cloud activities. While compliance is a subset of governance, they are closely intertwined. Governance establishes rules (policies) and processes that enable compliance. Compliance, in turn, ensures that governance objectives are met. Compliance can be seen as a specific outcome of effective governance. Compliance management and governance are closely related and mutually reinforcing:

- **Governance sets the tone**: Effective governance sets the tone for the organization, emphasizing ethical conduct, transparency, and accountability. It defines the roles and responsibilities of leadership, including the board of directors, in overseeing compliance.

- **Compliance supports governance**: Compliance management ensures that the organization follows laws, regulations, and ethical standards. It is a key component of governance as it helps operationalize the principles set by governance frameworks.

- **Alignment of goals**: Both compliance management and governance share the common goal of ensuring that the organization operates ethically, responsibly, and in accordance with legal requirements. They work together to achieve this goal.

In short, governance is **proactive** and **strategic**, focusing on defining objectives, policies, and decision-making frameworks. Compliance is **reactive** and **operational**, focusing on ensuring adherence to established rules and standards. An effective governance framework includes compliance as a core component. It establishes processes for monitoring, enforcing, and reporting on compliance.

Why are compliance and governance crucial in cloud security?

Compliance management and governance are foundational aspects of cloud security for several compelling reasons. Let us understand why:

- **Legal and regulatory requirements**: Cloud computing often involves the storage and processing of sensitive data. Compliance with data protection laws, industry regulations, and international standards such as GDPR, HIPAA, and the **International Organization for Standardization (ISO)** *27001* is mandatory. Failure to comply can result in legal consequences and financial penalties.

- **Risk management**: Compliance and governance frameworks help organizations manage risks associated with cloud security. They provide guidelines for assessing vulnerabilities, implementing controls, and responding to security incidents.

- **Data protection**: With the increasing emphasis on data privacy, compliance and governance ensure that data is handled responsibly, protecting the privacy of customers, partners, and employees.

- **Business continuity (BC)**: Effective governance practices, such as **disaster recovery (DR)** and BC planning, are essential for ensuring that cloud services remain available and secure in the face of unexpected disruptions or cyberattacks.

- **Reputation and trust**: Compliance and governance efforts build trust with stakeholders, including customers, investors, and partners. Organizations that can demonstrate their commitment to security and ethical practices enhance their reputation and competitiveness.

- **Efficiency and cost control**: Proper governance of cloud resources can lead to cost savings by optimizing resource utilization, reducing waste, and eliminating unnecessary expenditure. Compliance management ensures that cost-cutting measures do not compromise security or compliance.

Now that we understand the importance of compliance and governance in cloud security, let us understand some of the most commonly referred regulatory frameworks and compliance standards and their significance.

Regulatory frameworks and compliance standards

Regulatory frameworks and standards serve as a foundation for maintaining order, protecting the interests of stakeholders, and achieving specific objectives related to various aspects of business operations. They are crucial for ensuring the security, privacy, and integrity of data and services hosted in the cloud. These regulations ensure data security, privacy, and legal compliance in the cloud. Here are some common regulatory frameworks and compliance standards.

GDPR

GDPR is a comprehensive data protection and privacy regulation that was enacted by the **European Union (EU)** in 2018. GDPR was designed to harmonize data protection laws across EU member states, strengthen data privacy rights for individuals, and address challenges posed by the digital age and global data flows. Here are the key aspects of GDPR:

- **Scope**: GDPR applies to any organization, regardless of its location, that processes the personal data of individuals residing in the EU. This extraterritorial scope means that even non-EU organizations must comply if they handle EU citizens' data.

- **Data subject rights**: GDPR grants individuals several rights over their personal data, including the right to access their data, request corrections, object to processing, request deletion (the "right to be forgotten"), and data portability.

- **Consent**: Organizations must obtain clear and explicit consent from individuals before processing their personal data. Consent forms must be easy to understand and separate from other terms and conditions.

- **Data protection impact assessments (DPIAs)**: Organizations must conduct DPIAs for high-risk data processing activities. A DPIA helps assess the potential impact of data processing on individuals' privacy and identify mitigation measures.

- **Data protection officers (DPOs)**: Some organizations are required to appoint a DPO, especially if they process large amounts of personal data or engage in high-risk data activities.

- **Data breach notification**: Organizations are required to notify the pertinent **data protection authority (DPA)** of data breaches within a 72-hour timeframe from the moment they become aware of the breach. Data subjects must also be notified if the breach poses a risk to their rights and freedoms.

- **Accountability and governance**: GDPR places a strong emphasis on accountability. Organizations must implement appropriate data protection policies, procedures, and documentation. They are also required to demonstrate compliance with GDPR.

- **Cross-border data transfers**: Data transfers to countries outside the EU are allowed only if the destination country provides an "adequate level of data protection." **Standard contractual clauses (SCCs)** and **binding corporate rules (BCRs)** are mechanisms for ensuring lawful data transfers.

- **Penalties**: GDPR introduces severe penalties for non-compliance. Organizations can face fines of up to *€20 million* or *4% of their global annual revenue*, whichever is higher.

- **Privacy by design and default**: GDPR promotes the integration of data protection measures into the design and operation of systems, applications, and services. Organizations must implement privacy-enhancing technologies by default.

- **Data portability**: Individuals have the right to receive their personal data from organizations in a structured, commonly used, and machine-readable format, enabling them to transfer it to other **service providers (SPs)**.

DPA

A DPA is a legal contract that outlines the terms and conditions governing the processing of personal data between a *data controller* and a *data processor*. Here are the key elements and purposes of a DPA:

- **Roles and responsibilities**:

  - **Data controller**: The entity or individual that determines the purposes and means of processing personal data.

  - **Data processor**: The entity or individual that processes personal data on behalf of the data controller.

- **Purpose limitation**: The DPA specifies the purposes for which the data processor is allowed to process personal data. It should be limited to the purposes defined by the data controller.

- **Data security**: The agreement outlines the security measures and safeguards that the data processor must implement to protect personal data from unauthorized access, disclosure, alteration, and destruction.

- **Confidentiality**: The DPA includes provisions ensuring the confidentiality of the personal data being processed. It typically includes clauses preventing the data processor from disclosing the data to third parties without explicit consent from the data controller.

- **Sub-processing**: If the data processor intends to engage sub-processors (third parties) to assist in the data processing activities, the DPA specifies the conditions under which this is allowed and the obligations of the sub-processors.

- **Data subject rights**: The agreement often outlines the data processor's obligations regarding data subject rights, including assisting the data controller in responding to data subject requests, such as access, rectification, or erasure.

- **Data breach notification**: The DPA includes provisions regarding the data processor's obligation to notify the data controller of any data breaches promptly. It may specify the timeline and content of such notifications.

- **Data transfers**: If personal data is transferred to countries outside the jurisdiction of the data protection laws applicable to the data controller, the DPA addresses legal mechanisms and safeguards for such international data transfers.

- **Assistance with compliance**: The data processor agrees to assist the data controller in meeting its obligations under data protection laws. This may include providing necessary documentation, cooperating with audits, and facilitating compliance assessments.

- **Duration and termination**: The DPA specifies the duration of the agreement and the conditions under which it can be terminated. It often includes clauses for the return or deletion of personal data upon termination.

This agreement is a key component of ensuring compliance with the data protection regulations of GDPR. The DPA specifies the purposes for which the data processor is allowed to process personal data. It should be limited to the purposes defined by the data controller.

GDPR represents a significant shift in the way organizations handle personal data and prioritize individuals' privacy rights. Compliance with GDPR requires a thorough understanding of its principles and a commitment to implementing robust data protection measures, transparency, and accountability. For more details about it, refer to GDPR's official website: `https://gdpr.eu`.

HIPAA

HIPAA is a significant piece of legislation enacted in the US in 1996. HIPAA has had a profound impact on the healthcare industry, particularly concerning the handling of **protected health information (PHI)** and patients' privacy rights. The primary goal of HIPAA is to protect the privacy and security of individuals' PHI, including medical records, treatment history, health insurance information, and any other data that can be used to identify patients. Here's an explanation of HIPAA's key components and objectives:

- **Scope**: HIPAA applies to healthcare providers, health plans, healthcare clearinghouses, and their business associates who handle PHI.

- **HIPAA privacy rule**: This rule establishes standards for the use and disclosure of PHI by healthcare providers and health plans. It grants patients specific rights over their health information, including the right to access their records and the right to request corrections.

- **HIPAA security rule**: This rule sets forth security standards for **electronic PHI (ePHI)**. It requires covered entities to implement safeguards to protect ePHI against unauthorized access, breaches, and security threats. These safeguards include encryption, access controls, and security risk assessments.

- **Transactions and code sets**: HIPAA standardized electronic transactions and code sets to simplify and streamline healthcare billing and other administrative processes.

- **National provider identifier (NPI)**: HIPAA mandated the use of a unique NPI for healthcare providers, making it easier to track and manage billing information.

- **Breach Notification Rule**: The *Breach Notification Rule* under HIPAA mandates that covered entities must inform affected individuals, the US Department of **Health and Human Services (HHS)**, and potentially the media when an unauthorized disclosure of unsecured PHI takes place.

- **Enforcement and penalties**: HHS's **Office for Civil Rights (OCR)** enforces HIPAA compliance. Non-compliance can result in civil and criminal penalties, including fines ranging from thousands to millions of dollars, depending on the severity of the violation.

- **Patient rights**: HIPAA grants patients various rights over their PHI, including the right to access their health records, request corrections, and obtain copies.

- **Electronic health records (EHRs)**: HIPAA has promoted the adoption of EHRs to improve the efficiency and security of healthcare data management.

HIPAA is a critical regulation for the healthcare industry, aimed at safeguarding patient privacy and the confidentiality and security of their health information. Compliance with HIPAA is not optional; it is legally mandated for entities handling PHI in the US. Violations can lead to significant penalties, legal consequences, and damage to an organization's reputation. For more details about it, refer to HIPAA's official website: `https://www.hhs.gov/programs/hipaa/index.html`.

SOC 2

SOC 2 is a widely recognized framework for assessing and reporting on the security, availability, processing integrity, confidentiality, and privacy of data handled by service organizations. It was developed by the **American Institute of CPAs (AICPA)** to provide assurance to customers, stakeholders, and business partners that a service organization has effective controls in place to protect sensitive information and ensure the reliability of its systems and services. Here are the key components and features of SOC 2:

- **Trust Services Criteria (TSC)**: SOC 2 is built upon the TSC, which includes five key principles: *Security*, *Availability*, *Processing Integrity*, *Confidentiality*, and *Privacy*.

- **Type 1 versus Type 2 reports**: SOC 2 reports come in two types: *Type 1*, which provides an evaluation of the design of controls at a specific **point in time**, and *Type 2*, which includes a more detailed assessment of controls, covering a **period of time** (typically a minimum of 6 months) to assess their effectiveness.

- **Scope and coverage**: Service organizations can define the scope of their SOC 2 audit, specifying systems, processes, and services that are included within the assessment. This allows organizations to tailor the audit to their specific needs.

- **Third-party audits**: SOC 2 audits are conducted by independent third-party auditors who assess and verify the effectiveness of controls based on the chosen TSC.

- **Report distribution**: Service organizations that undergo a SOC 2 audit receive a detailed report from the auditor that can be shared with customers, business partners, and other stakeholders to demonstrate compliance and security measures.

- **Customer assurance**: SOC 2 compliance provides customers and partners with assurance that a service organization has implemented robust security and data protection controls, reducing risks associated with data breaches and system failures.

- **Continuous monitoring**: SOC 2 compliance is not a one-time event. It involves continuous monitoring and improvement of controls to ensure ongoing compliance with the chosen TSC.

- **Industry agnostic**: SOC 2 is applicable to service organizations across various industries, including technology, cloud services, data centers, healthcare, finance, and more.

- **Legal and regulatory compliance**: SOC 2 can help service organizations demonstrate compliance with legal and regulatory requirements related to data security and privacy.

In short, SOC 2 reports play a crucial role in building trust between service organizations and their customers by providing independent validation of controls and practices related to security, availability, processing integrity, confidentiality, and privacy. It is often a requirement for SPs handling sensitive data, such as **cloud SPs (CSPs)**, data centers, and **Software-as-a-Service (SaaS)** companies, to undergo SOC 2 audits to demonstrate their commitment to data security and compliance. For more details about it, refer to AICPA's official website: `https://us.aicpa.org/interestareas/frc/assuranceadvisoryservices/aicpasoc2report`.

Federal Risk and Authorization Management Program

The **Federal Risk and Authorization Management Program** (**FedRAMP**) is a US government-wide program designed to standardize security assessment, authorization, and continuous monitoring processes for cloud products and services used by federal agencies. FedRAMP aims to enhance the security posture of cloud solutions while streamlining the evaluation and authorization process, reducing duplication of efforts, and promoting the use of secure cloud technologies across the federal government. Key components and features of FedRAMP include:

- **Unified security standards**: FedRAMP establishes a set of unified security standards based on **National Institute of Standards and Technology** (**NIST**) guidelines, specifically NIST **Special Publication** (**SP**) *800-53*, tailored for cloud services. These standards provide a common baseline for assessing and authorizing cloud solutions.

- **Security assessment framework**: FedRAMP outlines a standardized process for security assessments, including penetration testing, vulnerability scanning, and risk assessments. This process ensures that cloud providers meet the required security controls.

- **Authorization tiers**: FedRAMP categorizes cloud services into three authorization tiers: *Low*, *Moderate*, and *High*, based on the sensitivity of the data and the associated security requirements. Federal agencies can choose cloud services based on their specific needs and the appropriate authorization level.

- **Joint Authorization Board (JAB)**: The FedRAMP program is overseen by the JAB, which consists of **chief information officers (CIOs)** from the **Department of Defense (DoD)**, **Department of Homeland Security (DHS)**, and **General Services Administration (GSA)**. The JAB grants provisional authorizations for cloud services, allowing multiple federal agencies to use them.

- **Agency authorization**: In addition to JAB authorizations, individual federal agencies can perform their own security assessments and issue authorizations for cloud services. Agencies can choose cloud solutions from the FedRAMP marketplace that align with their specific requirements.

- **Continuous monitoring**: FedRAMP emphasizes continuous monitoring of cloud services throughout their life cycle. This includes ongoing vulnerability assessments, security audits, and compliance checks to ensure that security controls remain effective.

- **FedRAMP marketplace**: The FedRAMP marketplace is a centralized repository of cloud service offerings that have achieved FedRAMP compliance. Federal agencies can use this marketplace to identify pre-authorized cloud solutions.

- **Compliance documentation**: CSPs seeking FedRAMP authorization must prepare extensive documentation, including a security assessment package and a **System Security Plan (SSP)**, to demonstrate compliance with security controls.

- **Annual reviews**: FedRAMP requires CSPs to undergo annual security assessments and updates to maintain their authorization. This ensures that security controls remain effective over time.

- **Collaboration with industry**: FedRAMP collaborates with CSPs and third-party assessment organizations to streamline the authorization process, reduce costs, and promote industry participation.

FedRAMP plays a crucial role in enabling federal agencies to leverage cloud technologies securely, improve cost efficiency, and modernize their IT infrastructure. By establishing standardized security requirements and authorization processes, FedRAMP helps ensure that government data is protected and compliant with federal regulations while promoting the adoption of cloud solutions that meet these standards. For more details about it, refer to FedRAMP's official website: `https://www.fedramp.gov/`.

California Consumer Privacy Act

The **California Consumer Privacy Act (CCPA)** is a comprehensive privacy law in the state of California, US. It was enacted to enhance the privacy rights and protections of California residents and grant them greater control over their personal information. CCPA is similar in some aspects to the EU's GDPR and has become a significant privacy framework in the US. Here are the key components and features of CCPA:

- **Scope**: CCPA applies to businesses that operate in California and meet certain criteria, such as having annual gross revenues exceeding $25 million, handling the personal information of at least 50,000 California consumers, or deriving 50% or more of their annual revenue from selling California consumers' personal information.

- **Consumer rights**: CCPA grants California consumers several rights regarding their personal information, including the following rights:

  - Know what personal information is collected, disclosed, or sold

  - Opt out of the sale of personal information

  - Access their personal information

  - Request the deletion of their personal information

  - Equal service and price, even if they exercise their privacy rights

- **Definitions of personal information**: CCPA defines personal information broadly, including not only traditional identifiers but also *online identifiers, browsing history, geolocation data*, and other information that can be reasonably linked to an individual.

- **Transparency and disclosure**: Businesses subject to CCPA must provide clear and conspicuous privacy notices to consumers, informing them about the types of personal information collected, the purposes for which it will be used, and the rights available to them.

- **Opt-out of sale**: CCPA requires businesses that sell personal information to provide consumers with an option to opt out of such sales. Businesses must also provide a *Do Not Sell My Personal Information* link on their websites.

- **Data access and deletion requests**: Businesses must establish procedures for consumers to submit requests to access or delete their personal information, and they must respond to these requests within specific timeframes.

- **Non-discrimination**: Businesses are prohibited from discriminating against consumers who exercise their privacy rights, such as by denying them goods or services, charging them different prices, or providing them with a lower quality of service.

- **Data security and safeguards**: While CCPA does not prescribe specific security standards, it requires businesses to implement reasonable security measures to protect personal information.

- **Enforcement and penalties**: The California Attorney General can enforce CCPA violations, with penalties ranging from fines to injunctions. In certain cases, consumers can also bring private lawsuits against businesses that fail to adequately protect their personal information.

- **Amendments and evolution**: CCPA is not static and may evolve over time. Amendments and adjustments to the law may occur to address emerging privacy concerns and issues.

CCPA has had a significant impact on how businesses collect, use, and protect personal information, not only in California but also beyond, as many organizations have extended CCPA-like privacy protections to consumers nationwide. Organizations subject to CCPA must understand their obligations, update their privacy practices, and be prepared to respond to consumer requests regarding their personal data. For more details about it, refer to CCPA's official website: `https://www.oag.ca.gov/privacy/ccpa`.

California Privacy Rights Act

The **California Privacy Rights Act** (**CPRA**) is a privacy law that builds upon and amends the CCPA. It was approved by Californian voters in November 2020 and is intended to strengthen privacy rights and consumer protection. Here are the key features and components of CPRA:

- **Key changes**: CPRA has established the **California Privacy Protection Agency** (**CPPA**), an independent regulatory body responsible for enforcing and implementing privacy laws.

- **Expanded consumer rights**: CPRA enhances certain consumer rights, introduces the right to correct inaccurate information, and introduces the concept of "sensitive personal information" with additional protections.

- **Applicability**: CPRA is slated to become enforceable on March, 2024. It generally applies to businesses that exceed certain thresholds related to data processing.

- **Enforcement and penalties**: The CPRA grants additional authority to the CPPA for enforcement. It includes higher penalties for violations involving the personal information of minors and increased fines for privacy-related violations.

- **Duration**: CPRA provides a transition period, and enforcement actions are expected to begin after the regulations are adopted and finalized.

CCPA has been in effect since *January 1, 2020*. CPRA introduces additional changes and enhancements to California's privacy landscape. As laws and regulations may evolve, it's advisable to check for the latest updates and compliance requirements.

Personal Data Protection Act

The **Personal Data Protection Act** (**PDPA**) is a legislation on data protection and privacy in Singapore, overseeing the gathering, utilization, disclosure, and safeguarding of personal data. The PDPA was enacted in 2012 and serves to regulate the handling of personal data by organizations in Singapore to safeguard individuals' privacy rights and ensure responsible data management practices. PDPA applies to all organizations, both public and private sectors, that collect, use, or disclose personal data in Singapore. This includes businesses, government agencies, nonprofit organizations, and healthcare providers. PDPA defines personal data broadly, encompassing any information that can be used to identify an individual, such as names, contact details, identification numbers, and even images. For more details, refer to `https://www.pdpc.gov.sg/Overview-of-PDPA/The-Legislation/Personal-Data-Protection-Act`.

Federal Information Security Management Act

The **Federal Information Security Management Act** (**FISMA**) is a US federal law enacted in 2002 as part of the Electronic Government Act. FISMA establishes a comprehensive framework for securing federal government information systems and ensuring the confidentiality, integrity, and availability of sensitive government data. The primary objectives of FISMA are to strengthen information security practices within federal agencies, promote consistent cybersecurity measures, and protect government information from threats and vulnerabilities. For more details about it, refer to `https://www.cisa.gov/topics/cyber-threats-and-advisories/federal-information-security-modernization-act`.

ISO 27001

ISO 27001, officially known as *ISO/IEC 27001:2013*, is an internationally recognized standard for **information security management systems (ISMS)**. It provides a systematic and risk-based approach for organizations to establish, implement, monitor, review, maintain, and improve the security of their information assets. *ISO 27001* is a key framework used by organizations to protect sensitive information and demonstrate their commitment to information security. Here are the key components and features of *ISO 27001*:

- **Scope and applicability**: *ISO 27001* can be applied to any organization, regardless of its size, industry, or sector. It is particularly relevant for organizations that handle sensitive information, such as personal data, **intellectual property (IP)**, financial data, and more.

- **Risk management**: *ISO 27001* is centered on a risk-based approach to information security. Organizations identify and assess information security risks and then implement controls to mitigate or manage those risks effectively.

- **PDCA (Plan-Do-Check-Act) cycle**: *ISO 27001* follows the PDCA cycle, which consists of four key phases:

  - **Plan**: Establish the ISMS, including defining objectives, scoping, risk assessment, and creating policies and procedures

  - **Do**: Implement and operate the ISMS by implementing controls, conducting awareness training, and documenting processes

  - **Check**: Monitor and review the ISMS through regular assessments, audits, and performance evaluations

  - **Act**: Continuously improve the ISMS by taking corrective and preventive actions based on the results of assessments and reviews

- **Information security controls**: *ISO 27001* provides a comprehensive list of security controls organized into 14 categories, known as *Annex A*. These controls cover areas such as access control, cryptography, physical security, IR, and more. *Annex A* can be accessed from here: `https://www.isms.online/iso-27001/annex-a/`.

- **Documentation and records**: *ISO 27001* requires organizations to maintain documentation and records of their information security policies, procedures, and activities. Proper documentation is crucial for demonstrating compliance.

- **Certification and compliance**: Organizations can seek *ISO 27001* certification through an accredited certification body. Certification demonstrates to stakeholders, customers, and partners that the organization has a robust ISMS in place.

- **Continuous improvement**: *ISO 27001* encourages organizations to continually improve their information security practices. This includes regularly reviewing risk assessments, monitoring security controls, and adapting to emerging threats and vulnerabilities.

- **Legal and regulatory compliance**: *ISO 27001* assists organizations in complying with legal and regulatory requirements related to information security, data protection, and privacy.

- **Management commitment**: *ISO 27001* emphasizes the importance of top management's commitment to information security. Leaders are expected to demonstrate their support for the ISMS and allocate necessary resources.

- **Third-party relationships**: Organizations are encouraged to extend the ISMS to third-party relationships, such as suppliers and SPs, to ensure the security of shared information.

- **Information security culture**: *ISO 27001* promotes the development of an organizational culture that values information security, including employee awareness and training.

ISO 27001 is considered a best practice for information security management and is widely adopted by organizations globally. Achieving *ISO 27001* certification demonstrates an organization's commitment to protecting its information assets, managing risks effectively, and continuously improving its information security posture. For more details, refer to `https://www.iso.org/obp/ui/#iso:std:iso-iec:27001:ed-3:v1:en`.

PCI DSS

PCI DSS is a set of security standards and requirements designed to protect the confidentiality and security of payment card data, including credit card and debit card information. PCI DSS was developed by the PCI **Security Standards Council** (**SSC**) to establish a common framework for securing cardholder data across the payment card industry. PCI DSS consists of 12 high-level security requirements, each with specific sub-requirements and controls. These requirements cover various aspects of information security, including network security, access controls, and data encryption. Here are the key components and features of PCI DSS:

- **Scope**: PCI DSS is applicable to any entity that stores, processes, or transmits payment card data. This includes merchants, SPs, payment processors, and other entities involved in card transactions.

- **Data classification**: PCI DSS distinguishes between sensitive and non-sensitive payment card data. Sensitive data includes the full cardholder's **primary account number** (**PAN**), while non-sensitive data includes the cardholder's name or the expiration date.

- **Network segmentation**: PCI DSS recommends or mandates network segmentation to isolate cardholder data from other parts of the network. This reduces the scope of compliance and minimizes the risk of data exposure.

- **Access controls**: PCI DSS requires strict access controls, including **role-based access control (RBAC)**, unique user IDs, and strong authentication mechanisms. It limits access to cardholder data on a need-to-know basis.

- **Encryption**: PCI DSS mandates the use of encryption for transmitting cardholder data over public networks and encrypting data at rest. Encryption protocols must be strong and well maintained.

- **Vulnerability management**: Organizations must implement and maintain vulnerability management programs, including regular scanning for vulnerabilities, patch management, and secure coding practices.

- **Security policies and procedures**: PCI DSS requires organizations to develop and maintain information security policies and procedures. These documents should address various aspects of security, including data protection, IR, and security awareness training.

- **Regular testing and assessment**: PCI DSS mandates regular security testing, including vulnerability scanning, penetration testing, and security assessments. These tests help identify and address security weaknesses.

- **Logging and monitoring**: Organizations must implement comprehensive logging and monitoring systems to track access to cardholder data and detect suspicious activities. Log data should be retained for a specified period.

- **IR plan (IRP)**: PCI DSS requires organizations to have a well-defined IRP to address security incidents promptly and effectively. This includes notifying stakeholders and authorities in case of a data breach.

- **Compliance validation**: To demonstrate compliance, organizations may undergo assessments conducted by **Qualified Security Assessors (QSAs)** or self-assessment using **Self-Assessment Questionnaires (SAQs)**. These assessments validate compliance with PCI DSS requirements.

Failure to adhere to PCI DSS may lead to financial penalties, legal ramifications, and harm to an organization's image and standing. Achieving and maintaining compliance with PCI DSS is essential for any entity involved in payment card transactions to protect cardholder data, reduce the risk of data breaches, and maintain the trust of customers and payment card companies. For more details, refer to `https://www.pcisecuritystandards.org/about_us/`.

NIST Cybersecurity Framework

The NIST **Cybersecurity Framework (CSF)** is essentially a comprehensive set of guidelines, best practices, and standards put together by NIST. Its primary purpose is to assist organizations in the management and improvement of their cybersecurity measures. This framework was born in response to *Executive Order 13636* (`https://www.cisa.gov/resources-tools/resources/executive-order-eo-13636-improving-critical-infrastructure-cybersecurity`), which essentially called for the development of a system to enhance the cybersecurity of critical infrastructure within the US. One of the significant advantages of this framework is its adaptability, making it an incredibly valuable tool for organizations looking to enhance their cybersecurity resilience. It consists of five core functions, each of which represents a different aspect of cybersecurity risk management:

- **Identify**: This function focuses on understanding and managing cybersecurity risks. Organizations are encouraged to identify and catalog their assets, assess vulnerabilities, and gain a comprehensive understanding of potential threats. It involves activities such as asset management, risk assessment, and the development of a risk management strategy.

- **Protect**: The *Protect* function emphasizes the implementation of safeguards to mitigate cybersecurity risks. It covers measures such as access control, data encryption, training and awareness programs, and security policies and procedures. The goal is to protect the organization's assets and data from potential threats.

- **Detect**: Detecting cybersecurity incidents in a timely manner is crucial. The *Detect* function involves continuous monitoring of systems and networks, intrusion detection, security event analysis, and IRP. It helps organizations identify threats and vulnerabilities as they occur.

- **Respond**: When a cybersecurity incident occurs, organizations must be prepared to respond effectively. The *Respond* function outlines the steps to take in the event of a security breach, including containment, eradication of the threat, and recovery efforts.

- **Recover**: The *Recover* function is centered on the restoration of regular operations following a cybersecurity incident. It includes activities such as BC planning, system backups, and communication with stakeholders. The goal is to ensure that the organization can recover quickly and effectively from disruptions.

Key features and concepts of the NIST CSF include:

- **Risk-based approach**: The framework is built on a risk management approach, helping organizations prioritize cybersecurity efforts based on their specific risks and needs.

- **Flexibility**: It is not prescriptive and does not mandate specific technologies or solutions. Instead, it provides a flexible structure that organizations can adapt to their unique circumstances.

- **Communication**: The framework provides a common language for discussing cybersecurity issues within organizations and with external stakeholders.

- **Measurement and improvement**: Organizations are encouraged to use the framework to assess their current cybersecurity posture, set improvement goals, and measure progress over time.

- **Adoption across sectors**: While initially developed for critical infrastructure, the NIST CSF has been adopted by organizations in various sectors, including government, healthcare, finance, and manufacturing.

> **Note**
>
> NIST is about to release a draft of the NIST CSF 2.0 for public comment, which also includes a discussion draft in the CSF 2.0 Draft Core for public comment by November 4, 2023. You can also acquire the NIST CSF 2.0 Reference Tool to examine the Draft CSF 2.0 Core, which encompasses functions, categories, subcategories, and implementation Examples. For the latest updated details on the framework, refer to the official website here: `https://www.nist.gov/cyberframework`.

Overall, the NIST CSF serves as a valuable tool for organizations of all sizes and types to assess, enhance, and communicate their cybersecurity efforts in an increasingly interconnected and digital world. It helps organizations better manage and mitigate cybersecurity risks to protect their assets, data, and operations.

Cloud Security Alliance Cloud Controls Matrix

The **Cloud Security Alliance Cloud Controls Matrix (CSA CCM)** is a framework and set of guidelines developed by the CSA to help organizations assess and manage the security of cloud computing environments. CCM provides a structured approach to understanding, implementing, and evaluating security controls for cloud-based systems. Here are the key components or functions of the framework:

- **Security control framework**: It offers a comprehensive framework of security controls and best practices specifically tailored to cloud computing environments. These controls help organizations address the unique security challenges of the cloud.

- **Risk assessment**: CSA CCM assists organizations in identifying, assessing, and mitigating security risks associated with cloud adoption. It helps organizations make informed decisions about cloud services and configurations.

- **Compliance and assurance**: The framework helps organizations demonstrate compliance with relevant industry standards and regulations by providing a roadmap for implementing security controls aligned with these requirements.

- **Standardization**: CSA CCM provides a standardized set of security controls that organizations can use to establish a baseline for securing cloud environments. This consistency aids in comparing security postures across CSPs.

The framework consists of 197 control objectives organized within 17 domains that encompass all essential aspects of cloud technology. This framework serves as a valuable tool for systematically evaluating cloud implementations and offers recommendations on which security measures should be adopted by different stakeholders within the cloud supply chain. The control framework is harmonized with the CSA Security Guidance for Cloud Computing, establishing it as the industry standard for ensuring cloud security and compliance.

The CCM guidelines include the following components:

- CCM v4 controls
- Control mappings
- **Consensus Assessments Initiative Questionnaire v4 (CAIQ v4)**
- Implementation guidelines
- Auditing guidelines
- CCM metrics
- CCM machine-readable formats (JSON/YAML/OSCAL)

Additionally, the download file also includes the *STAR Level 1 Security Questionnaire* based on CAIQ v4. You can download the guidelines and controls from the official website of CSA here: `https://cloudsecurityalliance.org/research/cloud-controls-matrix/`.

Center for Internet Security benchmark controls

The **Center for Internet Security** (**CIS**) benchmark controls are a set of best practice guidelines for securing various types of technology platforms and systems. These controls are developed and maintained by the CIS, a nonprofit organization dedicated to enhancing cybersecurity. CIS benchmark controls serve several important purposes; such as the following:

- **Security standards**: They offer comprehensive guidance for organizations aiming to strengthen the security of their IT environments.

- **Reducing vulnerabilities**: By implementing CIS benchmark controls, organizations can reduce vulnerabilities and security weaknesses in their technology platforms, thereby minimizing the risk of cyberattacks and data breaches.

- **Best practices**: These controls offer best practices and practical guidance for configuring and managing technology systems securely, making them valuable references for IT administrators and security professionals.

- **Scoring and compliance**: CIS Benchmarks include a scoring mechanism that allows organizations to assess their compliance with the recommended security settings. This scoring system helps quantify security posture and track improvements over time.

CIS benchmark controls also play a vital role in the overall cybersecurity ecosystem for the following reasons:

- **Adaptability**: While CIS benchmark controls provide a strong security baseline, organizations should consider customizing the controls to meet their specific needs and risk assessments. Not all recommendations may be applicable to every organization.

- **Alignment with standards**: CIS Benchmarks align with well-known security standards and frameworks, making them a valuable resource for organizations aiming to comply with broader industry requirements, such as NIST or ISO standards.

- **Community collaboration**: The development and maintenance of CIS benchmark controls involves collaboration with a community of cybersecurity experts, ensuring that the controls remain up to date and effective in addressing evolving threats.

- **Regular updates**: The cybersecurity landscape evolves continuously, and CIS Benchmarks are updated accordingly. Organizations should regularly check for updates to ensure they are following the most current best practices.

CIS benchmark controls provide organizations with a structured approach to enhancing their cybersecurity posture by offering specific recommendations and configurations for securing technology platforms and systems. CSPM solutions play a crucial role in helping organizations achieve and maintain compliance with these controls, especially in complex cloud environments. Refer to the CIS official website for more details: `https://www.cisecurity.org/`.

These are some of the most common frameworks that are comprehensively used in cybersecurity. Organizations must understand and adhere to these regulations based on their industry, location, and the nature of the data they handle. Compliance helps organizations protect sensitive information, maintain legal and contractual obligations, and build trust with customers and partners.

Next, let's explore some of the most popular frameworks developed by CSPs.

Cloud governance frameworks

CSPs often adhere to their own security and compliance standards. For example, **Amazon Web Services (AWS)**, Azure, and Google Cloud have established compliance programs and certifications (for example, AWS's **Well-Architected Framework (WAF)** and the **Microsoft cloud security benchmark (MCSB)**) to help organizations secure their cloud resources. Compliance with these regulatory frameworks and adherence to compliance standards in cloud security are crucial for organizations to mitigate security risks, protect sensitive data, and meet legal and contractual obligations. Failure to comply with these regulations and standards can lead to legal consequences, data breaches, and reputational damage.

Let us explore these frameworks.

AWS WAF

AWS WAF is a set of best practices and guidelines developed by AWS to help organizations design and build reliable, secure, efficient, and cost-effective cloud-based architectures. It serves as a blueprint for building and optimizing cloud solutions that align with business and customer needs while minimizing risks and maximizing the value of AWS services.

At its core, WAF focuses on five key pillars:

- **Operational Excellence**: This pillar emphasizes the need for efficient and reliable operations. It includes practices related to automating tasks, monitoring systems, responding to events, and continuously improving processes. The goal is to ensure that your cloud infrastructure runs smoothly and can adapt to changes in demand or conditions.

- **Security**: Security is paramount in any cloud architecture. This pillar helps you implement robust security measures to protect your data, applications, and systems. It involves practices such as access control, encryption, network security, and compliance with industry standards and regulations.

- **Reliability**: The *Reliability* pillar ensures that your cloud architecture can deliver the expected level of performance and availability. It focuses on designing for **fault tolerance** (**FT**), DR, and **high availability** (**HA**) to minimize downtime and disruptions.

- **Performance Efficiency**: This pillar aims to optimize the performance of your applications while managing costs. It involves selecting the right AWS resources for your workloads, monitoring performance, and scaling resources as needed. The goal is to deliver a great user experience without overspending on resources.

- **Cost Optimization**: Cost optimization is about maximizing the value of your cloud investment. It involves identifying cost drivers, optimizing resource utilization, and using AWS services and pricing models effectively. The goal is to achieve the desired performance and functionality at the lowest possible cost.

To implement this effectively, AWS provides a structured approach:

1. **Review**: Assess your existing architecture against the framework's principles to identify areas for improvement.

2. **Prioritize**: Determine which areas require the most immediate attention based on your business goals and constraints.

3. **Implement**: Make changes to your architecture based on identified priorities and best practices.

4. **Learn**: Continuously evaluate the impact of your changes and gather lessons learned to refine your architecture further.

In short, AWS WAF is a comprehensive approach to designing and managing cloud architectures that are secure, reliable, performant, and cost-effective. AWS also offers a Well-Architected Tool service, which provides a structured process for conducting reviews and assessments of your workloads against the framework's principles. To know everything about AWS WAF, refer to AWS' official website: `https://aws.amazon.com/architecture/well-architected`.

Now that we have a brief understanding of AWS WAF, let us dive deep into another popular benchmark known as MCSB.

MCSB

MCSB serves as a valuable resource for enhancing the security of your workloads, data, and services within Azure and multi-cloud environments. It offers a comprehensive framework of best practices and recommendations to bolster your cloud security posture, drawing insights from Microsoft's expertise and broader industry security guidance. The following diagram depicts how MCSB consolidates different frameworks (CIS, PCI DSS, and NIST) together for a comprehensive security approach for a multi-cloud environment:

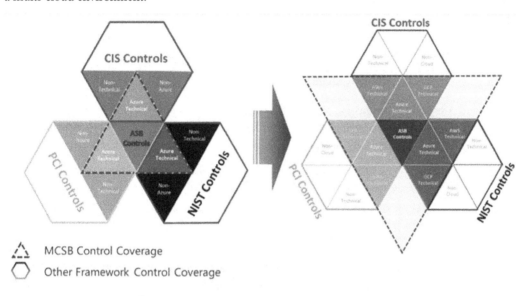

Figure 14.1 – MCSB (Source: https://learn.microsoft.com/en-us/security/benchmark/azure/overview)

Let us take a look at the key elements of MCSB.

Security controls

A security control serves as a broad and high-level description of a feature or action that requires attention, irrespective of the particular technology or implementation. These recommendations are relevant and can be applied across all your cloud workloads. They are crafted to assist you in implementing security measures in alignment with industry standards, including the likes of CIS Controls, NIST, PCI DSS, and more. For example, **identity and access management** (**IAM**) is one of the security control families. IAM contains specific actions that must be addressed to help ensure identity is protected.

Security baseline

A baseline involves applying a specific control to individual Azure services. Within this context, each organization defines its own benchmark recommendation, and Azure requires corresponding configurations to be implemented. These guidelines are tailored to specific workload types, encompassing areas such as computing, storage, networking, and identity management. They offer valuable insights on configuring your workloads securely.

> **Note**
>
> As of now (at the time of writing this section), Microsoft offers service baselines only for Azure.

The components that constitute MCSB include:

- **Cloud Adoption Framework**: This section provides insights into the security aspect of your cloud journey. It covers various aspects such as strategy, defining roles and responsibilities, Azure's top 10 security best practices, and even includes reference implementations.

- **Azure WAF**: Focusing on securing your workloads specifically within the Azure environment, this part of MCSB offers guidance on best practices.

- **Chief Information Security Officer (CISO) Workshop**: For those aiming to modernize their security practices in line with Zero Trust principles, this section offers program guidance and reference strategies to accelerate the process.

- **Other Industry and Cloud Service Providers' Standards**: MCSB doesn't exist in isolation. It takes into account established security best practices and frameworks from other industry leaders and CSPs. Examples include AWS WAF, CIS Controls, NIST, and PCI DSS, among others.

> **Note**
>
> MCSB is the evolution of the **Azure Security Benchmark** (**ASB**), which underwent a rebranding in October 2022. Security recommendations offered by Microsoft's CSPM solution, Defender for Cloud, are also completely integrated and aligned with MCSB.

You can conveniently access and download the MCSB recommendations in PDF or Excel format from the official Microsoft website, making it a valuable resource to help fortify your cloud security strategy. For more details, refer to `https://learn.microsoft.com/en-us/security/benchmark/azure/overview`.

Let us now understand at a very high-level how an organization can adapt cloud governance.

Adapting cloud governance to the organization's need

Every organization is unique, with its own set of objectives, challenges, and compliance requirements. Therefore, the key to successful cloud governance lies in adapting it to your organization's specific needs. Let us explore essential steps and considerations for tailoring cloud governance to fit your organization like a glove:

- **Understanding the cloud landscape**: Before diving into adapting compliance management and governance to the cloud, it's crucial to understand the cloud landscape thoroughly. Cloud computing encompasses various service models (for example, **Infrastructure as a Service (IaaS)**, **Platform as a Service (PaaS)**, and SaaS) and deployment models (for example, public, private, hybrid, and multi-cloud). Each has its implications for compliance and governance.

- **Identifying regulatory and compliance requirements**: Different industries and regions have specific regulatory requirements that organizations must adhere to. These regulations govern data privacy, security, and industry-specific standards. It's imperative to identify the relevant regulations and compliance standards that apply to your organization. These include GDPR, HIPAA, SOC 2, PCI DSS, or industry-specific guidelines.

- **Evaluating your current state**: Assess your organization's existing compliance management and governance practices. Which policies, procedures, and controls are currently in place? Are they suitable for a cloud environment, or do they require adaptation? Identify areas where your current practices align with compliance requirements and where adjustments are necessary.

- **Customizing policies and controls**: One of the most critical steps in adapting compliance management and governance to the cloud is customization. While industry standards and best practices provide a solid foundation, your organization's unique needs may require tailored policies and controls. This customization ensures that compliance efforts are aligned with your specific objectives and RT.

- **Data classification and protection**: In a cloud environment, data is at the heart of compliance and governance. Implement data classification frameworks to categorize data based on sensitivity and regulatory requirements. Apply encryption and access controls to safeguard data and define procedures for data retention and disposal that adhere to compliance standards.

- **Security in the cloud**: Cloud security is integral to compliance. Assess and customize security measures, including IAM, network security, and threat detection, to meet your organization's needs and compliance obligations. Utilize cloud-native security tools and services to enhance protection.

- **Auditing and monitoring**: Cloud environments offer robust monitoring and auditing capabilities. Customize monitoring and logging to track compliance-related activities, security incidents, and unauthorized access. Regularly review audit logs and perform compliance assessments to ensure ongoing adherence.

- **Vendor assessment and due diligence**: If you are using a CSP, conduct thorough vendor assessments and due diligence. Ensure that your cloud provider complies with necessary regulations and industry standards. Customize contractual agreements to address your specific compliance requirements.

- **Training and awareness**: Educate your personnel on the unique compliance considerations of the cloud environment. Develop training programs and awareness initiatives to ensure that employees understand their roles in maintaining compliance and governance.

- **Continuous improvement and adaptation**: Compliance management and governance are not static processes. Regularly review and adapt your strategies as your organization evolves, regulatory landscapes change, and new cloud technologies emerge. Stay informed about emerging threats and industry trends to ensure ongoing compliance.

- **Engaging stakeholders**: Collaborate with key stakeholders from legal, IT, security, and compliance teams to develop a cohesive approach to cloud compliance and governance. Establish clear lines of communication and responsibilities to foster a culture of compliance.

- **Seeking expertise**: If needed, consider seeking external expertise from cloud compliance and governance specialists or consultants. They can provide valuable insights, conduct assessments, and offer guidance tailored to your organization's unique requirements.

Adapting compliance management and governance to the cloud is a critical endeavor for organizations adopting the cloud. Customization is the key to success, ensuring that your compliance efforts align with your specific regulatory obligations and business objectives.

It is also extremely important to understand global and regional aspects of compliance needs. Let us dive deeper.

Global versus regional compliance considerations

Global and regional compliance considerations refer to the differences between regulatory requirements and standards that have a global scope and those that are specific to particular regions or countries. Organizations operating in multiple locations or serving diverse customer bases must navigate both global and regional compliance challenges to ensure they meet all relevant legal and regulatory obligations. Here's an explanation with an example.

Global regulations

Some compliance regulations, such as GDPR and *ISO 27001*, have global implications. Understanding these regulations is essential for organizations operating across international boundaries or serving global customer bases. Let us take an example of GDPR:

- **Scope**: GDPR is a global compliance regulation because it applies to any organization that processes the personal data of individuals residing in the EU, regardless of where the organization is located.

- **Focus**: GDPR emphasizes the protection of individuals' personal data, including their right to privacy, data breach notification, and the need for explicit consent to process personal information.

- **Impact**: Any organization worldwide that handles EU citizens' data must comply with GDPR. This means implementing stringent data protection measures, appointing DPOs, and conducting privacy impact assessments.

Regional variations

In addition to global regulations, many regions and countries have their own specific compliance requirements. It's vital to understand these regional variations and ensure that cloud operations comply with local laws and standards. Let us take an example of CCPA:

- **Scope**: CCPA is a regional compliance regulation because it applies only to businesses that collect personal information from California residents.

- **Focus**: CCPA grants Californian consumers specific rights regarding their personal information, including the right to know what data is collected, the right to request deletion of data, and the right to opt out of data sales.

- **Impact**: Organizations that do business with California residents must comply with CCPA, even if they are not physically located in California. This requires implementing mechanisms for data transparency, opt-out processes, and robust data protection measures specific to Californian customers.

Now that we understand global and regional aspects of compliance and governance, let us understand these requirements and how they are realized in the industry as best practices, with the help of some use cases, scenarios, and examples.

Use cases, scenarios, and examples

Compliance management and governance are essential aspects of organizations' operations, ensuring they adhere to relevant laws, regulations, and industry standards. Various frameworks and methodologies can be applied to facilitate these processes. Next are some use cases, scenarios, and examples of compliance management and governance concepts.

Use case #1 – Data protection and privacy

Data protection and privacy refer to the measures and principles designed to safeguard individuals' personal information and ensure that it is handled in a manner that respects their rights, maintains confidentiality, and prevents unauthorized access or misuse. These concepts are crucial in the digital age, where vast amounts of personal data are collected and processed.

Scenario: A multinational financial institution operating across various regions aims to enhance data protection and privacy compliance to safeguard sensitive customer information, comply with regional regulations (such as GDPR in Europe), and maintain customer trust.

Let's explore this concept with an example of GDPR and how it ensures data protection and privacy:

- **Lawfulness, fairness, and transparency**: Organizations must process personal data lawfully, fairly, and transparently. Individuals should know what data is being collected and for what purpose, and provide their consent when necessary.

  Example: An online retailer informs customers that their personal data, including purchase history and contact details, will be used to process orders and provide tailored product recommendations. Customers have the option to opt out or adjust privacy settings.

- **Purpose limitation**: Personal data should be collected for specified, explicit, and legitimate purposes and not further processed in a way that is incompatible with those purposes.

  Example: A healthcare provider collects patient data for the purpose of diagnosis and treatment. They cannot use this data for marketing without obtaining separate consent.

- **Data minimization**: Organizations should only collect and process data that is necessary for the stated purpose. Unnecessary data should not be collected.

  Example: A mobile app for weather updates only asks for the user's location data but does not request access to the device's contacts or photos.

- **Data accuracy**: Personal data should be accurate, and steps should be taken to ensure it remains up to date.

  Example: A bank periodically asks customers to verify and update their contact information to ensure that account statements and notifications reach the correct addresses.

- **Storage limitation**: Data should be retained in a manner that allows for the identification of data subjects only for the duration necessary to fulfill the purposes for which it is being processed.

  Example: An e-commerce platform retains customer purchase history for 5 years to handle returns and warranty claims but deletes payment card details immediately after processing the transaction.

- **Integrity and confidentiality**: Organizations must implement appropriate technical and organizational measures to ensure data security and protect against unauthorized access, disclosure, alteration, or destruction.

  Example: An IT company encrypts sensitive customer data and regularly conducts security audits to identify and rectify vulnerabilities.

- **Accountability and transparency**: Organizations are responsible for complying with GDPR's principles and must be able to demonstrate their compliance through documentation and transparency.

  Example: A data controller maintains records of data processing activities, conducts privacy impact assessments for high-risk processing activities, and appoints a DPO to oversee GDPR compliance.

- **Data subject rights**: GDPR grants individuals various rights, including the right to access their data, rectify inaccuracies, request erasure (the "right to be forgotten"), and object to processing under certain conditions.

    Example: A social media platform allows users to download their data, review and edit profile information, and delete their accounts.

Failure to comply with GDPR's data protection and privacy principles can result in substantial fines and legal consequences, emphasizing the importance of these principles in safeguarding individuals' personal information and ensuring responsible data handling.

Let us now see another use case that compels an organization to notify its customers and authority in case of a breach.

Use case #2 – Incident reporting and notification

Incident reporting and notification refers to the obligations and procedures that organizations must follow when a security incident or data breach occurs, as mandated by specific regulations and standards. Let's illustrate this concept with an example involving GDPR.

Scenario: Let us assume a fictitious European e-commerce company, "EuroKart," processes the personal data of customers within the EU. EuroKart discovers a data breach involving unauthorized access to customer accounts, potentially exposing personal information. Here's a step-by-step account of what happens:

- **Detection and assessment**: EuroKart's security team detects the breach during routine monitoring. They assess the scope, impact, and nature of the incident.

- **Internal reporting**: EuroKart follows internal incident reporting procedures, informing key stakeholders, including the DPO and senior management, about the breach. The incident is documented in detail.

- **Legal and regulatory assessment**: EuroKart's legal team collaborates with the DPO to evaluate the incident's compliance implications under GDPR. They determine if the breach meets the criteria for notification.

- **DPA notification**: Under GDPR, if the breach poses a risk to individuals' rights and freedoms, EuroKart must notify the relevant DPA within 72 hours of becoming aware of the breach. The notification includes:

    - A description of the breach

    - The categories and approximate number of affected individuals

    - Potential consequences of the breach

    - Measures taken or proposed to address the breach

- **Notification to affected individuals**: The organization must also notify the affected individuals directly if the breach is likely to result in a high risk to individuals' rights and freedoms. The notification includes:

  - A description of the breach

  - Likely consequences of the breach

  - Recommended measures to mitigate potential harm

  - Contact information for EuroKart's DPO or another point of contact

- **Documentation and compliance records**: EuroKart maintains detailed records of the breach, its assessment, notifications, and remediation efforts. This documentation is essential for demonstrating GDPR compliance during audits.

- **Communication and coordination**: EuroKart may need to communicate with law enforcement authorities such as the police if the breach involves criminal activity. Coordination with other stakeholders, such as third-party SPs, is also necessary.

- **Remediation and preventive measures**: EuroKart takes immediate steps to contain the breach, recover data, and prevent further unauthorized access. It conducts a post-incident analysis to identify vulnerabilities and implement measures to prevent future incidents.

In this example, GDPR serves as the regulatory framework, outlining specific requirements for **incident reporting and notification**. Compliance with GDPR ensures that EuroKart not only addresses the data breach promptly but also fulfills its legal obligations to protect individuals' data and inform both authorities and affected data subjects. Failure to comply with GDPR's incident reporting and notification requirements can result in significant fines and penalties.

Use case #3 – Compliance audits

Compliance audits refer to systematic and independent evaluations conducted by organizations to assess their adherence to established regulations, standards, and internal policies. Many regulatory frameworks require organizations to undergo regular audits or assessments to verify their compliance with security and privacy requirements. These audits are performed by third-party assessors or regulatory authorities and are critical to ensuring that organizations are operating in accordance with legal requirements and industry best practices. Let's explore this concept with an example in the context of PCI DSS.

Scenario: The same fictitious e-commerce company, "EuroKart," processes credit card payments from customers. To ensure the security of cardholder data, EuroKart must comply with the PCI DSS.

Here is how it works:

- **Audit planning**: EuroKart initiates a compliance audit by establishing a clear plan. This includes defining the scope of the audit, identifying relevant PCI DSS requirements, and scheduling audit activities.

- **Audit team**: EuroKart assembles an audit team that may include internal or external auditors with expertise in PCI DSS compliance. External auditors often bring a fresh perspective and specialized knowledge.

- **Data gathering**: The audit team collects relevant data, documents, and evidence related to EuroKart's **cardholder data environment** (**CDE**), security policies, procedures, and system configurations.

- **Assessment and testing**: The audit team evaluates EuroKart's controls and security measures against specific PCI DSS requirements. This involves conducting vulnerability scans, penetration tests, and reviews of security policies and procedures.

- **Interviews and documentation review**: Auditors interview employees and review documentation to understand how EuroKart manages cardholder data, implements security controls, and responds to security incidents.

- **Gap analysis**: Auditors identify gaps or deficiencies in EuroKart's compliance with PCI DSS requirements. They compare the current state to the standard's specifications.

- **Reporting and findings**: The audit team compiles its findings into a comprehensive audit report. This report includes:

  - Details of the audit scope and methodology

  - An assessment of compliance with specific PCI DSS requirements

  - A summary of findings, including any non-compliance issues or vulnerabilities

  - Recommendations for remediation and improvements

- **Remediation**: EuroKart uses the audit report to address identified issues. This may involve updating security policies, implementing additional security controls, or conducting employee training.

- **Follow-up**: Auditors may conduct follow-up assessments to verify that EuroKart has addressed identified deficiencies and is now in compliance with PCI DSS.

- **Documentation and compliance records**: EuroKart maintains all audit-related documentation and compliance records, which are crucial for demonstrating PCI DSS compliance to stakeholders and during future audits.

A compliance audit focused on PCI DSS ensures that EuroKart's processes and security controls meet the standard's requirements for handling credit card data. By regularly conducting these audits, EuroKart not only ensures its compliance but also enhances the security of cardholder information, reduces the risk of data breaches, and maintains the trust of customers and payment card companies.

Challenges, CSPM roles, and future trends

Effectively managing compliance and governance in a cloud environment is challenging due to its inherent complexity, dynamic nature, and the prevalence of multi-cloud and hybrid setups. Security risks, automation, and human error are constant concerns. Organizations must employ comprehensive strategies that incorporate tools, automation, regular audits, and cross-functional collaboration to strike a balance between cost control and compliance while ensuring the security and integrity of cloud resources.

Challenges in compliance and governance

Let us understand some of the most common challenges in effective compliance management and governance:

- **Regulatory complexity**: The ever-evolving regulatory landscape presents a major challenge. Navigating complex and frequently changing regulations can be daunting for organizations.

- **Data security and privacy**: The increasing frequency and sophistication of cyber threats make it challenging to protect sensitive data and maintain compliance with data protection and privacy regulations.

- **Cross-border operations**: Organizations operating in multiple jurisdictions must contend with differing regulatory frameworks, adding complexity to compliance efforts.

- **Resource constraints**: Many organizations face limitations in terms of financial and human resources allocated to compliance and governance activities.

- **Legacy systems**: Outdated technology and legacy systems hinder efficient compliance management. Modernizing these systems without disrupting operations is a significant challenge.

- **Cultural shifts**: Building a culture of compliance throughout an organization is also challenging. Ensuring that employees at all levels prioritize compliance is an ongoing effort.

- **Third-party risks**: Relying on third-party vendors and partners at B2B collaborations at the infrastructure level introduces compliance risks. Organizations must carefully monitor these third parties to ensure they meet compliance standards.

These are some of the most common challenges experienced by organizations while trying to meet compliance requirements. Let us now briefly recall how CSPM can be a proven boon for organizations in addressing these challenges and help achieve good scores in compliance management.

CSPM's role in effective compliance management and governance

Choosing a CSPM tool with thorough assessment can be a blessing, especially for an organization with a complex and multi-cloud environment. Here's what CSPM tools provide:

- **Compliance assurance**: CSPM tools enable organizations to define and enforce security policies and compliance standards across their cloud infrastructure. This ensures that cloud resources align with regulatory requirements and internal policies. By automating policy enforcement, CSPM tools help maintain consistent compliance, reducing the risk of non-compliance and associated penalties.

- **Continuous monitoring**: CSPM solutions continuously monitor cloud resources and configurations, keeping a vigilant eye on security postures. This real-time monitoring detects any deviations from compliance standards promptly. It provides organizations the ability to address issues as they arise, minimizing compliance gaps and security risks.

- **Risk assessment**: CSPM tools offer risk assessment capabilities, allowing organizations to identify security vulnerabilities and misconfigurations that could compromise compliance. These tools assign risk scores, helping prioritize remediation efforts to focus on the most critical compliance issues first.

- **Compliance reporting**: CSPM solutions generate comprehensive compliance reports and dashboards. These reports serve as a valuable resource during audits and regulatory assessments, providing clear visibility into the compliance status of cloud environments. By facilitating transparent reporting, CSPM tools aid in demonstrating adherence to compliance requirements.

- **Automation of remediation**: Many CSPM tools offer automated remediation capabilities. When non-compliance issues are identified, these tools can automatically rectify them or provide guidance on resolution. This automation accelerates the remediation process, ensuring a swift return to compliance.

- **Integration with cloud services**: CSPM tools seamlessly integrate with major CSPs, tapping into cloud-specific APIs and services. This integration ensures deep insights into the configuration and security of cloud resources, facilitating effective governance within the cloud environment.

CSPM plays an instrumental role in compliance and governance by automating policy enforcement, providing continuous monitoring, conducting risk assessments, facilitating compliance reporting, automating remediation, and seamlessly integrating with cloud services. These capabilities collectively empower organizations to maintain compliance with regulatory standards, internal policies, and best practices while bolstering the overall governance of their cloud environments.

Future trends in compliance and governance

Compliance and governance of cloud environments are continually evolving to meet the demands of an ever-changing technological landscape. Most advanced CSPM tools are getting equipped and will continue to do so to tackle new challenges in the cloud security domain. Here are some future trends that CSPM solutions are likely to leverage:

- **Zero Trust framework integration**: CSPM solutions will align closely with the Zero Trust security model, enabling continuous monitoring and verification of all users and devices accessing cloud resources. This will enhance security and compliance by implementing strict access controls and real-time risk assessments.

- **Artificial intelligence (AI)-powered compliance**: AI and **machine learning** (**ML**) will be increasingly used for automating compliance checks and risk assessments. AI can analyze vast amounts of data and identify compliance violations or security threats more efficiently than manual methods.

- **Regulatory compliance automation**: CSPM tools will become more adept at automating compliance checks specific to various regulations and standards. They will offer preconfigured compliance templates and workflows for standards such as GDPR, HIPAA, and more, making it easier for organizations to maintain compliance.

- **Serverless and container security**: As serverless computing and containerization become more prevalent in cloud environments, governance will need to address the unique security challenges these technologies present. Policies for secure container orchestration and serverless function execution will be crucial.

- **Governance as Code (GaC)**: Similar to **Infrastructure as Code** (**IaC**), GaC will become popular for codifying governance policies and rules. This approach enables automated governance enforcement alongside infrastructure provisioning.

- **Supply chain governance**: There will be an increased focus on securing the entire cloud supply chain, from third-party services to software dependencies. Organizations will need to assess the security and compliance of every component in the supply chain.

- **Contextual threat intelligence (TI)**: Advanced CSPM solutions will incorporate contextual TI, allowing organizations to assess compliance risks in the context of known and emerging threats. This will enhance proactive threat detection and remediation.

- **Compliance reporting enhancements**: Future CSPM tools will offer more advanced compliance reporting features, including customizable dashboards, trend analysis, and executive summaries. These features will make it easier for organizations to communicate compliance status to stakeholders.

- **Blockchain-based audit trails**: Some CSPM tools may explore blockchain technology to create immutable audit trails and logs. This can enhance the integrity and transparency of compliance records.

- **Integration with DevOps pipelines**: CSPM tools will seamlessly integrate with DevOps pipelines, allowing for automated security and compliance checks throughout the **software development life cycle (SDLC)**. This DevSecOps approach will promote security and compliance by design.

- **Collaborative workflows**: CSPM tools will facilitate collaboration among security, compliance, and operations teams, streamlining workflows and fostering cross-functional communication.

These future trends represent the direction in which advanced CSPM tools are heading to meet the growing demands of cloud compliance and governance. Leveraging these trends, organizations can enhance their ability to secure cloud environments, maintain compliance, and effectively manage risk in an increasingly complex cloud landscape.

Summary

In this chapter, we have explored wide aspects of compliance management and governance within the realm of cloud security. We began by defining compliance management and governance, highlighting their symbiotic relationship. Compliance management involves adhering to regulatory requirements and industry standards, while governance encompasses the broader set of policies and practices that guide an organization's operations and security. We delved into the importance of compliance frameworks and standards, which provide structured guidelines for organizations to follow. These frameworks, such as *ISO 27001* and *NIST SP 800-53*, serve as essential blueprints for achieving compliance and maintaining robust governance.

A note to readers

As we move forward in this journey of mastering CSPM, remember that knowledge is most valuable when put into action. Take the insights and strategies you've gained in this chapter on compliance management and governance and apply them to your cloud security practices. By doing so, you'll not only fortify your organization's defenses but also contribute to the broader mission of ensuring a safer and more secure digital landscape for all. Stay vigilant, stay secure, and let's dive into the world of security alerts and monitoring together in the next chapter. We encourage you to carry forward the knowledge gained from this chapter as you continue your exploration of cloud security and CSPM. Compliance and governance are not just concepts; they are the cornerstones of a secure and resilient cloud environment.

Throughout this chapter, we have underscored a fundamental truth: compliance and governance are not just checkboxes to be marked; they are the bedrock upon which cloud security stands. In an ever-evolving landscape of regulations, threats, and technologies, organizations that prioritize compliance and governance are better equipped to protect their assets, build trust with customers, and thrive in the cloud. As you embark on your journey to mastering CSPM and navigating the complex world of cloud security, remember that compliance management and governance are your steadfast allies. They provide the structure, guidance, and assurance needed to safeguard your cloud assets and data in an ever-connected digital world.

In our next chapter, we'll venture into the dynamic realm of security alerts and monitoring. We'll explore how proactive monitoring and swift responses to security alerts are crucial for maintaining the integrity and resilience of your cloud environment. Get ready to delve into the tools, techniques, and best practices that empower you to stay one step ahead of emerging threats.

15

Security Alerts and Monitoring

As organizations continue to embrace cloud computing and expand their digital footprint, mostly without a proper security-by-design approach, the attack surface grows larger, making it imperative to implement robust security measures. Security alerts and monitoring serve as the eyes and ears of your cloud environment. Being constantly vigilant regarding signs of unauthorized access, suspicious activities, and potential vulnerabilities is one of the most critical needs. These capabilities are indispensable in maintaining a robust security posture, meeting compliance requirements, and safeguarding valuable data and resources.

Throughout this chapter, we will navigate the complex world of security alerts and monitoring within the context of CSPM. We will discuss the significance of real-time threat detection, the types of alerts you should be monitoring for, and the technologies and tools at your disposal. Moreover, we will provide practical insights and best practices for configuring and fine-tuning alerting systems to strike the right balance between vigilance and alert fatigue. CSPM not only encompasses proactive measures such as configuration management and policy enforcement but also relies heavily on the ability to detect, respond, and adapt to security threats in real time. This is where *security alerts and monitoring* comes to the forefront—a vital pillar of CSPM that allows organizations to maintain an active defense posture in the face of evolving cyber threats by integrating with existing monitoring solutions. Furthermore, we will delve into the fundamental principles and practical strategies that will empower you to take control of your cloud security posture in an increasingly volatile digital landscape.

We'll cover the following main topics:

- Security alerts and monitoring overview
- Building an effective alerting strategy
- Leveraging cloud-native monitoring solutions
- Compliance and auditing through monitoring
- Emerging trends in security alerts and monitoring
- Case study and lessons learned

Let's get started!

Security alerts and monitoring overview

At its core, CSPM is a comprehensive approach to securing cloud environments. It brings a range of strategies and practices aimed at identifying and mitigating security risks and vulnerabilities. However, CSPM extends beyond merely configuring cloud resources securely or defining access control policies. It is also about maintaining continuous vigilance over your cloud infrastructure to ensure that it remains secure over time. Security alerts and monitoring serve as the watchful eyes and keen ears of your cloud environment, constantly scanning for potential threats, deviations from security policies, and signs of unauthorized access. They act as the first line of defense against emerging security risks.

Consider a scenario where an unauthorized user attempts to gain access to sensitive data stored in the cloud. Without effective monitoring and alerting mechanisms in place, this intrusion could go unnoticed until considerable damage has occurred. Security alerts and monitoring, however, can detect such activities in real time or near real time, triggering immediate responses to thwart potential breaches. Beyond the reactive aspect of incident detection, security alerts and monitoring are instrumental in maintaining proactive control. It helps organizations pre-emptively identify misconfigurations, policy violations, and anomalies that might otherwise go unnoticed until they're exploited by malicious actors. Security alerts and monitoring are like the sentinels standing guard over your cloud infrastructure, ensuring that it remains resilient and secure in the face of ever-evolving threats. They play a pivotal role in maintaining a robust security posture, meeting compliance requirements, and safeguarding your valuable data and resources.

So, let's understand the significance of security alerts and monitoring in CSPM as it is a fundamental step toward mastering the art of cloud security in an ever-evolving digital landscape.

Real-world scenarios illustrating the consequences of inadequate monitoring

Let's look at a few real-world scenarios that illustrate the severe consequences that can result from inadequately monitoring cloud environments within the context of CSPM.

Scenario 1 – data breach due to a misconfigured S3 bucket

In this scenario, a well-known technology company, despite having implemented robust security measures for its cloud infrastructure, neglected to set up proper monitoring and alerting for its Amazon S3 storage buckets. An employee mistakenly configured one of the S3 buckets to be publicly accessible instead of restricting access to authorized users only.

Consequence: Hackers discovered misconfiguration and accessed sensitive customer data, including **personally identifiable information** (**PII**). The breach led to legal ramifications, a loss of customer trust, and severe damage to the company's reputation.

Scenario 2 – insider threat goes unnoticed

A financial institution, focused on external threats, did not invest in comprehensive monitoring for internal users within its cloud environment. An employee with access to sensitive financial data decided to misuse their privileges for personal gain.

Consequence: The insider's activities went unnoticed for months, during which they siphoned off a substantial amount of money. The lack of monitoring not only led to financial losses but also eroded trust among customers and shareholders when the incident eventually became known.

Scenario 3 – continuous cryptocurrency mining in cloud servers

A mid-sized e-commerce company failed to establish proper monitoring for its virtual servers running in the cloud. Unknown to the IT team, an attacker had gained access to a few servers and was using them for cryptocurrency mining, consuming significant computing resources.

Consequence: Over time, the increased cloud costs went unnoticed, as did the performance degradation affecting the company's website and online shopping experience. This lack of monitoring led to both financial losses and a negative impact on the customer experience.

Scenario 4 – compliance violations leading to fines

A healthcare organization transitioned its patient data to the cloud but did not implement continuous monitoring for compliance with healthcare regulations. As a result, sensitive patient data was at risk of exposure.

Consequence: An audit by regulatory authorities revealed multiple compliance violations, resulting in substantial fines and mandatory corrective actions. The lack of monitoring costs organizations financially and endangers patient privacy.

These real-world scenarios emphasize the critical importance of effective monitoring and alerting within CSPM. Inadequate monitoring can lead to data breaches, financial losses, compliance violations, and reputational damage, all of which could have been mitigated or prevented with vigilant monitoring and timely alerts. These examples highlight the necessity of implementing robust security alerts and monitoring practices to protect cloud environments effectively.

Distinguishing between security alerts, incidents, and anomalies

Distinguishing between security alerts, incidents, and anomalies is crucial for effective security monitoring and incident response. These terms represent different aspects of cybersecurity and are often used to categorize and manage security-related events in a cloud environment, as well as in broader IT security contexts. Let's look at how they differ.

Security alerts

Security alerts are notifications that are generated by security monitoring tools or systems when predefined criteria or conditions are met. These criteria involve detecting specific patterns, behaviors, or events that may indicate a security threat or policy violation.

Purpose: Security alerts serve as early warnings of potential security issues. They are the initial indicators that something unusual or suspicious may be happening within a system or network.

Example: An alert is triggered when a user fails to log in after multiple attempts, indicating a potential brute-force attack on an account.

Incidents

Incidents are confirmed security events that have been investigated and determined to be actual security breaches, policy violations, or other security-related issues. Incidents are typically escalated for further analysis, containment, and response. Incidents represent actionable, validated cases that require intervention. They are incidents of security concern that demand immediate attention and remediation efforts.

Example: Investigating alerts for multiple failed login attempts confirmed that an unauthorized user gained access to an account. This is now classified as a security incident.

Anomalies

Anomalies are deviations from established patterns or baselines. They may not necessarily indicate a security threat on their own, but they can be indicative of potential issues that require further investigation. Anomalies are observed as deviations from the norm, and they serve as a starting point for investigation. They may or may not lead to security alerts or incidents, but they are essential for detecting subtle changes in system behavior.

Example: An anomaly is detected when a user who typically logs in from one geographic location suddenly logs in from a different country. While this may not be an incident, it warrants further investigation to ensure the account has not been compromised.

In short, security alerts are the initial triggers that are generated by monitoring systems to indicate potential security concerns. Incidents are confirmed security breaches or violations that require immediate action. Anomalies are deviations from normal behavior that may or may not lead to alerts or incidents but serve as early indicators of potential issues. Effectively managing these concepts is critical for maintaining a robust security posture and responding proactively to security threats in a cloud environment.

Common categories of security alerts

Security alerts can cover a wide range of categories, each designed to detect specific types of threats or violations within a cloud environment or an IT infrastructure. Here are some common categories of security alerts:

- **Intrusion attempts**: Alerts in this category signal potential unauthorized access or intrusion attempts into a system, network, or application.

  Example: Alerts triggered by repeated failed login attempts, unusual or suspicious network traffic patterns, or known attack patterns, such as SQL injection attempts.

- **Policy violations**: These alerts indicate violations of established security policies, configurations, or access controls.

  Example: Alerts that are triggered when a user or application accesses restricted resources, circumvents authentication mechanisms, or violates data access policies.

- **Malware and virus detection**: Alerts related to the detection of malicious software or viruses within the environment.

  Example: Alerts that are triggered when malware is identified during file uploads and downloads or when suspicious processes or behaviors indicative of malware activity are observed.

- **Data exfiltration**: Alerts in this category identify the unauthorized transfer or theft of sensitive data from the organization's network or systems.

  Example: Alerts that are triggered when large volumes of data are sent to external or unusual destinations, or when sensitive files are accessed and copied by unauthorized users.

- **Anomalous behavior**: These alerts detect deviations from normal patterns of user or system behavior.

  Example: Alerts that are triggered when a user logs in from an unusual location, performs actions inconsistent with their typical behavior, or exhibits behavior indicative of insider threats.

- **Distributed denial of service (DDoS) attacks**: Alerts in this category identify attempts to overwhelm systems or networks, causing disruptions in service availability.

  Examples: Alerts are triggered when a sudden increase in network traffic is detected. This is indicative of a potential DDoS attack.

- **Security certificate issues**: These alerts focus on problems with digital certificates, such as expired or invalid certificates, which can indicate potential security risks.

  Example: Alerts are triggered when SSL/TLS certificate expiration dates are approaching or when certificates are found to be mismatched or signed by untrusted authorities.

- **Privilege escalation attempts**: Alerts related to attempts to gain unauthorized access to higher-level privileges within systems or applications.

  Examples: Alerts are triggered when a user or application attempts to escalate their permissions or manipulate access control lists.

- **Suspicious network traffic**: Alerts in this category detect unusual or potentially malicious network traffic patterns.

  Examples: Alerts are triggered by traffic associated with known malware command and control servers, or traffic patterns inconsistent with normal network behavior.

- **Vulnerability exploitation attempts**: Alerts identify attempts to exploit known vulnerabilities in software or systems.

  Examples: Alerts are triggered when an attacker scans or probes for vulnerabilities or when specific exploit signatures are detected in network traffic.

These common categories of security alerts provide organizations with a broad spectrum of threat detection capabilities, enabling them to monitor, detect, and respond to a wide range of security risks and incidents within their cloud environments and IT infrastructure.

Building an effective alerting strategy

Building an effective alerting strategy is essential for maintaining robust security in a cloud environment as part of the effective implementation of CSPM. One crucial aspect of this strategy is setting clear security objectives and risk thresholds. Let's delve into what this means and why it matters.

Setting clear security objectives and risk thresholds

Security objectives are specific, measurable goals that an organization sets to achieve its desired level of security. These objectives should align with the organization's overall security strategy and compliance requirements. Clear security objectives provide a roadmap for what an organization aims to achieve in terms of security. They help define the scope and purpose of security monitoring and alerting. Without well-defined objectives, it is challenging to determine which security events or incidents should trigger alerts.

Example: Security objectives could include goals such as "ensure that all access to sensitive customer data is logged and monitored, or "minimize the mean time to detect and respond to security incidents to less than 30 minutes."

Setting risk thresholds

Risk thresholds are predetermined levels of risk that an organization is willing to tolerate or accept before acting on it. They help organizations differentiate between acceptable and unacceptable risks. Risk thresholds serve as a critical component of the alerting strategy by helping organizations prioritize which alerts require immediate attention and which can be monitored passively. They ensure that resources are allocated efficiently to address the most significant security risks.

Example: An organization might set a risk threshold for a specific alert, stating that if the alert's severity or impact exceeds a certain level (for example, a criticality of 7 on a scale of 1 to 10), immediate action is required. Alerts that fall below this threshold may undergo further investigation but not demand an immediate response.

Why it matters

By setting clear security objectives, organizations can concentrate their monitoring efforts on areas that are critical to achieving those objectives. This prevents resource wastage on irrelevant alerts and activities:

- **Prioritize the response**: Risk thresholds help organizations prioritize their incident response efforts. Alerts exceeding the threshold are deemed high-priority and receive immediate attention, reducing response time for critical incidents.

- **Align with compliance**: Security objectives often align with compliance requirements, ensuring that the organization meets regulatory obligations. Risk thresholds help demonstrate a proactive approach to risk management.

- **Improve decision-making**: Clear objectives and risk thresholds facilitate informed decision-making. Security teams can make well-founded judgments about whether to investigate, mitigate, or accept certain security events based on their alignment with these criteria.

Building an effective alerting strategy within CSPM involves defining clear security objectives and risk thresholds. This not only provides direction for security monitoring efforts but also ensures that organizations can efficiently allocate resources and respond to security events in a manner aligned with their overarching security goals and risk tolerance levels.

Defining alerting criteria tailored to your organization's needs

Defining alerting criteria tailored to your organization's needs is a critical aspect of building a robust security alerting strategy within the context of CSPM. Let's explain this concept in more detail.

Defining alerting criteria

Alerting criteria refers to the specific conditions, thresholds, or triggers that determine when a security alert should be generated. These criteria can vary widely based on the organization's objectives, risk tolerance, and the nature of its cloud environment.

The alerting criteria should align closely with the security objectives and goals set by your organization. They should reflect what you consider as **threats, vulnerabilities,** or **deviations** from secure configurations within your cloud environment. Consider the impact of security alerts on your organization's day-today operations. The alerting criteria should be designed to flag events that are relevant to your critical business processes and systems.

Risk profile – tailored to your organization's needs

Your organization's risk profile plays a significant role in defining alerting criteria. If your industry or business processes are highly regulated or involve sensitive data, you may have stricter alerting criteria than a less regulated industry. Different industries face unique threats. Tailoring alert criteria involves understanding the specific threats that are most pertinent to your industry and configuring alerts to detect them effectively. Determine the relative importance of various alerts. Not all security incidents are equal in terms of their potential impact. Tailoring alerting criteria allows you to prioritize alerts based on their severity and relevance. Consider the resources available for monitoring and incident response. Alerting criteria should be tailored to what your security team can effectively manage without becoming overwhelmed.

Why it matters

Alerts that are tailored to your organization's needs are more likely to identify threats that are specific to your environment, reducing false positives and enhancing the chances of detecting actual security incidents. Customized alerting criteria ensure that your security team does not waste time investigating irrelevant or low-priority alerts, allowing them to focus on real threats. By aligning alerting criteria with your organization's capabilities, you can optimize the allocation of resources, making the most of your security personnel and technology investments. Tailored alerting criteria can help demonstrate compliance with industry-specific regulations and standards as they reflect the specific security requirements relevant to your sector. It involves customizing the parameters and conditions that trigger security alerts to align with your organization's unique requirements and priorities.

In conclusion, defining alerting criteria tailored to your organization's needs ensures that the alerts generated are relevant, actionable, and aligned with your organization's objectives, helping you maintain a strong security posture in your cloud environment.

Avoiding alert fatigue – Best practices in alert tuning and prioritization

Avoiding alert fatigue is crucial in maintaining an effective security monitoring system within the context of CSPM. Alert fatigue occurs when security professionals are inundated with a high volume of alerts, many of which are false positives or low-priority events. This can lead to reduced response effectiveness and increased stress among security teams. Here are some best practices in alert tuning and prioritization to mitigate alert fatigue:

* **Understand the business context**: Identify and prioritize the **critical assets** and systems within your cloud environment. Alerts related to these assets should be given higher priority. Understand what **normal** behavior looks like in your environment. This knowledge will help you distinguish between legitimate deviations and potential threats.

- **Implement robust baseline monitoring**: Create **baseline** profiles for network traffic, user behavior, and system performance. Alerts should be triggered when deviations from these baselines occur. Leverage **machine learning** and **anomaly detection** techniques to automatically adapt to changes in your environment and reduce false positives.

- **Fine-tune alerting thresholds**: Adjust alerting thresholds to strike a balance between detecting real threats and reducing false alarms. Thresholds should be aligned with your risk tolerance. Implement graduated alerting levels based on the severity and context of an event. Low-severity alerts can be aggregated or deprioritized.

- **Prioritize alerts effectively**: Assign **severity levels** to alerts based on their potential impact. High-severity alerts should demand immediate attention, while low-severity alerts can be investigated later. Prioritize alerts based on the **level of risk** they pose to your organization. Focus on alerts that could result in significant data breaches or financial losses.

- **Correlation and enrichment**: Implement alert correlation to group-related alerts into incidents. This reduces noise and provides a more comprehensive view of an incident. Enhance alerts with additional context, such as threat intelligence feeds, to help analysts assess their significance quickly.

- **Automation and playbooks**: Implement automated responses for routine tasks and alerts, freeing up security analysts to focus on more complex threats. Develop incident response playbooks that outline steps to be taken for specific types of alerts. This streamlines the response process and reduces decision-making time.

- **Regular review and feedback**: Conduct regular reviews of alerting configurations and incident response processes. Continuously adjust alert criteria based on the feedback and lessons learned from past incidents.

- **Training and education**: Invest in ongoing training and education for security personnel to keep them updated on the latest threats and best practices in alert handling.

- **Collaboration and communication**: Foster collaboration between security teams, IT operations, and other relevant departments to enhance understanding and alignment on alert priorities.

- **Feedback and documentation**: Maintain thorough documentation of alerting criteria, response procedures, and any changes made to alert configurations. Establish a **feedback loop** where security analysts can provide input on the effectiveness of alerts and suggest improvements.

In short, organizations can significantly reduce alert fatigue, improve the efficiency of their security monitoring efforts, and enhance their ability to respond effectively to genuine security threats within their cloud environments by following the aforementioned best practices.

Leveraging cloud-native monitoring solutions

In today's fast-paced digital landscape, cloud-native monitoring solutions have become a cornerstone of effective cybersecurity. They offer real-time visibility into your cloud infrastructure, allowing you to proactively manage and secure your resources. Since CSPM tools are also mostly cloud-native, and bring the deep visibility of multi-cloud environments, it is important to explore whether CSPM can be used as monitoring solutions. Let us find out how along with some other important topics.

Can CSPM tools be used as cloud-native monitoring solutions?

CSPM tools are primarily designed to ensure the secure configuration of cloud resources and compliance with security policies within cloud environments. While CSPM tools play a crucial role in enhancing cloud security, they are not typically used as direct replacements for cloud-native monitoring solutions, **Security Information and Event Management** (**SIEM**) systems, or **Security Orchestration, Automation, and Response** (**SOAR**) platforms. Let's understand why.

CSPM focus and use case

CSPM tools focus on identifying misconfigurations, vulnerabilities, and compliance violations within cloud environments. They are primarily concerned with the configuration of cloud resources, access controls, and security group settings.

Use case: CSPM is used to improve the security posture of cloud environments by preventing misconfigurations, enforcing security policies, and ensuring compliance with industry standards and regulatory requirements. It primarily focuses on security and compliance.

Cloud-native monitoring solutions focus and use case

Cloud-native monitoring solutions, on the other hand, provide real-time visibility into the performance, availability, and behavior of cloud-native services, applications, and infrastructure components. They collect and analyze metrics, logs, and events generated by cloud resources to ensure optimal operation and troubleshoot issues.

Use case: Cloud-native monitoring solutions are used for performance monitoring, troubleshooting, capacity planning, and resource optimization. They provide insights into the operational aspects of cloud resources and help maintain service availability. Here are some examples:

- **SIEM integration**: Organizations often integrate CSPM tools with SIEM systems to centralize security event data from cloud environments and correlate it with data from other IT assets. This integration enhances security monitoring and threat detection capabilities.

- **SOAR integration**: Similarly, CSPM can be integrated with SOAR platforms to automate response actions when security misconfigurations or vulnerabilities are detected. SOAR helps orchestrate incident response workflows efficiently.

> **Important**
>
> CSPM tools are not cloud-native monitoring solutions in the traditional sense, but they are essential components of a comprehensive cloud security strategy. Organizations often use CSPM tools alongside cloud-native monitoring solutions such as SIEM systems and SOAR platforms to create a holistic security ecosystem. This combination allows them to address security, compliance, performance, and incident response needs effectively in their cloud environments.

In short, CSPM tools are not substitutes for cloud-native monitoring solutions such as SIEM and SOAR but rather complementary tools that focus on different aspects of cloud security and compliance. Integrating CSPM with these solutions can enhance an organization's overall cloud security and monitoring capabilities.

Third-party SIEM solutions

With this transition to the cloud, the need for robust security monitoring and alerting has become paramount. This is where third-party SIEM solutions come into play, acting as crucial components of an organization's security toolkit.

Evaluating the need for third-party SIEM solutions

CSPM tools are excellent at ensuring that your cloud resources are configured securely, compliant with industry standards, and adhere to your organization's security policies. They are designed to identify and rectify misconfigurations and vulnerabilities within your cloud infrastructure. As we've already established, CSPM tools typically focus on the cloud environment itself, leaving a potential gap in holistic security monitoring. This gap arises because CSPM tools cannot provide the comprehensive threat visibility required to detect and respond to security incidents that span across both cloud and on-premises environments. Third-party SIEM solutions step in to bridge this gap by offering broader security event monitoring capabilities. They collect and analyze data from various sources, providing insights into potential security threats and incidents that go beyond the scope of CSPM tools. Let's look at some important things to consider.

Choosing the right SIEM platform that integrates well with CSPM

Selecting the right SIEM platform is a critical decision when you wish to integrate with your CSPM solution. Here are some key considerations:

- **Compatibility**: Ensure that the SIEM platform is compatible with your CSPM tools and cloud environment providers. Compatibility issues can hinder seamless integration and data sharing.

- **Scalability**: As your organization grows, so does the volume of security data that's generated. Choose a SIEM solution that can scale alongside your CSPM needs.

- **Advanced analytics**: Look for SIEM platforms with advanced analytics and machine learning capabilities to detect and respond to evolving threats effectively.

- **Compliance**: If your organization operates within a regulated industry, ensure that the SIEM solution can support compliance reporting and auditing requirements.

- **Customization**: The ability to customize alerts, reports, and dashboards to suit your specific CSPM needs can be a significant advantage.

In most cases, organizations already have SIEM solutions in place before they opt for CSPM solutions, so it is important to assess the CSPM tool in a way that integrates well with existing monitoring solutions.

Integrating SIEM with CSPM for comprehensive threat visibility

To effectively monitor and safeguard cloud environments, integrating a SIEM solution with CSPM becomes a strategic imperative and is about connecting these two distinct but complementary tools to achieve comprehensive threat visibility. Here is why it is essential:

- **Holistic monitoring**: SIEM allows organizations to monitor not only cloud configurations but also security events and incidents. This holistic approach ensures that potential threats across the entire IT landscape, including the cloud, are captured and analyzed.

- **Advanced threat detection**: SIEM leverages its advanced correlation and analytics capabilities to identify complex threats that may span multiple cloud services and resources. By combining CSPM alerts with SIEM data, organizations gain a more in-depth understanding of these threats.

- **Rapid incident response**: The integration streamlines incident response. When CSPM detects a misconfiguration or vulnerability, it can trigger an alert within the SIEM. SIEM, in turn, can automate response actions or notify the security team, leading to faster incident resolution.

- **Compliance management**: SIEM provides robust compliance reporting capabilities. By integrating CSPM data into SIEM, organizations can create compliance reports that encompass both configuration checks and security events, simplifying the audit process.

The integration of SIEM with CSPM is a strategic move to enhance cloud security. It combines CSPM's focus on secure configurations with SIEM's event analysis capabilities, offering organizations a powerful solution for detecting, responding to, and mitigating threats across their entire IT landscape, including the cloud.

Considerations for integration

While the benefits of integrating SIEM with cloud environments are clear, there are some key considerations:

- **Data mapping**: Ensure that CSPM alerts are correctly mapped to the SIEM's data structure for effective correlation

- **Automation**: Develop automated workflows for incident response to maximize the value of the integration

- **Scalability**: Consider scalability needs, as cloud environments can grow rapidly
- **Monitoring policies**: Align CSPM and SIEM monitoring policies to avoid duplication and ensure comprehensive coverage

In short, integrating SIEM with cloud environments is a critical step in achieving comprehensive threat visibility. It combines CSPM's focus on secure configurations with SIEM's event analysis capabilities, providing organizations with a robust solution for detecting and responding to threats across their entire IT landscape, including the cloud. This integration is a strategic move toward building a resilient and proactive cybersecurity posture.

Now, let's understand another critical aspect of effective alerts and monitoring: automated incident response.

Automated incident response

Automated incident response, a critical component of CSPM, leverages the synergy between security alerts and predefined response workflows to enable real-time incident containment and mitigation. Let's explore how this dynamic process unfolds.

The synergy between security alerts and automated incident response

Imagine CSPM as the vigilant guardian of your cloud environment, continuously monitoring for misconfigurations, vulnerabilities, and compliance violations. When it identifies anomalies or policy breaches, CSPM generates security alerts. However, alerts alone are just the first step in the security journey. The synergy between security alerts and automated incident response is where the real magic happens. Automated incident response systems (also known as SOAR), which are often integrated with CSPM, kick into action upon receiving these alerts. They follow predefined playbooks and response workflows to assess the situation and take appropriate actions.

Implementing playbooks and response workflows

Playbooks and response workflows are the heart of automated incident response. They are predefined sets of actions and decisions that guide the response process when a security alert is triggered. These playbooks are carefully crafted to handle different types of incidents, from minor policy violations to critical security breaches.

For instance, when CSPM alerts about an unauthorized change in cloud access permissions, the playbook can include steps such as the following:

1. Identify the affected resource.
2. Verify the change and its potential impact.
3. Isolate the resource to prevent further harm.
4. Notify the security team for investigation.

Organizations should ensure that incident response is consistent, efficient, and well-informed by defining these steps in advance. It reduces the risk of human error and accelerates the time it takes to contain and mitigate threats.

Real-time incident containment and mitigation strategies

Automated incident response goes beyond acknowledgment; it is about real-time containment and mitigation. In the preceding example, isolating the affected resource is a crucial step to prevent further unauthorized access or data breaches. The automation system can execute this action swiftly, reducing the window of vulnerability.

Furthermore, the system can gather additional information, such as log data and user activity, to aid in the investigation. It can also initiate remediation procedures, such as rolling back changes to a previously known good state. The overall goal is to contain the incident, mitigate the damage, and restore normal operations as quickly as possible.

In summary, automated incident response is the bridge that connects security alerts to swift action. It relies on predefined playbooks and workflows to orchestrate responses to security incidents identified by CSPM.

By automating these responses, organizations can enhance their ability to detect, contain, and mitigate threats in real time, strengthening their overall security posture in the ever-changing landscape of cloud security.

Compliance and auditing through monitoring

Compliance and auditing through monitoring are vital aspects of modern cybersecurity and risk management. Organizations are often subject to various regulatory requirements, industry standards, and internal policies that mandate a certain level of security and data protection. Monitoring plays a key role in ensuring compliance and providing evidence to auditors and regulators that these requirements are met. Let's dive deep into the topic.

Meeting compliance requirements through continuous monitoring

In today's digital landscape, compliance with industry standards and regulatory requirements is non-negotiable. Organizations must adhere to specific rules and best practices to safeguard their data and maintain trust with customers and stakeholders. Achieving compliance involves not only setting up the right security policies but also ensuring that they are consistently enforced. This is where CSPM comes into play. CSPM tools are purpose-built to assist organizations in meeting compliance requirements by continuously monitoring cloud environments for security misconfigurations, vulnerabilities, and adherence to predefined security policies. For example, suppose an organization is subject to the **General Data Protection Regulation (GDPR)** and must protect the privacy of customer data stored in the cloud. CSPM can monitor the cloud environment for any configuration issues that might lead to data exposure, such as improperly configured access controls or encryption settings. It can generate alerts and reports in real time whenever non-compliant conditions are detected.

Demonstrating CSPM effectiveness to auditors and regulators

Auditors and regulators play a critical role in ensuring that organizations are meeting compliance standards. They require evidence that security controls are in place and effective. CSPM serves as a powerful ally in this process by providing concrete data and documentation to demonstrate compliance.

When auditors or regulators assess an organization's cloud security, CSPM tools can generate detailed reports that show the following:

- A historical record of security configurations and changes

- Evidence of compliance checks and alerts

- Documentation of corrective actions that have been taken in response to alerts

- Consistent monitoring and enforcement of security policies

These reports provide auditors with a clear picture of an organization's commitment to compliance and its ability to maintain a secure cloud environment. They also enable organizations to proactively address any compliance issues before they become major concerns during audits.

Automating compliance checks and reporting

One of the significant advantages of CSPM is its ability to automate compliance checks and reporting. Instead of relying on manual audits that are time-consuming and error-prone, organizations can configure CSPM tools to perform regular checks against compliance standards automatically. For instance, CSPM can automate checks for compliance with standards such as the **Payment Card Industry Data Security Standard (PCI DSS)** or the **Health Insurance Portability and Accountability Act (HIPAA)**. When non-compliance is detected, the tool can trigger alerts, initiate corrective actions, and generate compliance reports on a predefined schedule. This automation streamlines the compliance process, reduces the risk of human error, and ensures that organizations maintain a consistent state of compliance.

In short, CSPM plays a crucial role in helping organizations meet compliance requirements through continuous monitoring, demonstrating its effectiveness to auditors and regulators, and automating compliance checks and reporting. By integrating CSPM into their cloud security strategy, organizations can not only enhance their security posture but also streamline the often complex and challenging process of compliance management in the cloud era.

Emerging trends in security alerts and monitoring

Staying ahead of emerging threats and vulnerabilities is a constant challenge in the ever-evolving world of cybersecurity. One of the areas witnessing significant transformation is security alerts and monitoring, with CSPM emerging as a critical player. Let's explore the latest trends in security alerts and monitoring, with a focus on how CSPM is shaping the landscape.

Real-time visibility across multi-cloud environments

As organizations increasingly adopt multi-cloud strategies, the need for real-time visibility into their cloud environments has surged. CSPM solutions are at the forefront of this trend, providing insights for continuous monitoring and instant alerts for any misconfigurations or security policy violations across diverse cloud platforms. This real-time visibility enables rapid response to potential threats and vulnerabilities, helping organizations maintain a secure cloud posture.

Artificial intelligence-driven threat detection and anomaly analysis

Artificial intelligence (**AI**) and **machine learning** (**ML**) are revolutionizing the way security alerts and monitoring operate. CSPM tools are leveraging AI to identify abnormal behaviors and patterns within cloud environments. This proactive approach to threat detection can pinpoint potential risks before they escalate into security incidents. By analyzing vast datasets, AI-powered CSPM solutions can enhance the accuracy and efficiency of security alerts. For example, Microsoft has recently announced *Microsoft Security Copilot*, through which Microsoft aims to empower the cybersecurity space. Security tools such as Microsoft Sentinel, Microsoft Defender, Intune, and more will be enriched with Security Copilot so that the security team can use generative AI to help detect threats, manage incidents, and improve security posture. Security Copilot is still in preview mode; go to `https://www.microsoft.com/en-us/security/business/ai-machine-learning/microsoft-security-copilot` to learn more.

Cloud-native security monitoring

With the shift to cloud-native architectures and serverless computing, security monitoring strategies are evolving accordingly. CSPM solutions are adapting to this change by offering cloud-native security monitoring capabilities. They focus on the unique security challenges posed by cloud-native environments, such as monitoring serverless functions, containerized applications, and microservices. This trend ensures that organizations maintain a comprehensive view of their cloud security, regardless of their infrastructure's complexity.

Automated remediation and orchestration

Security alerts are only as valuable as the actions taken in response to them. CSPM solutions are now incorporating automated remediation and orchestration features. When a security alert is triggered, these tools can automate the remediation process, swiftly rectifying misconfigurations or vulnerabilities. This reduces the burden on security teams and minimizes exposure to potential threats.

Cloud compliance and governance

As regulatory requirements become more stringent, security monitoring has expanded to include compliance and governance aspects. CSPM solutions are evolving to include compliance monitoring, allowing organizations to assess their cloud resources against industry standards and regulatory frameworks. This ensures that security alerts are focused on threat detection and adherence to compliance requirements.

Integration with SIEM solutions

Another noteworthy trend is the integration of CSPM with SIEM solutions. SIEM platforms provide a broader view of security events across an organization's entire IT environment, including cloud and on-premises resources. By integrating CSPM with SIEM, organizations can centralize their security data and gain a holistic view of their security posture, enhancing their ability to detect and respond to security incidents effectively.

Emerging trends in security alerts and monitoring are closely tied to the evolving threat landscape and the increasing complexity of cloud environments. CSPM solutions are playing a pivotal role in addressing these challenges by providing real-time visibility, leveraging AI-driven threat detection, adapting to cloud-native architectures, automating remediation, ensuring compliance, and integrating with SIEM platforms.

Case study and lessons learned

The integration of CSPM and SIEM is crucial in fortifying the organization's security posture, showcasing the effectiveness of proactive measures and advanced technologies in mitigating cyber threats. Let's understand this topic with a case study and explore some lessons learned from this activity.

Case study – streamlined threat detection and incident response with CSPM and SIEM

Let's delve into a case study that demonstrates the implementation of an effective security alerts and monitoring setup using a CSPM tool in conjunction with an organization's existing SIEM and SOAR tools.

Scenario: In this case study, we will explore how a global financial services organization, XYZ Corp., harnessed the power of CSPM, integrated it with its SIEM/SOAR tools, and achieved a highly efficient and responsive security alerts and monitoring setup.

Background

XYZ Corp. operates in a highly regulated industry and manages a vast cloud infrastructure to support its financial services. They recognized the need to strengthen their cloud security posture and accelerate incident detection and response, which led them to adopt CSPM.

Challenges

XYZ Corp. faced several challenges related to security alerts and monitoring:

- **Complex cloud environment**: Their multi-cloud environment made it challenging to gain centralized visibility into security configurations

- **Alert overload**: Existing SIEM generated numerous alerts, making it difficult to distinguish genuine threats from false positives

- **Manual incident response**: Their incident response process was manual, leading to slower response times

Implementation of CSPM with SIEM and SOAR

XYZ Corp. embarked on a comprehensive solution involving CSPM and SIEM.

They integrated CSPM with their cloud providers, allowing continuous monitoring of cloud configurations and activity. CSPM was configured to generate custom alerts based on specific compliance requirements and security policies, reducing alert fatigue. CSPM was seamlessly integrated with their existing SIEM platform, which allowed for centralized monitoring and correlation of security events. XYZ Corp. also integrated an additional SOAR capability of existing SIEM solutions into their setup, enabling automated incident response and orchestration of security actions.

Case highlights

Let's understand the highlights of this case study:

- **Early detection of unauthorized access**: CSPM detected an unauthorized attempt to access a critical cloud server. The CSPM alert categorized the incident as high-risk and provided detailed information about the suspicious activity.

- **Automated response**: The SOAR tool, connected to CSPM and SIEM, received the alert and automatically initiated an incident response workflow. It isolated the affected server, revoked unauthorized access, and initiated forensic data collection.

- **Incident investigation and correlation**: Simultaneously, SIEM correlated the CSPM alert with other security events, revealing that the unauthorized access was part of a broader attack. SIEM provided context, indicating that this might be an **advanced persistent threat** (**APT**).

- **Efficient incident resolution**: With the integrated setup, the incident response team quickly identified and contained the APT, preventing data exfiltration and minimizing potential damage.

Here are the *lessons learned* and potential future enhancements:

- **Streamlined workflow**: XYZ Corp. realized the importance of a streamlined workflow, where CSPM's early alerts triggered automated responses through SOAR and were further investigated using SIEM

- **Continuous monitoring**: They adopted a proactive approach by implementing continuous monitoring with CSPM, which proved invaluable in early threat detection

- **Staff training**: The security team received training to maximize the effectiveness of CSPM, SIEM, and SOAR tool integration

In conclusion, XYZ Corp.'s case study illustrates the power of CSPM in conjunction with SIEM and SOAR tools to streamline security alerts and monitoring. This integrated setup allowed for early threat detection, automated incident response, and efficient investigation, enhancing their cloud security posture and resilience against sophisticated threats. This case study emphasizes the importance of mastering CSPM in a comprehensive security strategy for cloud environments.

Implementing proactive resilience using alerts and monitoring

This case study describes the reactive approach of how you can set up an effective resilience system. Implementing resilience using alert and monitoring features proactively rather than reactively involves setting up systems that not only detect issues when they occur but also anticipate and prevent potential disruptions:

- **Define key performance indicators (KPIs) and service-level objectives (SLOs)**: Clearly define KPIs and SLOs that align with your organization's goals and user expectations. Establish thresholds for normal operation and performance.

  Implementation: Use monitoring tools to track these KPIs in real time. Set up alerts to notify teams when metrics approach or breach predefined thresholds, indicating potential issues before they impact the user experience.

- **Predictive analytics and anomaly detection**: Implement predictive analytics using machine learning algorithms to forecast trends and identify potential anomalies in your system's behavior.

  Implementation: Use anomaly detection algorithms to analyze historical data and predict expected performance patterns. When deviations occur, trigger alerts to investigate and mitigate issues before they escalate.

- **Continuous monitoring for security**: Integrate security monitoring into your resilience strategy. Monitor for unusual or suspicious activities that may indicate a security threat.

  Implementation: Utilize SIEM systems to monitor logs and detect anomalies. Set up alerts for potential security breaches and take immediate action to prevent or mitigate them.

- **Automation of response mechanisms**: Automate responses to common issues or known patterns to reduce manual intervention and response time.

  Implementation: Implement automation scripts and workflows triggered by alerts. These automated responses can include scaling resources, rerouting traffic, or applying predefined fixes to known issues.

- **Incident response planning**: Develop comprehensive incident response plans that outline steps to be taken when alerts are triggered. Train response teams to ensure quick and effective actions.

  Implementation: Conduct regular drills and simulations to test the incident response plans. Update the plans based on lessons learned from simulations and real incidents to continuously improve response efficiency.

- **Capacity planning and scalability**: Regularly assess the capacity needs of your system based on user growth, data volume, and other factors. Plan for scalability to accommodate increasing demands.

  Implementation: Use monitoring tools to track resource utilization and performance metrics. Set up alerts to signal when resources are approaching capacity limits, allowing for proactive scaling to prevent performance degradation.

- **User experience monitoring**: Focus on monitoring user experience metrics, such as page load times and transaction success rates, to ensure optimal service delivery.

  Implementation: Utilize synthetic monitoring tools and real-user monitoring to track user interactions. Set up alerts for deviations from expected user experience benchmarks to address issues before users are significantly impacted.

- **Regular reviews and optimization**: Conduct regular reviews of your monitoring and alerting systems to ensure they align with evolving business needs and technological advancements.

  Implementation: Periodically reassess the relevance of your alerts, KPIs, and monitoring strategies. Optimize configurations based on lessons learned from incidents and changes in the technology landscape.

By adopting a proactive approach to alerting and monitoring, organizations can identify and address potential issues before they have a significant impact, ultimately enhancing the resilience of their systems and services.

Summary

In this chapter, we started by delving into the concept of security alerts and why they are the first line of defense in identifying potential threats and vulnerabilities within the cloud. From the nuances of alert types to the importance of contextualization, we explored how CSPM tools generate and manage these critical signals. We also ventured into the realm of continuous monitoring, where CSPM tools tirelessly scrutinize cloud configurations, access controls, and adherence to security policies. We uncovered how continuous monitoring is the cornerstone of maintaining a robust security posture in cloud environments. Through automation, it can respond swiftly to potential risks, minimizing the impact of security incidents. We also discussed the evolution of security monitoring, from traditional on-premises solutions to cloud-native strategies.

As cloud adoption continues to soar, mastering CSPM becomes a strategic imperative for organizations worldwide. Moreover, this chapter highlighted the symbiotic relationship between CSPM and other security tools, such as SIEM and SOAR. These integrations are pivotal in achieving comprehensive threat visibility, orchestrating automated incident responses, and demonstrating compliance to auditors and regulators. In mastering these concepts, we equip ourselves with the knowledge and tools needed to navigate the complex terrain of cloud security, ensuring that our cloud environments remain resilient and impervious to emerging threats.

In the next chapter, we will learn about **Infrastructure as Code (IaC)** in the context of CSPM.

Further reading

To learn more about the topics that were covered in this chapter, take a look at the following resources:

- *Security alerts and monitoring powered with AI*: `https://www.microsoft.com/en-us/security/business/ai-machine-learning/microsoft-security-copilot`
- *Security alerts and incidents*: `https://learn.microsoft.com/en-us/azure/defender-for-cloud/alerts-overview`

Part 4: Advanced Topics and Future Trends

In this part, you will embark on a journey into the cutting-edge aspects of CSPM. You will explore the integration of CSPM with **Infrastructure as Code** (**IaC**) for seamless deployment practices. We then move forward to DevSecOps and workflow automation, optimizing security within operational workflows. After that, we delve into CSPM-related technologies for an expansive understanding of complementary tools. Concluding with insights into future trends and challenges, this part is tailored for those ready to explore the forefront of cloud security.

This part has the following chapters:

- *Chapter 16, Integrating CSPM with IaC*
- *Chapter 17, DevSecOps – Workflow Automation*
- *Chapter 18, CSPM-Related Technologies*
- *Chapter 19, Future Trends and Challenges*

16

Integrating CSPM with IaC

In today's fast-paced world of cloud computing and digital transformation, the need for efficient, scalable, and reliable infrastructure management has never been more critical. As organizations strive to deliver applications and services at scale, the traditional manual methods of infrastructure provisioning and management have become bottlenecks, hindering agility and innovation, and with huge security concerns too. Imagine a world where provisioning servers, configuring network resources, and managing the complex web infrastructure required to support modern applications is as simple as writing lines of code. This is where **Infrastructure as Code (IaC)** comes into action. In this chapter, we will uncover its principles, dissect its benefits, and examine the tools and technologies that make it all possible. Along the way, we will delve into best practices, design patterns, and real-world case studies to illustrate how IaC is transforming the way organizations approach infrastructure management. We will also explore how **cloud security posture management (CSPM)** and IaC can integrate and help organizations identify and mitigate security risks early in the development and deployment process.

As we navigate this chapter, we invite you to explore this new shift where infrastructure is as agile as the software it supports, where innovation knows no bounds, and where the complexities of managing infrastructure fade into the background, allowing your organization to focus on what truly matters—delivering value to your customers and stakeholders. So, let us explore this further, as we lay the foundation for a deep dive into IaC and its role in CSPM.

We will cover the following main topics:

- Understanding IaC
- CSPM and IaC integration
- Best practices and design patterns

Let us get started!

Understanding IaC

At its core, IaC is a revolutionary approach that treats infrastructure not as a set of physical components but as code. It relies on the principles of automation, version control, and collaboration, offering a way to define, deploy, and manage infrastructure elements programmatically. It enables organizations to build, scale, and modify infrastructure with unprecedented speed and precision. IaC represents a paradigm shift in how we think about and manage infrastructure. It empowers organizations to break free from the constraints of manual processes, reduce human errors, and achieve a level of flexibility and scalability that was once unimaginable. Let us understand this in detail.

What is IaC?

IaC is a methodology that involves defining and provisioning infrastructure using code, typically in a high-level, human-readable format, such as YAML or JSON. It is a modern approach to managing and provisioning infrastructure for software applications and services using code, just like you would write code for your software. Instead of manually configuring servers, networks, and other infrastructure components, IaC allows you to define and manage these resources through code, making the process more automated, consistent, and scalable. Let us understand with an example.

Imagine you are a software developer working on a web application, and you need to set up a web server to host your application. With traditional manual infrastructure management, you would need to log in to a server, install the necessary software, configure security settings, and so on. It is a time-consuming and error-prone process. Now, with IaC, you can define your server infrastructure using code. Let us say you are using a tool such as Terraform, a popular IaC tool. You would write code in a file (usually with a `.tf` extension) that describes the infrastructure you need. This is how the code will look:

```
# Define an AWS provider block to specify your AWS credentials and
region
provider "aws" {
  region = "us-east-1"
}

# Create an AWS EC2 instance for the web server
resource "aws_instance" "web_server" {
  ami           = "ami-0c55b159cbfafe1f0"  # Amazon Linux 2 AMI
  instance_type = "t2.micro"
  tags = {
    Name = "my-web-server"
  }
}
# Define a security group to allow incoming HTTP (port 80) traffic
resource "aws_security_group" "web_security_group" {
  name          = "web-sg"
```

```
  description = "Allow incoming HTTP traffic"
  # Inbound rule to allow HTTP traffic
  ingress {
    from_port   = 80
    to_port     = 80
    protocol    = "tcp"
    cidr_blocks = ["0.0.0.0/0"]
  }
  # Outbound rule to allow all traffic (for simplicity)
  egress {
    from_port   = 0
    to_port     = 0
    protocol    = "-1"
    cidr_blocks = ["0.0.0.0/0"]
  }
}
```

In this example, we do the following:

- We start by defining the **Amazon Web Services** (**AWS**) provider block, specifying the AWS region where we want to create resources

- We create an AWS **Elastic Compute Cloud** (**EC2**) instance named web_server using the specified Amazon Linux 2 **Amazon Machine Image** (**AMI**) and a t2.micro instance type

- We add tags to the EC2 instance for better identification

- We define a security group named web_security_group with an inbound rule allowing incoming HTTP (port 80) traffic and an outbound rule allowing all outbound traffic for simplicity

> **Important note**
>
> Keep in mind that this example is for demonstration purposes. In a production environment, you would want to limit ingress IP ranges by specifying the actual IP ranges that should have access to your EC2 instance over HTTPS and not HTTP. Additionally, you should configure the necessary SSL/TLS certificates and any other security measures required for secure HTTPS communication.

To apply this code, you would use Terraform commands such as terraform init to initialize the project and terraform apply to create resources on AWS. This code will create an EC2 instance and a security group with the specified configuration.

How did IaC evolve, and what problems does it solve?

IaC has evolved in response to the challenges and complexities of managing modern IT infrastructure. Its development has been shaped by various factors and the need to address specific problems in the realm of infrastructure management. Let us understand how IaC has evolved and the problems it solves:

- **Complexity of infrastructure**: Traditional infrastructure management involved manually configuring and provisioning servers, networks, and other components. As technology advanced, infrastructures became more complex, making manual management error-prone and time-consuming. IaC emerged as a solution to simplify and streamline this complexity.

- **Agile and DevOps practices**: The rise of Agile and DevOps methodologies emphasized the need for rapid and automated infrastructure provisioning to match the pace of software development and deployment. IaC aligns with these practices by enabling infrastructure changes to be made as code and integrated into the development pipeline.

- **Cloud computing**: The adoption of cloud computing introduced new challenges in managing virtualized resources that could be provisioned and deprovisioned on demand. IaC became essential in the cloud environment as it allowed for the dynamic, automated creation and management of cloud resources.

- **Configuration drift**: In traditional environments, manual configurations often led to "configuration drift," where infrastructure components in different environments (for example, development, staging, and production) became inconsistent. IaC mitigates this problem by ensuring that configurations are consistent across environments, reducing security risks and operational issues.

- **Disaster recovery (DR) and redundancy**: Ensuring **high availability** (**HA**) and DR is challenging without automation. IaC helps in creating and maintaining redundant and resilient infrastructures, which is crucial for **business continuity** (**BC**).

- **Security and compliance**: Managing security and compliance in large, dynamic infrastructures can be daunting. IaC allows security best practices and compliance policies to be codified and consistently enforced across all resources, reducing security vulnerabilities and compliance risks.

- **Collaboration and documentation**: Collaboration among IT teams is essential, but manual processes can lead to knowledge silos and miscommunication. IaC serves as documentation for infrastructure configuration and promotes collaboration through version control and code review processes.

- **Scaling and cost efficiency**: As businesses grow, they require scalable and cost-effective infrastructures. IaC enables the easy scaling of resources up or down based on demand, optimizing infrastructure costs.

- **Vendor agnosticism**: Organizations often use multiple cloud providers or have hybrid cloud environments. IaC tools provide vendor-agnostic solutions, allowing organizations to manage infrastructure consistently across different platforms.

- **Change management (CM)**: IaC tools offer CM capabilities, enabling organizations to track and audit infrastructure changes. This is crucial for accountability, auditing, and compliance.

In short, IaC evolved to address challenges associated with the increasing complexity, agility, and scalability requirements of modern IT infrastructures. By codifying infrastructure, IaC enhances efficiency, reliability, and resilience while reducing human error and operational overhead. It has become a fundamental practice for organizations seeking to modernize their infrastructure management processes and embrace cloud-native, DevOps-driven approaches.

Key principles and benefits

IaC is a game-changing approach in the world of IT infrastructure management. It is all about treating your infrastructure, such as servers, networks, and databases, as if they were pieces of software code. This shift in thinking brings several key principles and benefits. Here are the key principles and associated benefits of using IaC.

Automation

Automation is at the heart of IaC. It involves using scripts or configuration files to define and manage infrastructure components, such as servers, networks, and storage. Automation reduces manual intervention, speeds up deployment, and minimizes human errors. Let us understand the key benefits in detail:

- **Provisioning and deployment**: IaC streamlines the process of creating and deploying infrastructure resources. Instead of manually configuring servers and network settings, you define these configurations in code. When you need to provide infrastructure, you execute the code, and the automation takes care of setting up the resources according to your specifications.

- **Speed**: Automation accelerates the deployment of infrastructure components. Manual provisioning can be time-consuming and error-prone, especially in complex environments. With IaC, you can deploy infrastructure quickly, enabling faster development and testing cycles, and delivering applications and services to users more rapidly.

- **Minimized human errors**: Automating infrastructure tasks reduces the risk of human errors. When humans manually configure systems, mistakes can happen due to oversight or inconsistencies. IaC ensures that configurations are consistent and repeatable, minimizing the likelihood of errors that can lead to downtime or security vulnerabilities.

- **Consistency across environments**: IaC promotes consistency by enabling you to define infrastructure configurations in code. This consistency ensures that development, testing, and production environments match each other closely, reducing the "it works on my machine" problem and making it easier to troubleshoot issues that may arise.

- **Scalability**: Automation allows you to scale your infrastructure up or down in response to changing demands. Whether you need to add more servers to handle increased traffic or reduce resources during off-peak hours, you can adjust your IaC code to reflect these changes, and the automation will execute the adjustments consistently.

- **Adaptability**: As your requirements evolve, IaC makes it easy to adapt your infrastructure. Instead of making manual changes that may introduce inconsistencies, you can modify your infrastructure code to reflect new requirements or technologies. This adaptability is crucial for staying competitive and responsive in a fast-changing technological landscape.

- **Version control**: Automation in IaC goes hand in hand with **version control systems** (**VCSs**) such as Git. By storing your infrastructure code in version control, you gain the ability to track changes, collaborate with team members, and roll back to previous configurations if issues arise. This ensures that your infrastructure is well managed and documented.

- **Predictability**: Because infrastructure is defined as code, changes and configurations are predictable. You know exactly what your infrastructure will look like after each change, which is vital for maintaining the reliability and stability of your systems.

Security as Code

Security as Code (**SaC**) is a crucial aspect of IaC that emphasizes integrating security practices into the entire life cycle of infrastructure provisioning and management. This approach ensures that security is not an afterthought but is considered from the very beginning. Let's look at the key benefits:

- **Infrastructure security policies**: Using IaC, you can define and document your organization's security policies as code. These policies can include requirements for network configurations, data encryption, access controls, and compliance standards. By encoding security policies in code, you make them explicit and enforceable.

- **Automated security checks**: You can also implement automated security checks within your IaC pipeline. These checks can include static code analysis, vulnerability scanning, and compliance audits. Automated tools can scan your IaC code for security issues and misconfigurations, helping you catch potential problems early in the development process.

- **Role-based access control** (**RBAC**): You can also use code to define and enforce RBAC policies for your infrastructure resources. You can ensure that access permissions are based on the **principle of least privilege** (**PoLP**), where users or systems have only the permissions necessary to perform their specific tasks.

- **Secrets management**: Using IaC, you can avoid hardcoding secrets in your IaC code. Instead, leverage secrets management tools and integrations to securely retrieve and inject secrets into your infrastructure at runtime.

- **Immutable infrastructure**: You can also embrace the concept of immutable infrastructure, where instances are replaced instead of patched. When security vulnerabilities are identified, new instances with the latest security patches should be deployed automatically, reducing the window of vulnerability.

> **What is immutable infrastructure?**
>
> Immutable infrastructure is an approach to managing infrastructure where changes and updates are made by creating entirely new instances rather than modifying existing ones. This approach offers predictability, rollback safety, improved security, and consistency in deployments. It enhances infrastructure reliability and security by ensuring that each instance is a precise, unchangeable copy of the others, reducing the risk of configuration drift and vulnerabilities that can arise when modifying existing configurations. In combination with IaC, immutable infrastructure streamlines infrastructure management, making it more agile, secure, and reliable through automation and code-driven practices.

Cost optimization

Cost optimization refers to the practice of effectively managing and reducing expenses associated with your cloud-based infrastructure deployments. IaC offers several strategies and benefits for achieving cost optimization:

- **Resource right-sizing**: IaC allows you to provision infrastructure resources precisely according to your requirements. You can define the size and capacity of resources, such as **virtual machines (VMs)**, databases, and storage, based on the actual workload needs. By avoiding over-provisioning, you can save on unnecessary costs. Here's an example to illustrate the concept.

  Let's say you have a web application that experiences varying levels of traffic throughout the day. During peak hours, you expect higher user activity, and during off-peak hours, the traffic is much lower. Without IaC, you might manually provision a fixed number of VMs to handle the maximum expected load during peak hours. This could result in over-provisioning during periods of lower demand, leading to wasted resources and increased costs.

  With IaC, you can dynamically adjust the infrastructure based on the workload. For example, using a tool such as Terraform or AWS CloudFormation, you can define your infrastructure requirements in code. Here's a simplified Terraform example:

  ```
  resource "aws_instance" "web_server" {
    count         = var.instance_count
    instance_type = "t2.micro"
    ami           = "ami-xxxxxxxxxxxxxx"
  }
  variable "instance_count" {
    default = 3
  }
  ```

  In this example, you define an AWS EC2 instance with a specific instance type and AMI. The `count` parameter allows you to easily scale the number of instances based on the workload. During peak hours, you might increase the `instance_count` value to handle more traffic, and during off-peak hours, you can decrease it to save on costs.

- **Auto-scaling**: IaC enables you to set up auto-scaling policies that automatically add or remove resources in response to changing demand. This ensures that you have enough resources to handle traffic spikes without paying for unused capacity during periods of low demand.

- **Resource tagging and visibility**: IaC allows you to tag resources for better cost tracking and allocation. By properly tagging resources, you can gain insights into which departments, projects, or teams are consuming resources and allocate costs accordingly.

- **Reserved instances**: IaC can help you identify opportunities to purchase reserved instances or reserved capacity, which can lead to significant cost savings compared to on-demand pricing. You can use IaC to automate the procurement and management of these reservations. Here's an explanation with an example.

Imagine you have an application running on AWS, and it consists of a fleet of EC2 instances that need to be available 24/7 to handle varying workloads. You can define your infrastructure requirements in code, as explained in the *Resource right-sizing* list point. Now, let's say your application has a consistent workload, and you can predict the number of instances you need to run 24/7. With this knowledge, you can leverage reserved instances. Reserved instances involve committing to a 1- or 3-year term in exchange for a significant discount compared to on-demand pricing.

IaC allows you to automate the procurement of reserved instances by modifying your infrastructure code to include the reservation details. Here's an example:

```
resource "aws_instance" "web_server" {
  count           = var.instance_count
  instance_type = "t2.micro"
  ami            = "ami-xxxxxxxxxxxxxx"
  lifecycle {
    create_before_destroy = true
  }
  reserved_instances {
    count           = var.instance_count
    offering_type = "standard"
  }
}
variable "instance_count" {
  default = 3
}
```

In this example, the `reserved_instances` block has been added to specify the details of the reserved instances. `offering_type` is set to `"standard"`, indicating a standard reserved instance offering. By incorporating such changes into your IaC code, you can automate the purchase of reserved instances, ensuring that your infrastructure is cost-optimized with long-term commitments that lead to substantial savings over on-demand pricing.

- **Cost monitoring and reporting**: IaC scripts can include configurations for monitoring resource usage and cost. You can set up alerts and automated reports to keep an eye on your cloud spending and take corrective actions when costs exceed predefined thresholds.

Portability

Portability is the ability to use the same IaC code base across various cloud providers and on-premises environments without the need for extensive modifications. This portability is a significant advantage because it offers flexibility and reduces the risk of vendor lock-in. Let us understand this in detail:

- **Cross-platform compatibility**: IaC code is typically designed to be platform-agnostic, meaning it can work on different cloud platforms and on-premises servers with minimal adjustments. This compatibility is achieved by abstracting the infrastructure configuration, allowing you to define resources and their properties in a way that can be understood and executed by multiple environments.

- **Reduced vendor lock-in**: Vendor lock-in occurs when an organization becomes heavily dependent on a specific cloud provider's services and technologies, making it challenging to switch to an alternative provider. IaC mitigates this risk by enabling you to write code that is not tightly coupled to any one cloud provider. If the need arises to migrate to a different cloud or on-premises environment, you can adapt your IaC code with relatively minimal effort, reducing barriers to migration.

- **Flexibility**: Portability through IaC provides flexibility in choosing the most suitable cloud provider or environment for your specific needs. It allows you to take advantage of cost differences, regional availability, or unique features offered by different providers without undergoing a complete infrastructure overhaul.

- **Consistency across environments**: IaC ensures that your infrastructure configuration remains consistent across different environments. Whether you are deploying to AWS, Azure, or an on-premises data center, you can maintain the same infrastructure configuration, reducing the risk of configuration drift and simplifying management.

- **DR and redundancy**: Portability is also beneficial for DR and redundancy strategies. If one cloud provider experiences an outage or disruption, you can quickly switch to another provider or environment where your IaC code is compatible, ensuring BC.

- **Testing and development**: Developers and DevOps teams can use the same IaC code base in development, testing, and production environments, ensuring that code behaves consistently across the entire **software development life cycle** (**SDLC**).

In short, automation is one of the biggest benefits of using IaC. It accelerates deployment, reduces errors, ensures consistency, and enables quick adaptation to changing requirements, making it a cornerstone of modern infrastructure management practices.

These are just a few core principles and key benefits of using IaC. IaC allows organizations to respond swiftly to changing requirements, enabling them to experiment with new configurations and technologies without the burden of manual reconfiguration. This agility accelerates development cycles, supports innovation, and helps organizations stay competitive by quickly adapting to evolving technology landscapes and market demands. Let us now dive deep into key IaC tools and technologies.

Key IaC tools and technologies

IaC has gained popularity, and various tools and technologies have emerged to facilitate the implementation of IaC practices. These tools help automate the provisioning, configuration, and management of infrastructure resources. Here are some key IaC tools and technologies.

Terraform by HashiCorp

Terraform is one of the most popular open source IaC tools. It is developed by HashiCorp, which uses a declarative configuration language called **HashiCorp Configuration Language** (**HCL**) or JSON to define infrastructure. With Terraform, you can deliver IaC by codifying cloud **application programming interfaces** (**APIs**) into declarative configuration files. You can enable self-service infrastructure provisioning using IaC and seamlessly integrate with VCS, **IT service management** (**ITSM**), and **Continuous Integration/Continuous Deployment** (**CI/CD**) pipelines. It is widely used for multi-cloud deployment and to manage network infrastructure, such as updating load balancer member pools or applying firewall policies. HashiCorp also provides a business plan that includes functionalities such as identifying configuration drift, **single sign-on** (**SSO**) support, audit trail logs, an option for hosting your agents, and customizable concurrency settings. Specific pricing details for the business plan can be obtained from the official website: `https://www.terraform.io/`.

Ansible by Red Hat

Ansible is a widely embraced open source automation tool used as an IaC by Red Hat. It has the capability to set up systems, distribute software, and coordinate more advanced IT operations such as continuous deployments or seamless, zero-downtime rolling updates. Ansible is agentless, which means it does not require any software agents to be installed on the target machines. Instead, it communicates with remote hosts using SSH (for Linux/Unix) or WinRM (for Windows) protocols. This reduces the complexity of managing agents and makes Ansible easy to deploy and use. Ansible is widely used for multi-cloud environments and is suitable for a range of environments, spanning from modest configurations featuring just a few instances to sprawling enterprise setups encompassing thousands of instances. Beyond just infrastructure orchestration, Ansible seamlessly extends its capabilities to configuration management and facilitates swift application deployments, making it a versatile and favored choice for automating diverse IT operations. For more details about Ansible, refer to the official website: `https://www.redhat.com/en/technologies/management/ansible`.

Puppet

Puppet is an open source configuration management and automation tool that helps IT teams manage IaC. It allows you to define and enforce the desired state of your infrastructure using declarative code, making it easier to automate tasks, ensure consistency, and scale your infrastructure efficiently. Puppet is widely used in IT operations, particularly for configuration management, software deployment, and compliance enforcement. Puppet uses a declarative approach where you define the desired configuration state, and Puppet takes care of ensuring that the system matches that state. Puppet uses agent software (Puppet Agent) installed on target nodes to manage them, allowing for secure and efficient communication between the Puppet master and agents. It is highly extensible, allowing you to create custom modules and facts to adapt it to your specific needs. It also provides reporting and auditing capabilities, making it possible to track changes to your infrastructure and ensure compliance with desired configurations. Puppet can integrate with various tools and services, including cloud providers, VCSs, and external data sources. For more details about the tool and its extensive use cases, please refer to the official website: `https://www.puppet.com/`.

Chef

Chef is another popular open source configuration management and automation tool used for managing and provisioning IaC. Similar to Puppet and Ansible, Chef helps IT teams automate infrastructure management, ensuring consistency and scalability across diverse environments. Chef uses a "cookbook" approach, where configurations are defined in reusable scripts known as cookbooks and recipes. It supports both declarative and procedural automation, allowing for fine-grained control over configuration management. Chef uses an agent (Chef Client) that runs on managed nodes to apply configurations. It communicates with a central Chef Server to retrieve and apply recipes. Chef is highly extensible, allowing you to create custom cookbooks and resources to meet specific infrastructure requirements. Chef uses a policy-driven approach to manage infrastructure. You can define policies for your infrastructure in code, and Chef ensures those policies are enforced. As with other IaC tools, it also integrates with various tools and services, including cloud platforms, source control systems, and monitoring solutions. For more details about the tool and its extensive use cases, please refer to the official website: `https://www.chef.io/products/chef-infra`.

Packer

Packer is an open source tool developed by HashiCorp that specializes in creating *machine images* for different platforms in a consistent and automated way. Machine images are essentially preconfigured templates of VMs or containers that include the operating system, software, and configurations required for specific tasks or applications. It is designed to work with a wide range of platforms, including virtualization platforms such as VMware or VirtualBox, cloud providers, and container technologies (for example, Docker). This means you can use Packer to create machine images tailored for different deployment targets. Packer uses configuration files written in JSON or HCL to define how to build machine images. These configuration files specify the base image, provisioners (scripts or tools for customizing the image), and postprocessors (actions to take after image creation), among other settings. Packer also automates the process of creating machine images, reducing manual intervention and ensuring that images are consistent and reproducible. It can integrate with other automation and orchestration tools such as Ansible, Puppet, or Chef to configure and provision the image during the build process. Packer can perform parallel builds, allowing you to create multiple machine images concurrently. This can significantly speed up the image creation process, especially when you need to build images for multiple platforms or configurations. It also supports image optimization to reduce the image size and improve performance. You can use it to clean up temporary files, remove unnecessary packages, and ensure that the image is optimized for its intended use. Packer can help enforce security and compliance standards by ensuring that images are built from approved sources and follow specific configuration guidelines. For more details about the tool and its extensive use cases, please refer to the official website: `https://www.packer.io/`.

> **Nomad**
>
> **Nomad** is another tool also developed by HashiCorp and is a scheduler and orchestrator for deploying applications and services across multiple environments.

Docker Compose

Docker Compose is a tool that facilitates the management of multi-container Docker applications. While it's not strictly a part of traditional IaC, it plays an important role in defining and orchestrating the application's IaC when working with containerized applications. It simplifies the process of defining and running multi-container Docker applications by allowing you to specify the configuration of these containers in a human-readable YAML file. Docker Compose files can be stored in a VCS such as Git, just as with other IaC code. This enables collaboration among team members, version tracking, and the ability to roll back to previous configurations when needed. Docker Compose promotes the portability of your applications and infrastructure configurations. The same Docker Compose file can be used across different environments (development, testing, and production) with minimal modifications, ensuring consistency and reducing the "*it works on my machine*" problem. It can be integrated with container orchestration tools such as Kubernetes and Docker Swarm for managing containers in a distributed environment. This allows you to extend the IaC principles to container orchestration and scaling. For more details about the tool and its extensive use cases, please refer to the official website: `https://docs.docker.com/compose/`.

Kubernetes

Kubernetes (often abbreviated as **K8s**) is not typically considered an IaC tool in the same way as tools such as Terraform, Ansible, or Puppet. Instead, Kubernetes is categorized as an open source container orchestration platform, and it does incorporate some IaC principles and practices in its configuration management approach, such as defining infrastructure configurations in code (YAML), version control, automation, and infrastructure repeatability. Kubernetes manifests specify the desired state of your application infrastructure, and tools such as Kustomize and Helm can further enhance the declarative nature of Kubernetes configuration management. It's a powerful platform for automating and orchestrating container deployments at scale, and it is often used alongside IaC tools to manage the underlying infrastructure. The open source project is managed by the **Cloud Native Computing Foundation (CNCF)**. For more details about the tool and its extensive use cases, please refer to the official website: `https://kubernetes.io/`.

SaltStack (Salt)

SaltStack, also referred to as **Salt**, is an open source configuration management and orchestration tool. It is unique for its use of remote execution and event-driven automation. Salt employs a master-minion architecture where a master server communicates with minion agents running on target systems. It uses YAML for configuration files, making them human-readable. Salt allows for remote execution of tasks, making it highly efficient for managing large-scale infrastructures. Salt uses an event bus for real-time communication, enabling event-driven automation. It can execute tasks in parallel across multiple systems, improving scalability and performance. Salt is known for its flexibility and ability to adapt to complex infrastructure needs. For more details about the tool and its extensive use cases, please refer to the official website: `https://saltproject.io/`.

Now that we have learned about quite a few cloud provider-agnostic tools, let us learn briefly about some of the most popular IaC tools/services offered by cloud providers.

IaC offerings by cloud providers

Cloud computing heavily relies on IaC, which allows you to provision and manage infrastructure resources using code and automation. Various cloud providers offer IaC solutions and services that help streamline the process of defining, deploying, and managing infrastructure resources. Let us take a look at some of the IaC offerings by major cloud providers.

AWS CloudFormation

AWS CloudFormation is like a blueprint for your cloud infrastructure. It lets you define your entire AWS environment as code using easy-to-read templates, written in YAML or JSON. With CloudFormation, you can specify everything you need, from servers and databases to networks and security settings, in a single document. Then, AWS takes care of creating and managing those resources for you, ensuring your infrastructure is consistent, reproducible, and easily scalable. It's a powerful tool for automating and streamlining the provisioning and management of your AWS resources, all while following the principles of IaC.

Microsoft ARM templates

Azure provides **Azure Resource Manager (ARM)** templates, which are JSON files that can be used with Azure DevOps for CD and infrastructure automation. ARM templates enable you to automate the deployment of Azure resources, making it easier to create, modify, and manage complex Azure infrastructures consistently and reproducibly. Just as with AWS CloudFormation, ARM templates are declarative, allowing you to specify what you want, and Azure takes care of figuring out how to make it happen. This approach promotes IaC principles and infrastructure consistency and supports the automation and scalability requirements of modern cloud environments.

Google Cloud Deployment Manager

Google Cloud provides **Deployment Manager** for IaC. It uses YAML or Python configurations to define Google Cloud resource deployments. Deployment Manager is tailored for managing Google Cloud resources. You can repeatedly deploy the same configuration to create and manage resources consistently, which is essential for maintaining IaC. It integrates seamlessly with other GCP services, making it easy to manage various resources, including VMs, databases, storage, and networking. Google Cloud **Identity and Access Management** (**IAM**) can be used to control who has access to create or modify deployments, ensuring security and compliance.

Alibaba Cloud ROS

Alibaba Cloud's **Resource Orchestration Service** (**ROS**) is similar to AWS CloudFormation and allows users to define, provision, and manage cloud infrastructure using declarative templates written in JSON or YAML format. ROS templates describe the desired state of Alibaba Cloud resources, including VMs, databases, networking configurations, and other cloud services. These templates are written in a structured format and can be version-controlled for easy tracking and collaboration. ROS templates define dependencies between resources, ensuring that resources are provisioned in the correct order to meet application requirements.

Oracle Cloud Infrastructure Resource Manager

Oracle Cloud offers Resource Manager, which allows you to define and deploy IaC using Terraform templates. It provides version control and collaboration features.

These are some of the most common IaC tools available to use; most of them come with an open source version, and some also offer enterprise versions with dedicated support. These tools vary in their approach, capabilities, and compatibility with different cloud providers and environments. The choice of an IaC tool depends on factors such as the organization's infrastructure needs, existing technology stack, cloud provider preferences, and the complexity of the infrastructure to be managed.

Let us now dive deeper into the core topic of this chapter: how do CSPM and IaC work together to enhance security posture?

CSPM and IaC integration

Integrating IaC and CSPM is crucial for ensuring security in cloud environments.

How IaC and CSPM enhance security posture together

CSPM and IaC integration is a powerful approach to ensuring "shift left" security, which means addressing security concerns as early as possible in the SDLC. Let us now understand how CSPM and IaC integration can be a boon, especially for organizations with complex infrastructure, and can help achieve shift left security with other use cases:

- **Early security assessment**: CSPM tools can be integrated into IaC pipelines and development workflows. IaC templates and configurations are scanned for security vulnerabilities and compliance violations before deployment. This early assessment allows teams to identify and address security issues at the code and configuration stage, reducing the risk of vulnerabilities making their way into production.

  For example: AWS CloudFormation templates can define granular IAM permissions, while Terraform scripts can specify secure **Simple Storage Service** (**S3**) bucket policies. CSPM tools then scan these IaC scripts, identifying security issues, compliance violations, and access problems early in the development process, ensuring that cloud resources are provisioned securely and aligned with established security policies.

- **Automated remediation**: CSPM tools can automate the remediation of security findings. When vulnerabilities or misconfigurations are detected in IaC code, CSPM tools can automatically generate remediation recommendations or, in some cases, automatically apply fixes. This automation ensures that security issues are resolved quickly, reducing manual intervention.

  For example: An IaC script defines security groups and their associated rules. It includes rules for ingress and egress traffic. If a CSPM tool identifies a security group with overly permissive rules during continuous monitoring, it can trigger an alert. The CSPM tool, integrated with the IaC pipeline, can automatically update the IaC script to tighten the security group rules and remediate the issue.

- **Ensuring encryption**: In an IaC script, resources such as Amazon S3 buckets or Azure Blob storage containers are provisioned. The script specifies encryption settings for these resources. The CSPM tool continuously scans the cloud environment and detects unencrypted storage resources, which can pose a security risk. Upon detection of unencrypted resources, the CSPM tool can trigger a remediation action by modifying the IaC script to enable encryption settings for those resources.

- **Key rotation and rotation policies**: IaC scripts define the creation and management of cryptographic keys for data encryption and signing. The CSPM tool monitors the usage of cryptographic keys and checks for expired or outdated keys. When the CSPM tool identifies an expired key, it can trigger an update in the IaC script to rotate the key, ensuring that encryption remains secure.

- **Policy enforcement (policy as code, or PaC)**: Security policies can be defined as code within IaC scripts. This includes policies related to access controls, encryption, network security, and compliance standards. CSPM tools provide a framework for codifying security policies specific to your cloud environment. These policies are continuously enforced and checked against live infrastructure, ensuring ongoing compliance and security adherence. This proactive approach prevents non-compliant configurations from being deployed.

- **Resource tagging and categorization**: Tags to cloud resources for categorization, management, and cost-tracking purposes are assigned using IaC scripts. The CSPM tool checks for resources without appropriate tags or resources with sensitive data that lack proper categorization. Upon detection of tag-related issues, the CSPM tool can initiate an IaC script modification to ensure that all resources are correctly tagged, enhancing resource management and security.

- **Visibility and collaboration**: CSPM tools provide visibility and collaboration features for security teams and developers. Security teams gain insights into IaC security posture and can collaborate with development teams to resolve issues. Developers receive feedback and guidance on security best practices early in the development process, fostering a culture of shared responsibility for security.

- **Enforcing compliance standards**: IaC scripts incorporate compliance policies and standards specific to the organization's industry and regulatory requirements. The CSPM tool continuously assesses cloud resources against these compliance standards and identifies non-compliant resources. When CSPM identifies non-compliant resources, it can trigger updates to the IaC scripts to bring the resources into compliance automatically.

- **User access controls**: IaC defines user access controls and permissions using IAM policies. It specifies which users or roles have access to various cloud resources. The CSPM tool monitors IAM policies for over-permissive access, such as overly broad permissions or users with excessive privileges. When CSPM detects such policy violations, it can initiate an automated remediation process by modifying the IaC script to restrict permissions and remove excessive access.

In short, CSPM and IaC integration plays a pivotal role in achieving shift left security by proactively addressing security concerns during the development and deployment of cloud infrastructure. These examples and use cases demonstrate how IaC scripts and CSPM tools can work together to enhance cloud security.

Potential integration challenges and strategies to overcome

While integrating IaC and CSPM offers significant benefits, it also comes with its own set of challenges. Here are some potential challenges organizations may face when integrating IaC and CSPM:

- **Complexity of IaC scripts**: IaC scripts can become complex, especially in large-scale cloud environments. Managing and maintaining these scripts can be challenging, and they may contain security misconfigurations themselves.

Strategy: Implement strong coding practices, modularize scripts, and conduct regular code reviews to ensure that IaC scripts remain clean, efficient, and secure.

- **Automated remediation risks**: Automated remediation initiated by CSPM tools may introduce unintended consequences or disrupt services if not carefully configured. There is a risk of automation making incorrect changes to IaC scripts.

  Strategy: Implement safeguards and testing procedures to validate automated remediation actions before they are applied. Establish clear rollback procedures in case of unexpected issues.

- **Integration complexity**: Integrating CSPM tools with IaC pipelines and workflows can be complex and require additional infrastructure and configuration.

  Strategy: Invest in robust integration strategies and consider leveraging third-party tools or platforms that facilitate this integration. Engage with vendors or cloud providers that offer built-in CSPM capabilities.

- **Communication and collaboration**: Ensuring effective communication and collaboration between development, operations, and security teams can be challenging. Teams may have different priorities and processes.

  Strategy: Foster a culture of collaboration, conduct cross-team training, and establish clear communication channels to ensure that security findings from CSPM are shared and addressed promptly.

- **Policy conflicts**: IaC scripts and CSPM policies may conflict, especially when security policies are enforced in both. Overlapping policies can lead to confusion and unintended changes.

  Strategy: Define clear roles and responsibilities for policy management. Ensure that policies in IaC scripts and CSPM tools are well documented and that potential conflicts are identified and resolved proactively.

- **Resource life cycle management**: Managing the entire life cycle of cloud resources, including deprovisioning, can be complex when IaC scripts are primarily focused on provisioning.

  Strategy: Develop IaC scripts and CSPM policies that include resource life cycle management, including decommissioning and deprovisioning procedures to prevent "zombie" resources.

Human and cultural aspects of challenges

Organizational resistance to change can be a significant obstacle when implementing IaC practices. Many employees may be accustomed to traditional manual processes and may resist the shift toward automated infrastructure management. Overcoming this challenge involves providing comprehensive training, securing executive support, and initiating small-scale IaC pilot projects to demonstrate its benefits, ultimately fostering a culture of adaptability and continuous improvement within the organization.

Organizational resistance to change

Organizations often face resistance to change when going through transition, whether it's a shift left approach using IaC or embracing agile methodologies. Employees are accustomed to manual processes and resist adopting automated approaches. Here are some strategies to overcome this:

- **Education and training**: Provide comprehensive training and resources to employees to help them understand the benefits of IaC and how it simplifies their tasks
- **Executive buy-in**: Secure support and buy-in from leadership to communicate the importance of IaC adoption throughout the organization
- **Pilot projects**: Begin with small-scale IaC projects as pilots to demonstrate their advantages in a controlled environment
- **CM**: Implement CM practices to address employee concerns and encourage a culture of continuous improvement

Siloed teams

In some organizations, development, operations, and security teams operate in silos, which can hinder the collaboration required for IaC's success. The following strategies can help alleviate this:

- **Cross-functional teams**: Encourage cross-functional collaboration between development, operations, and security teams. Foster a DevOps culture where these teams work together seamlessly.
- **Shared goals**: Define shared goals and objectives to align teams toward a common purpose.
- **Regular communication**: Establish regular communication channels to facilitate information sharing and collaboration.
- **Training**: Provide training and resources to help teams acquire the necessary skills to work with IaC.

In conclusion, while integrating IaC and CSPM can be challenging, these challenges can be addressed through careful planning, collaboration, automation, and best practices. The benefits of enhanced security, compliance, and efficiency make the effort worthwhile for organizations operating in cloud environments.

Best practices and design patterns

Adhering to best practices and design patterns is essential for creating reliable, efficient, and maintainable cloud environments for successful IaC adoption and smooth integration with CSPM. Let us delve into some fundamental principles that can greatly enhance your IaC implementations.

DRY principle – Reducing redundancy in IaC code

The **Don't Repeat Yourself** (**DRY**) principle is a cornerstone of software development, and it holds just as much relevance in the realm of IaC. At its core, DRY encourages you to eliminate redundancy and repetition in your code. This means avoiding duplication of configuration settings and code blocks. By adhering to DRY, you achieve efficiency as you save time and effort by defining configurations and resources only once, reducing the chance of inconsistencies. When changes are required, you make them in one place, ensuring that updates propagate across your infrastructure, which enhances maintainability. Your IaC code becomes more readable and comprehensible, making it easier for your team to collaborate and troubleshoot.

Separation of concerns – Organizing code for maintainability and scalability

IaC projects can quickly become complex as cloud environments grow. **Separation of concerns** (**SoC**) is a design pattern that advocates breaking your code into modular, self-contained components. This practice offers several advantages:

- **Modularity**: You can work on individual components independently, making it easier to manage and maintain your infrastructure. Modular IaC simplifies CSPM scans, making it easier to pinpoint security issues within specific components or services.

- **Scalability**: As your cloud infrastructure scales, a well-organized code base can accommodate growth more effectively.

- **Debugging**: Isolating issues becomes simpler when code is divided into smaller, logically organized units.

Testing and validation – Ensuring the reliability of your IaC code

Testing and validation are crucial for verifying that your IaC code behaves as expected. Comprehensive testing can help you with the following:

- **Catching errors early**: Identify and rectify issues before deploying code to production environments

- **Enhancing reliability**: Ensure that your infrastructure is robust and resilient

- **Compliance**: Validate that your infrastructure adheres to security and compliance requirements

- **Documentation**: Testing provides living documentation, showcasing the intended behavior of your infrastructure

Infrastructure as Data – Leveraging data-driven approaches for configuration

The concept of IaD emphasizes treating configuration data as a first-class citizen in your IaC. By doing so, your infrastructure can adapt more easily to changes, thanks to dynamic, data-driven configurations making it *flexible*. Configuration data can be reused across multiple environments, streamlining deployments and making it reusable, and configuration data becomes more *manageable* when it's stored and versioned separately.

In short, these best practices and design patterns can be of great help. By embracing these principles, you'll not only integrate CSPM very well with IaC but also enhance the security and reliability of your cloud infrastructure.

Summary

This chapter explores the critical integration of IaC into CI/CD pipelines, demonstrating how organizations can automate and streamline the provisioning and management of cloud infrastructure. The chapter emphasizes the selection of appropriate IaC tools, setting up version control, automating testing processes, and defining CI and CD workflows. It highlights the significance of continuous monitoring, feedback loops, documentation, and training while discussing the seamless incorporation of IaC into development pipelines. The integration of IaC and CI/CD is presented as a fundamental strategy for enhancing the reliability, security, and scalability of cloud environments while fostering a culture of automation and collaboration within organizations.

In the next chapter, we will delve into the critical intersection of **Development, Security, and Operations** (**DevSecOps**). This chapter will guide you through the automation of security processes and best practices in the IaC pipeline. Topics covered will include integrating security checks into the CI/CD workflow, leveraging vulnerability scanning tools, and embedding security policies into IaC scripts.

Further reading

To learn more about the topics covered in this chapter, please visit the following links:

- *Automate infrastructure workflows* (https://www.redhat.com/en/resources/infrastructure-automation-ebook)
- *Deploy to Azure infrastructure with GitHub Actions* (https://learn.microsoft.com/en-us/devops/deliver/iac-github-actions)
- *Best Infrastructure as Code (IaC) Tools [By Use Case]* (https://www.wiz.io/academy/best-infrastructure-as-code-tools-by-use-case)

17

DevSecOps – Workflow Automation

In the fast-paced world of modern software development, security is no longer an afterthought but an integral part of the process. DevSecOps is not just about adding security to the DevOps pipeline; it's a mindset that strives to make security an inherent part of every stage of the software development life cycle. In other words, it's about **shifting left** – moving security practices to the earliest stages of development rather than tacking them on at the end. The significance of DevSecOps lies in its ability to enhance software security, reduce vulnerabilities, and increase the speed of development. It empowers organizations to build and deploy secure software with agility, ensuring that security is no longer a bottleneck or a separate process but an integral part of the entire development cycle.

CSPM plays a vital role in DevSecOps by providing a framework for securing cloud assets, infrastructure, and applications. Modern CSPM integrates seamlessly with DevSecOps practices to ensure that security is not compromised in the rush to deliver software quickly. By automating security checks and policy enforcement in the cloud, CSPM bridges the gap between security and development teams, making the entire process more efficient and secure.

Speed and security go hand in hand when it comes to DevSecOps. Manual security checks and cumbersome, error-prone processes are not sustainable. This is where workflow automations come into play. Workflow automations in DevSecOps encompass the use of tools, scripts, and pipelines to automate repetitive and time-consuming security tasks. It ensures that security practices are consistent and reliable, and also don't slow down the development and deployment of software. Automating security checks, compliance audits, asset discovery, and incident response not only speeds up the development cycle but also reduces the likelihood of human error, ensuring that security is not compromised.

In this chapter, we'll delve into the various ways DevSecOps teams can leverage workflow automations to improve their security posture. We'll explore the significance of DevSecOps and its role in modern software development. You'll gain a deep understanding of how CSPM fits into the DevSecOps landscape and why it's a crucial component. We'll also delve into the need for workflow automations in DevSecOps, covering the challenges and benefits of automation in ensuring both speed and security. By the end of this chapter, you'll have a clear understanding of the core concepts, tools, and best practices that underpin successfully integrating workflow automations into your DevSecOps processes. This knowledge will empower you to build a more secure and efficient software development pipeline.

We will cover the following main topics:

- Understanding DevSecOps
- Key automation concepts
- Workflow automation in CSPM
- Implementing workflow automations
- Case studies and best practices
- Security and compliance in DevSecOps automation
- Future trends and emerging technologies

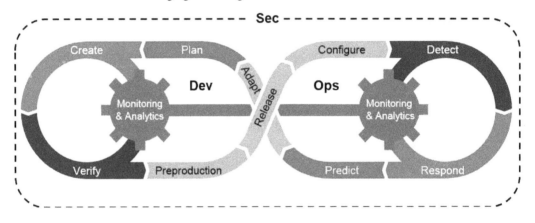

Figure 17.1 – DevSecOps (https://images.idgesg.net/images/article/2018/01/ devsecops-gartner-image-100745815-orig.jpg)

Let's take a look at the key elements and principles of DevSecOps:

- **Security as a culture**: DevSecOps promotes a culture where security is not just the responsibility of a dedicated security team but is embraced by everyone involved in the software development and deployment process. It encourages a shared sense of responsibility for security, from developers to operations personnel.

- **Shift-left approach**: The traditional approach to security involves checking for vulnerabilities and addressing them late in the software development cycle. DevSecOps advocates for a *shift-left* approach, meaning security considerations are brought forward to the earliest stages of development. This helps in identifying and addressing security issues at a stage where they are easier and more cost-effective to fix.

What is the shift-right approach?

Shift-right involves extending testing activities to the right, or later stages, in the development life cycle. It often refers to testing that occurs in production or in environments that closely resemble the production environment. The goal of shift-right is to identify issues that may only surface in a production environment, such as performance or scalability problems. It also aims to gather insights from real user interactions and production data. Practices such as A/B testing (also known as split testing), canary releases, and monitoring in production are examples of shift-right activities. Both shift-left and shift-right are valuable and can complement each other. While shift-left helps catch and fix issues early in the development process, shift-right provides insights into real-world behavior and performance.

- **Automation**: Automation is a cornerstone of DevSecOps. Security checks, testing, and compliance enforcement are automated wherever possible. This ensures that security is consistent, reliable, and not a bottleneck in the software delivery pipeline.

- **Continuous integration and continuous deployment** (**CI/CD**): DevSecOps integrates security practices into CI/CD pipelines. These pipelines automate the building, testing, and deployment of software, ensuring that security checks are performed at every stage of the process.

- **Collaboration**: Teams that have typically worked in silos, such as development, security, and operations, collaborate more closely in a DevSecOps environment. Security professionals work with developers to identify and remediate vulnerabilities, while operations teams ensure that security policies are consistently applied in production environments.

- **Security as code**: Just as infrastructure can be managed as code (*Infrastructure as Code*), security policies and configurations can be defined and managed as code. This allows for version control, tracking changes, and ensuring consistent security settings across environments.

- **Continuous monitoring and response**: In a DevSecOps environment, continuous monitoring for security threats and incidents is crucial. Security teams are prepared to respond to security incidents in real time and remediate vulnerabilities promptly.

- **Compliance and regulations**: DevSecOps ensures that software and systems comply with industry regulations and internal standards. This is particularly important in highly regulated industries such as finance and healthcare.

By implementing DevSecOps practices, organizations can achieve several important goals, including the following:

- **Faster and more secure software development**: DevSecOps accelerates the development and deployment of software while maintaining a prominent level of security

- **Early detection and mitigation of vulnerabilities**: Security issues are identified and addressed earlier in the development process, reducing the risk of security breaches

- **Improved collaboration**: Collaboration between different teams fosters a better understanding of security concerns and leads to better security outcomes
- **Enhanced compliance**: DevSecOps practices help organizations maintain compliance with industry regulations and security standards

In short, DevSecOps is a holistic approach that combines development, security, and operations to create a culture of security that is both agile and robust, making software development and deployment more efficient and secure.

DevOps versus DevSecOps – Key differences and principles

DevOps and DevSecOps share many similarities, but they also have some fundamental differences that set them apart. **DevOps**, short for **Development and Operations**, is a set of practices and principles that aim to improve collaboration and communication between software development and IT operations teams. The primary focus of DevOps is to streamline the software delivery process, increase deployment frequency, and achieve faster time-to-market.

In contrast, DevSecOps integrates security into the DevOps methodology, making security considerations an intrinsic part of every stage of the software development life cycle. DevSecOps seeks to create a culture where security is not a separate entity but a shared responsibility among all teams involved in software development and delivery.

Here are the key differences between DevOps and DevSecOps:

- DevOps emphasizes collaboration between development and operations teams, while DevSecOps extends this collaboration to include security teams
- DevOps is primarily concerned with speed and agility, whereas DevSecOps places equal importance on security
- DevOps assumes that security is the responsibility of a separate security team, while DevSecOps integrates security practices into every step of the DevOps pipeline

The DevSecOps life cycle

The DevSecOps life cycle is a structured approach that outlines how security practices are integrated throughout the software development and deployment process. It typically consists of the following stages:

- **Plan**: In this initial phase, security requirements and considerations are incorporated into the project planning. Security experts collaborate with developers and operations to define security policies, standards, and objectives.
- **Code**: During the coding phase, developers write code with security in mind. They follow secure coding practices, use libraries and frameworks with known security features, and conduct code reviews to identify and rectify security vulnerabilities.

- **Build**: The build phase involves compiling the code and creating executable software. DevSecOps teams use automated security testing tools to scan the code for vulnerabilities, ensuring that the build process does not introduce security issues.

- **Test**: This stage focuses on comprehensive security testing. It includes **dynamic application security testing (DAST)**, **static application security testing (SAST)**, penetration testing, and other security assessments to identify and remediate vulnerabilities.

- **Deploy**: Security is maintained during the deployment phase by using secure configuration management and containerization techniques. Security policies and access controls are enforced, and continuous monitoring begins.

- **Operate**: Continuous monitoring and real-time security assessments are vital in the operational phase. Any security incidents or anomalies are detected and addressed promptly.

- **Monitor and respond**: DevSecOps teams monitor the system's security, gather feedback, and respond to incidents in real time. Security experts work in tandem with development and operations teams to ensure that any vulnerabilities or threats are mitigated.

The importance of CI/CD pipelines

CI/CD pipelines are at the heart of DevSecOps. These pipelines automate the software delivery process, from code integration to deployment. CI ensures that code changes are continuously integrated into the main code base, while CD automates the process of deploying code changes to production. In DevSecOps, CI/CD pipelines are designed to include security checks and tests at every stage. This ensures that security is not compromised in the rush to deploy new features or updates. Automated security testing tools, vulnerability scanning, and policy enforcement are integrated into the CI/CD pipeline to detect and remediate security issues as early as possible.

The role of security in DevSecOps

Security in DevSecOps goes beyond traditional security practices. It involves a shift-left approach, meaning security is addressed from the earliest stages of development. Security is not just a gatekeeper; it is an enabler of faster and safer software delivery.

Here are the key roles of security in DevSecOps:

- **Security automation**: Security practices are automated to keep up with the speed of development and ensure consistent security checks

- **Collaboration**: Security teams collaborate closely with development and operations teams, sharing knowledge and responsibilities

- **Policy enforcement**: Security policies are defined and enforced throughout the software development process, reducing the risk of security breaches

- **Vulnerability management**: Security teams actively identify and remediate vulnerabilities, ensuring that the software is as secure as possible

- **Incident response**: DevSecOps teams are prepared to respond to security incidents promptly, minimizing the impact of potential breaches

In short, DevSecOps represents a change in thinking in software development and delivery, where security is not just a component but an integral part of the process. By understanding the differences, life cycle, and role of security in DevSecOps, organizations can create a culture of security that enhances both speed and safety in software development.

Key automation concepts

In the world of DevSecOps and CSPM, automation tools and frameworks are the backbone of efficiency and security. These tools are designed to streamline and simplify repetitive, time-consuming tasks while ensuring that security and compliance standards are consistently met. They cover a wide range of functions, including configuration management, testing, monitoring, and incident response.

Some of the popular automation tools and frameworks in the DevSecOps and CSPM domain include Ansible, Terraform, Kubernetes, Jenkins, and security-specific tools such as Nessus, Qualys, and OpenSCAP. These tools allow organizations to automate various aspects of security and compliance management, making it easier to maintain a strong security posture in dynamic cloud environments.

The relationship between CSPM and workflow automation

CSPM and workflow automation are closely intertwined. CSPM focuses on identifying and mitigating security risks and vulnerabilities within cloud infrastructure and services. Workflow automation, on the other hand, revolves around automating the processes and tasks related to security and compliance. The relationship between CSPM and workflow automation can be summarized as follows:

- CSPM provides the foundation for identifying security and compliance issues in cloud environments

- Workflow automation tools and frameworks enable the automatic execution of tasks related to remediating these issues

- CSPM identifies problems, and workflow automation tools facilitate the rapid response and resolution of these problems

By integrating CSPM and workflow automation, organizations can ensure that their cloud infrastructure remains secure and compliant. This not only reduces the risk of security breaches but also streamlines security management by automating many of the necessary actions.

Benefits of automation in security and compliance

The adoption of automation in security and compliance brings forth a multitude of benefits for organizations:

- **Consistency**: Automation ensures that security and compliance checks are consistently performed across all systems and environments. This reduces the risk of human error and security gaps caused by oversight.

- **Speed**: Automated security checks and policy enforcement happen in real time or as part of CI/CD pipelines, allowing organizations to maintain prominent levels of security without slowing down development and deployment processes.

- **Efficiency**: Automation frees up human resources from mundane, repetitive tasks, allowing security professionals to focus on more critical and strategic activities.

- **Scalability**: Automated solutions can easily scale to meet the demands of growing cloud environments, which is essential for organizations with dynamic infrastructure needs.

- **Reduction in downtime**: Automation can swiftly respond to incidents and vulnerabilities, minimizing system downtime and reducing the impact of security breaches.

- **Cost savings**: While there are initial setup costs, the long-term cost savings through automation are significant. Fewer manual interventions mean fewer labor costs and potential losses due to security incidents.

- **Compliance assurance**: Automation tools can continuously monitor and enforce compliance, ensuring that organizations adhere to industry regulations and internal security standards.

Common automation challenges and their solutions

Despite the many advantages of automation, organizations encounter some usual challenges in implementing and maintaining automated security and compliance processes. Here are a few of these challenges and potential solutions:

- **Complexity**: Implementing automation tools can be complex. To address this, organizations should invest in proper training and documentation to help teams effectively use these tools.

- **Integration**: Ensuring that automation tools and frameworks seamlessly integrate with existing systems and cloud environments can be challenging. Employing best practices and thorough planning can help streamline the integration process.

- **Monitoring and maintenance**: Automated systems require ongoing monitoring and maintenance to ensure they remain effective. Regularly reviewing and updating automation scripts and rules is essential.

- **Security of automation tools**: The very tools that are used for automation need to be secured against potential threats. Robust access controls, encryption, and security best practices should be applied to these tools.

- **Resource constraints**: Organizations may face resource constraints when implementing automation. Collaborative efforts among different teams can help manage these constraints and ensure a successful implementation.

Once these automation concepts are understood well, organizations can harness the full potential of automation to enhance security and compliance in the fast-paced world of DevSecOps and CSPM.

Workflow automation in CSPM

One of the fundamental goals of implementing CSPM is to ensure that your cloud infrastructure remains secure and compliant. To achieve this, modern CSPM tools are integrated with DevSecOps pipelines, where automation plays a crucial role. Integrating CSPM tools with DevSecOps pipelines allows for the seamless execution of security and compliance checks at every stage of the software development and deployment process. This integration ensures that security remains a priority, from code development and testing to deployment and monitoring.

By incorporating CSPM checks into the CI/CD pipeline, organizations can automatically scan code, configurations, and infrastructure for security issues. This early detection and immediate remediation help maintain a strong security posture throughout the software development life cycle.

Automating compliance checks and policy enforcement

Automation in CSPM extends to the automation of compliance checks and policy enforcement. Organizations usually need to adhere to industry regulations, internal security policies, and best practices. Automating compliance checks ensures that cloud resources and configurations consistently meet these standards. Automation tools, scripts, and policies can be designed to continuously monitor cloud infrastructure for compliance violations. When non-compliance is detected, the automation framework can trigger alerts or take corrective actions automatically. This proactive approach helps maintain compliance and reduces the risk of security breaches and associated penalties.

Dynamic asset discovery and tracking

In cloud environments, assets can be dynamic, frequently changing as resources are created, modified, or decommissioned. It is crucial to have a real-time understanding of your assets and their security postures. CSPM solutions often include automated asset discovery and tracking capabilities.

Automated asset discovery tools scan your cloud environment to identify and record assets, such as virtual machines, storage resources, databases, and network components. Tracking and monitoring these assets in real time provides visibility into their security status, making it easier to identify and address security vulnerabilities.

Incident response and remediation automation

In an era of evolving security threats, rapid incident response is critical. Automation plays a significant role in incident response and remediation. When a security incident occurs, an automated response system can be triggered to take immediate action.

For example, if a security breach or vulnerability is detected, automated incident response can quarantine affected resources, roll back changes, and initiate forensics investigations. By automating these processes, organizations can reduce the time it takes to respond to incidents, limiting the potential impact and reducing the manual workload on security teams.

Real-time monitoring and alerting

Automation in CSPM enables real-time monitoring and alerting, which is essential for identifying and responding to security threats promptly. Automated monitoring tools continuously scan cloud resources, configurations, and logs, looking for suspicious activities or deviations from security policies. When a potential security issue is detected, the system can trigger automated alerts to notify security teams or initiate predefined responses. Real-time monitoring and alerting are invaluable for identifying and addressing security incidents in their early stages, preventing security breaches, and minimizing the damage they can cause.

In summary, workflow automation is an integral part of CSPM. It allows organizations to seamlessly integrate security and compliance checks into their DevSecOps pipelines, enforce compliance, discover and track dynamic assets, automate incident response, and maintain real-time monitoring and alerting capabilities. By leveraging automation in CSPM, organizations can enhance their security posture and respond swiftly to evolving security threats in cloud environments.

Implementing workflow automations

The successful implementation of workflow automations with CSPM begins with selecting the right automation tools. There is a wide array of tools and platforms available, each with its strengths and use cases. The selection process involves understanding the specific needs and challenges of your organization, aligning them with the capabilities of the available tools, and considering factors such as scalability, compatibility, and ease of integration. Choosing the right automation tools is critical. Whether it is for continuous compliance monitoring, real-time incident response, or asset discovery, the selected tools should align with your CSPM goals. An assessment of the tool's features, support, and community involvement can help you make informed decisions.

Setting up and configuring automation pipelines

Once the automation tools have been selected, the next step is setting up and configuring automation pipelines. Automation pipelines are the workflows that execute various tasks automatically. They can range from simple one-task pipelines to complex, multi-stage processes involving different tools and integrations.

Configuring these pipelines involves defining the sequence of tasks, specifying triggers (events that initiate the automation), setting up dependencies, and establishing the flow of data and information between different steps. It is essential to ensure that the automation pipeline aligns with your organization's security policies and procedures.

Writing scripts and playbooks for CSPM automation

Automation in CSPM involves writing scripts or playbooks that define how tasks are performed. These scripts are instructions that automation tools follow to execute actions. They can include tasks such as security checks, policy enforcement, incident response, and asset tracking.

Scripts and playbooks need to be well-documented, modular, and adaptable. They should also consider error handling, logging, and scalability. Scripting languages such as Python, PowerShell, and YAML play a significant role in automating CSPM tasks. Writing efficient and maintainable scripts is crucial for the long-term success of your automation efforts.

Testing and validating automation workflows

Before deploying automation workflows in a production environment, it is essential to rigorously test and validate them. This phase helps identify and address issues, ensuring that automation functions as intended and does not introduce vulnerabilities or risks.

Testing involves simulating different scenarios and edge cases to evaluate how the automation responds. It also entails validating that the outputs match the expected results. Security and compliance checks should be an integral part of the testing process.

Continuous testing and validation are essential as new features, cloud environments, or policies may require making adjustments to the automation workflows. Implementing automated testing processes as part of your automation framework can help maintain the reliability and effectiveness of your CSPM automation.

Scaling automation for enterprise-level CSPM

As organizations grow and their cloud environments expand, the demands on CSPM automation increase. Implementing automation at an enterprise level requires scalability and flexibility. It is essential to plan for this scalability from the beginning of your automation efforts.

Scaling automation involves ensuring that it can handle a growing number of resources, systems, and cloud services. This might require load balancing, distributed automation agents, and resource-efficient architecture. Furthermore, it is crucial to have a monitoring and management strategy to oversee automation at an enterprise scale. Automated monitoring, alerting, and reporting can provide insights into the performance and security of your CSPM automation framework.

In summary, implementing workflow automations tools with CSPM requires careful planning, tool selection, configuration, scripting, testing, and scalability considerations. By approaching these steps methodically, organizations can establish a robust and reliable automation framework that enhances security and compliance while adapting to the evolving needs of their cloud environments.

Case studies, best practices, and lessons learned

Automation not only improves security but also enhances operational efficiency and agility. It allows organizations to maintain a strong security posture while managing complex and dynamic cloud environments. Let's look at how case studies would look.

Netflix's automated security guardrails

Netflix, a global leader in streaming services, relies heavily on cloud infrastructure. They developed an open source security automation tool called *Security Monkey* (now known as *Repokid*) to automate their CSPM efforts. This tool scans AWS configurations, identifies security misconfigurations, and automatically remediates them by applying security guardrails. For example, it ensures that S3 buckets are not publicly accessible and that permissions adhere to predefined policies. By implementing this automation, Netflix has significantly enhanced its security posture while managing the vast number of cloud resources it uses. For more details on this tool, refer to `https://github.com/Netflix/Repokid`.

Google's BeyondProd – zero-trust security model

Google, a global technology giant, implemented a zero-trust security model called BeyondProd to enhance the security of its cloud-native applications. As part of BeyondProd, Google incorporated automated security guardrails that leverage CSPM principles. They developed a suite of tools and processes to enforce the following security policies in their cloud environment:

- **Automated access controls**: Implemented automated access controls to ensure the principle of least privilege across cloud resources
- **Continuous monitoring**: Utilized automated monitoring tools to detect and respond to anomalous activities in real time
- **Automated incident response**: Integrated automated incident response workflows to contain and remediate security incidents

This was the outcome:

- **Enhanced cloud security**: BeyondProd, with its automated security guardrails, significantly strengthened Google's cloud security posture
- **Adaptability to scale**: The automated approach allowed Google to scale security measures effectively as their cloud infrastructure continued to grow

For more details, please refer to **BeyondProd | Documentation | Google Cloud**.

These examples highlight how various companies have embraced CSPM and automated security guardrails within their DevSecOps practices to bolster their cloud security and maintain agility in their operations. You can also find several use cases on the CSPM vendor's website explaining how their customers/partners improved their security posture.

Best practices for implementing and maintaining automation in DevSecOps

Implementing and maintaining automation in DevSecOps involves a combination of technological, cultural, and process-oriented considerations. Here are some best practices to guide you in effectively implementing and sustaining automation in a DevSecOps environment:

- **Define clear objectives**: Clearly define the objectives of your automation efforts, whether it is improving security, compliance, or efficiency. Having well-defined goals ensures everyone is on the same page.

- **Collaboration across teams**: Encourage collaboration and communication between development, security, and operations teams. A united approach to automation is essential for its success.

- **Continuous testing and validation**: Regularly test and validate your automation workflows to ensure they function as intended. Automation is dynamic, and ongoing testing helps maintain reliability.

- **Security-centric design**: Incorporate security best practices into your automation design. This includes securing automation code and access controls, and ensuring that security remains a priority throughout the automation life cycle.

- **Comprehensive documentation**: Maintain thorough documentation for your automation scripts, playbooks, and workflows. Well-documented automation helps with understanding, troubleshooting, and scaling.

- **Monitoring and alerting**: Implement automated monitoring and alerting to proactively identify issues with your automation. Timely alerts enable you to address problems as they arise, preventing potential security incidents.

Lessons learned from DevSecOps and CSPM automation adoption

Let's look at some common lessons learned from organizations that have embraced DevSecOps and CSPM automation:

- **Cultural transformation**: The shift to DevSecOps and CSPM automation is not just a technological change; it is a cultural transformation. Emphasize collaboration, shared responsibility, and adaptability in your organization's culture.

- **Start small, scale gradually**: Begin with manageable automation tasks and scale up as you gain confidence and experience. This gradual approach minimizes risks associated with large-scale automation projects.

- **Scalability planning**: Consider scalability from the outset. As your organization and cloud environments expand, ensure that your automation can accommodate the growing workload.

- **Continuous learning**: DevSecOps and CSPM automation are dynamic fields. Continuous learning and staying up to date with evolving security threats and best practices are essential.

- **Human element:** While automation is a valuable asset, the human element remains indispensable. Security professionals, developers, and operations teams play a crucial role in ensuring the success of automation efforts.

In summary, the case studies, best practices, and lessons learned from organizations that have embraced DevSecOps and CSPM automation provide practical insights into the benefits and challenges of these approaches. By following best practices and learning from others' experiences, organizations can navigate their automation journey effectively, enhancing security, compliance, and operational efficiency.

Security and compliance in DevSecOps automation

Security and compliance are critical aspects of DevSecOps automation, ensuring that automated processes not only enhance efficiency but also maintain the highest standards of security and regulatory adherence. This section provides an overview of how to address security and compliance within your DevSecOps automation.

Ensuring the security of automation pipelines

When implementing DevSecOps automation, ensuring the security of your automation pipelines is paramount. Here are some key considerations:

- **Access control**: Implement robust access controls to limit who can modify or execute automation workflows. Ensure that only authorized personnel have access to critical automation components.

- **Secure code practices**: Apply secure coding practices to the automation scripts, playbooks, and configurations. This includes validating inputs, escaping user-generated data, and avoiding hardcoded secrets.

- **Encryption**: Use encryption to protect sensitive data, both in transit and at rest. This is especially important when transferring credentials and secrets within the automation pipeline.

- **Authentication and authorization**: Employ strong authentication and authorization mechanisms to verify the identity of users and grant them appropriate permissions within the automation workflow.

- **Version control**: Keep automation code and configurations under version control. This allows you to track changes, roll back to previous versions in case of issues, and maintain a secure code base.

Compliance with regulatory requirements in automated processes

Maintaining compliance with regulatory requirements is a crucial aspect of DevSecOps automation. To achieve this, you must implement the following features:

- **Policy enforcement**: Implement automated policy checks to ensure that your automation workflows adhere to industry regulations and internal compliance standards.

- **Audit trails**: Maintain comprehensive audit trails of all automated processes. This enables you to trace back and demonstrate compliance in the event of an audit.

- **Compliance as code**: Define compliance requirements and policies as code that can be versioned, reviewed, and integrated into automation workflows. This approach ensures consistency and traceability.

- **Regular assessments**: Continuously assess your automated processes to identify and remediate any compliance gaps promptly. Implement scheduled compliance checks as part of your automation.

Handling secrets and sensitive data securely in automation

Safely handling secrets and sensitive data is critical to the security of your automation. Consider the following:

- **Secret management**: Employ a robust secret management system to securely store and retrieve sensitive data such as API keys, passwords, and cryptographic keys. Avoid hardcoding secrets directly into automation scripts.

- **Rotation and expiry**: Implement regular rotation and expiry of secrets. This reduces the risk of long-term exposure in case of a security breach.

- **Least privilege**: Follow the principle of least privilege. Ensure that automation scripts and processes only have the permissions they need to perform their tasks, minimizing the exposure of sensitive data.

- **Secure transmission**: Encrypt sensitive data in transit, especially when it is being shared between automation components or stored in databases.

Continuous monitoring and auditing of automated workflows

The continuous monitoring and auditing of automated workflows are essential for maintaining a secure and compliant DevSecOps environment:

- **Real-time monitoring**: Implement real-time monitoring and alerting to detect any unusual or potentially harmful activities within your automation pipelines.

- **Logging and auditing**: Maintain detailed logs of all automation activities. These logs should capture not only successful executions but also any errors or exceptions.

- **Automated auditing**: Set up automated auditing processes to periodically review your automation configurations and code for security and compliance.

- **Incident response plans**: Prepare incident response plans specifically for automation-related incidents. This should include actions to take in case of security breaches, unauthorized access, or other anomalies in your automation.

By focusing on these key considerations in the realm of security and compliance in DevSecOps automation, organizations can maintain a robust, safe, and compliant automated environment while continuing to benefit from the efficiency and agility that automation offers.

Future trends and emerging technologies

The shift to agile development methodologies and DevOps practices has now become an industry standard, emphasizing speed and efficiency, making automation essential to maintain security without hindering development velocity. Moreover, the migration to cloud environments, although advantageous, introduces new security complexities, requiring organizations to adapt their security practices, hence paving the way for CSPM and DevSecOps automation. The rising awareness of data privacy and consumer rights places organizations under greater pressure to ensure the security of customer data, fostering the need for robust security measures and automation in data protection. As organizations that effectively implement automation in DevSecOps and CSPM gain a competitive edge by responding more swiftly to threats, reducing security incidents, and enhancing operational efficiency, the compelling drive for this significant transformation is not merely an industry necessity but a strategic imperative.

The evolving landscape of DevSecOps and CSPM

The landscape of DevSecOps and CSPM is continually evolving, with several key trends and developments:

- **Shift-left security**: There is a growing emphasis on integrating security at the earliest stages of the software development life cycle, ensuring that security is considered from the very beginning of application design and coding.

- **Microservices architecture**: The adoption of microservices architecture is on the rise. This architecture allows for more agility and scalability but also presents new challenges for security and automation due to its distributed nature.

- **Compliance as code**: Organizations are increasingly adopting the practice of defining compliance requirements and policies as code, making it easier to enforce and audit compliance within automated processes.

- **Cloud-native security**: The focus is shifting from traditional network security to cloud-native security solutions. Technologies such as cloud security orchestration and cloud workload protection are becoming essential in securing cloud-native environments.

Artificial intelligence (AI) and machine learning (ML) in CSPM automation

The integration of AI and ML into CSPM automation is a significant trend:

- **Anomaly detection**: AI and ML are used to detect anomalies and security threats in real time. These technologies can identify deviations from expected behavior and automatically trigger responses.

- **Predictive analysis**: Predictive analytics powered by AI can forecast potential security risks and vulnerabilities based on historical data, enabling organizations to take proactive measures.

- **Behavior analysis**: ML models analyze user and system behavior patterns to identify unusual activities that may indicate security breaches or policy violations.

- **Automation enhancement**: AI-driven automation enhances the efficiency of CSPM processes by automating response actions based on intelligent analysis, reducing the burden on security teams.

The role of containers and serverless in automated security

Containers and serverless computing technologies are transforming the way organizations approach automated security:

- **Container security**: The rise of containers has prompted the development of security solutions tailored to containerized environments. DevSecOps practices are evolving to secure containerized applications from development to deployment.

- **Serverless security**: With serverless computing, the responsibility for infrastructure management shifts to cloud providers, placing a greater focus on securing the code and functions within serverless applications.

- **Immutable infrastructure**: Containers and serverless architecture often lead to the adoption of immutable infrastructure practices. This approach simplifies security patching and compliance enforcement by deploying entirely new instances instead of modifying existing ones.

Predictions for the future of DevSecOps automation

Several predictions for the future of DevSecOps automation include the following:

- **Continuous compliance**: Compliance automation will become more sophisticated, enabling continuous monitoring and enforcement of compliance standards throughout the software development and deployment process

- **Zero-trust security**: The zero-trust security model will gain wider adoption, emphasizing strict access controls and verification for every user and device seeking access to an organization's network

- **Multi-cloud security**: With the increasing adoption of multi-cloud strategies, there will be a growing need for consistent security and compliance measures across multiple cloud platforms

- **Maturity models**: Organizations will increasingly adopt DevSecOps maturity models to assess and improve their automation and security practices, providing a structured framework for gradual improvements

- **DevSecOps as a service**: The rise of DevSecOps as a service, offered by cloud providers and specialized vendors, will provide organizations with pre-built automation solutions, reducing the need for custom development and management

In short, the future of DevSecOps and CSPM has a dynamic landscape, with the integration of AI and ML, the influence of container and serverless technologies, and a continued focus on security and compliance. As organizations adapt to these emerging trends and technologies, they will be better equipped to address evolving security challenges and the increasing complexity of cloud environments.

Summary

In this chapter, we delved into the dynamic world of DevSecOps and CSPM with a particular focus on workflow automations. We began by exploring the significance of DevSecOps, understanding its principles, and the crucial role of CSPM within it. We emphasized the need for automation in this evolving landscape, where security, compliance, and operational efficiency are paramount. The key takeaway is the vital role that CSPM and automation play in the modern landscape of DevSecOps. CSPM ensures that your cloud environment adheres to security best practices and regulatory standards, while automation streamlines these processes, making them not only more efficient but also more effective.

Automation allows you to proactively identify and remediate security issues, reduces human error, and enhances the agility of your organization in responding to threats. The landscape is evolving rapidly, and embracing automation is not just a best practice but also a strategic imperative. Start small, identify areas where automation can make a difference, and gradually expand your automation efforts. Learn from the lessons of successful organizations and keep an eye on emerging technologies and trends to stay at the forefront of security and compliance.

In the next chapter, we will dive deep into security recommendations.

Further reading

If you're interested in diving deeper into DevSecOps and CSPM automation, here is a curated list of books and websites that offer valuable insights and practical guidance:

*   Books:

    *   *The DevOps Handbook: How to Create World-Class Agility, Reliability, & Security in Technology Organizations*, by Gene Kim, Jez Humble, Patrick Debois, and John Willis

    *   *DevSecOps: Securing Software in the DevOps World*, by Shannon Lietz, Daniel Kennedy, and Rugged DevOps, Inc.

    *   *Site Reliability Engineering: How Google Runs Production Systems*, by Niall Richard Murphy, Betsy Beyer, Chris Jones, and Jennifer Petoff

*   Websites and blogs:

    *   **DevOps.com**: A comprehensive resource for DevOps and DevSecOps news, articles, webinars, and best practices (DevOps – The Web's Largest Collection of DevOps Content)

    *   **The DevOps Institute**: This site offers certifications, articles, and resources on DevOps practices, including DevSecOps (DevOps Certifications — DevOps Institute)

    *   **National Institute of Standards and Technology (NIST) Cybersecurity Framework**: NIST provides valuable resources on cybersecurity and compliance standards (Cybersecurity Framework | NIST)

18
CSPM-Related Technologies

Cloud security posture management (**CSPM**) provides a solid foundation for securing your cloud infrastructure; however, it's crucial to understand that it's not the sole player in the overall cloud security space. As cloud technologies continue to evolve, so do the threats and vulnerabilities associated with them. To stay ahead and ensure comprehensive cloud security, organizations must embrace a broader perspective that extends beyond CSPM. This chapter serves as your guide to the complementary tools and strategies that bolster your cloud security posture. We'll explore the cloud security ecosystem and essential technologies such as **cloud access security brokers** (**CASBs**), **cloud workload protection platforms** (**CWPPs**), **cloud-native application protection platforms** (**CNAPPs**), **cloud identity and entitlement management** (**CIEM**), and **data security posture management** (**DSPM**). These technologies can work in synergy with CSPM, creating a layered defense that ensures your cloud environment remains resilient. As we dive deep into each of these technologies, we'll uncover their unique contributions to cloud security, offering practical insights, real-world use cases, and integration strategies.

By the end of this chapter, you'll have a comprehensive understanding of how CASBs, CWPPs, CNAPPs, CIEM, DSPM, and emerging cloud security technologies can enhance your cloud security strategy.

The following main topics will be covered:

- Understanding the cloud security ecosystem
- CNAPPs
- CWPPs
- CASBs
- DSPM
- CIEM

Let us get started!

Understanding the cloud security ecosystem

The cloud security ecosystem refers to an interconnected and interdependent set of technologies, tools, processes, and practices that collectively work to ensure the security, compliance, and resilience of cloud computing environments:

Figure 18.1 – Cloud security ecosystem

Before we dive deep into each component of the ecosystem in detail, let us understand why CSPM is not enough to protect cloud resources.

Why is CSPM not enough?

While CSPM is a crucial component within this ecosystem, it cannot be the sole solution for all aspects of cloud security. It is worth understanding the reasons why CSPM cannot be enough:

- **Scope of CSPM**: CSPM primarily focuses on ensuring the secure configuration and compliance of cloud infrastructure. It is designed to identify and address misconfigurations that could expose vulnerabilities. However, cloud security involves multiple dimensions, including data protection, identity management, network security, and application security, which go beyond the scope of CSPM.

- **Limited to configuration issues**: CSPM is highly effective in addressing configuration-related issues, such as ensuring that cloud services are configured according to security best practices and compliance standards. However, it doesn't cover all aspects of security, such as monitoring for malicious activities, protecting against advanced threats, or securing applications and data.

- **Data encryption and privacy**: CSPM does not directly handle data encryption or privacy measures. While it can help identify misconfigurations that might impact data security, the encryption of sensitive data in transit and at rest is a separate concern that requires additional solutions and practices.

- **Application security**: Securing cloud-native applications, including those built using microservices, containers, and serverless computing, is beyond the primary focus of CSPM. Application-level security, including secure coding practices, runtime protection, and vulnerability management within applications, requires specialized solutions such as **web application firewalls (WAFs)** and CNAPP.

- **Identity and access management (IAM)**: CSPM is not designed to manage user access or handle identity-related security issues. IAM solutions are crucial for managing user identities, controlling access to cloud resources, and ensuring that only authorized individuals have the right permissions.

- **Network security controls**: While CSPM ensures that cloud configurations align with security policies, it does not handle network security controls directly. Network security measures, such as firewalls and **intrusion detection/prevention systems (IDSs/IPSs)**, are critical for protecting against network-based threats.

- **Incident response (IR) and monitoring**: CSPM is not a dedicated IR or monitoring solution. It lacks the capabilities to actively monitor suspicious activities, detect security incidents, and orchestrate responses to security events.

- **Adaptability to emerging threats**: CSPM is not designed to address emerging threats or zero-day vulnerabilities proactively. Dealing with advanced threats requires solutions with **threat intelligence (TI)** capabilities, **machine learning (ML)**, and behavioral analysis.

In short, even though CSPM plays a crucial role in maintaining a secure cloud posture by addressing misconfigurations and ensuring compliance, it is not a *one-size-fits-all* solution for the diverse and complex landscape of cloud security. A comprehensive approach involves integrating CSPM with other components within the cloud security ecosystem to create a layered defense strategy that covers multiple facets of security, including data protection, network security, application security, and IR.

Now that we understand the reasons why CSPM is not enough to protect cloud workloads holistically, let us dive deep into each component of the ecosystem in detail.

CNAPPs

Gartner defines CNAPPs as follows (https://www.gartner.com/reviews/market/cloud-native-application-protection-platforms):

> *"...a unified and tightly integrated set of security and compliance capabilities designed to secure and protect cloud-native applications across development and production. CNAPPs consolidate a large number of previously siloed capabilities, including container scanning, cloud security posture management, infrastructure as code scanning, cloud infrastructure entitlement management, runtime cloud workload protection, and runtime vulnerability/configuration scanning."*

CNAPPs represent the forefront of cloud security, providing a cutting-edge solution. They seamlessly integrate security and compliance functionalities, aiming to detect, identify, and address contemporary threats in cloud security, spanning from the development phase to runtime.

CNAPPs offer a consolidated experience for enterprises, amalgamating insights and fostering collaborative efforts among developers, DevOps teams, security teams, and analysts within the **Security Operations Center (SOC)**. The goal is to mitigate excessive risks associated with cloud-native applications and embed security throughout the **Continuous Integration and Continuous Delivery (CI/CD)** life cycle. The following diagram depicts how a CNAPP consolidates other security solutions to provide holistic security:

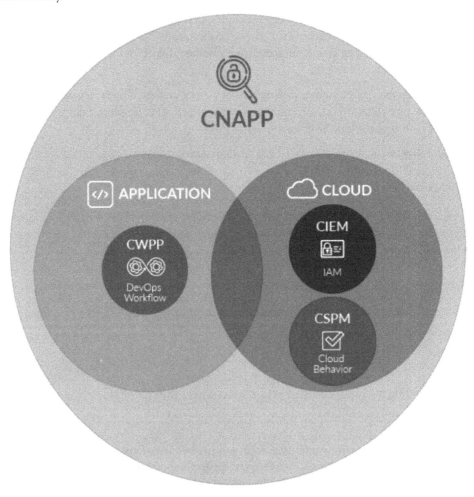

Figure 18.2 – CNAPP (source: https://sysdig.com/wp-content/uploads/CNAPP-LCN_3.png)

Why is a CNAPP important?

The necessity for a comprehensive CNAPP has become imperative to address the escalating demand for robust cloud security consolidation and an enhanced **software development life cycle (SDLC)**. As cloud computing adoption surges and modern applications become increasingly intricate, conventional security measures often prove insufficient in effectively thwarting sophisticated cyber threats. A CNAPP incorporates security principles such as *shift left* and *shield right*, forming a holistic security strategy throughout the application life cycle. Through the implementation of "shift left," organizations can deploy security controls, vulnerability scanning, and compliance checks from the initial stages of the application development process. The "shield right" concept concentrates on real-time detection and response to security incidents during the runtime phase of the application. Despite diligent efforts to secure applications during development, the presence of vulnerabilities or the emergence of new threats necessitates the adoption and integration of these two fundamental concepts within a CNAPP:

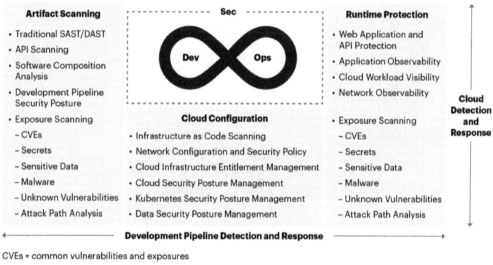

CVEs = common vulnerabilities and exposures

Source: Gartner

785751_C

Gartner

Figure 18.3 – CNAPP detailed overview (source: https://www.paloaltonetworks.com/
blog/prisma-cloud/get-to-know-cloud-native-application-protection-platforms/)

Gartner, through the preceding diagram, provides overall CNAPP capabilities and security features spanning from development to runtime.

How does a CNAPP work?

A CNAPP facilitates the consolidation of cloud security by integrating the need for real-time risk visibility, cloud risk awareness, and development artifact risk awareness into a unified platform. To achieve this cohesive set of functionalities, CNAPPs typically adhere to two distinct instrumentation paradigms: agent-based and agentless. The agent-based approach operates close to the workloads, requiring the deployment of an agent (commonly called a sensor or probe) alongside the workloads on the instrumented machine. This placement on the same host provides real-time visibility into the runtime and enables access to system-level context information, which would otherwise be unavailable.

On the other hand, the agentless approach utilizes the APIs provided by cloud providers to collect relevant context without the need for an agent to run alongside the workloads. It often utilizes the capability to take snapshots, allowing security scans to be deferred on a **point-in-time** (**PIT**) copy, leaving the original workload unaltered. While this method may lack the in-depth runtime insights offered by an agent, it provides a seamless solution for addressing issues that do not require real-time data, such as constructing an asset inventory or identifying known vulnerabilities and anomalous behavior in audit logs.

An effective CNAPP solution should incorporate both instrumentation approaches to maximize its efficacy. Utilize the agent for real-time visibility into the runtime and enhanced access to system-level context information, while employing the agentless approach to identify known vulnerabilities and anomalous behavior in audit logs.

CNAPP and CSPM correlation

CNAPP and CSPM contribute to a comprehensive cloud security strategy, addressing both application-level and infrastructure-level security concerns in the dynamic and complex landscape of cloud computing. CSPM can be called a subset of a CNAPP.

CWPPs

A CWPP is a comprehensive security solution designed to secure and protect the workloads and applications running in cloud environments. The term "*cloud workload*" refers to **virtual machines** (**VMs**), containers, serverless functions, storage, networking capabilities, and other cloud-native services needed by applications in the cloud. CWPP solutions play a crucial role in addressing unique security challenges associated with dynamic, scalable, and often ephemeral cloud workloads. The following Gartner diagram summarizes the key capabilities of a CWPP tool:

CWPP

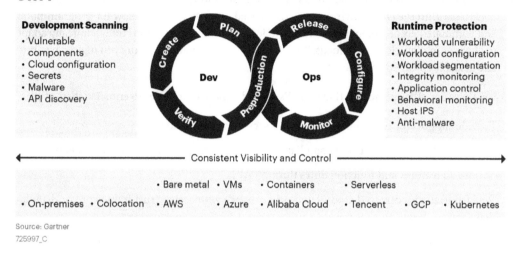

Source: Gartner
725997_C

Figure 18.4 – CWPP capabilities (source: https://www.gartner.com/resources/725900/725997/
Figure_1_Cloud_Workload_Protection_Platform_Capabilities.png)

Let us now explore the key capabilities of a CWPP.

CWPP key capabilities

Gartner (https://www.gartner.com/en/documents/3983483) defines CWPPs as *"security solutions designed to protect cloud workloads, which consist of applications, services, and processes running in cloud environments."* Gartner identifies four essential features or capabilities of CWPP solutions:

- **Hypervisor-based security**: CWPP solutions should provide security capabilities at the hypervisor level. This involves protecting virtualized workloads by leveraging security features integrated into the hypervisor layer. This capability is particularly important in virtualized and multi-tenant cloud environments where workloads are often isolated using hypervisor technology.

- **Cloud-native application protection**: CWPP solutions must be capable of securing cloud-native applications, including those built using microservices, containers, and serverless computing. Cloud-native application protection involves ensuring the security of the entire application stack, from the underlying infrastructure to the application code and data.

- **Integration with DevOps processes**: CWPP solutions should seamlessly integrate with DevOps processes and tools to support the dynamic and agile nature of cloud environments. This includes automation, CI/CD pipelines, and collaboration between development and operations teams. Integration with DevOps processes ensures that security is an integral part of the application life cycle.

- **API-based security controls**: CWPP solutions should leverage APIs to enforce security controls within the cloud environment. API-based security controls allow for programmatic and automated enforcement of security policies, enabling organizations to dynamically adapt to changes in their cloud workloads. This is crucial for maintaining security in highly dynamic and scalable cloud environments.

Moreover, there are other principles that CWPPs should adhere to in order to enhance their utility:

- Provide support for both containerized and serverless workloads

- Extend workload scanning and compliance measures into development environments

- Expose all features and functionalities through APIs

- Replace strategies centered around antivirus reliance with a zero-trust framework or default-deny approach during runtime

- Ensure consistent visibility and control across all workloads, irrespective of their scale, architecture, or geographical location

- Facilitate integration with CSPM solutions, enabling the detection and remediation of potentially hazardous misconfigurations

These key capabilities reflect the evolving nature of cloud workloads and the need for security solutions that can adapt to the dynamic and diverse cloud landscape. Organizations seeking effective cloud workload protection should evaluate CWPP solutions based on these key capabilities to ensure they meet the specific requirements of their cloud environments.

Why are CWPP solutions important?

CWPP solutions are crucial in the modern cybersecurity landscape for several reasons:

- **Dynamic cloud environments**: As organizations increasingly migrate their workloads to the cloud, the dynamic and scalable nature of cloud environments poses unique security challenges. CWPP solutions are designed to adapt to the dynamic nature of cloud workloads, providing security without hindering the agility and flexibility that cloud computing offers.

- **Protection against evolving threats**: Cyber threats are constantly evolving, and traditional security measures may not be sufficient to address modern attack vectors. CWPP solutions are specifically designed to protect cloud workloads against a wide range of threats, including malware, data breaches, and vulnerabilities inherent in cloud configurations.

- **Cloud-native application security**: With the rise of cloud-native applications, traditional security approaches may fall short of providing adequate protection. CWPP solutions focus on securing cloud-native applications, including those using microservices, containers, and serverless computing, ensuring the entire application stack is safeguarded.

- **Visibility and compliance**: CWPP solutions offer consistent visibility and control across diverse workloads, regardless of their size, design, or location. This visibility is essential for monitoring and ensuring compliance with security policies, industry regulations, and organizational standards.

- **Integration with DevOps processes**: In cloud environments, DevOps practices are prevalent, emphasizing collaboration and automation between development and operations teams. CWPP solutions integrate seamlessly with DevOps processes, ensuring that security is an integral part of the development life cycle and supporting CI/CD practices.

- **API-based security controls**: CWPP solutions leverage APIs for security controls, allowing for programmatic and automated enforcement of security policies. This is essential for adapting to the dynamic nature of cloud workloads and supporting automation in security processes.

- **Zero-trust framework**: CWPP solutions adopt a zero-trust framework or default-deny approach during runtime, moving away from traditional antivirus-centric strategies. This approach enhances security by treating all transactions, communications, and access as potentially untrusted, requiring verification and authorization.

- **Integration with CSPM**: CWPP solutions integrate with CSPM solutions to address the full spectrum of cloud security. This integration enables the detection and remediation of risky misconfigurations, providing a comprehensive approach to cloud security.

In essence, CWPP solutions play a critical role in ensuring the security, compliance, and resilience of cloud workloads in the face of evolving cybersecurity threats and the dynamic nature of cloud computing environments. They provide organizations with the tools and capabilities needed to secure their applications and data as they embrace the benefits of cloud technology. Let us now understand the layers of a CWPP.

Eight layers of CWPP controls

The eight layers of CWPP controls, as defined by Gartner (`https://www.gartner.com/en/documents/4003465`), represent a comprehensive set of security measures designed to protect cloud workloads across various aspects. Each layer focuses on a specific area of security, contributing to the overall resilience and defense against cyber threats in dynamic cloud environments. Let us look at the purpose of each layer:

- **Hardening**: Hardening involves strengthening the security of the underlying operating systems and applications within cloud workloads. This includes applying security best practices, disabling unnecessary services, and configuring settings to minimize potential vulnerabilities.

- **Configuration**: Configuration control ensures that cloud workloads adhere to security configurations and compliance standards. It involves verifying that settings and configurations align with security policies, reducing the risk of misconfigurations that could expose vulnerabilities.

- **Vulnerability management**: Vulnerability management focuses on identifying and addressing vulnerabilities within cloud workloads. This layer includes continuous scanning for potential weaknesses and timely application of patches or remediation to mitigate the risk of exploitation.

- **Network firewalling**: Network firewalling establishes and enforces policies to control incoming and outgoing network traffic for cloud workloads. This layer is crucial for preventing unauthorized access and protecting against network-based attacks.

- **Visibility and micro-segmentation**: Visibility and micro-segmentation enhance control and monitoring within cloud workloads. It involves gaining comprehensive visibility into network traffic and implementing micro-segmentation to isolate and compartmentalize workloads, limiting the lateral movement of threats.

- **System integrity assurance**: System integrity assurance ensures the integrity and trustworthiness of the cloud workload's operating system and critical components. This layer involves monitoring for any unauthorized changes or deviations from the expected system state.

- **Application control and allowlisting**: Application control and allowlisting involve defining and enforcing policies regarding which applications are allowed to run within cloud workloads. This helps prevent the execution of unauthorized or malicious applications.

- **Exploitation prevention and memory protection**: This layer focuses on preventing the exploitation of vulnerabilities within the cloud workload's applications and memory. It includes measures to detect and block malicious activities attempting to exploit vulnerabilities and protections against memory-based attacks.

These eight layers collectively create a multi-faceted defense strategy for cloud workloads, addressing various dimensions of security, from configuration and vulnerability management to network controls and application-level security. Implementing controls across these layers helps organizations establish a robust security posture in their cloud environments, protecting against a diverse range of cyber threats.

How does a CWPP work?

A CWPP works by implementing a set of security measures specifically designed to safeguard cloud workloads, which include applications, services, and processes running in cloud environments. The primary objective is to detect, prevent, and respond to security threats in a dynamic and scalable cloud infrastructure. To understand it better, let us take some use cases where a CWPP protects your workload:

- **Malware prevention**: CWPP solutions include mechanisms to prevent, detect, and remediate malware within cloud workloads

  Example: Real-time scanning and behavioral analysis to identify and block malicious code attempting to infiltrate cloud workloads

- **Intrusion detection and prevention**: CWPP solutions monitor and protect against unauthorized access, activities, and potential security breaches within cloud workloads

  Example: **Network IDS** (**NIDS**) and IPS designed to identify and block suspicious network traffic or activities

- **Data loss prevention (DLP)**: A CWPP helps prevent the unauthorized exposure or leakage of sensitive data from cloud workloads

  Example: Encryption of sensitive data, monitoring and blocking the transmission of confidential information outside predefined boundaries

- **Vulnerability management**: CWPP solutions identify, manage, and remediate vulnerabilities within the applications and components of cloud workloads to reduce the risk of exploitation

  Example: Regular scanning for software vulnerabilities and providing patches or recommendations for remediation

- **Behavioral analytics**: CWPP solutions provide behavioral analysis to detect anomalous activities or deviations from normal behavior within cloud workloads

  Example: ML algorithms analyzing user and application behavior to identify and respond to unusual patterns indicative of a potential security threat

- **Micro-segmentation**: CWPP solutions also offer micro-segmentation capabilities to enhance network security by isolating and segmenting workloads from one another

  Example: Creating network segments to restrict lateral movement within a cloud environment, limiting the impact of a security compromise

CWPPs versus CSPM – Differences and crossover

While both CWPPs and CSPM are integral components of the cloud security ecosystem, they have distinct focuses and address different aspects of an organization's cloud infrastructure and applications. Here are the key differences between CWPPs and CSPM based on five components – focus, capabilities, scope, use case, and integrations:

- **Focus**: A CWPP primarily focuses on protecting individual workloads or applications within the cloud. It is concerned with securing the runtime environment, including the operating system, applications, and data associated with a specific workload. CSPM, meanwhile, is focused on the overall security posture and configuration of the entire cloud environment. It looks at the broader picture, covering multiple workloads, services, and configurations.

- **Capabilities**: CWPPs' core capabilities are identifying and managing vulnerabilities within specific workloads, detecting and preventing malware from impacting the integrity of workloads, ensuring secure configurations of individual workloads, addressing security concerns within the application layer of specific workloads, and runtime protection, which means providing security measures during the execution of workloads. CSPM's core capabilities are ensuring that cloud resources are configured securely according to best practices and compliance standards, identifying and assessing risks associated with the overall cloud infrastructure, detecting and remediating misconfigurations that could expose vulnerabilities, and ensuring compliance with industry regulations and organizational security policies.

- **Scope**: A CWPP deals with securing the specific elements of a cloud environment where applications and workloads reside. It involves protection against malware, intrusion prevention, and DLP within these workloads, while CSPM brings a broader scope, including the entire cloud infrastructure. It involves ensuring that configurations across various cloud services are secure, monitoring compliance with policies, and managing vulnerabilities at an infrastructure level.

- **Deployment stage**: A CWPP focuses on the runtime phase, securing applications and workloads during their execution in the cloud environment. CSPM primarily operates during the pre-runtime or configuration stages, identifying and managing security risks before or during the deployment of resources in the cloud.

  Here are some example use cases:

  - *CWPP*: Protecting a cloud-based application from malware, ensuring that only authorized users have access, and preventing data leakage from specific workloads

  - *CSPM*: Ensuring that all cloud resources are configured securely, identifying vulnerabilities in the cloud infrastructure, and monitoring compliance with industry regulations and security policies

- **Integration**: CWPPs and CSPM have distinct focuses, but they are often used together as complementary solutions. In fact, the majority of CSPM vendors also offer CWPP features under the same umbrella as CSPM, with an additional licensing cost. Integrating both can provide a layered approach to cloud security, addressing both the security of individual workloads and the overall security posture of the cloud environment. A CWPP integrates with other security solutions focused on protecting individual workloads and applications.

In summary, while CWPPs and CSPM both contribute to cloud security, a CWPP is more focused on protecting individual workloads during runtime, while CSPM is concerned with the broader security posture of the entire cloud infrastructure, including configurations, compliance, and vulnerabilities. Organizations often use both solutions in tandem to achieve comprehensive security coverage for their cloud environments.

What is endpoint detection and response?

Endpoint detection and response (**EDR**) is a cybersecurity technology designed to monitor and secure endpoints, such as computers and mobile devices, against advanced threats. EDR tools provide real-time monitoring, threat detection using advanced algorithms, and IR capabilities to rapidly identify and mitigate potential security risks. With features such as forensic analysis, detailed visibility into endpoint activities, and integration with broader security ecosystems, EDR enhances an organization's ability to detect and respond to sophisticated cyber threats, offering a crucial layer of defense in safeguarding against attacks on endpoints within a network.

How are EDR and CWPPs related?

EDR and CWPPs are both cybersecurity solutions that play crucial roles in securing modern IT environments, but they focus on different aspects of the overall security landscape.

EDR is primarily concerned with securing individual computing devices or endpoints such as desktops, laptops, servers, and mobile devices. It involves real-time monitoring and analysis of endpoint activities to detect and respond to security incidents. EDR solutions use advanced techniques such as behavioral analysis and ML to identify suspicious behavior and potential threats on endpoints. The goal is to provide rapid detection, investigation, and response capabilities to mitigate security incidents at the endpoint level.

A **CWPP**, on the other hand, is focused on securing workloads and applications in cloud environments. As organizations increasingly migrate their applications and data to the cloud, protecting these workloads becomes paramount. CWPP solutions are designed to offer security for cloud-native applications, ensuring the integrity and confidentiality of data stored and processed in the cloud. They often include features such as vulnerability management, threat detection, and workload runtime protection to safeguard against various cyber threats targeting cloud workloads. EDR addresses security concerns at the endpoint level, covering devices such as computers and mobile devices, while a CWPP is tailored for securing workloads and applications specifically in cloud environments. Both are essential components of a comprehensive cybersecurity strategy, especially in the context of the evolving threat landscape and the widespread adoption of cloud technologies.

Now that we understand CWPPs, let us dive deep into another important component, called a CASB.

CASBs

A CASB is a critical component of the cloud security ecosystem that plays a pivotal role in safeguarding an organization's data and applications in cloud environments. CASB solutions act as intermediaries between an organization's on-premises infrastructure and **cloud service providers** (**CSPs**), offering visibility, control, and security enforcement over cloud-based applications and data. The term *CASB* was coined by Gartner, a leading research and advisory company. A CASB plays a pivotal role in addressing security challenges associated with the migration of data and services to the cloud. As mentioned, it acts as an intermediary between users and cloud service providers, offering features such as **user and entity behavior analytics** (**UEBA**), data encryption, threat protection, and compliance management. A CASB is crucial in helping organizations secure their cloud environments, safeguard sensitive data, and ensure compliance with data protection regulations, all while enabling the benefits of cloud technology and services without compromising security.

Four pillars of a CASB

CASBs are multifaceted security solutions that help organizations secure their interactions with cloud services. They typically operate based on four key pillars:

Figure 18.5 – Four pillars of a CASB

Let's briefly discuss them:

- **Visibility**: A CASB solution provides organizations with insights into their cloud ecosystem. It offers visibility into which cloud services are being used, by whom, and for what purposes:

    - **Comprehensive visibility**: It is a cornerstone of effective security management. CASB solutions consolidate the oversight of users, devices, files, and connections into a unified platform, empowering IT administrators to monitor activities across all third-party applications and enforce specific controls. For example, allowing access to approved apps solely from authorized devices or implementing restrictions on sensitive data access.

    - **Shadow IT discovery**: This refers to the process of identifying and managing the use of unauthorized or unapproved applications or services within an organization. As cloud adoption is at an all-time high, shadow IT becomes obvious because employees or departments independently adopt technology solutions without the knowledge or approval of the IT department. CASB solutions help identify and control the use of cloud applications and services, including those not sanctioned by IT.

    - **Risk reporting**: Unveiling enhanced visibility also enables CASBs to monitor and promptly report security risks. For instance, if a user logs in to a company's cloud service from two geographically distant locations within a brief time frame, the CASB will promptly flag this event and take immediate action, such as blocking the unauthorized login. This term is often referred to as "*impossible travel activities.*"

- **Data security**: CASBs help protect sensitive data stored and transmitted through cloud services. They offer functionalities such as data encryption, DLP, and access controls. CASBs can enforce policies to prevent data leakage, ensuring that sensitive information remains secure, even in the cloud environment. They can also provide encryption for data at rest and in transit, adding an extra layer of security.

- **Threat protection**: CASBs monitor user behavior and network traffic in real time to detect and mitigate security threats. They use features such as UEBA, anomaly detection, and contextual analysis to identify potential threats, such as unauthorized access or suspicious activities. CASBs can respond by enforcing security policies, blocking malicious activity, and providing alerts or reports to security teams. This proactive threat protection helps organizations safeguard their cloud environments from various cyber threats.

- **Compliance**: CASBs assist organizations in complying with industry regulations and internal policies related to data security and privacy. They offer features for auditing, reporting, and compliance management. CASBs can generate detailed reports to demonstrate compliance with standards such as the **General Data Protection Regulation (GDPR)**, the **Health Insurance Portability and Accountability Act (HIPAA)**, or the **Payment Card Industry Data Security Standard (PCI DSS)**. They also help enforce governance policies by allowing organizations to set and monitor access controls, permissions, and other security policies across their cloud services, ensuring that security and compliance standards are met.

Purpose and key benefits of CASBs

CASBs play a crucial role in enhancing the security of cloud environments by providing visibility, control, and security features. The main purpose of using CASBs comes from their key capabilities, which include the following:

- **Visibility and discovery**: CASBs offer visibility into the use of cloud services across the organization, discovering shadow IT and unauthorized cloud applications

  Benefits: Enables organizations to understand and control the usage of cloud services, ensuring compliance with security policies

- **DLP**: Monitors and prevents the unauthorized sharing or leakage of sensitive data in the cloud

  Benefits: Protects sensitive information, **intellectual property (IP)**, and compliance-related data from being exposed or misused

- **Access control and authentication**: Enforces access policies, ensuring that only authorized users and devices can access cloud resources

  Benefits: Strengthens authentication mechanisms, prevents unauthorized access, and supports **conditional access (CA)** policies

- **Encryption**: Provides encryption for data at rest, in transit, and during processing within cloud applications

  Benefits: Enhances data privacy and protection, especially when data is stored or transmitted in the cloud

- **Threat protection**: Detects and mitigates security threats such as malware, ransomware, and phishing attacks within cloud environments

  Benefits: Enhances the overall security posture by preventing malicious activities and maintaining the integrity of cloud applications

- **Compliance monitoring and reporting**: Monitors cloud usage for compliance with industry regulations and organizational policies

  Benefits: Helps organizations maintain regulatory compliance, avoid penalties, and adhere to internal security standards

- **UEBA**: Analyzes user behavior within cloud applications to detect anomalies and potential security incidents

  Benefits: Improves the ability to identify insider threats, compromised accounts, and other suspicious activities

- **Secure collaboration**: Facilitates secure collaboration by controlling file sharing, collaboration features, and access permissions within cloud applications

  Benefits: Ensures that collaboration tools are used securely, preventing accidental exposure of sensitive data

- **API security and integration**: Integrates with cloud service APIs to extend security controls and visibility

  Benefits: Enhances security capabilities by leveraging direct integrations with cloud providers, allowing for more granular control and monitoring

- **IR and forensics**: Assists in IR activities and provides forensic capabilities to investigate security incidents

  Benefits: Enables organizations to respond quickly to security incidents, investigate root causes, and implement corrective measures

- **Proxy and gateway functionality**: Acts as a proxy or gateway between users and cloud services, allowing for real-time inspection and enforcement of security policies

  Benefits: Provides a centralized point for enforcing security controls and monitoring traffic between users and cloud applications

- **Integration with IAM**: Integrates with IAM solutions to enforce consistent access controls and policies across on-premises and cloud environments

  Benefits: Strengthens identity-centric security measures and ensures a unified approach to access management

These key capabilities collectively empower organizations to secure their use of cloud services, protect sensitive data, and maintain compliance with security standards and regulations. CASBs serve as a critical component in the overall cloud security strategy.

How does a CASB work?

CASBs operate through a comprehensive three-part process to enhance visibility and control over enterprise data in the cloud. The three parts are as follows:

- **Discovery phase**: In this phase, CASBs identify all cloud applications in use and associate them with employees

- **Classification phase**: CASBs assess each application, identify associated data, and calculate a risk factor

- **Remediation phase**: CASBs craft tailored security policies for enterprises, addressing specific needs

Additionally, CASBs actively identify and remediate incoming threats or policy violations, ensuring a secure and compliant cloud environment for organizations.

Deployment methods of CASBs

Deploying and utilizing CASBs is straightforward. Although the predominant deployment for CASBs is in the cloud, there are alternatives for on-premises setups. CASBs function through three distinct deployment models, with multimode CASBs employing all three, providing enhanced flexibility and robust protection. Here are three ways to deploy CASBs:

- **API scanning**: Accessible for authorized enterprise applications, API scanning serves as a discreet security measure for data at rest in the cloud; however, it lacks real-time prevention capabilities.

- **Forward proxy**: The forward proxy provides real-time DLP for both authorized and unauthorized applications but is limited to supervised devices. Also, it cannot scan data at rest.

- **Reverse proxy**: A reverse proxy redirects all user traffic, making it suitable for both supervised and unsupervised devices. While it delivers real-time DLP, this functionality is exclusive to approved applications.

CSPM versus CASBs – Differences and crossover

By now, it is evident that a CASB is primarily focused on securing user interactions with cloud applications, offering features such as real-time DLP, user authentication, and threat protection. In contrast, CSPM concentrates on the broader security posture of an organization's entire cloud environment, identifying and remediating misconfigurations, and ensuring compliance with industry standards. While a CASB is geared toward user-driven activities, CSPM addresses infrastructure security. However, they *overlap* when integrated, providing a comprehensive cloud security strategy. For instance, a CASB can enforce security policies for user interactions, while CSPM identifies and corrects misconfigurations in the underlying infrastructure, resulting in a unified and robust defense against a spectrum of cloud security risks.

Now that we understand CASBs, let us understand another comparatively new term, *DSPM*, which is mostly complemented with CSPM by vendors.

DSPM

Gartner identified the term *DSPM* first in its *2022 Hype Circle for Data Security* and defines it as follows (`https://www.gartner.com/reviews/market/data-security-posture-management`):

"Data security posture management (DSPM) provides visibility as to where sensitive data is, who has access to that data, how it has been used, and what the security posture of the data stored, or application is. It does that by assessing the current state of data security, identifying potential risks and vulnerabilities, implementing security controls to mitigate these risks, and regularly monitoring and updating the security posture to ensure it remains effective. As a result, it enables businesses to maintain the confidentiality, integrity, and availability of sensitive data. The typical users of DSPM include Information Technology (IT) departments, security teams, compliance teams, and executive leadership."

DSPM is a data-first approach to securing sensitive data across multiple cloud environments and services.

Key features of DSPM

DSPM helps organizations to identify, classify, protect, and monitor their data assets, and to address security and compliance issues. Some of the features of DSPM are as follows:

- **Data discovery**: DSPM locates and catalogs data sources throughout the organization, such as databases, filesystems, cloud storage, and third-party applications.

- **Data classification**: DSPM assigns labels to data according to their sensitivity and importance, such as **personally identifiable information** (**PII**), financial data, or IP addresses.

- **Data flow mapping**: DSPM tracks how data moves within the organization and identifies potential risks and vulnerabilities.

- **Data encryption and tokenization**: DSPM applies encryption to data at rest and in transit, using industry-standard algorithms and keys. It also provides robust tokenization capabilities.

- **Access control**: DSPM enforces granular policies and permissions to control who can access, modify, or delete data.

- **DLP**: DSPM prevents data leakage or exfiltration by blocking unauthorized data transfers or downloads.

- **Monitoring**: DSPM continuously monitors data activity and generates alerts and reports on any anomalies or incidents.

DSPM versus CSPM – A security focus shift from infrastructure to data security risks

DSPM and CSPM are closely related yet distinct security paradigms. Grasping their key disparities is essential for organizations aiming to make well-informed decisions about their security stance.

The difference between both technologies lies in their core philosophy toward the cloud security approach. **CSPM** concentrates on discovering and addressing vulnerabilities in cloud infrastructure, particularly in compute units such as VMs and containers, as well as in **Platform as a service (PaaS)** implementations. On the other hand, **DSPM** is dedicated to identifying and addressing vulnerabilities at the data level. As organizations expand their cloud usage, both CSPM and DSPM become essential, with CSPM ensuring the security of cloud infrastructure assets and DSPM safeguarding the data contained within those assets, collectively enhancing the overall cloud security posture.

These disparities are foundational in defining the specific roles and functions of DSPM and CSPM within an organization's security strategy. While DSPM protects data regardless of its location, CSPM focuses on securing the cloud environment itself. Understanding these distinctions is crucial for tailoring an effective security posture that comprehensively addresses both data and cloud security.

How can DSPM and CSPM complement each other?

DSPM and CSPM can complement each other by providing different layers of security for an organization's data and cloud environment. DSPM can provide data-level protection, while CSPM can provide infrastructure-level protection. DSPM can also provide context and prioritization for CSPM alerts, by identifying which data is at risk and how critical it is. CSPM can also support DSPM by ensuring that the cloud environment is configured and maintained according to best practices and standards.

As vendors have already started offering DSPM features under the umbrella of CSPM as a unified solution, this comprehensive offering brings a distinctive advantage by enabling the identification of data vulnerabilities within the cloud infrastructure. This collaborative approach empowers organizations to detect and respond to threats early in the data life cycle, triggering alerts and actions for suspicious data access, unconventional configurations, or unauthorized access to cloud resources. This proactive threat detection significantly enhances the overall security posture, mitigating the impact of potential security incidents.

By subscribing to both DSPM and CSPM, organizations can achieve a holistic and robust security posture for their data and cloud environments. They can also reduce the risk of data breaches, comply with regulations, and optimize their security operations.

Let us dive deep into another recent advancement in the cloud security space, called CIEM.

CIEM

CIEM focuses on managing and securing permissions and entitlements within cloud environments. It involves monitoring and controlling access rights, permissions, and configurations related to cloud resources to ensure security, compliance, and the **principle of least privilege** (**PoLP**).

CIEM solutions help organizations address challenges associated with misconfigurations, excessive permissions, and potential security risks within cloud infrastructure. By providing visibility into entitlements and implementing controls, CIEM aims to enhance security posture and mitigate the risks associated with unauthorized access or misuse of cloud resources. *Microsoft*, *Tenable*, *CyberArk*, and *BeyondTrust* are some vendors offering CIEM tools.

Key capabilities of CIEM

CIEM is designed to address the challenges associated with managing permissions and entitlements within cloud environments. Key capabilities of CIEM include the following:

- **Entitlement monitoring**: CIEM tools monitor and analyze permissions and entitlements associated with cloud resources. This includes user roles, access rights, and configurations.

- **Permission gaps detection**: CIEM helps identify any gaps or disparities between necessary privileges and the actual permissions granted, reducing the risk of overprivileged accounts.

- **Relationship visualization**: CIEM visualizes and exposes complex relationships between identities and roles, helping organizations understand and manage access relationships.

- **Policy modifications**: CIEM enables policy adjustments to remove access risks, ensuring that users have the necessary permissions without unnecessary over privileges.

- **Alerts for suspicious activity**: CIEM tools detect and alert on suspicious access activities, privilege escalation, and potential security incidents associated with unauthorized access or credential abuse.

CSPM and CIEM overlapping points

While CIEM and CSPM have distinct focuses, there are overlapping points where their functionalities complement each other:

- **Access control and configuration**: Both CIEM and CSPM contribute to access control by monitoring and managing permissions (CIEM) and configurations (CSPM) to ensure a secure and compliant cloud environment

- **Risk mitigation**: Both CIEM and CSPM contribute to identifying and mitigating risks associated with the cloud environment, whether it's through managing entitlements (CIEM) or addressing misconfigurations (CSPM)

CIEM and CSPM have distinct focuses; they can complement each other when integrated into a comprehensive cloud security strategy. CIEM addresses access-related security concerns, while CSPM addresses configuration-related security challenges, providing a more holistic approach to cloud security. Organizations may choose to implement both to cover different aspects of their cloud security needs.

Summary

In this chapter, we explored key components within the cloud security ecosystem, shedding light on the roles of CNAPPs, CIEM, CASBs, CWPPs, and DSPM. The cloud security ecosystem presented as a comprehensive framework to tackle the evolving challenges of securing cloud environments. CNAPPs take center stage by offering a unified approach to secure cloud-native applications, while CIEM is highlighted for its crucial role in managing and securing access entitlements within cloud infrastructures. CASBs emerge as a pivotal bridge between on-premises and cloud environments, providing visibility and control over cloud-based applications. CWPPs are discussed for their essential role in safeguarding cloud workloads from diverse threats and ensuring the overall security of applications and data in the cloud. This chapter provides a holistic view of these technologies, offering valuable insights into building a robust and integrated cloud security strategy.

In the next chapter, we will dive deep into the future trends and challenges related to CSPM technologies and the cloud security ecosystem.

Further reading

To learn more about the topics covered in this chapter, please visit the following links:

- *Top 20 use cases for CASBs*: https://query.prod.cms.rt.microsoft.com/cms/api/am/binary/RE3nibJ

- *What is Data Security Posture Management (DSPM)?*: https://www.ibm.com/topics/data-security-posture-management

- *The Big Guide to Data Security Posture Management (DSPM)*: https://www.dig.security/post/the-big-guide-to-data-security-posture-management-dspm

19

Future Trends and Challenges

The past decade has witnessed a transformative journey in the realm of cloud security, marking a shift from skepticism and cautious adoption to a widespread reliance on cloud services. As organizations embrace the agility and scalability offered by the cloud, security concerns that once posed significant barriers have given way to innovative solutions and robust frameworks. The landscape has evolved dynamically, reshaping the way we perceive and manage security in the digital age.

In this ever-evolving landscape, the security of cloud environments is facing new challenges and opportunities. As organizations increasingly migrate operations to the cloud, the complexities of securing these dynamic environments have grown in tandem. The traditional perimeter-based security model, effective in the on-premises era, has become insufficient in the face of distributed and scalable cloud architectures. Recognizing this shift, the paradigm has moved toward a more proactive and comprehensive approach known as CSPM.

This concluding chapter delves into the critical importance of anticipating future trends and challenges in CSPM. Beyond a mere response to current security needs, CSPM represents a strategic foresight, allowing organizations not only to adapt to the present but also to proactively address emerging risks. As we explore the future of cloud security, understanding the significance of staying ahead of the curve becomes paramount. The evolving threat landscape necessitates a dynamic and adaptive approach, and CSPM stands as a linchpin in ensuring the security and resilience of cloud environments. Let's embark on a journey to uncover the future trends and challenges that will shape the landscape of CSPM.

We'll cover the following main topics:

- Emerging technologies impacting CSPM
- Regulatory landscape
- Evolving threat landscape
- Integration challenges
- User awareness and training
- Automation and orchestration

- Case studies and best practices
- Collaboration and information sharing

Let's get started!

Emerging technologies impacting CSPM

The CSPM landscape is being significantly shaped by a wave of emerging technologies, each presenting unique challenges and opportunities. These technologies are not only transforming the way we secure cloud environments but also redefining the strategies employed to anticipate and mitigate potential threats. Let's try to understand some of these emerging technologies and their impact on the security landscape.

Quantum computing and its potential threat to encryption

The advent of quantum computing poses both promises and threats to the field of cloud. Quantum computers, with their unprecedented processing power, have the potential to break traditional encryption algorithms, raising concerns about the future integrity of data stored in the cloud. Quantum computing has the potential to revolutionize various fields, including cryptography. While quantum computers offer exciting possibilities for solving certain complex problems much faster than classical computers, they also pose a potential threat to widely used encryption algorithms such as **Advanced Encryption Standard** (**AES**) and **Rivest-Shamir-Adleman** (**RSA**). Quantum computing introduces unique challenges to traditional cryptographic techniques, and adapting CSPM strategies to withstand the quantum threat is crucial.

Implications of quantum computing on cloud security

Here are the implications and strategies for addressing quantum computing in the context of CSPM:

- **Cryptographic vulnerabilities**: Quantum computers could potentially break widely used encryption algorithms, leading to data exposure and integrity issues. If large-scale, fault-tolerant quantum computers become available, they could compromise the security of current encryption methods, making data encrypted with widely used algorithms vulnerable to decryption. This threat has led to the development of *post-quantum cryptography*, which focuses on cryptographic algorithms that are believed to be secure even in the presence of powerful quantum computers.

- **Key management risks**: Quantum computers may compromise the security of cryptographic keys, leading to unauthorized access. It is advisable to enhance CSPM products and practices to monitor and manage key life cycles, ensuring the use of quantum-safe key exchange protocols. Implement key rotation policies that account for quantum threats.

- **Configuration weaknesses**: Misconfigurations in cryptographic settings can introduce security risks. CSPM tools will be expected to enforce standardized cryptographic configurations, including the use of quantum-resistant algorithms. Continuously monitor configurations to detect and remediate potential weaknesses.

- **Data confidentiality concerns**: Current encryption methods may become insecure, jeopardizing the confidentiality of sensitive data. Due to this, existing CSPM tools may not be super-efficient in detecting and highlighting this concern, so it will become imperative to implement CSPM practices to identify and update encryption policies so that they use quantum-resistant algorithms.

Note

It is important to note that quantum computers capable of breaking current encryption standards are still largely theoretical and face significant technical challenges, such as error correction and maintaining stable qubits over a sufficiently prolonged period. Researchers and organizations are actively working on developing quantum-resistant cryptographic algorithms to ensure the security of information in a post-quantum era. While the timeline for the development of practical quantum computers remains uncertain, the potential threat to encryption has spurred efforts to prepare for a future in which quantum computing becomes a reality. Organizations are advised to stay informed about developments in quantum computing and to adopt cryptographic algorithms that are resilient to quantum attacks as they become available.

Strategies to overcome potential challenges in quantum computing

Now that we understand the potential threats posed by quantum computing, let's look at strategies to overcome these challenges in the context of CSPM:

- **Quantum-resistant algorithm adoption**: Stay informed about quantum-resistant cryptographic algorithms and update CSPM tools to support the identification and enforcement of these algorithms. Establish policies that mandate the use of quantum-safe encryption in the cloud environment.

- **Continuous monitoring for quantum threats**: Enhance CSPM tools to continuously monitor cryptographic activities for signs of quantum threats. Implement real-time alerts for any suspicious or anomalous behavior related to quantum attacks.

- **Incident response planning for quantum threats**: Update incident response plans so that they include scenarios related to quantum threats. Define specific response actions in case of suspected quantum-related security incidents. Integrate CSPM tools into incident response workflows.

- **Automated encryption policy enforcement**: Leverage CSPM automation capabilities to enforce encryption policies consistently across the cloud environment. Automate the deployment of quantum-resistant cryptographic algorithms and configurations.

- **Key management automation**: Automate key management processes within CSPM to ensure the secure generation, distribution, and rotation of cryptographic keys. Implement automated key rotation policies that consider the impact of quantum threats.

- **Integration with quantum-safe technologies**: Collaborate with vendors and integrate CSPM tools with emerging quantum-safe technologies. Ensure that CSPM solutions can adapt to the evolving landscape of quantum-resistant cryptography.

- **User education and training**: Educate cloud security teams about the implications of quantum computing on cryptographic practices. Provide training on how to configure and manage quantum-resistant cryptographic techniques using CSPM tools.

- **Policy alignment with quantum standards**: Align CSPM policies with emerging quantum-safe cryptographic standards. Ensure that security policies and configurations are updated as per the latest developments in quantum-resistant cryptography.

Adapting CSPM strategies to withstand the quantum threat would require a combination of proactive planning, continuous monitoring, and the integration of quantum-resistant technologies. Organizations need to stay informed about advancements in quantum-safe cryptography and update their CSPM practices accordingly to maintain the security of cloud environments in a post-quantum era.

AI and ML in enhancing CSPM capabilities

AI and ML are becoming integral to bolstering CSPM capabilities. These technologies enable proactive threat detection, anomaly identification, and automated response mechanisms. By analyzing vast datasets and patterns, AI and ML empower CSPM solutions to evolve from reactive to predictive, staying one step ahead of potential security risks. The transformative impact of AI and ML on CSPM has started proving to be profound in terms of significantly enhancing the ability to maintain a secure cloud posture. For example, Microsoft's recent announcement of a security copilot feature as one of its security offerings is one example of integrating AI/ML to enhance security products. Other product vendors such as Prisma Cloud by Palo Alto, Wiz, and ORCA CSPM have also announced such enhancements. The evolving role of intelligent automation in CSPM brings about several key benefits.

Real-time threat detection and response

Real-time threat detection and response are critical components of effective cybersecurity, and when applied to CSPM, they play a crucial role in identifying and mitigating security risks in cloud environments.

Here's how real-time threat detection and response works in the context of CSPM:

- **AI-driven threat detection**: ML algorithms can analyze vast amounts of data in real time, identifying patterns indicative of security threats. This enables CSPM solutions to detect and respond to potential incidents promptly.

- **Automated incident response**: Intelligent automation can trigger predefined response actions, allowing for swift and automated responses to security events without requiring manual intervention.

Continuous monitoring and adaptability

Continuous monitoring and adaptability involve ongoing surveillance of a system or environment, coupled with the ability to adapt and respond to changes or emerging threats. Here are how these concepts apply to CSPM:

- **Continuous compliance monitoring**: AI-powered CSPM tools can continuously monitor cloud environments for compliance with security policies and industry regulations, providing real-time insights into the compliance status

- **Adaptive security posture**: ML models can adapt and learn from new data, ensuring that security postures evolve in response to changing threat landscapes and dynamic cloud environments

Dynamic risk assessment

Dynamic risk assessment is a continuous and adaptive process that involves evaluating and re-evaluating potential risks in real time based on the evolving threat landscape and changes within a system or environment. In the context of CSPM, dynamic risk assessment plays a crucial role in identifying and prioritizing security risks to an organization's cloud infrastructure. The following are some of the key roles in which dynamic risk assessment contributes:

- **Predictive risk analysis**: ML algorithms can predict potential security risks by analyzing historical and real-time data. This allows organizations to proactively address risks before they escalate.

- **Risk prioritization**: Intelligent automation helps in prioritizing security risks based on their severity, allowing security teams to focus on the most critical issues first.

Context-aware security analysis

Context-aware security analysis is crucial for accurately assessing the severity and impact of security incidents. Here are some examples:

- **Contextual understanding**: AI enhances the context-aware analysis of security incidents, reducing false positives by considering the specific context of activities within the cloud environment

- **Behavioral analytics**: ML models can analyze user and entity behavior, helping to distinguish between normal and suspicious activities

Automated policy enforcement

Intelligent automated policy enforcement can significantly improve the security posture by ensuring that cloud resources and configurations adhere to predefined security policies and compliance standards. This automation helps organizations maintain a secure and compliant posture in their cloud environments, such as the following:

- **Automated remediation**: Intelligent automation can enforce security policies by automatically remediating non-compliant configurations or security vulnerabilities, ensuring that cloud resources adhere to predefined security standards

- **Policy optimization**: ML algorithms can optimize security policies based on evolving threats and the changing nature of the cloud environment

Enhanced User and Entity Behavior Analytics (UEBA)

AI and ML can play a pivotal role in enhancing UEBA by providing advanced capabilities for analyzing, modeling, and predicting user and entity behaviors within a system. Some of the capabilities are as follows:

- **Insider threat detection**: AI and ML can enable more accurate detection of insider threats by analyzing user behavior and identifying anomalous patterns
- **Adaptive access control**: Intelligent automation can dynamically adjust access controls based on user behavior, reducing the risk of unauthorized access

Efficiency and scalability

AI and ML can significantly enhance efficiency and scalability in various domains, including CSPM. Here are some examples:

- **Automated scaling**: AI and ML enable CSPM solutions to efficiently scale to handle large and complex cloud environments. This ensures that security monitoring and response capabilities keep pace with the dynamic nature of cloud infrastructure.
- **Scale automated threat detection**: ML algorithms can analyze vast datasets in real time to detect patterns indicative of security threats. Automated threat detection scales easily to handle a growing volume of data and an increasing number of potential threats without a linear increase in human resources.

Continuous improvement

Implementing CSPM by leveraging AI and ML can enhance the effectiveness, accuracy, and adaptability of security measures over time. Here's how AI and ML contribute to the continuous improvement of CSPM:

- **Self-learning systems**: ML-powered CSPM solutions continuously learn from new data and security incidents, improving over time and adapting to emerging threats
- **Feedback loop integration**: Intelligent automation incorporates feedback from security analysts, enabling the system to iteratively refine its algorithms and response mechanisms

The evolving role of intelligent automation in CSPM is marked by a shift toward proactive and adaptive security measures. By using AI and ML-leveraged CSPM tools, organizations can not only detect and respond to security threats more effectively but also maintain a resilient and secure posture in the face of evolving cyber threats and cloud environments.

The Internet of Things (IoT) and its implications for CSPM

IoT refers to a network of interconnected devices, objects, and systems that communicate and share data over the internet. These devices, often embedded with sensors and actuators, collect and exchange data, enabling them to interact and make intelligent decisions. The implications of IoT for CSPM are significant, introducing both opportunities and challenges. As these devices become ubiquitous in both personal and enterprise environments, CSPM must adapt to address the unique security challenges posed by the IoT ecosystem.

Let's explore the integration challenges and security considerations associated with the growing presence of IoT devices, emphasizing the need for a comprehensive approach to CSPM that encompasses the diverse landscape of connected devices:

- **Increased attack surface**: IoT devices introduce additional entry points and vulnerabilities into the network. CSPM tools need to extend their coverage to include IoT devices and their associated configurations.

- **Diverse device ecosystem**: A wide variety of devices with different operating systems, firmware, and security postures. CSPM solutions need to adapt to the diversity of IoT devices, ensuring comprehensive coverage and visibility.

- **Data privacy and compliance**: IoT devices often handle sensitive data, raising privacy and compliance concerns. Compliance monitoring and data protection become crucial, requiring CSPM to integrate IoT-related compliance checks.

- **Real-time monitoring requirements**: IoT devices often operate in real-time environments, requiring continuous monitoring. The real-time monitoring capabilities of CSPM tools need to extend to IoT devices to promptly detect and respond to security incidents.

- **Identity and access management**: Managing identities and access to many diverse IoT devices can be challenging. CSPM solutions need to integrate robust identity and access management mechanisms to secure IoT device access.

- **Device life cycle management**: IoT devices have varied life cycles and may be difficult to update or patch. Ensuring secure onboarding, monitoring, and decommissioning of IoT devices becomes a priority for CSPM.

- **Network security challenges**: IoT devices can introduce vulnerabilities into the network infrastructure. CSPM tools need to address network security issues related to IoT devices, including segmentation, encryption, and intrusion detection.

- **Edge computing security**: IoT often involves edge computing, which brings security considerations closer to the device. CSPM solutions should extend their security controls to cover edge computing environments and address specific edge-related risks.

- **IoT-specific threats**: IoT introduces new threat vectors, including device manipulation, data spoofing, and physical attacks. CSPM tools need to be equipped to detect and respond to IoT-specific threats through behavior analysis and anomaly detection.

- **Integration with IoT security platforms**: Many organizations use specialized IoT security platforms. CSPM solutions should integrate or collaborate with IoT security platforms to provide comprehensive security coverage.

- **Regulatory compliance**: Compliance requirements may differ for IoT devices in various industries. CSPM tools should support industry-specific compliance checks and adapt to evolving regulatory frameworks for IoT security.

- **Data encryption and integrity**: Ensuring the confidentiality and integrity of data transmitted by IoT devices is critical. CSPM tools need to enforce encryption protocols and verify data integrity for IoT communication.

In summary, the increasing prevalence of IoT devices in organizations introduces complexities and security challenges that CSPM must address. CSPM tools need to evolve to encompass the unique characteristics of IoT environments, ensuring comprehensive security coverage and effective risk management. This includes addressing issues related to device diversity, data privacy, real-time monitoring, and collaboration with specialized IoT security solutions.

Blockchain and its role in securing cloud environments

Blockchain is a distributed ledger technology that provides a secure, transparent, and tamper-resistant way to record transactions and manage data across a network of participants. Each participant in the network has a copy of the entire blockchain, and transactions are added to the ledger through a consensus mechanism, making it difficult for any single entity to manipulate or alter the data. In the context of CSPM, blockchain can play a role in enhancing the security of cloud environments in several ways, such as the following:

- **Immutable audit trail**: Blockchain creates an immutable and transparent record of changes made to cloud configurations, policies, and access controls. It can provide a secure audit trail for CSPM, allowing organizations to trace and verify changes made to their cloud environment. This helps in identifying unauthorized modifications and ensuring compliance.

- **Decentralized consensus**: Blockchain relies on decentralized consensus mechanisms, making it resistant to single points of failure or manipulation. It can enhance the reliability of CSPM by reducing the risk of unauthorized alterations or malicious activities. The decentralized nature of blockchain makes it harder for attackers to compromise the integrity of the system.

- **Smart contracts for policy automation**: Smart contracts, which self-execute code on the blockchain, can be utilized to automate and enforce security policies in cloud environments. Blockchain can enable the creation of programmable and automated security policies within CSPM. Smart contracts can automatically trigger actions based on predefined conditions, enhancing the responsiveness of security measures.

- **Enhanced data integrity**: Blockchain's cryptographic hash functions ensure the integrity of data stored in the ledger. By leveraging blockchain to store critical security information, CSPM can ensure the integrity of data, preventing unauthorized alterations or tampering. This is particularly relevant for logs, configurations, and other security-related data.

- **Secure identity management**: Blockchain can be used for decentralized and secure identity management, ensuring the authenticity of users and devices accessing cloud resources. This can strengthen access controls in CSPM by providing a robust and decentralized identity verification mechanism. This reduces the risk of unauthorized access and identity-related security incidents.

- **Supply chain security**: Blockchain can be applied to secure the supply chain of cloud services, ensuring the integrity of software and configurations from development to deployment. This will enhance the security of cloud environments by verifying the authenticity and integrity of software components and configurations. This is crucial for preventing supply chain attacks and ensuring the trustworthiness of cloud services.

- **Decentralized threat intelligence sharing**: Blockchain facilitates secure and decentralized sharing of threat intelligence among different cloud environments and organizations. This will improve the collective security posture by allowing organizations to share threat intelligence without compromising the confidentiality of sensitive information. This collaboration helps in identifying and mitigating threats more effectively.

- **Transparent compliance verification**: Blockchain's transparency allows for real-time verification of compliance with security policies and regulatory requirements. This simplifies the compliance auditing process for CSPM, providing a transparent and unforgeable record of security-related activities. This helps organizations demonstrate adherence to regulatory standards.

- **Resilience against Distributed Denial of Service (DDoS) attacks**: Blockchain's distributed nature makes it more resilient against DDoS attacks and enhances the availability and reliability of CSPM services by reducing susceptibility to DDoS attacks. This ensures that security monitoring and response capabilities remain operational during an attack.

- **Tokenization for access control**: Blockchain-based tokenization can be employed for secure and decentralized access control in cloud environments. This improves access management in CSPM by using tokens to authenticate and authorize users and devices. This enhances security and reduces the risk of unauthorized access.

It is important to mention that even though blockchain technology offers promising security benefits for CSPM, its implementation should be *carefully considered* based on the specific use case, regulatory requirements, and the organization's overall security strategy. Blockchain is not a *one-size-fits-all* solution, and its adoption should be aligned with the unique needs and challenges of the cloud environment in question.

Now that we have understood the impacts of some of the emerging technologies in the cloud security landscape, let's dive deep into the future trends and challenges in the regulatory landscape in the context of CSPM.

Regulatory landscape

The future trends and challenges in the regulatory landscape in the context of CSPM are shaped by the evolving nature of technology, cybersecurity threats, and the need for comprehensive and adaptable regulatory frameworks. Here are some key trends and challenges:

- **Convergence of regulations**: There is a growing recognition of the need for harmonization and convergence of cybersecurity regulations globally. Efforts may be made to create common standards to simplify compliance for organizations operating in multiple jurisdictions. Achieving consensus on global standards and ensuring their effective implementation across diverse regulatory environments can be challenging. Organizations may face complexities in adapting CSPM solutions to meet varying regional requirements.

- **Increased emphasis on data protection**: The importance of data protection is likely to intensify, with more stringent regulations governing the collection, processing, and storage of personal and sensitive data. Enhanced rights for individuals and greater transparency may become key components of future regulations. Adapting CSPM solutions to effectively protect sensitive data while ensuring encryption, access controls, and compliance with evolving data protection laws poses a challenge for organizations.

- **Zero-trust security framework adoption**: The zero-trust security model, which assumes no implicit trust, is gaining traction. Future regulations may encourage or mandate the adoption of zero-trust principles in CSPM to enhance the overall security posture. Implementing zero trust requires a fundamental shift in cybersecurity strategies. CSPM solutions need to align with zero-trust principles, emphasizing continuous monitoring and strict access controls.

- **Focus on supply chain security**: There is a growing awareness of the vulnerabilities within supply chains, leading to increased regulatory scrutiny of supply chain security. Regulations may require organizations to demonstrate the security of their entire supply chain ecosystem. Ensuring the security of the end-to-end supply chain, including third-party services and vendors, requires robust CSPM practices. Organizations must adapt CSPM solutions to monitor and secure complex supply chain environments.

- **Quantum-safe security measures**: The development of quantum computing poses a threat to traditional encryption methods. Future regulations may encourage the adoption of quantum-safe cryptographic algorithms to protect against the potential risks posed by quantum computing. Preparing CSPM solutions for the post-quantum era involves revisiting encryption strategies and implementing quantum-resistant measures, which may require updates to existing regulatory compliance standards.

- **Continuous compliance monitoring and automation**: There is a shift toward continuous compliance monitoring and automation in response to the dynamic nature of cybersecurity threats. Future regulations may emphasize real-time monitoring and automated responses to security incidents. Adapting CSPM solutions to provide continuous, real-time visibility into the security posture of cloud environments and automating compliance checks requires investing in advanced technologies and processes.

- **Accountability and incident response**: Future regulations may place increased emphasis on accountability, requiring organizations to demonstrate proactive cybersecurity measures and robust incident response capabilities. Timely reporting of security incidents may become a regulatory requirement. Organizations must enhance their incident response capabilities and ensure that CSPM solutions support efficient detection, response, and reporting of security incidents in compliance with regulatory time frames.

In navigating these future trends and challenges, organizations leveraging CSPM solutions must prioritize proactive compliance strategies, stay informed about evolving regulations, and invest in technologies and practices that enhance their overall security posture in the dynamic regulatory landscape. Continuous adaptation and a comprehensive approach to cybersecurity will be essential in addressing the complexities of future CSPM regulatory requirements.

Evolving threat landscape

The evolving threat landscape refers to the dynamic and constantly changing nature of cybersecurity threats and risks that organizations face. It includes the various tactics, techniques, and procedures used by malicious actors to compromise the confidentiality, integrity, or availability of information systems and data. The future trends and challenges in the context of the evolving threat landscape are influenced by technological advancements, changes in attack methods, and the shifting priorities of cyber criminals. Let's look at the key aspects of the evolving threat landscape:

- **Advanced persistent threats (APTs)**: Cyberattacks are expected to become more sophisticated, with threat actors employing advanced techniques such as AI, ML, and automation. This sophistication will allow attackers to evade traditional security measures and launch more targeted and efficient attacks. APTs, which are sophisticated and targeted cyberattacks conducted by well-funded and highly skilled threat actors, are expected to be more prominent and are characterized by their *persistence*, *stealth*, and *intent* to remain undetected within a targeted network over an extended period. These attacks are often associated with *nation states*, *state-sponsored* groups, or advanced cybercriminal organizations. Organizations will have to continually enhance their cybersecurity defenses to detect and mitigate advanced threats. This includes implementing advanced threat detection tools and staying abreast of emerging attack methodologies.

- **Rise of ransomware**: Ransomware attacks have become increasingly prevalent and are expected to be even more sophisticated. Attackers often target critical infrastructure, organizations, and individuals, encrypting data and demanding ransom payments for its release. Organizations will be required to understand the importance of robust backup and recovery mechanisms, user awareness training, and proactive security measures to prevent and respond to these types of attacks.

- **Supply chain vulnerabilities**: As trends suggest, cybercriminals will continue targeting the supply chain to compromise organizations indirectly. This includes exploiting vulnerabilities in third-party vendors, suppliers, or service providers to gain unauthorized access to targeted entities. Organizations will have to assess and manage the security posture of their supply chain partners, implement strict access controls, and conduct thorough risk assessments to identify and mitigate potential vulnerabilities.

- **Cloud security challenges**: With the widespread adoption of cloud services, threat actors will continue focusing on exploiting vulnerabilities in cloud infrastructure. Misconfigurations, inadequate access controls, and insecure **application programming interfaces** (**APIs**) are common targets. Organizations must prioritize cloud security, implement robust identity and access management, conduct regular security assessments, and stay informed about the specific threats associated with cloud environments.

- **Targeted nation-state attacks**: Nation-state actors engage in cyber espionage, cyber warfare, and economic espionage. These sophisticated and well-funded attackers target governments, critical infrastructure, and organizations to gain strategic advantages. The world has witnessed some of the most sophisticated targeted nation-state attacks in the recent *Russia-Ukraine* war and the *Israel-Palestine* war. Organizations, especially those operating in critical sectors, need to implement advanced threat intelligence, conduct regular cybersecurity assessments, and collaborate with government agencies to defend against nation-state threats.

- **IoT exploitation**: The increased adoption of IoT devices will continue expanding the attack surface for cybercriminals. Insecure IoT devices, often lacking proper security measures, are targeted for various purposes, including launching DDoS attacks. Organizations must secure IoT devices through robust authentication, encryption, and regular firmware updates. Network segmentation and monitoring are essential to mitigate the risks associated with compromised IoT devices.

- **Social engineering and phishing**: Social engineering and phishing attacks continue to be prevalent, with attackers using increasingly convincing tactics to deceive individuals into disclosing sensitive information or clicking on malicious links. Ongoing user education, awareness training, and the deployment of advanced email filtering and threat detection technologies are essential to mitigate the risks associated with social engineering and phishing.

- **Emergence of insider threats**: Insider threats, whether malicious or unintentional, will continue posing a significant risk to organizations. Malicious insiders may intentionally compromise security, while unintentional insider threats may result from human error or negligence. Organizations will have to implement strategies for monitoring and mitigating insider threats, including user behavior analytics, robust access controls, and employee training on security best practices.

In response to the evolving threat landscape, organizations will have no other choice but to adopt a proactive and adaptive cybersecurity strategy. This involves continuous monitoring, threat intelligence analysis, regular security assessments, and the implementation of advanced technologies to detect and respond to emerging threats effectively. Staying informed about the latest cybersecurity trends and collaborating with the broader cybersecurity community will be even more crucial elements of a resilient defense against evolving threats.

Zero-day vulnerabilities and their implications for CSPM

Zero-day vulnerabilities refer to software vulnerabilities that are unknown to the vendor or developers and, therefore, have no official patch or fix available. These vulnerabilities pose a significant risk because attackers can exploit them before the software vendor becomes aware of the issue and releases a security update. In the context of CSPM, zero-day vulnerabilities can have several implications:

- **Increased risk of exploitation**: Zero-day vulnerabilities are valuable to attackers because they offer a window of opportunity to exploit a software weakness before it is patched. CSPM solutions need to be vigilant in monitoring cloud environments for any signs of suspicious activity that may indicate exploitation of zero-day vulnerabilities. This requires advanced threat detection capabilities and continuous monitoring.

- **Limited preemptive protection**: Since zero-day vulnerabilities are unknown to security vendors and developers, traditional security measures such as antivirus signatures or intrusion detection systems may not provide preemptive protection. CSPM solutions must focus on anomaly detection, behavioral analysis, and heuristic approaches to identify potential indicators of compromise or unusual patterns in the cloud environment that may suggest zero-day exploitation.

- **Potential impact on cloud services**: Exploitation of zero-day vulnerabilities can lead to unauthorized access, data breaches, and disruption of cloud services. CSPM tools need to enhance their monitoring capabilities to detect unusual behavior, unauthorized access attempts, or any deviations from the established security postures within cloud environments.

- **The need for rapid response**: As there is no official patch available for zero-day vulnerabilities, organizations must respond quickly to mitigate the risk. This may involve implementing temporary workarounds, isolating affected systems, or deploying compensating controls. CSPM solutions should facilitate rapid incident response by providing real-time visibility into the cloud environment, enabling security teams to identify and respond to potential threats associated with zero-day vulnerabilities promptly.

- **Continuous monitoring and vulnerability assessment**: Continuously monitoring cloud environments and regular vulnerability assessments are crucial to identify and address potential weaknesses, including zero-day vulnerabilities. CSPM solutions must integrate with vulnerability assessment tools and perform continuous monitoring to identify any deviations from the secure configuration, unauthorized changes, or suspicious activities that may indicate exploitation of unknown vulnerabilities.

- **Collaboration with cloud service providers (CSPs)**: Organizations often rely on CSPs for the security of underlying infrastructure and services. In the case of zero-day vulnerabilities, collaboration with CSPs is essential to address potential risks. CSPM solutions should integrate with CSPs' security services and leverage their threat intelligence to enhance detection capabilities. Additionally, organizations should have communication channels in place to report and address zero-day vulnerabilities with their CSPs.

- **Threat intelligence integration**: Access to up-to-date threat intelligence is crucial for identifying zero-day vulnerabilities and understanding the potential impact on specific cloud environments. CSPM solutions should integrate with threat intelligence feeds to stay informed about emerging threats, including zero-day vulnerabilities. This integration enhances the ability to detect and respond to potential threats effectively.

It is important to address the implications of zero-day vulnerabilities for CSPM. This requires a combination of advanced monitoring, rapid incident response capabilities, collaboration with cloud service providers, and integration with threat intelligence.

Skills and talent gap

Addressing the human factor in CSPM is essential for ensuring that individuals within an organization contribute effectively to maintaining a secure cloud environment. The human factor involves the actions, behaviors, and decisions of people that can impact the security of cloud configurations. As CSPM continues to play a crucial role in securing cloud environments, organizations face challenges related to a shortage of skilled professionals in cloud security. Addressing these skills and the talent gap is essential for ensuring the effective implementation and management of CSPM solutions. This section provides an overview of the challenges, followed by strategies to bridge the gap.

Key challenges

The skill gap and talent challenges in the cloud security space significantly impact organizations' abilities to effectively secure their cloud environments. Here are some of the skill gap and talent challenges that organizations face:

- **Shortage of skilled professionals**: The demand for skilled professionals in cloud security, including CSPM, often exceeds the available talent pool. The rapidly evolving nature of cloud technologies further intensifies this shortage.

- **Recruiting challenges**: Identifying and recruiting qualified candidates with specific expertise in CSPM is challenging. The unique skill set required, including knowledge of cloud environments and security protocols, adds complexity to the hiring process.

- **Retention issues**: Once skilled professionals are onboarded, retaining them becomes a challenge. The competitive landscape and the allure of new opportunities lead to higher turnover rates.

- **Continuous learning and adaptation**: Cloud security is a dynamic field with evolving technologies and threat landscapes. Keeping the workforce continuously updated with the latest skills and knowledge is a persistent challenge.

Strategies for bridging the gap

Bridging the skills and talent gap in cloud security and related areas requires a strategic and proactive approach. Here are strategies that organizations can adopt to address the gap and build a skilled workforce:

- **Upskilling existing IT teams**: Invest in training and upskilling programs for existing IT teams to enhance their expertise in cloud security and CSPM. This can involve workshops, online courses, and certifications.

- **Cross-training initiatives**: Implement cross-training initiatives to transition existing IT professionals with relevant skills (such as network or system administrators) into roles focused on CSPM. Leverage their foundational knowledge and provide specialized training.

- **Collaboration with educational institutions**: Forge partnerships with educational institutions to create specialized programs or certifications in cloud security and CSPM. Encourage students to pursue careers in this field and establish internship programs.

- **Certification programs**: Support employees in obtaining relevant certifications in cloud security and CSPM. Certifications such as **Certified Cloud Security Professional (CCSP)** or vendor-specific certifications can validate and enhance skills.

- **Talent pipeline development**: Establish a talent pipeline by engaging with entry-level professionals and recent graduates. Offer mentorship programs and internships to nurture and develop a pool of skilled individuals interested in cloud security.

- **Competitive compensation and benefits**: To attract and retain top talent, offer competitive compensation packages and attractive benefits. Recognize the specialized skills required for CSPM roles and align remuneration accordingly.

- **Professional development opportunities**: Provide ongoing professional development opportunities for employees, including access to conferences, workshops, and industry events. Encourage participation in webinars and forums to stay abreast of industry trends.

- **Promote a positive work environment**: Create a positive and inclusive work environment that fosters collaboration, innovation, and continuous learning. A supportive culture can contribute to higher employee satisfaction and retention.

- **Outsourcing and managed services**: Consider outsourcing certain aspects of CSPM or leveraging managed services. This can help alleviate immediate skill shortages while providing time for in-house teams to upskill.

- **Diversity and inclusion initiatives**: Embrace diversity and inclusion initiatives to attract a broader range of talent. Diverse teams often bring a variety of perspectives and creative solutions to complex challenges.

In summary, addressing the skills and talent gap in CSPM requires a multi-faceted approach. Organizations must invest in both recruitment strategies and upskilling programs for existing teams to build a skilled workforce capable of navigating the evolving landscape of cloud security. Continuous support for professional development and a proactive talent management strategy are critical for long-term success in managing CSPM effectively.

User awareness and training

User awareness and training are crucial components of a comprehensive strategy for securing cloud environments through CSPM. Educating users about the unique challenges and best practices associated with cloud security helps reduce the risk of misconfigurations, data breaches, and other security incidents. Let's explore some important aspects associated with user awareness and training in terms of future trends and challenges.

The importance of user education in maintaining a secure cloud posture

Educating cloud users and IT professionals plays a critical role in maintaining a secure cloud posture. The expanding attack surface and dynamic nature of cloud environments make it imperative for organizations to empower their users with the knowledge and skills needed to contribute to a secure cloud posture. Future trends and challenges in this area include the following:

- **Increased user awareness**: The importance of user awareness is expected to grow as organizations recognize that employees at all levels can impact the security of cloud environments. Educating users about the evolving threat landscape and the specific security implications of their actions in the cloud requires continuous efforts.

- **Focus on cloud-specific threats**: User education will increasingly emphasize cloud-specific threats and security best practices tailored to the unique features of cloud environments. Keeping up with the evolving nature of cloud services and associated threats can be challenging.

- **Phishing and social engineering awareness**: Training programs will intensify their focus on recognizing and mitigating cloud-related phishing attacks and social engineering tactics that target cloud credentials. They will also address the sophisticated nature of phishing attacks and ensure that users remain vigilant in the face of evolving social engineering techniques.

- **Secure cloud collaboration**: With the growing emphasis on remote work and collaborative cloud tools, education will extend to secure cloud collaboration, including file sharing, permissions, and data handling. It will involve balancing collaboration and security, ensuring that users understand the implications of their collaboration choices, and implementing secure workflows.

- **User-driven security culture**: Organizations will strive to cultivate a security culture where users actively contribute to maintaining a secure cloud posture and feel a sense of responsibility for security. Shifting organizational culture requires ongoing efforts, leadership buy-in, and a commitment to integrating security into everyday practices.

- **Integration with CSPM tools**: User education programs will integrate with CSPM tools, providing real-time guidance and alerts to users about potential security risks and policy violations. It also involves integrating educational content seamlessly with CSPM tools and ensuring that users can easily access relevant information during their cloud interactions.

Training programs for IT professionals and end users

Training programs for IT professionals and end users are essential components of a robust CSPM strategy. These programs ensure that individuals across the organization possess the knowledge and skills needed to effectively secure cloud environments. Here is a guide to designing training programs tailored to both IT professionals and end users:

- **Comprehensive training curricula**: Training programs for IT professionals and end users will become more comprehensive, covering a wide range of cloud security topics, including CSPM best practices. Though every cloud provider offers a comprehensive learning portal, designing and maintaining comprehensive curricula that address the diverse needs of different user groups and roles within the organization requires effort.

- **Hands-on simulation and exercises**: Training programs will increasingly incorporate hands-on simulations and exercises, allowing users to practice securing cloud environments in a controlled environment. Providing realistic and up-to-date simulations that mimic the complexity of real-world cloud security scenarios will be challenging.

- **Role-based training**: Training programs will tailor content based on the roles and responsibilities of different user groups, ensuring relevance and effectiveness. Identifying and categorizing the specific knowledge and skills required for distinct roles within the organization will be daunting tasks.

- **Continuous learning platforms**: Organizations will adopt continuous learning platforms that offer ongoing training opportunities, enabling users to stay informed about the latest cloud security developments. It ensures that continuous learning platforms remain engaging and that users actively participate in ongoing educational activities.

- **Integration with cloud service providers**: Training programs will integrate with cloud service providers' educational resources, leveraging vendor-specific content to enhance user knowledge of cloud platforms. Training content must be adapted to changes in CSPs' features and interfaces to ensure accuracy and relevance.

- **Cultural shift toward security**: Organizations will work toward a cultural shift where security is integrated into the daily activities of users, reducing the likelihood of unintentional security incidents. This will result in organizations overcoming resistance to change and ensuring that security becomes a shared responsibility across the organization.

- **Human-centric security design**: Security solutions and policies will be designed with a human-centric approach while considering user workflows and minimizing the likelihood of errors. It will also balance usability with security requirements and ensure that security measures do not hinder productivity.

In summary, the importance of user education in maintaining a secure cloud posture is expected to grow as cloud environments evolve. Organizations need to invest in comprehensive training programs that address the specific needs of IT professionals and end users while also addressing the human factor in cloud security. This approach will contribute to building a security-aware culture and reducing the overall risk of security breaches in the cloud.

Case studies and best practices

Let's delve into some case studies and best practices in the context of CSPM.

Lessons learned from successful CSPM deployments

Successful CSPM deployments have taught organizations the importance of achieving comprehensive visibility in their cloud environments, embracing continuous monitoring to promptly detect and address security misconfigurations, automating remediation processes to keep up with the dynamic nature of the cloud, integrating with DevOps practices to embed security throughout the development life cycle, customizing policy enforcement to meet unique security requirements, leveraging UEBA to identify abnormal activities, ensuring scalability and flexibility to accommodate the growth of cloud resources, establishing centralized governance for consistent policy enforcement, conducting regular audits and assessments to stay proactive, and fostering user education and awareness to enhance overall security. Collectively, these lessons emphasize the need for a holistic and adaptive approach that aligns with the dynamic nature of cloud environments and involves a combination of technology, processes, and collaboration across organizational teams.

Lessons learned from unsuccessful CSPM deployments

Unsuccessful CSPM deployments have highlighted critical pitfalls, such as the following:

- Overlooking shadow IT activities and failing to manage unapproved cloud instances
- Insufficient training and awareness programs, which leads to security team gaps
- Inadequate centralized governance, resulting in inconsistent security policies and a lack of real-time compliance monitoring, which leads to regulatory and policy violations

These shortcomings underscore the importance of accounting for the full scope of cloud activities and investing in continuous training to keep security teams abreast of evolving threats and best practices. Implementing robust governance structures for policy enforcement and prioritizing real-time compliance checks helps prevent regulatory breaches.

These lessons emphasize the need for a proactive, well-coordinated, and comprehensive approach to CSPM to avoid common pitfalls and mitigate risks effectively.

Best practices for staying ahead of emerging threats in CSPM

Here are some best practices to consider:

- Staying ahead of emerging threats in CSPM requires a proactive and adaptive approach
- Implementing regular threat intelligence integration into CSPM tools allows organizations to stay informed about evolving cyber threats
- Leveraging ML and AI for anomaly detection helps with identifying and responding to unusual patterns or behaviors in real time
- Embracing container security best practices ensures that specific challenges associated with containerized environments are effectively addressed
- Adopting a zero-trust security model, which involves continuous verification of users and devices accessing cloud resources, enhances the overall security posture
- Investing in cloud-native security solutions and staying abreast of technological advancements in CSPM ensures that organizations can swiftly adapt to the changing threat landscape

Additionally, conducting regular security training and drills helps teams prepare for and respond effectively to emerging threats, fostering a proactive security culture within the organization. By learning from both successful and unsuccessful CSPM deployments and adopting best practices, organizations can navigate the evolving landscape of cloud security, mitigate risks, and stay ahead of emerging threats in cloud environments.

Summary

This concluding chapter provided a comprehensive exploration of the dynamic landscape of CSPM, emphasizing the critical importance of anticipating future trends and challenges. From the transformative impact of emerging technologies such as quantum computing, AI, and blockchain, to the nuanced considerations of regulatory landscapes and evolving threat landscapes, this chapter navigated the intricate facets of securing cloud environments. It shed light on the integration challenges, user awareness, and training imperatives, while also delving into the realm of automation and orchestration. The inclusion of case studies and best practices offered valuable insights derived from real-world CSPM implementations, providing you with a practical foundation. As the digital landscape continues to evolve, this chapter serves as a guide, equipping security professionals with the knowledge and strategies needed to navigate the complexities of CSPM and stay ahead of emerging threats.

Further reading

To learn more about the topics that were covered in this chapter, take a look at the following resources:

- *Blockchain Security in Cloud Computing: Use Cases, Challenges, and Solutions*: `https://www.mdpi.com/2073-8994/9/8/164`

- *The Evolving Landscape of CSPM: Trends and Predictions for the Future*: `https://ts2.space/en/the-evolving-landscape-of-cspm-trends-and-predictions-for-the-future`

Index

www.packtpub.com

Subscribe to our online digital library for full access to over 7,000 books and videos, as well as industry leading tools to help you plan your personal development and advance your career. For more information, please visit our website.

Why subscribe?

- Spend less time learning and more time coding with practical eBooks and Videos from over 4,000 industry professionals

- Improve your learning with Skill Plans built especially for you

- Get a free eBook or video every month

- Fully searchable for easy access to vital information

- Copy and paste, print, and bookmark content

Did you know that Packt offers eBook versions of every book published, with PDF and ePub files available? You can upgrade to the eBook version at packtpub.com and as a print book customer, you are entitled to a discount on the eBook copy. Get in touch with us at customercare@packtpub.com for more details.

At www.packtpub.com, you can also read a collection of free technical articles, sign up for a range of free newsletters, and receive exclusive discounts and offers on Packt books and eBooks.

Other Books You May Enjoy

If you enjoyed this book, you may be interested in these other books by Packt:

Building and Automating Penetration Testing Labs in the Cloud

Joshua Arvin Lat

ISBN: 978-1-83763-239-8

- Build vulnerable-by-design labs that mimic modern cloud environments
- Find out how to manage the risks associated with cloud lab environments
- Use infrastructure as code to automate lab infrastructure deployments
- Validate vulnerabilities present in penetration testing labs
- Find out how to manage the costs of running labs on AWS, Azure, and GCP
- Set up IAM privilege escalation labs for advanced penetration testing
- Use generative AI tools to generate infrastructure as code templates
- Import the Kali Linux Generic Cloud Image to the cloud with ease

Cloud Auditing Best Practices

Shinesa Cambric, Michael Ratemo

ISBN: 978-1-80324-377-1

- Understand the cloud shared responsibility and role of an IT auditor
- Explore change management and integrate it with DevSecOps processes
- Understand the value of performing cloud control assessments
- Learn tips and tricks to perform an advanced and effective auditing program
- Enhance visibility by monitoring and assessing cloud environments
- Examine IAM, network, infrastructure, and logging controls
- Use policy and compliance automation with tools such as Terraform

Packt is searching for authors like you

If you're interested in becoming an author for Packt, please visit `authors.packtpub.com` and apply today. We have worked with thousands of developers and tech professionals, just like you, to help them share their insight with the global tech community. You can make a general application, apply for a specific hot topic that we are recruiting an author for, or submit your own idea.

Share Your Thoughts

Now you've finished *Mastering Cloud Security Posture Management (CSPM)*, we'd love to hear your thoughts! Scan the QR code below to go straight to the Amazon review page for this book and share your feedback or leave a review on the site that you purchased it from.

`https://packt.link/r/1837638403`

Your review is important to us and the tech community and will help us make sure we're delivering excellent quality content.

Download a free PDF copy of this book

Thanks for purchasing this book!

Do you like to read on the go but are unable to carry your print books everywhere?

Is your eBook purchase not compatible with the device of your choice?

Don't worry, now with every Packt book you get a DRM-free PDF version of that book at no cost.

Read anywhere, any place, on any device. Search, copy, and paste code from your favorite technical books directly into your application.

The perks don't stop there, you can get exclusive access to discounts, newsletters, and great free content in your inbox daily

Follow these simple steps to get the benefits:

1. Scan the QR code or visit the link below

https://packt.link/free-ebook/9781837638406

2. Submit your proof of purchase
3. That's it! We'll send your free PDF and other benefits to your email directly

www.ingramcontent.com/pod-product-compliance
Lightning Source LLC
Chambersburg PA
CBHW060644060326
40690CB00020B/4505